Alexander F. Kirkpatrick

The Book of Psalms

With introduction and notes

Alexander F. Kirkpatrick
The Book of Psalms
With introduction and notes

ISBN/EAN: 9783744779647

Printed in Europe, USA, Canada, Australia, Japan

Cover: Foto ©Lupo / pixelio.de

More available books at **www.hansebooks.com**

The Cambridge Bible for Schools and Colleges.

THE BOOK OF
PSALMS.
(I—XLI)

Cambridge:
PRINTED BY C. J. CLAY, M.A. & SONS,
AT THE UNIVERSITY PRESS.

PREFACE
BY THE GENERAL EDITOR.

THE General Editor of *The Cambridge Bible for Schools* thinks it right to say that he does not hold himself responsible either for the interpretation of particular passages which the Editors of the several Books have adopted, or for any opinion on points of doctrine that they may have expressed. In the New Testament more especially questions arise of the deepest theological import, on which the ablest and most conscientious interpreters have differed and always will differ. His aim has been in all such cases to leave each Contributor to the unfettered exercise of his own judgment, only taking care that mere controversy should as far as possible be avoided. He has contented himself chiefly with a careful revision of the notes, with pointing out omissions, with suggesting occasionally a reconsideration of some question, or a fuller treatment of difficult passages, and the like.

Beyond this he has not attempted to interfere, feeling it better that each Commentary should have its own individual character, and being convinced that freshness and variety of treatment are more than a compensation for any lack of uniformity in the Series.

CONTENTS.

		PAGES
I. INTRODUCTION.		
I.	The Book of Psalms	ix—xii
II.	The Position, Names, Numbering, and Divisions of the Psalter	xii—xvii
III.	The Titles of the Psalms	xvii—xxxi
IV.	The Authorship and Age of the Psalms	xxxi—xxxviii
V.	The Collection and Growth of the Psalter	xxxix—xliv
VI.	The Form of Hebrew Poetry	xliv—xlviii
VII.	The Hebrew Text, the Ancient Versions, and the English Versions	xlix—lvii
VIII.	The Messianic Hope	lviii—lxvii
IX.	On some points in the Theology of the Psalms	lxvii—lxxix
II. TEXT AND NOTES		1—220
III. APPENDICES		221—224
INDEX		225

*** The Text adopted in this Edition is that of Dr Scrivener's *Cambridge Paragraph Bible*. A few variations from the ordinary Text, chiefly in the spelling of certain words, and in the use of italics, will be noticed. For the principles adopted by Dr Scrivener as regards the printing of the Text see his Introduction to the *Paragraph Bible*, published by the Cambridge University Press.

The choice and flower of all things profitable in other books the Psalms do both more briefly contain, and more movingly also express, by reason of that poetical form wherewith they are written... What is there necessary for man to know which the Psalms are not able to teach? They are to beginners an easy and familiar introduction, a mighty augmentation of all virtue and knowledge in such as are entered before, a strong confirmation to the most perfect among others. Heroical magnanimity, exquisite justice, grave moderation, exact wisdom, repentance unfeigned, unwearied patience, the mysteries of God, the sufferings of Christ, the terrors of wrath, the comforts of grace, the works of Providence over this world, and the promised joys of that world which is to come, all good necessarily to be either known or done or had, this one celestial fountain yieldeth. Let there be any grief or disease incident into the soul of man, any wound or sickness named, for which there is not in this treasure-house a present comfortable remedy at all times ready to be found.

R. HOOKER.

INTRODUCTION.

CHAPTER I.

THE BOOK OF PSALMS.

Lyric poetry is the most ancient kind of poetry, and Hebrew poetry is mainly lyric. Neither epic nor dramatic poetry flourished in ancient Israel. Some indeed of the historical Psalms may be said to have an epic colouring, but they belong to the class of didactic narrative: Job and the Song of Songs may be called in a sense dramatic, but they do not appear to have been intended for performance on the stage. The only independent branch of poetry in Israel was Gnomic or Proverbial poetry, which in the hands of the 'Wise Men' attained to a rich development, and must have exercised an important influence on the education of the people.

The Old Testament is the religious history of Israel, and the poetry preserved in the Book of Psalms is, as might be expected, religious poetry. Secular poetry no doubt existed[1], but it has not come down to us. The Psalter then is a collection of religious lyrics. Lyric poetry is defined as "that which directly expresses the individual emotions of the poet;" and religious lyric poetry is the expression of those emotions and feelings as they are stirred by the thought of God and directed God-wards. This is the common characteristic of the Psalms in all their

---

[1] Such as the drinking songs referred to in Amos vi. 5 (R.V.); Is. v. 12: harvest and vintage songs (Is. xvi. 10, 11; Jer. xlviii. 33): parables (Judg. ix. 8 ff.). Solomon's 'thousand and five songs' were probably of a secular character (1 Kings iv. 32). Poems like Exod. xv and Judg. v are essentially religious.

manifold variety. Some are directly addressed to God, as petition or thanksgiving or praise: some are the communings of the soul with God, expressing its faith, its hope, its love, its needs, its fears, its aspirations, its joys, its triumphs: some celebrate the 'marvellous works' of God in nature and in history: some reflect upon the perplexing problems of life and their relation to the divine government of the world: but God is as it were the sun around which all revolves, and His light and heat illuminate and animate the whole.

The Psalms stand in an intimate relation to the whole of the Old Testament. They are the inspired response of the human heart to God's revelation of Himself, in Law and History and Prophecy and Philosophy.

The Psalmists celebrate *the moral law* as the guide of human conduct; they welcome *the ordinances of worship* and rejoice in the privilege of access to the presence of God in the Temple, as the crowning joy of life.

History supplies its lessons of God's goodness and man's ingratitude. The recollection of the past is a warning for the present, the support of faith in the hour of trial, the ground of comfort in times of calamity.

The Psalms are closely connected with *Prophecy*. The term 'prophesying' is applied to the expression of religious fervour in chant and hymn (1 Sam. x. 10 ff.; xix. 20 ff.: 1 Chr. xxv. 1—3); and David's chief musicians, Heman, Asaph and Jeduthun, are called 'seers' (1 Chr. xxv. 5; 2 Chr. xxix. 30; xxxv. 15). Sacred poetry often rises to prophetic foresight, while prophecy passes into lyric poetry[1]. The passion for truth and righteousness, and the unquenchable belief that Jehovah's moral government of the world is working, surely if slowly, towards a glorious consummation in the establishment of His universal sovereignty, animate and inspire Psalmists not less than Prophets.

Several Psalms reflect the influence of the '*Wisdom*' or religious philosophy of Israel, both in its practical and in its speculative aspects. The moral lessons for every-day life collected in the Book of Proverbs, and the discussion of the

[1] E.g. Is. xii, xxv, xxvi; Hab. iii.

problems of the world in Job and Ecclesiastes, find their echo in the poetry of the Psalter.

The importance of the Psalter for a just appreciation of the history of Israel is obvious. How meagre an idea of the higher religious life of Israel should we derive from the Historical Books apart from the Prophets: how imperfect still would be the picture drawn from the Historical Books and the Prophets without the warmth of colouring added to it by the Psalms. These alone give us a glimpse into the inner religion of the best spirits in the nation, and bear witness to the faith, the love, the devotion of pious souls even under the limitations of the Old Covenant.

Hence it is essential to study the Psalms critically and historically; to endeavour to ascertain their original meaning and to assign them to their proper place in the history and development of revelation; not only in order to give life and reality to the Psalms themselves, and to understand them better; but for the sake of the light which they throw upon the religious history of Israel, and the course of God's dealings with His people.

The inquiry is however one of extreme difficulty. The widest diversity of opinion prevails as to the date and authorship of the Psalms, and we must often be content to acknowledge that a Psalm cannot be assigned to a definite period, still less to a particular author, with any degree of certainty.

But after all, the critical and historical study of the Psalms is but a preliminary to the higher study of their spiritual meaning and their devotional use. The Psalter has been through all the centuries and will ever continue to be the one unique and inexhaustible treasury of devotion for the individual and for the Church. Through its guidance the soul learns to commune with God: it supplies the most fitting language for common worship.

To some it may seem almost a sacrilege to apply the methods of criticism to such a book. It may be disappointing to find that many Psalms once supposed to be David's must be relegated to a far later age; perplexing to find familiar renderings condemned, and long current interpretations abandoned.

But Holy Scripture conveys divine truth through the medium of human language, and it is our duty to investigate to the full the meaning and the force of that language. Criticism is not the enemy but the handmaid of devotion. As we learn to understand more of the original meaning of the Psalms for those who wrote and used them, we shall learn more of their true meaning for ourselves.

But that meaning is not limited to the 'original' sense, if by this is meant only that which the writers could recognise in their own words. Every true poet's words contain far more than he himself at the moment intends. And the words of these inspired poets were so shaped and moulded by the Holy Spirit that they might grow and expand with the growth of revelation, and "gather wealth in the course of ages." The Psalms belong indeed to the Old and not to the New Testament. They are the product of the Jewish and not of the Christian Church. But "the Psalter in its spiritual fulness belongs to no special time;" and the old words are 'fulfilled' in Christ. The Christian Church may, nay must, use them as they are illuminated by the light of the Gospel. And if the saying, "pectus est quod facit theologum[1]," is true of the study of the Bible generally, it is most true of the study of that book which has well been called "the Bible within the Bible," the very "heart of the Bible."

CHAPTER II.

THE POSITION, NAMES, NUMBERING, AND DIVISIONS OF THE PSALTER.

1. *The position of the Psalter in the Old Testament.* The Hebrew title of the Old Testament indicates the three great divisions, in which, from very early times[2], the Canonical

---

[1] "It is the heart which makes the theologian."
[2] This triple division is recognised in the Prologue to Ecclesiasticus, written about B.C. 132 by the author's grandson, who translated the book from Hebrew into Greek. "Whereas many and great things have been delivered unto us by means of (διὰ) the law and the prophets and the others that have followed after them ..... my grand-

Books were arranged by the Jewish Church:—*Law, Prophets, Writings*. The Book of Psalms belongs to the third of these divisions, the *Writings* or *Hagiographa*. But its position in the group has not always been the same. In the MSS. of the German type, which our printed editions follow, the Psalms stand first, followed by Proverbs and Job. That this was the ancient order is at least a probable inference from Luke xxiv. 44 where "the Psalms" stands by the side of "the Law" and "the Prophets" as the title of the Hagiographa in general[1].

The order of the books of the O.T. in our English Bibles is that which had come to be adopted in the Vulgate by the sixteenth century. It corresponds more nearly to the arrangement of the LXX found in the Vatican MS. than to that of the Hebrew, but differs from it in placing Job before the Psalter instead of after the Song of Songs, and in placing the Minor Prophets after instead of before the Major Prophets, and arranging them as they stand in the Hebrew text.

2. *Names of the Psalter.* The Septuagint translators employed the word ψαλμός[2], *psalm*, to render the Heb. word *mizmor*, which was the technical term for a song with musical accompaniment (p. xvii). The collection was styled simply *Psalms*, as in the Vatican MS. (ψαλμοί, cp. Luke xxiv. 44), or *the Book of Psalms* (Luke xx. 42), or in later times the *Psalter*,

father Jesus, when he had diligently given himself to the reading of the law and the prophets and the other books of our fathers (τῶν ἄλλων πατρίων βιβλίων)... was drawn on also himself to write something pertaining to instruction and wisdom." And again, apologising for the imperfections of his version, he says: "For words spoken in Hebrew have not precisely the same force, when they are translated into another tongue: and not only this treatise, but even the law and the prophecies and the rest of the books (τὰ λοιπὰ τῶν βιβλίων) differ in no small degree when they are spoken in their own language." The clear distinction which is here drawn between the Canonical books and Ecclesiasticus, and the reference to the Greek Version of the O.T. as already in existence, should be carefully noticed.

[1] Comp. too Philo (B.C. 20—A.D. 50) *de vita contempl.* (ii. 475): νόμους καὶ λόγια θεσπισθέντα διὰ προφητῶν καὶ ὕμνους καὶ τὰ ἄλλα οἷς ἐπιστήμη καὶ εὐσέβεια συναύξονται καὶ τελειοῦνται. "Laws and oracles delivered by prophets and hymns and the other writings by which knowledge and piety are increased and perfected."

[2] ψαλμός denotes (1) the music of a stringed instrument; (2) a song sung to the accompaniment of such music.

ψαλτήρ or ψαλτήριον[1]. The Greek words have come down to us through the Latin *psalmus, psalterium*.

The title of the collection in the Hebrew Bible is *Book of Praises* or simply *Praises: Sepher Tehillim* abbreviated into *Tillim* or *Tillin*[2]. This title was known to Hippolytus[3] and Origen[4] in the first half of the third century A.D., and to Jerome[5]. Only one Psalm (cxlv) bears the title *A Praise*, and the name *Book of Praises* probably originated in the use of the collection as the hymn-book of the Second Temple[6]. But no more fitting name could be found for a book, of which a predominant characteristic is praise and thanksgiving, and which ends with a diapason of Hallelujahs.

Another title, possibly that of the earliest collection of Davidic Psalms, was *Tephilloth* or *Prayers* (lxxii. 20). Only five Psalms, xvii, lxxxvi, xc, cii, cxlii, are so entitled; but again, although some Psalms (e.g. i, ii) contain no direct address to God, the title is a suitable one. Prayer in its widest sense includes all elevation of the mind to God[7]. Hannah's thanksgiving and Habakkuk's ode are both described as prayer (1 Sam. ii. 1, Hab. iii. 1).

3. *Numbering of the Psalms.* The Massoretic Text and the LXX both reckon a total of 150 Psalms. The 151st Psalm, which is added in the LXX, is expressly said to be "outside

---

[1] ψαλτήριον meant originally a *stringed instrument*, a *psaltery* (frequently in the LXX), and was afterwards applied to a *collection of psalms*, a *psalter*. In this sense it is used by Hippolytus, Athanasius, Epiphanius, and stands as the title of the Psalms in the Alexandrine MS.

[2] The word is derived from the same root as *Hallelujah*, and the verb is frequently used in connexion with the Temple Service (1 Chron. xvi. 4 &c.).

[3] p. 188, ed. Lagarde. Ἑβραῖοι περιέγραψαν τὴν βίβλον Σέφρα θελείμ. The genuineness of the fragment of Hippolytus which treats of the inscriptions, authorship, divisions, and order of the Psalms, is however doubtful. See Dr Salmon in the *Dict. of Christian Biography*, iii. 103.

[4] In Euseb. *Hist. Eccl.* vi. 25 (ed. Burton) Σφαρθελλείμ.

[5] In the Preface to his *Psalterium iuxta Hebraeos* (p. 2, ed. Lagarde): "titulus ipse Hebraicus *sephar tallim*, quod interpretatur *volumen hymnorum*."

[6] Cp. Neh. xii. 46.

[7] "Lege totum Psalterium...nihil erit nisi ad Deum in cunctis operibus deprecatio." S. Jerome *contra Pelag.* i. 5.

the number[1]." But this reckoning has not been uniformly observed. Some ancient Jewish authorities reckon 149, others 147 Psalms, the latter number, as the Jerusalem Talmud says, "according to the years of our father Jacob." These totals are obtained by uniting one or all of the pairs i, ii: ix, x : cxiv, cxv. Although the Hebrew and the LXX agree in the total, they differ in the details of the numeration. The LXX unites ix and x, cxiv and cxv, and divides cxvi and cxlvii. It may be useful to subjoin a comparative table, for while our modern English versions follow the Hebrew reckoning, the Vulgate and the older English Versions (e.g. Wycliffe and Coverdale) and modern Roman Catholic versions based upon it, follow that of the LXX.

Hebrew (Later English Versions).		LXX (Vulgate. Older English Versions. Rom. Cath. Versions).
i—viii.	=	i—viii.
ix, x.	=	ix.
xi—cxiii.	=	x—cxii.
cxiv, cxv.	=	cxiii.
cxvi.	=	cxiv, cxv.
cxvii—cxlvi.	=	cxvi—cxlv.
cxlvii.	=	cxlvi, cxlvii.
cxlviii—cl.	=	cxlviii—cl.

[1] This Psalm appears to have been translated from a Hebrew original, but the contrast between it and the canonical Psalms is so noteworthy that it seems worth while to append a version of it.

"This Psalm was written by David with his own hand (and it is outside the number) when he fought in single combat with Goliath.

1. I was little among my brethren,
   and the youngest in my father's house;
   I fed my father's sheep.
2. My hands made a harp,
   my fingers contrived a psaltery.
3. And who will declare unto my Lord?
   He is the Lord, it is He that heareth.
4. He sent His angel,
   and took me from my father's sheep,
   and anointed me with the oil of his anointing.
5. My brethren were comely and tall,
   and in them the Lord had no pleasure.
6. I went forth to meet the Philistine,
   and he cursed me by his idols.
7. But I drew the sword from his side, and beheaded him,
   and took away the reproach from the children of Israel."

Thus for the greater part of the Psalter the numeration of the LXX is one behind that of the Hebrew.

The English reader should also remember that the title of a Psalm, when it consists of more than one or two words, is reckoned as a verse, and sometimes (e.g. in Ps. li) as two verses, in the Hebrew text. Attention to this is necessary in using the references of commentaries, which like that of Delitzsch, follow the numbering of the verses in the original.

4. *Divisions of the Psalter.* The Psalter has from ancient times been divided into five books:

> Book i = Pss. i—xli:
> „ ii = Pss. xlii—lxxii:
> „ iii = Pss. lxxiii—lxxxix:
> „ iv = Pss. xc—cvi:
> „ v = Pss. cvii—cl.

These divisions are indicated not merely by headings in the Massoretic text, which have been introduced into the Revised Version, but by doxologies at the close of the first four books (xli. 13, lxxii. 18, 19, lxxxix. 52, cvi. 48), which obviously form no part of the Psalms to which they are appended. No special doxology is added to Ps. cl. It is in itself an appropriate concluding doxology for the whole Psalter.

This five-fold division is earlier than the LXX, which contains the doxologies. It is often referred to by Jewish and Christian authorities, and compared to the five books of the Pentateuch.

Thus the *Midrash*[1] on Ps. i. 1: "Moses gave the Israelites the five books of the Law, and to correspond to these David gave them the Book of Psalms containing five books."

Hippolytus [?] (ed. Lagarde, p. 193): "Let it not escape your notice...that the Hebrews divided the Psalter also into five books, that it might be a second Pentateuch."

Jerome, in the *Prologus Galeatus:* "Tertius ordo Hagiographa possidet. Et primus liber incipit a Job. Secundus a David, quem quinque incisionibus (*sections*) et uno Psalmorum

---

[1] An ancient Jewish commentary, probably however in its present form not earlier than the 10th century A.D.

volumine comprehendunt." No doubt he chose this form of expression carefully, for in his preface to the Psalter he somewhat passionately affirms the unity of the Book.

The division is referred to by most of the Fathers, some of whom, as Ambrose, explain it allegorically; others, as Gregory of Nyssa, find in the several books so many steps rising to moral perfection. As will be shewn presently, the division of the books in part corresponds to older collections out of which the Psalter was formed, in part is purely artificial.

CHAPTER III.

THE TITLES OF THE PSALMS.

To nearly all the Psalms in the first three Books, and to some of those in the fourth and fifth Books, are prefixed titles, designating either (1) the character of the poem, or (2) matters connected with its musical setting, or (3) its liturgical use, or (4) the author, or perhaps more strictly, the collection from which the Psalm was taken, or (5) the historical occasion for which it was written or which it illustrates.

Such titles may occur separately or in combination. Many of them are extremely obscure, and their meanings can only be conjectured. All that will be attempted here is to give the most probable explanations. An elaborate discussion of the innumerable interpretations which have been proposed would be mere waste of time. Some special titles which occur but once will be discussed in the introduction to the Psalms to which they belong.

1. *Titles descriptive of the character of the poem.*

Psalm[1]. *Mizmōr*, rendered *Psalm*, is a technical term found only in the titles of the Psalter. It is prefixed to 57 Psalms, and with few exceptions, preceded or followed by the name of the author, generally that of David. The verb from which *Mizmōr* is derived occurs frequently in the Psalter (e.g. vii. 17, xlvii. 6, 7, cxlix. 3) but rarely elsewhere

[1] מִזְמוֹר: LXX ψαλμός: Vulg. *Psalmus*.

(Judg. v. 3; [2 Sam. xxii. 50; 1 Chr. xvi. 9]; Is. xii. 5). It appears originally to have meant *to make music*, like the Lat. *canere*, but came to be applied specially to instrumental music, as distinguished from vocal music. *Mizmōr* then means *a piece of music*, a song with instrumental accompaniment.

Song[1]. *Shīr*, rendered *song*, is the general term for a song or canticle. It occurs 30 times in the titles, generally preceded or followed by *Mizmōr*, and not unfrequently in the text of the Psalms (e.g. xxviii. 7, xl. 3, cxxxvii. 3, 4), and in other books. It is applied to secular as well as sacred songs (Gen. xxxi. 27; Jud. v. 12; 1 Kings iv. 32; Is. xxx. 29; Neh. xii. 27, 36, 46).

Maschīl[2] is found as the title of thirteen[3] Psalms, eleven of which are in Books ii and iii. The meaning is obscure. (*a*) It has been explained to mean *a didactic psalm*. Comp. the use of the cognate verb in xxxii. 8, 'I will instruct thee.' But of the Psalms which bear the title only xxxii and lxxviii are specifically 'didactic.' (*b*) Delitzsch supposes it to mean *a meditation*. (*c*) Most probable however is Ewald's explanation, *a skilful psalm*. The word is used in Ps. xlvii. 7, 'sing ye praises *with understanding*' (Heb. *maschīl*), R.V. marg., *in a skilful psalm*. It may have denoted something more definite than the ordinary *Mizmōr*, a psalm with musical setting of a specially delicate and artistic character.

Michtam occurs in the title of six Psalms, preceded or followed by *of David*[4]. It is probably, like *Maschīl*, a musical term, the meaning of which cannot now be determined. A few of the many explanations which have been given may be mentioned: (1) That of the LXX and Theodotion, στηλογραφία or εἰς στηλογραφίαν, *an inscription* or *for an inscription*. Cp. the Targ. *an excellent inscription* or *writing*. Hence Delitzsch explains, *a*

---

[1] שִׁיר: LXX in titles usually ᾠδή, in text ᾠδή or ᾆσμα.

[2] מַשְׂכִּיל: LXX συνέσεως or εἰς σύνεσιν: Vulg. *intellectus* or *ad intellectum*: Jer. *eruditio*.

[3] xxxii. xlii. xliv. xlv. lii. liii. liv. lv. lxxiv. lxxviii. lxxxviii. lxxxix. cxlii.

[4] xvi. lvi—lx.

poem of epigrammatic character, containing pithy or expressive sayings. (2) In defiance of all grammar and analogy Aquila Symmachus and Jerome render the word as an epithet of David, *the humble and sincere* or *blameless*. (3) *A golden Psalm* (A.V. marg.), with reference to the preciousness of its contents, like the *golden sayings* (χρυσᾶ ἔπη) of Pythagoras. (4) An unpublished poem. (5) A Psalm of hidden, mysterious meaning.

Shiggaion[1] occurs in the title of Ps. vii, and the Prayer of Habakkuk is said to be *set to Shigionoth*. The word is derived from a verb which means *to wander*, and it probably denotes a particular style of poetry or music, or it may include both, and mean 'a dithyrambic poem in wild ecstatic wandering rhythms, with corresponding music.'

A Prayer stands as the title of five Psalms (xvii. lxxxvi. xc. cii. cxlii). Cp. lxxii. 20; 1 Sam. ii. 1; Hab. iii. 1.

A Praise is the title of one Psalm only (cxlv).

2. *Titles connected with the musical setting or performance.*

To the chief Musician[2]: R.V. **For the Chief Musician**: is prefixed to fifty-five Psalms, of which only two (lxvi, lxvii) are anonymous, and most bear the name of David. Fifty-two of these are in Books I—III, and three in Book V. It is found also in the subscription to Habakkuk's Prayer (Hab. iii. 19). The verb, of which the word is a participle, is used in Chronicles and Ezra in the sense of *superintending* (1 Chr. xxiii. 4; 2 Chr. xxxiv. 12; Ezra iii. 8, 9), and in 1 Chr. xv. 21 in the

---

[1] שִׁגָּיוֹן plur. שִׁגְיֹנוֹת: LXX in Ps. vii simply ψαλμός, in Hab. μετὰ ᾠδῆς. Jer. *ignoratio*, following Symm. ἀγνόημα. Aq. ψ. ὑπὲρ ἀγνοίας, supposing it to refer to the contents of the Psalm.

[2] לַמְנַצֵּחַ (*lam'naççeach*). The Targum renders it *for praise*, giving the general sense. But the other Ancient Versions were completely at a loss. The LXX renders εἰς τὸ τέλος, Vulg. *in finem*, 'unto the end' or 'for ever,' confusing the word with לָנֶצַח (*lāneçach*). The other Greek Versions and Jerome connected it with the sense of *victory*, which is one of the meanings of the root. Thus Aquila τῷ νικοποιῷ, 'for the victor.' Symmachus, ἐπινίκιος, 'a song of victory:' Theodotion, εἰς τὸ νῖκος, 'for the victory:' Jerome, *victori*. So too the LXX in Hab. iii. 19, τοῦ νικῆσαι. These renderings gave the ingenuity of the Fathers great opportunities for allegorical interpretations.

specific sense of *leading* (R.V.) the music. There can be little doubt that the word means the *precentor*, or *conductor* of the Temple choir, who trained the choir and led the music, and denotes the destination of the Psalm for use in the Temple Services. Why it appears so rarely in the later books, where the Psalms are mainly of a liturgical character, must remain matter of conjecture. The explanation commonly given, that it was unnecessary, because the destination of these Psalms was obvious, is hardly satisfactory. Many of the Psalms in Books I—III which have it prefixed to them, are clearly intended for public use. Possibly it was a term belonging to the older collections, which had gone out of use in later times. Certainly the translators of the LXX had lost all clue to its meaning.

Selah. This term, though not belonging to the titles, may conveniently be discussed here.

The word is found 71 times in the Psalter, 3 times in Habakkuk iii, and nowhere else. In 16 Psalms it occurs once; in 15 twice; in 7 (and in Hab. iii) three times: in one, four times. Of these Psalms 9 are in Book I: 17 in Book II: 11 in Book III; none in Book IV: 2 only in Book V. It is to be further noted that all these Psalms, with the exception of the anonymous lxvi and lxvii, bear the name of David or of the Levitical singers (the sons of Korah, Asaph, Heman, Ethan); and all bear indications of being intended to be set to music. The majority of them (28 of the 39: cp. Hab. iii. 19) have, 'For the Chief Musician' in the title, frequently with a further specification of the instruments or melody (iv. ix. xlvi. liv. lv. lvii. lix. lx. lxi. lxii. lxvii. lxxv. lxxvi. lxxvii. lxxxi. lxxxiv. lxxxviii. Hab. iii. 19). Of the remaining eleven, eight are designated *mizmōr*, 'psalm', two *maschīl*, and one *shiggaion*.

It may fairly be inferred from these facts that Selah is a technical term of great antiquity, having reference to musical accompaniment. Its precise meaning, however, is quite uncertain. There are two main lines of ancient tradition:

(*a*) By the LXX always, and by Symmachus and Theodotion generally, it is rendered διάψαλμα[1] (*diapsalma*), which may

[1] The word is also found twice in the Psalms of Solomon (xvii. 31; xviii. 10).

denote either louder playing, *forte;* or, more probably, *an instrumental interlude*[1], while the singing ceased. The Syriac (with a few exceptions) gives an abbreviation of the Greek word. The Vulgate omits it entirely.

(*b*) The most ancient Jewish traditions interpret the word to mean *for ever*. So the Targum, with some variety of rendering, Aquila, the 'Fifth' and 'Sixth' Greek versions, Symmachus, Theodotion, and the Syriac occasionally; and Jerome, who renders *semper*[2].

Of these ancient renderings, that of the LXX probably preserves a true tradition as to the usage of *Selah:* but the meaning 'always' is based on no known etymology, and is obviously unsuitable in the majority of passages.

Of the multitude of modern explanations only the most reasonable and most generally accepted need be mentioned here. According to this explanation *Selah* is derived from a root meaning *to raise*, and signifies 'Up!'

It is then a direction to the musicians to strike up, either with a louder accompaniment, or with an interlude while the singing ceased. This explanation is supported by the conjunction of *Selah* in Ps. ix. 16 with *Higgaion*, a term used of instrumental music (Ps. xcii. 3, 'a solemn sound'). It is moreover confirmed by an examination of the passages in which *Selah* occurs. In the majority of cases it is found at the end of a strophe, or before the introduction of some fresh thought, where an interlude would be most natural (Ps. iii. 2, 4, 8; xxiv. 6, 10; xliv. 8; xlvi. 3, 7, 11; lxvi. 4, 7, 15); or before some appeal or utterance which would be distinguished from what preceded and emphasised by an interlude or by a stronger accompaniment (Ps. vii. 5; l. 6; lx. 4; lxxv. 3; lxxxi. 7; lxxxiii. 8). There

---

[1] Cp. διαύλιον, an interlude on the flute.

[2] For an interesting account of the various opinions held in his day consult his letter to Marcella (Opp. i. col. 135, ed. Vallarsi). He decides in favour of the rendering *semper*, 'always,' because it is that given by Aquila, 'the most careful interpreter of the meanings of Hebrew words,' and says that it is designed 'to connect what precedes with what follows, or to shew that what has been said is everlasting': and compares the use of the word with that of *Amen* or *Shalom* (peace), to mark the end of a passage, and confirm its contents.

are no doubt many instances which do not appear to come under these general principles; but the Hebrew idea of what was fitting by way of accompaniment may have differed from ours; and in some cases the accuracy of the Massoretic Text is doubtful. The Septuagint does not always agree with it in the insertion or omission of *Selah*, and an obscure technical term would be specially liable to be omitted or wrongly inserted.

Two terms refer to *musical instruments*.

On Neginôth[1]: R.V. **on stringed instruments**: occurs six times in the Psalter[2]: and in Hab. iii. 19 we find *on my stringed instruments*. **Upon Neginah**: R.V. **on a stringed instrument** (lxi): may be a variation of the expression, or may indicate the melody to which the Psalm was to be sung[3]. The word is derived from a verb meaning *to play on stringed instruments* (1 Sam. xvi. 16—18, 23). The meaning *stringed instruments* is peculiar to these titles: elsewhere it denotes *song* (Job xxx. 9; Ps. lxxvii. 6; Is. xxxviii. 20). The title no doubt indicates that the Psalm was to be accompanied by stringed instruments, perhaps by these only.

Upon Nehilôth[4]: R.V. **with the Nehiloth**, or (marg.) *wind instruments:* in Ps. v only. Probably *flutes* of some kind are meant. For the use of these in sacred music see Is. xxx. 29 (*a pipe*): 1 Sam. x. 5; 1 Kings i. 40.

Two terms probably indicate the *character* or *pitch* of the music.

Upon Alāmôth[5]: R.V. **set to A.**: is found in the title of Ps.

---

[1] בִּנְגִינוֹת: LXX. ἐν ψαλμοῖς (iv): ἐν ὕμνοις generally: in Hab. ἐν τῇ ᾠδῇ αὐτοῦ: Vulg. *in carminibus:* Jer. *in psalmis*. Symm. διὰ ψαλτηρίων.

[2] Pss. iv. vi. liv. lv. lxvii. lxxvi.

[3] The Heb. is עַל נְגִינַת which may mean *set to neginath*, or, *the song of...:* some word of definition being lost.

[4] אֶל הַנְּחִילוֹת. The Greek and Latin versions are quite astray, referring the word to the contents of the Psalm. The LXX and Theodotion: ὑπὲρ τῆς κληρονομούσης: Vulg. *pro ea quae hereditatem consequitur*. Aq. ἀπὸ (?) κληροδοσιῶν: Symm. ὑπὲρ κληρουχιῶν: Jer. *super hereditatibus*.

[5] The ancient Versions were again at fault. The LXX renders: ὑπὲρ

xlvi, and may possibly once have stood in the title of Ps. ix, and as a subscription to Ps. xlviii, or in the title of Ps. xlix. See the notes there. The term appears to mean *in the manner of maidens*, or, *for maidens' voices: soprano*.

Upon Sheminith[1]: R.V. **set to the S.**, i.e. as marg., *the eighth* (Pss. vi and xii): probably denotes that the setting was to be an octave lower, or, on the lower octave; *tenor* or *bass*. Both terms occur together in 1 Chr. xv. 19—21. Heman, Asaph, and Jeduthun were appointed "with cymbals of brass to sound aloud": eight other Levites, "with psalteries set to Alamoth"; and six "with harps set to the Sheminith, to lead."

Upon Gittith[2]: R.V. **set to the Gittith**: occurs in the titles of Pss. viii, lxxxi, lxxxiv. In form *Gittith* is a fem. adj. derived from *Gath*, and may mean either (1) some Gittite instrument: so the Targ. 'the harp which David brought from Gath': or (2) a Gittite melody; possibly, as has been conjectured, the march of the Gittite guard (2 Sam. xv. 18).

To Jeduthun[3]: R.V. **after the manner of J.** (lxii, lxxvii): probably means that the Psalm was set to some melody composed by or called after David's chief musician (1 Chr. xvi. 41). In the title of Ps. xxxix Jeduthun appears to be named as the chief musician intended.

A series of obscure titles probably indicate the *melody* to which the Psalm was to be sung by a reference to the opening words of some well-known song. Such are the titles of

Ps. ix: **set to Muth-labben** (R.V.).

Ps. xxii: **set to Ayyéleth hash-Shahar**, i.e. *the hind of the morning*.

τῶν κρυφίων: Vulg. *pro occultis:* Symm. ὑπὲρ τῶν αἰωνίων: Aq. ἐπὶ νεανιοτήτων: and so Jer. *pro iuventutibus.*

[1] עַל הַשְּׁמִינִית. The LXX literally ὑπὲρ τῆς ὀγδόης: Vulg. *pro octava*. Both terms are allegorically explained by the Fathers, of the mysteries of the faith, the octave of eternity, &c. &c.

[2] עַל הַגִּתִּית. The LXX and Symm. have ὑπὲρ τῶν ληνῶν: Vulg. and Jer. *pro torcularibus*, 'for the wine-presses', reading גִּתּוֹת for גִּתִּית. Hence some have explained the title, 'set to the melody of a vintage song.' Aq. and Symm. render the Massoretic text: ὑπὲρ τῆς γεϑϑίτιδος.

[3] עַל יְדוּתוּן.

Pss. xlv, lxix: **set to Shoshannim** (R.V.), i.e. *Lilies.* Ps. lx: **set to Shushan Eduth** (R.V.), i.e. *The lily of testimony.* Ps. lxxx: **set to Shoshannim Eduth** (R.V.), i.e. *Lilies, a testimony.*

Ps. lvi: **set to Yonath elem rechōkīm**, i.e. *The silent dove of them that are afar off:* or, as read with different vowels, *The dove of the distant terebinths.*

Four Psalms (lvii—lix, lxxv) are entitled, [**set to**] **Al-tashcheth** i.e. *Destroy not.*

The titles of Ps. liii: **set to Mahalath**: and lxxxviii: **set to Mahalath Leannōth**: are extremely obscure, but probably belong to this class.

For further details see the notes in each case.

3. A few titles refer to *the liturgical use of the Psalm.* In the time of the Second Temple, each day of the week had its special Psalm, which was sung at the offering of the morning sacrifice[1]. Thus Ps. xcii is entitled "A Psalm, a Song **for the Sabbath day**." This is the only reference to the daily psalms in the Heb. text: but in the LXX, Ps. xxiv is assigned to the first day of the week (τῆς μιᾶς σαββάτων); Ps. xlviii to the second day (δευτέρᾳ σαββάτου); Ps. xciv to the fourth day (τετράδι σαββάτων); Ps. xciii to the sixth day of the week, "when the earth had been filled with inhabitants" (εἰς τὴν ἡμέραν τοῦ προσαββάτου, ὅτε κατῴκισται ἡ γῆ). The Old Latin Version further refers Ps. lxxxi to the fifth day (*quinta sabbati*). These titles agree with the arrangement given in the Mishna (*Tamid*, vii. 3), according to which the Psalm for the third day was Ps. lxxxii.

The title of Pss. xxxviii and lxx **to bring to remembrance**, or, as R.V. marg., **to make memorial**, may indicate that they were sung at the offering of incense: and that of Ps. c, **A Psalm of thanksgiving** (R.V.), marg. *for the thank-offering*, may mark that it was sung when thank-offerings (lvi. 12) were offered.

The title of Ps. xxx, **A Song at the Dedication of the House**, may refer to its use at the Festival of the Dedication.

To teach is part of the title prefixed to Ps. lx. A comparison of Deut. xxxi. 19 and 2 Sam. i. 18 makes it probable that it was to be learnt by heart and recited on public occasions.

---

[1] Cp. Ecclus. l. 14 ff. for a description of the service.

INTRODUCTION.

On these titles see further in the notes on the particular Psalms.

A song of Degrees, rather, **A Song of the Ascents** (or, **of the Going up**), is the title prefixed to 15 Psalms (cxx—cxxxiv), which appear to have formed a separate collection, bearing the title *Songs of the Goings up* (or, *of the Going up*), which was afterwards transferred to each separate Psalm.

Various explanations of this title have been proposed.

(1) The LXX renders, ᾠδὴ τῶν ἀναβαθμῶν: Vulg. and Jer., *canticum graduum*, 'a song of steps.' It has been supposed that they were so called because they were sung upon the flight of 15 steps which led from the Court of the Women to the Court of the Men in the Second Temple. But Delitzsch has shewn that the passage of the Talmud quoted in support of this explanation really says nothing at all about the singing of these Psalms upon the steps, or the derivation of the name from them, but merely compares the number of the Psalms with that of the steps.

(2) An explanation which has found considerable favour in modern times regards the term as denoting a particular kind of 'ascending' structure, in which each verse takes up and repeats a word or clause from the preceding verse. Ps. cxxi offers a good example of this structure; but apart from the fact that no trace can be found of this technical meaning of the word '*ascent*' elsewhere, the structure is neither peculiar to these Psalms nor characteristic of all of them.

(3) As 'the ascent' or 'going up' was the regular term for the Return from Babylon (Ezra vii. 9), some have supposed that these psalms were sung by the returning exiles on their march. So the Syriac Version, and probably Aq. Symm. and Theod., who render ᾆσμα τῶν ἀναβάσεων or εἰς τὰς ἀναβάσεις. But the contents of many of the Psalms do not favour this explanation.

(4) 'To go up' was the regular term for making pilgrimage to Jerusalem at the great festivals (1 Sam. i. 3; Ps. cxxii. 4). 'The songs of the goings up' may have been the name for those which were sung on these occasions. We know that the pilgrims went up with singing (Is. xxx. 29; Ps. xlii. 4), and many of these

Psalms are well suited for such occasions[1]; while others, though not so obviously appropriate, might well have been employed for the purpose. This is on the whole the most probable explanation, although the substantive 'going up' is not used elsewhere in this technical sense.

4. *Titles relating to Authorship.* These are regularly introduced by a preposition denoting *of* or *belonging to*, the so-called '*lamed* auctoris.'

(*a*) One Psalm (xc) bears the name of **Moses**.

(*b*) 73 Psalms bear the name of **David**: viz. all those in Book I, except i and ii, which are prefatory; x, which is part of ix; and xxxiii, which appears to be a later addition: 18 in Book II. (li—lxv, lxviii—lxx); one in Book III. (lxxxvi); two in Book IV. (ci, ciii); 15 in Book V. (cviii—cx, cxxii, cxxiv, cxxxi, cxxxiii, cxxxviii—cxlv).

(*c*) Two (lxxii, cxxvii) bear the name of **Solomon**.

(*d*) 12 (l, lxxiii—lxxxiii) bear the name of **Asaph**, one of David's principal musicians (1 Chr. vi. 39, xv. 17, xvi. 5 ff.; 2 Chr. v. 12).

(*e*) To **the sons of Korah** are attributed 10 or 11: xlii [xliii], xliv—xlix. lxxxiv. lxxxv. lxxxvii. lxxxviii. [?], for according to analogy the title is to be rendered as in R.V., **of the sons of K.**; not, as in A.V., *for the sons of K.*

(*f*) The sages **Heman the Ezrachite** and **Ethan the Ezrachite** (1 Kings iv. 31) have each a psalm attributed to them (lxxxviii, lxxxix).

5. *Titles describing the occasion of the Psalm* are prefixed to 13 psalms, all of which bear the name of David. Pss. vii. lix. lvi. xxxiv. lii. lvii. cxlii. liv. are referred to the period of his persecution by Saul: xviii to the climax of his reign; Ps. lx to the Syro-Ammonite war; Ps. li to his fall; Pss. iii and lxiii to his flight from Absalom.

The Value of the Titles. We have now to inquire whether these titles give any authentic information, or must be regarded as late additions, largely, if not wholly, untrustworthy.

(i) With regard to the *musical titles* it is often asserted that

---

[1] E.g. cxxi—cxxiii. cxxv. cxxvii. cxxviii. cxxxii—cxxxiv.

they represent the usages of the Second Temple, and were added by some post-exilic editor. This may be true of some; but as a general statement it is hardly justified by the evidence.

(1) Although, as might be expected, light is thrown upon them by the description of David's musical services in 1 Chron., it is by no means the case that they are merely borrowed from that book. Many of them are not to be found there.

(2) We have positive evidence for the use of titles and terms of the kind in pre-exilic times from Hab. iii. 1, 19.

(3) It is precisely in the later Psalms which bear every appearance of being intended for the Temple worship, that the musical titles and terms are rare or entirely wanting.

(4) The Septuagint translators found them in the text, but were unable to understand even their general purport. This may possibly have been due to ignorance of the technical terms of Palestinian music in Egypt, and in any case only indicates a relatively high antiquity, but it must be taken into account.

The most natural inference from these considerations appears to be that while the liturgical titles belong to the services of the Second Temple, and may in some cases (e.g. Ps. xxx) have been added at a very late date, the musical titles may very probably be referred to the period before the exile. After the Return they ceased to be used, and in the second century B.C. they were no longer intelligible.

(ii) We may now proceed to consider the titles relating to *authorship and occasion*. It is frequently asserted that these must be neglected as wholly untrustworthy for reasons such as the following:

(1) The variations found in MSS. and Versions shew that they were not regarded as an integral part of the text, but were liable to alteration by the transcribers, like the titles of the books of the N.T., or the subscriptions to the Pauline Epistles.

(2) The fact that only Moses, David, Solomon, and David's singers are mentioned is supposed to be due to the tendency of tradition to connect everything with famous names.

(3) It is thought strange that none of the prophets, in particular Jeremiah, whose writings so remarkably resemble many of the Psalms, are mentioned.

(4) The historical notices are almost all taken from the Books of Samuel, and are in most cases inappropriate.

(5) Many of the titles are demonstrated to be erroneous by the contents and language of the Psalms to which they are prefixed. Many Psalms ascribed to David assume situations and circumstances wholly unlike any in which he can be supposed to have been placed: some (e.g. lxix. ciii) refer to the destruction of Jerusalem: the language of others (e.g. cxxxix) is unquestionably late: some (e.g. lxxxvi) are mere compilations.

On these and similar grounds modern critics are disposed to reject the titles entirely. But while it is clear that in many cases the titles cannot be right, much may be said in favour of allowing them a certain significance and a relative authority.

(1) The titles are not to be peremptorily condemned as a whole, because MSS. and Versions do not unanimously support some of them[1]. The text itself was liable to alteration in early times, but it is not therefore to be suspected where the documentary evidence is unanimous, unless the strongest internal evidence points to an error anterior to our existing authorities.

(2) Titles of a similar kind are prefixed to poems found elsewhere in the O. T., e.g. Ex. xv. 1: 1 Sam. ii. 1; 2 Sam. i. 17, 18; xxii. 1, xxiii. 1; Is. xxxviii. 9; Hab. iii. 1. These are no doubt due in many cases to the compilers of the books in which they are found, but they are evidence for the antiquity of the custom of prefixing titles to poems.

(3) The infrequency of titles in the later books (iv, v) is at least an indication that they were not an arbitrary addition of

---

[1] The extent of the variations may easily be exaggerated. A few Heb. MSS. assign lxvi. lxvii. to David. In the LXX David's name is prefixed to xxxiii. xliii. lxvii. lxxi. xci. xciii—xcix. civ. cxxxvii. Historical notices are added to xxvii. xciii. xcvi. xcvii. cxliii. cxliv. Jeremiah's name (as well as David's) is prefixed to cxxxvii in some MSS (not אב), and the names of Haggai and Zechariah to cxxxviii (not in א, in A Zechariah only), cxlvi—cxlviii. In cxxii. cxxiv. cod. א, and in cxxxi. cxxxiii. codd. A and א agree with the Heb. text in retaining *David*, though it is omitted by the ordinary editions. In cxxvii *Solomon* is omitted in the best MSS.

the latest compilers of the Psalter, but rested on some authority, documentary or traditional.

(4) Some at any rate of the titles, e.g. those of vii and lx, are not derived from the historical books now extant, but from some independent source.

It appears then that while on the one hand the titles cannot be regarded as in all cases giving certain and trustworthy information concerning the authorship of the Psalms, on the other hand they are not to be one and all peremptorily rejected as purely arbitrary and conjectural.

What then is their value? It seems probable that they indicate the source from which the Psalms were derived rather than the opinion of the collector as to their authorship.

In regard to the Psalms of the Sons of Korah this is clearly the case. The title *A Psalm of the Sons of Korah* cannot mean that the Psalm was composed by a plurality of authors. It must be part of the title of the collection from which these Psalms were derived. Such a collection may have been called, "*The Book of the Songs of the Sons of Korah*," and have contained Psalms written by members of the guild or family of Korah and preserved in a collection, made probably for liturgical purposes, which bore their name.

Similarly the title, "A Psalm of David," may have been derived from the general title of the collection from which the Psalms in question were taken:—"*The Book of the Prayers of David.*" The collection may have been so named from its most eminent poet, although the works of other poets were subsequently added to it. Just as in later times the whole Psalter came to be spoken of as the Psalms of David, from its founder and principal author, so in earlier times the smaller collection of which only the origin and nucleus was due to David, came to bear his name, and when that collection was incorporated in the Psalter, his name was placed at the head of each Psalm taken from it[1].

The compiler of the Second Book may also have taken the Davidic Psalms which it contains from some earlier collection,

---

[1] We commonly speak of Newman's *Lyra Apostolica*, though five other writers contributed to it.

possibly a historical work in which many of them were connected with particular episodes in the life of David. The earlier histories were often illustrated by the insertion of poems, e.g. Judg. v: 1 Sam. ii: 2 Sam. xxii.

Even the compilers of Books IV and V may have found the Psalms which are there attributed to David in some earlier collection bearing his name, or assigned to him by current tradition.

Further it is quite possible that imitations of Davidic Psalms, such for example as Ps. lxxxvi, may have been called by his name, without the slightest intention of fraud. In 1 Chr. xvi we find a Psalm compiled from other Psalms suggested as an appropriate thanksgiving for the occasion, though it does not appear to be expressly attributed to David[1].

Again, it is possible that Psalms were written by different poets to illustrate particular episodes in the life of David, or to express the thoughts which might be supposed to have been in his mind upon certain occasions. These might easily have had his name affixed to them, without the slightest intention of passing them off as his for the sake of giving them currency and authority. Similarly the title "A Psalm of Asaph" may indicate that the Psalm was taken from a collection founded by David's famous minstrel. Such a collection would have been preserved and used by the guild or family of Asaph, and added to from time to time, though it still retained the name of its founder.

While then the titles of the Psalms cannot be supposed to give certain information as to their authors, and many of the Psalms bearing the name of David or Asaph cannot have been written by them, we are not justified in rejecting the titles as blind and worthless conjectures. A sober criticism will allow them a certain weight, as giving, in general at least, some information as to the source from which the Psalms were derived, which is not to be rejected without good reason.

In criticising the title of a Psalm by the light of its contents much caution is necessary. The possibility of alterations and additions to the original poem must be taken into account.

[1] See the R.V. of 1 Chr. xvi. 7.

It is probable that many of the Psalms were not at once committed to writing, but like other oriental poetry, transmitted orally[1]. The comparison of Ps. xviii with 2 Sam. xxii shews that the text has in some cases suffered from accidental errors of transcription, while in others it appears to bear marks of intentional revision. The comparison of Ps. liii with Ps. xiv, and of Ps. cviii with Pss. lvii and lx, shews that editors did not scruple to alter earlier Psalms, or to combine portions of them, for their own special purposes. Additions seem to have been made with a view of adapting Psalms for liturgical use. Such processes, which can be definitely traced in some instances, have no doubt been in operation elsewhere.

CHAPTER IV.

THE AUTHORSHIP AND AGE OF THE PSALMS.

It is obvious from what has been said in the preceding chapter that great uncertainty must necessarily rest upon the authorship of the Psalms. When once it is admitted, as it must be admitted, that the titles cannot be absolutely relied on, we are launched upon a sea of uncertainty. Internal evidence, whether of thought, or style, or language, is a precarious guide. The same Psalm has been confidently assigned by one critic to David, by another to the age of the Maccabees[2].

---

[1] Arabic poetry was preserved by the *ráwís*, or *reciters*. "The custom of committing verse to writing did not begin till near the end of the first century after the Flight. The whole of the old poetry was preserved by oral tradition only." Lyall's *Ancient Arabian Poetry*, p. xxxv.

[2] The question is often asked by the English reader why language does not determine the date of the books of the O.T. within at any rate comparatively definite limits. But (1) the remains of Hebrew literature of which the date is admitted as certain are too scanty to give much material for forming a judgment: (2) the Massoretic vocalisation, while here and there preserving ancient forms, has obscured distinctions under the uniform pronunciation of a later age: (3) the possibility of imitation of ancient models in a later age must be taken into account.

Important as it is for the full interpretation of many Psalms to know the circumstances under which they were written, and for the elucidation of the religious history of Israel to determine the age to which they belong, the Psalms as a whole suffer less from this uncertainty than might be expected. Their interest is human and universal. They appeal to the experience of all ages. Still the endeavour must be made to ascertain to what period of the history a Psalm belongs.

An uncritical age attributed the whole Psalter to David. Modern criticism has gone to the opposite extreme, and is disposed to refer the whole Psalter, or at least the greater part of it, to the period after the return from Babylon[1].

It would be strange indeed if none of those sacred "songs of Zion," the fame of which was so well known to her Babylonian captors (Ps. cxxxvii. 3, 4), had survived. But further, it is difficult to believe that the tradition of the Jewish Church was entirely wrong in assigning the foundation of the Psalter to David and regarding him as the most eminent religious poet of the nation.

His skill as poet and musician, and his interest in the development of religious music, are attested by the earliest records[2]. Later times pointed to him as the founder of the services of the sanctuary[3]. The leaders of the return from the exile believed themselves to be restoring his institutions[4].

But in particular, the incorporation of Ps. xviii in the Book of Samuel as a specimen of David's poetry illustrating his character and genius is the strongest evidence in favour of

---

[1] So, for example, Wellhausen in Bleek's *Introduction*, p. 507 (ed. 1876): "Since the Psalter belongs to the Hagiographa, and is the hymn-book of the congregation of the Second Temple...the question is not whether it contains any post-exilic Psalms, but whether it contains any pre-exilic Psalms." Similarly Reuss: "Our doubts do not go so far as to deny the possibility of referring a single one of the poems in the present collection of Synagogue hymns to the period of the kingdom. But we have no decisive proofs for such antiquity." *History of the O.T.* § 282.

[2] See 1 Sam. xvi. 17 ff.; xviii. 10; 2 Sam. i. 17 ff.; iii. 33 ff.; vi. 5, 15; xxii. 1; xxiii. 1 ff.; Amos vi. 5.

[3] 2 Chr. xxix. 30.

[4] Ezra iii. 10; Neh. xii. 24, 36, 46.

regarding David as the founder of the Psalter. That Psalm is there circumstantially ascribed to David, and there is no sufficient ground for placing the compilation of the Book of Samuel at so late a date that its evidence on this point can be set aside as a mere tradition which had sprung up in the course of centuries.

But if Ps. xviii must be acknowledged to be the work of David, important consequences follow. For depth of devotion, simplicity of trust, joyousness of gratitude, and confidence of hope, not less than for its natural force and poetic beauty, that Psalm has few rivals. It has all the freshness of creative genius. It can hardly have been the solitary production of its author. If such a Psalm could have been written by David, so might many others; and it is reasonable to inquire with regard to those which bear his name whether they may not actually have been composed by him.

Both poetry and music existed before David's time, and poetry had been carried to a high development in such compositions as Ex. xv and Judg. v. But with David a new era of religious poetry commenced. The personal element entered into it. It became the instrument of the soul's communion with God. David's natural poetic powers were awakened by his training in the schools of the prophets under Samuel[1]. The manifold vicissitudes of his life gave him an unparalleled depth and variety of experience. Chosen by God to be the founder of the kingdom of promise, he must still pass through trials and persecutions and dangers to the throne. When he had reached the zenith of his fame, he fell through pride and self-reliance, and by sharp chastisement must learn the grievousness of sin. But genius and circumstances alone could not have produced the Psalms. In his "last words" he himself declared,

> "The spirit of the LORD spake in me,
> And his word was upon my tongue."

Unique natural genius, trained and called into action by the discipline of an unique life, must still be quickened and illuminated by the supernal inspiration of the Holy Spirit, before it

[1] Comp. Delitzsch, *The Psalms*, Introd. § iii.

could strike out the strains, which were to be the pattern and model of religious poetry for all the ages.

It has often been asserted that the David of the Psalms is an entirely different character from the David of history. The devout singer and the rough warrior cannot, it is said[1], be the same person. But a great nature is necessarily many sided; and in early ages it is possible for traits of character which to us seem irreconcilable to coexist in the same individual. And the difference is often exaggerated. Not a few of the Psalms illustrate and are illustrated by the history of David's life; and in that history, fragmentary and incomplete as it necessarily is, are to be found abundant traces of the religious side of his character; of the confidence which in the midst of danger and difficulty threw itself unperplexed upon God; of the patience which could await God's time instead of rushing to revenge; of the simple faith which ascribed all success and advancement to God; of the hope which looked trustingly forward into the unknown future, in calm assurance that God would fulfil His promises; last but not least, of the penitence which humbled itself in unfeigned sorrow for sin.

It may have been the case, as Delitzsch supposes[2], that the reigns of Jehoshaphat and Hezekiah were marked by fresh outbursts of Psalm poetry. Under both these kings great national deliverances called for fresh expressions of praise and thanksgiving (2 Ch. xx; 2 Kings xviii. ff.): Jehoshaphat exerted himself for the religious education of the country (2 Chr. xvii. 7 ff.): the collection of Proverbs, made under the direction of Hezekiah, attests his interest in literature (Prov. xxv. 1).

A few Psalms date from the time of the destruction of Jerusalem and the earlier years of the exile. Some may be from the pen of Jeremiah, who has been credited by some critics with the authorship of a considerable number[3].

With the Return from the Exile Psalmody revived. The harp

---

[1] e.g. by Reuss, § 157.   [2] Introd. § iii.
[3] This appears to be due partly to the fact that so much of his personal and inner life is known to us from his autobiography; partly to his familiarity with existing literature and his free use of it, which results in numerous parallels between his prophecies and the Psalms.

which had been hung up on the willows of Babylon was strung once more. Fresh hymns were written for the services of the restored Temple[1]. The renewed study of the Law under Ezra and Nehemiah bore fruit in such meditations as Ps. cxix.

Did the Psalter still continue to receive further enrichment? The question has been warmly debated in ancient and modern times, whether any of the Psalms belong to the Maccabaean age. Prophecy was silent (1 Macc. iv. 46, &c.); but might not the great revival of national spirit naturally have found expression in poetry? and do not some of the Psalms clearly refer to the circumstances of that period?

Some critics would refer the whole of the last three books as well as many Psalms in the earlier books to that period, and bring down the completion of the collection to the reign of John Hyrcanus (B.C. 135—107) or Alexander Jannaeus (B.C. 105—79)[2].

The real question is, however, a much narrower one. The Psalms which have been most confidently and generally referred to the age of the Maccabees are xliv. lxxiv. lxxix. and lx. lxxx. lxxxiii; with a few others. These are thought to present features which belong to that age, and to no other; e.g. in Ps. xliv the description of the nation as suffering, though it has been faithful to God; in lxxiv the destruction of the synagogues, the profanation of the Temple, and the cessation of prophecy: and the quotation of lxxix. 2, 3 in 1 Macc. vii. 16, 17 with reference to the massacre of the Assideans by the usurping high-priest Alcimus, is supposed to imply that it was written on the occasion.

---

[1] Yet some of the Temple Psalms in the later books of the Psalter may have been revivals or adaptations of ancient hymns. An incidental reference in Jer. xxxiii. 11 shews that the doxology, "Give thanks to the LORD of hosts, for the LORD is good, for his mercy endureth for ever," was the characteristic formula of thanksgiving before the Captivity. Yet it is found only in the later books (iv and v) of the Psalter (Ps. c. 4, 5; cvi. 1; &c.), in Psalms which would generally be regarded as post-exilic.

[2] "The Psalms preserved to us," says Reuss, "are for the most part the work of the generation which suffered under Antiochus, fought with Judah and Jonathan, and then under Simon enjoyed victory and rest, praising God in gratitude and humility." *Hist. of O. T.* § 474.

The question is one of exegesis, and a detailed examination of the characteristics of these Psalms must be deferred to the commentary on them. It will then be seen whether they cannot be as well or better referred to the Chaldean or Persian period, or even a much earlier time. Moreover it has well been pointed out that some distinctive features of the Maccabaean period are conspicuously absent from these Psalms. "They do not contain the slightest trace of those internal divisions of the people which were the most marked features of the Maccabaean struggle. The dangers then were as much from within as from without; and party jealousies brought the divine cause to the greatest peril. It is incredible that a series of Maccabaean Psalms should contain no allusion to a system of enforced idolatry, or to a temporising priesthood, or to a faithless multitude[1]."

The preliminary question may however be discussed here, whether the history of the Psalter and the Canon does not exclude the possibility of such late additions.

(1) As the author of the Book of Chronicles (1 Chr. xvi. 8 ff.), in combining portions of Pss. cv, xcvi, cvi, includes as a part of cvi the doxology which marks the end of the fourth Book, it has been argued that the Psalter must have been already known to him in its five-fold division. This is extremely doubtful, and even if it is admitted, it cannot prove that the Psalter was finally complete, and closed against the admission of fresh Psalms.

(2) More important is the fact that all the Psalms which are most confidently set down as Maccabaean belong to the 'Elohistic' collection, which was anterior to the collections contained in Books IV and V[2]. Moreover some of them have musical titles, in contrast to the practice of the last collection. Is it conceivable that the LXX translators should have been so entirely at fault as to the meaning of the titles of lx and lxxx, if they were almost contemporary compositions?

(3) The Prologue to Ecclesiasticus speaks of the Canonical Books as already distinguished from other writings in the time of the author's grandfather, and of the Greek translation as already existing; and though again this statement does not

---

[1] Dr (now Bp) Westcott in Smith's *Dict. of the Bible*, ii. 168.
[2] See below, p. xl ff.

amount to proof that the Canon was finally closed, it raises a strong presumption against the admission of fresh writings at so late a date as B.C. 150 or even 100. The Second Book of Maccabees speaks of the care which Judas took to collect the sacred writings which had been dispersed or lost in the war (2 Macc. ii. 14), but no hint is given that the collection included new works.

(4) If the *Psalms of Solomon*[1] could be referred to the Maccabaean age, they would afford an almost conclusive proof that the whole of the Psalter belongs to a much earlier time. But it is now generally agreed that this work belongs to the period after the conquest of Jerusalem by Pompey in B.C. 63, and was completed soon after his death in B.C. 48[2]. Even if the Psalms of Solomon are to be placed at this later date, the argument does not altogether lose its force[3]. For they were written only a century after the standard of independence was raised by Mattathias, and less than half a century after the time at which the Psalter is supposed to have received its latest additions. But the contrast is immense. They are separated from the Psalter by an impassable gulf. "The spirit which the Psalms breathe is entirely that of Pharisaic Judaism. They are pervaded by an earnest moral tone and a sincere piety. But the righteousness which they preach and the dearth of which they deplore is, all through, the righteousness which consists in complying with all the Pharisaic prescriptions[4]." Their development of the doctrine of the Resurrection and the Messianic expectation separates them widely from the canonical Psalms. Where for example can we find parallels in the Psalter to language like the following with reference to the Resurrection?

---

[1] A collection of 18 Psalms, written in Hebrew, probably in Palestine, and now extant in a Greek version, which may be found in Fritzsche's *Libri Vet. Test. Pseudepigraphi Selecti*. A new edition, with translation and notes, has recently been published by Prof. Ryle and Mr James.
[2] See Schürer's *Hist. of the Jewish People in the time of Jesus Christ*, Div. ii. § 32 (Vol. iii. p. 17 ff. E. T.).
[3] The development of this argument by Bp Westcott in Smith's *Dict. of the Bible*, ii. 168, on the hypothesis of the Maccabaean date of these Psalms, should still be consulted.
[4] Schürer, p. 21.

"The destruction of the sinner shall be for ever,
and he shall not be remembered, when He visiteth the righteous.
This is the portion of sinners for ever.
But they that fear the Lord shall arise unto life eternal,
and their life shall be in the light of the Lord and shall fail
    no more" (iii. 13—16).
"For the Lord will spare His saints,
and their transgressions will He blot out by correction:
for the life of the righteous is for ever,
but sinners shall be carried away to destruction
and their memorial shall no more be found" (xiii. 9, 10).

Equally remarkable is the expression of the Messianic hope:
"Behold, O Lord, and raise up unto them their king,
the son of David, at the time which thou knowest, O God,
that he may reign over Israel thy servant.
And gird him with strength to break in pieces unrighteous
    rulers" (xvii. 23, 24).

    *   *   *   *

"And in his days there is no unrighteousness in the midst of
    them,
for all are holy, and their king is the anointed lord[1]" (v. 36).

    *   *   *   *

"And he himself is pure from sin, to rule over a great people;
to rebuke rulers and to destroy sinners by the might of a word.
And he shall not be feeble in his days, relying upon his God,
for God made him mighty in the holy spirit,
and wise in the counsel of understanding with strength and
    righteousness" (*vv.* 41, 42).

These considerations are sufficient, taken all together, to make us hesitate to assign Psalms to the Maccabaean period, except on the most cogent internal evidence. The discussion of such evidence must necessarily be deferred to the notes on each Psalm. Few commentators however deny the possibility, and most maintain the certainty, of the existence of Maccabaean Psalms in the Psalter.

[1] χριστὸς κύριος: cp. Lam. iv. 20 (LXX).

CHAPTER V.

THE COLLECTION AND GROWTH OF THE PSALTER.

INTERNAL evidence makes it certain that the Psalter grew up gradually from the union of earlier collections of Psalms. The various strata of which it is composed can to some extent be distinguished. Three principal divisions, marked by well-defined characteristics, may be observed. They appear to have arisen in successive chronological order, but such a supposition need not exclude the possibility that the earlier collection received late additions, or that the later collection may contain early Psalms.

(i) The First Division is coextensive with Book I (Pss. i—xli). All the Psalms in it have titles, with the exception of i. ii. x. xxxiii, and are described as Psalms "of David." The exceptions are easily accounted for. Pss. i and ii are introductory, and probably did not belong to the original collection. Ps. x was part of Ps. ix, or was written as a pendant to it. Ps. xxxiii appears to be of distinctly later date, inserted as an illustration of the last verse of Ps. xxxii.

(ii) The Second Division corresponds to Books II and III (Ps. xlii—lxxxix). All the Psalms in it, except xliii (which is really part of xlii) and lxxi, bear titles. It consists of (*a*) seven Psalms (or eight, if xlii and xliii are both reckoned) "of the sons of Korah" (xlii—xlix): (*b*) a Psalm "of Asaph" (l): (*c*) ten Psalms, all except lxvi, lxvii, "of David" (li—lxx): (*d*) an anonymous Psalm (lxxi), and a Psalm "of Solomon" (lxxii)[1]: (*e*) eleven Psalms "of Asaph" (lxxiii—lxxxiii): (*f*) a

[1] It has been conjectured by Ewald that Pss. li—lxxii originally stood after xli, so that the arrangement was (1) Davidic Psalms, i—xli; li—lxxii: (2) Levitical Psalms: (*a*) Korahite, xlii—xlix; (*b*) Asaphite, l, lxxiii—lxxxiii; (*c*) Korahite supplement, lxxxiv—lxxxix. The hypothesis is ingenious. It brings the Davidic Psalms together, and makes the note to lxxii. 20 more natural; and it connects the isolated Psalm of Asaph (l) with the rest of the group.

But it is clear that Books ii and iii formed a collection independent of Book i: and the editor may have wished to separate the mass of

supplement containing three Psalms "of the sons of Korah" (lxxxiv. lxxxv. lxxxvii); one "of David," which is manifestly a cento from other Psalms (lxxxvi); one "of Heman the Ezrahite" (lxxxviii); and one "of Ethan the Ezrahite" (lxxxix).

(iii) The Third Division corresponds to Books IV and V (Pss. xc—cl). In this division many Psalms have no title at all, and only a few bear the name of an author. In Book IV, Ps. xc bears the name of Moses: Pss. ci and ciii that of David. In Book V, Pss. cviii—cx. cxxii. cxxiv. cxxxi. cxxxiii. cxxxviii—cxlv, bear the name of David: cxxvii that of Solomon. Of the rest the majority have no title, or only that of a subordinate collection (e.g. 'A Song of Ascents').

We may now proceed to examine the characteristics of these divisions. The greater part of the Second Division is remarkably distinguished from the First and Third by the use of the Divine Names. Psalms xlii—lxxxiii are 'Elohistic'; that is to say, they employ the appellative *Elōhīm* = '*God*,' in the place and almost to the exclusion of the proper name *Jehovah*, represented in the A. V. by *LORD*.

In Pss. i—xli, *Elohim* occurs absolutely[1] only 15 times, and in some of these cases it is required by the sense[2]. *Jehovah* on the other hand occurs 272 times.

In Pss. xlii—lxxxiii, the proportion is reversed. *Elohim* occurs 200 times, *Jehovah* only 43 times (exclusive of the doxology, lxxii. 18); while in Pss. lxxxiv—lxxxix *Elohim* occurs only 7 times, Jehovah 31 times.

---

the Asaphite Psalms from the Korahite Psalms by placing the Davidic Psalms between them, while he put l. next to li. on account of the similarity of its teaching on sacrifice. The note to lxxii. 20 is true for his collection; and it does not necessarily imply that none but Davidic Psalms have preceded. Cp. Job xxxi. 40.

[1] By 'absolutely' is meant, without either a pronoun attached to it ('my God' and the like) or a qualifying word grammatically connected with it ('God of my righteousness,' 'God of my salvation,' and the like). The English reader must remember that three Hebrew words, *El*, *Elōah*, and *Elōhīm*, are represented by *God* in the A.V. *El* occurs absolutely 11 times in division i, 29 times in division ii, 14 times in division iii. *Elōah* is rare in the Psalter.

[2] E.g. ix. 17; x. 4, 13; xiv. 1, 2, 5; xxxvi. 1, 7. In iii. 2 the reading is doubtful. See note there.

INTRODUCTION. xli

In Pss. xc—cl, *Jehovah* occurs 339 times, while *Elōhīm* (of the true God) is to be found only in Ps. cviii, which is taken direct from two Psalms in the Elohistic group, and in cxliv. 9, in a Psalm which is evidently compiled from various sources.

It may also be noted that *Adōnāī*='*Lord*' occurs much more frequently in the Second Division (31 times), than in the First (10 times), or Third (8 times).

This use of *Elōhīm* cannot be explained on internal grounds. It stands precisely as *Jehovah* does elsewhere, and not unfrequently the substitution leads to awkwardness of expression. Thus, for example, Ps. l. 7 is taken from Ex. xx. 2; lxviii. 1, 2, 7, 8 are based upon Num. x. 35; Judg. v. 4, 5, 31; lxxi. 19 is from Ex. xv. 11; and in each case *Elōhīm* takes the place of *Jehovah*. More striking still is the fact that in two Psalms which are repeated from Book I. (liii=xiv; lxx=xl. 14 ff.), the alteration is made, though in Ps. lxx *Jehovah* still occurs twice.

To what then is this peculiarity due? Is it characteristic of a particular style of writing? or is it the work of an editor or compiler?

It seems certain (1) from the alteration in Psalms adopted from Book I, (2) from the variety of the sources from which the Psalms in this group are derived, that the change is, in part at least, due to the hand of an editor. It may no doubt have been the usage of certain writers. It has been suggested that it was a custom in the family of Asaph, connected possibly with the musical or liturgical use of the Psalms. But even if the peculiarity is due in some instances to the author, there can be little doubt that it is due, in the group as a whole, to the collector or editor.

A guess might be hazarded that the collection was thus adapted for the use of the exiles, with a view to avoid the repetition of the Sacred Name in a heathen land. But no positive result can be arrived at. The relation of the 'Elohistic' Psalms to the 'Elohistic' documents in the Pentateuch is also an obscure question, which needs further investigation.

It seems clear, however, that the substitution of *Elōhīm* for *Jehovah* was not due to the superstitious avoidance of the use of the Sacred Name in later times. Books IV and V are composed of Psalms the majority of which are unquestionably of later date than those in the Elohistic group. But in these books the name *Jehovah* is used throughout, with the exception noted above. The compiler of Book V knew the Elohistic Psalms in their present form: and so apparently did the compiler of Ps. lxxxvi, as may be inferred from a comparison of *v.* 14 with liv. 4 f.

The argument for the original independence of the three divisions which is derived from the use of the names of God is corroborated:

(*a*) By the repetition in the Second Division of Psalms found in the First, and in the Third of Psalms found in the Second. Thus liii=xiv: lxx=xl. 15 ff.: cviii=lvii. 7—11, lx. 5—12.

(*b*) By the note appended to Ps. lxxii., "the prayers of David the son of Jesse are ended[1]." This note, whether taken over from an earlier collection by the editor of Books II and III, or inserted by him, appears to shew that he knew of no more Davidic Psalms, or at any rate that his collection contained no more. Clearly therefore his collection must have been independent of Books IV and V, which contain several more Psalms ascribed to David.

(*c*) By the difference already noticed in regard to titles. In this respect the Third Division is markedly distinguished from the First and Second. In these the Psalms with but few easily explained exceptions have titles, giving the name of the author or the collection from which the Psalm was taken, in many cases the occasion, and some musical or liturgical description or direction. But in the Third Division the majority of the Psalms are anonymous; musical and liturgical directions are rare; and titles of the obscure character of many of those in Divisions I and II are entirely absent. Moreover the musical term *Selah*, which occurs 17 times in Division I, and 50 times in Division II, is found but four times in Division III, and then in two Psalms ascribed to David (cxl. cxliii).

(*d*) By the character of the contents of the three divisions. Speaking broadly and generally, the Psalms of the First Division are *personal*, those of the Second, *national*, those of the Third,

---

[1] Comp. Job xxxi. 40.

liturgical. There are numerous exceptions, but it is in the First Division that personal prayers and thanksgivings are chiefly to be found: in the Second, prayers in special times of national calamity (xliv. lx. lxxiv. lxxix. lxxx. lxxxiii. lxxxix), and thanksgivings in times of national deliverance (xlvi. xlvii. xlviii. lxxv. lxxvi. lxv—lxviii): in the Third, Psalms of praise and thanksgiving for general use in the Temple services (xcii. xcv—c. cv—cvii. cxi—cxviii. cxx—cxxxvi. cxlvi—cl).

The various steps in the formation of the Psalter may have been somewhat as follows:

(1) An original collection, which bore the name *Psalms* (or, *Prayers*) *of David*, from its first and greatest poet, though poems by other writers were not excluded from it. It has already been suggested (p. xxix) that the general title of the collection was subsequently transferred to each separate Psalm in the First Group which was taken from it. To this 'Davidic' collection Psalms i and ii were prefixed as an introduction.

(2) Next, the 'Elohistic' collection was formed by the union of two selections of Levitical Psalms from the Korahite and Asaphite hymnaries with another selection of 'Davidic' Psalms. To this collection was added an appendix of Korahite and other Psalms (lxxxiv—lxxxix), which were not altered by the Elohistic editor.

(3) Finally, the Temple Psalms of the Return were collected, with a gleaning of earlier Psalms, some of which were believed to have been written by David, or were taken from a collection bearing his name.

The date of these collections cannot be determined with certainty. The nucleus of the First Collection may have been formed by Solomon, or certainly early in the regal period, though it appears to have received later additions. Nothing in the collection (not even xiv. 7) necessarily refers to the Exile or the Return.

The Second Collection contains Psalms of the middle period of the Kingdom, but the appendix at any rate cannot have been completed till the Return (lxxxv).

The Third Collection may be placed in the time of Ezra and

Nehemiah[1]. The Chronicler was familiar with it, and possibly found the doxology at the close of Ps. cvi already in its place (see p. xxxvi).

The possibility of much later additions has already been discussed (p. xxxv ff.).

Other collections no doubt preceded these. Such were 'The Book of Songs of the Sons of Korah,' 'The Songs of Asaph,' 'The Songs of Ascents.' Pss. xcii—c, with the exception perhaps of Ps. xciv, are marked by a common character, and may have formed a separate collection. The 'Hallelujah Psalms,' civ—cvi. cxi—cxviii. cxxxv. cxlvi—cl, may have been taken from some 'Book of Praise.'

The arrangement of the Psalms in the several books appears to have been determined partly by their arrangement in the smaller collections from which they were taken, where their order may have been fixed by considerations of date and authorship; partly by similarity of character and contents. Thus for example, we find groups of *Maschil* Psalms (xlii—xlv. lii—lv. lxxxviii, lxxxix), and *Michtam* Psalms (lvi—lx). Resemblance in character may account for the juxtaposition of l and li: xxxiii takes up xxxii. 11: xxxiv and xxxv both speak of 'the angel of the LORD,' who is mentioned nowhere else in the Psalter. The title of xxxvi links it to xxxv. 27 ('servant of the LORD'): that of lvi may connect it with lv. 6.

CHAPTER VI.

THE FORM OF HEBREW POETRY.

ANCIENT Hebrew poetry possesses neither metre nor rhyme[2]. Its essential characteristic is **rhythm**, which makes itself ap-

---

[1] Cp. the statement in 2 Macc. ii. 13. "Neemias founding a library gathered together...the writings of David" (τὰ τοῦ Δαυίδ).

[2] When Philo, Josephus, Eusebius, Jerome, and other early writers, compared Hebrew poetry with Greek and Latin metres, and spoke of hexameters and pentameters, sapphics, or trimeter and tetrameter iambics, they were using familiar language loosely. Various attempts have been made to discover a metrical system in the Psalms, on the basis of quantity, or of number of syllables or accents. Most of them involve

parent both in the rhythmical cadence of each separate clause, and in the rhythmical balance of clauses when they are combined in a verse.

The Hebrew language is characterised by a vigorous terseness and power of condensation which cannot be preserved in English. Hence the clauses of Hebrew poetry are as a rule short. They consist sometimes of two words only, most frequently of three words, but not seldom of more than three words.

The rhythm of the clause often reflects the thought which it expresses. Thus, for example, the lively animated rhythm of the opening stanza (*vv.* 1—3) of Ps. ii vividly suggests the tumultuous gathering of the nations; while the stately measure of *v.* 4 presents the contrast of the calm and unmoved majesty of Jehovah enthroned in heaven. Or again, the evening hymn Ps. iv sinks to rest in its concluding verse with a rhythm as reposeful as the assurance which it expresses.

The rhythm of clauses however, together with many other features of Hebrew poetry, such as assonance and alliteration, distinctive use of words and constructions, and so forth, chiefly concerns the student of the original. But the rhythmical balance of clauses combined in a verse admits of being reproduced in translation, and can to a large extent be appreciated by the English reader. Owing to this peculiar nature of its form, Hebrew poetry loses less in translation than poetry which depends for much of its charm upon rhymes or metres which cannot be reproduced in another language.

This balanced symmetry of form and sense is known as *parallelism of clauses* (*parallelismus membrorum*) or simply, *parallelism*. It satisfies the love of regular and harmonious movement which is natural to the human mind, and was specially adapted to the primitive method of antiphonal chant-

---

the abandonment of the Massoretic vocalisation, and invoke the aid of 'a whole arsenal of licences.' Happily they do not concern the English reader.

Rhyme is found occasionally (e.g. viii. 3 [*Heb.* 4]; cvi. 4—7), but it appears to be accidental rather than intentional, and is never systematically employed. Both rhyme and metre have been used in medieval and modern Jewish poetry from the 7th cent. A.D. onwards.

ing (Ex. xv. 1, 20, 21; 1 Sam. xviii. 7). Such poetry is not sharply distinguished from elevated prose. Many passages in the prophets are written in poetical style, and exhibit the features of parallelism as plainly as any of the Psalms[1].

The law of parallelism in Hebrew poetry has an exegetical value. It can often be appealed to in order to determine the construction or connexion of words, to elucidate the sense, or to decide a doubtful reading. The arrangement of the text in lines, adopted by Dr Scrivener in the standard edition of the A. V. from which the text in this edition is taken, and in the Revised Version, makes this characteristic of Hebrew poetry more plainly perceptible to the English reader.

The various forms of parallelism are generally classified under three principal heads:

(1) *Synonymous parallelism*, when the same fundamental thought is repeated in different words in the second line of a couplet. Thus in Ps. cxiv. 1:

"When Israel went forth out of Egypt,
 The house of Jacob from a people of strange language:"

and the same construction is maintained throughout the Psalm. Every page of the Psalter supplies abundant examples.

(2) *Antithetic* or *contrasted parallelism*, when the thought expressed in the first line of a couplet is corroborated or elucidated by the affirmation of its opposite in the second line. This form of parallelism is specially suited to Gnomic Poetry, and is particularly characteristic of the oldest collection of proverbs in the Book of Proverbs (chaps. x—xxii. 16). Thus for example:

"Every wise woman buildeth her house:
 But folly plucketh it down with her own hands" (Prov. xiv. 1).

But it is by no means rare in the Psalms, e.g. i. 6,

"For the LORD knoweth the way of the righteous:
 But the way of the wicked shall perish."

(3) *Synthetic* or *constructive parallelism*. Under this head are classed the numerous instances in which the two lines of

[1] E.g. Is. lx. 1—3; lxv. 13, 14; Hos. xi. 8, 9; Nah. i. 2.

the couplet stand in the relation of cause and consequence, protasis and apodosis, proposition and qualification or supplement, or almost any logical or constructional relation; or in which the parallelism is one of form only without any logical relation between the clauses.

The simplest and most common form of parallelism is the couplet or distich: but this may be expanded into a tristich (triplet) or a tetrastich (quatrain) or even longer combinations, in a variety of ways. Thus the three lines of a verse may be synonymous:

> "The floods have lifted up, O LORD,
> The floods have lifted up their voice;
> The floods lift up their waves" (Ps. xciii. 3).

Or two only of the lines may be synonymous, while the third is introductory (Ps. iii. 7), or supplementary (ii. 2), or antithetic (liv. 3).

Similarly in tetrastichs (usually including two verses) we find four synonymous lines, as in xci. 5, 6. Or the first line may be parallel to the third, the second to the fourth, as in xxvii. 3:

> "Though an host should encamp against me,
> My heart shall not fear:
> Though war should rise against me,
> Even then will I be confident."

Or two synonymous lines may be contrasted with two synonymous lines, as in xxxvii. 35, 36:

> "I have seen the wicked in his terribleness,
> And spreading himself like a green tree in its native soil:
> And I passed by, and lo! he was not,
> Yea, I sought him, but he could not be found."

Even longer combinations than tetrastichs sometimes occur; and on the other hand single lines are found, for the most part as introductions or conclusions. While maintaining its fundamental characteristic of rhythm, Hebrew poetry admits of the greatest freedom and variety of form.

Strophical arrangement. Series of verses are, as might be expected, combined, and many Psalms consist of distinct groups of verses. Such groups may conveniently be called *stanzas* or *strophes*, but the terms must not be supposed to imply that the same metrical or rhythmical structure recurs in each, as in Greek or Latin poetry. The strophes in a Psalm do not even necessarily consist of the same number of lines or verses.

Such divisions are sometimes clearly marked by a refrain, as in Pss. xlii—xliii. xlvi. lvii: or by alphabetical arrangement, as in cxix: or by *Selah*, denoting probably a musical interlude, as in Pss. iii and iv. But more frequently there is no external mark of the division, though it is clearly indicated by the structure and contents of the Psalm, as in Ps. ii.

Alphabetic or *Acrostic Psalms.*

Eight or nine Psalms[1] present various forms of alphabetic structure (Pss. ix. x. xxv. xxxiv. xxxvii. cxi. cxii. cxix. cxlv). In cxi and cxii each letter begins a line, and the lines are arranged in eight distichs and two tristichs.

In Pss. xxv. xxxiv. cxlv. Prov. xxxi. Lam. iv., each letter begins a distich, in Lam. i. ii. a tristich. In Pss. xxxvii each letter begins a pair of verses, commonly containing four, sometimes five, lines. In Lam. iii each verse in a stanza of three verses, and in Ps. cxix each verse in a stanza of eight verses, begins with the same letter, and the letters are taken in regular succession.

Such an arrangement, artificial though it seems, does not necessarily fetter a poet more than an elaborate metre or rhyme. It is not to be regarded as 'a compensation for the vanished spirit of poetry.' It was probably intended as an aid to memory, and is chiefly employed in Psalms of a proverbial character to connect detached thoughts, or when, as in Ps. cxix and in Lamentations, the poet needs some artificial bond to link together a number of variations upon one theme.

The elaborate development of the system in Lamentations proves that alphabetic structure is not in itself a proof of a very late date[2].

---

[1] Also Lam. i—iv: Prov. xxxi. 10—31. Bickell has pointed out traces of alphabetic structure in Nah. i. 2—10: and shewn that the original of Ecclesiasticus li. 13—30 was alphabetic.

[2] The early Roman poet Ennius wrote acrostics (Cicero, *de Divina-*

CHAPTER VII.

THE HEBREW TEXT, THE ANCIENT VERSIONS, AND THE ENGLISH VERSIONS.

i. *The Hebrew Text.* A few words on the character of the Hebrew Text are necessary in order to justify the occasional departures from it, which will be met with in this commentary.

The extant Hebrew MSS. of the O.T. are all comparatively recent. The oldest of which the age is known with certainty bears date A.D. 916; the majority are of the 12th to the 16th centuries. They all present substantially the same text[1], commonly called the Massoretic Text[2]. Thus while we possess MSS. of the N.T. written less than three centuries after the date of the earliest of the books, our oldest MS. of the O.T. is more than ten centuries posterior to the date of the latest of the books which it contains; and while our MSS. of the N.T. present a great variety of readings, those of the O.T. are practically unanimous in supporting the same text.

This unanimity was long supposed to be due to the jealous care with which the Jewish scribes had preserved the sacred text from the earliest times. But careful examination makes it clear that this is not the case. Since the rise of the schools of the 'Massoretes,' in the seventh and eighth centuries A.D., the text has, no doubt, been preserved with scrupulous exactness. But the recension which they adopted, whether originally

tione, ii. 54, § 111); and they are said to have been invented in Greece by the comedian Epicharmus (B.C. 540—450). We may compare the *alliteration*, which is a common feature of early poetry.

[1] The variations between them are (roughly speaking) not greater than the variations between the different editions of the A.V. which have appeared since 1611, and they concern for the most part unimportant points of orthography.

[2] *Massōrā* means (1) *tradition* in general: (2) specially, tradition concerning the text of the O.T., and in particular the elaborate system of rules and *memoria technica* by which the later scribes sought to guard the text from corruption. Those who devoted themselves to this study were called 'masters of Massōrā', or 'Massoretes'; and the term 'Massoretic' is applied to the text which their labours were designed to preserve.

derived from a single MS., as some suppose, or from a comparison of MSS. held in estimation at the time, unquestionably contains not a few errors, which had crept in during the long course of its previous history[1]. The proof of this lies in the following facts :—

(1) There are many passages in which the Massoretic Text cannot be translated without doing violence to the laws of grammar, or is irreconcilable with the context or with other passages.

(2) Parallel passages (e.g. Ps. xviii and 2 Sam. xxii) differ in such a way as to make it evident that the variations are due partly to accidental mistakes in transcription, partly to intentional revision.

(3) The Ancient Versions represent various readings, which in many cases bear a strong stamp of probability upon them, and often lessen or remove the difficulties of the Massoretic Text.

The Massoretic Text as a whole is undoubtedly superior to any of the Ancient Versions : but we are amply justified in calling in the aid of those Versions, and in particular the Septuagint, wherever that text appears to be defective: and even where it is not in itself suspicious, but some of the Ancient Versions offer a different reading, that reading may deserve to be taken into account.

In some few cases, where there is reason to suspect corruption anterior to all extant documentary authorities, it may even be allowable to resort to conjectural emendation, and such emendations will occasionally be mentioned.

---

[1] The history of the Hebrew text may be divided into four periods. (1) The first of these periods was marked by the exclusive use of the archaic character: (2) the second, from the time of Ezra to the destruction of Jerusalem, saw the archaic character completely superseded by the square character, as the Hebrew language was superseded by Aramaic : (3) in the third period, from the Fall of Jerusalem to the end of the fifth century, the consonantal text was fixed : (4) in the fourth period, the exegetical tradition of the proper method of reading the text was stereotyped by the addition of the vowels, and an elaborate system of rules invented to secure the accurate transmission of the text even in the minutest particulars.

Two further points must be mentioned here in order to explain some of the notes:

(1) Hebrew, like other Semitic languages, was originally written without any vowels, except such long vowels as were represented by consonants. In the earlier stages of the language even these were sparingly used. The present elaborate system of vowel marks or 'points,' commonly called the 'Massoretic punctuation' or 'vocalisation,' was not reduced to writing until the seventh or eighth century A.D. It stereotyped the pronunciation and reading of the O.T. then current, and in many respects represents a far older tradition. But in a vowelless, or as it is called 'unpointed,' text, many words may be read in different ways, and the Massoretic punctuation does not appear in all cases to give the true way of reading the consonants.

(2) In some passages the traditional method of *reading* (Q'rī) did not agree with the consonants of the *written text* (K'thībh). In such cases the Massoretes did not alter the text, but appended a marginal note, giving the consonants with which the vowels shewn in the text were to be read. It should be clearly understood that the *Q'rī* or marginal reading is the accepted reading of the Jewish textual tradition. But internal evidence, and the evidence of the Ancient Versions, lead us to prefer sometimes the *Q'rī* and sometimes the *K'thībh*. See for example Ps. xxiv. 4, where A.V. and R.V. rightly follow the *K'thībh*, and desert the Jewish tradition: or Ps. c. 3, where A.V. unfortunately followed the *K'thībh*, and R.V. has happily taken the *Q'rī*.

ii. *The Ancient Versions of the O. T.* These possess a fresh interest for the English reader, since the R.V. has given occasional references to them in its margin.

(i) *The Septuagint.* The oldest and most valuable of them is the Greek Version, commonly called the SEPTUAGINT (Sept. or LXX), or Version of the Seventy Elders. It derives its name from the tradition that the translation of the Pentateuch was made by seventy or seventy-two elders, despatched from Jerusalem to Alexandria at the request of Ptolemy Philadelphus (B.C. 283— 247). But the 'Letter of Aristeas,' on which this story rests, is undoubtedly a forgery, and all that can be asserted about the origin of the Septuagint is that it was made (1) in Egypt, and probably at Alexandria, (2) at different times and by different hands during the third and second centuries B.C., (3) before the vowel-points had been added to the Hebrew text, or that text had finally taken its present form.

The Pentateuch was probably translated first under the earlier Ptolemies: and the grandson of Jesus the son of Sirach, about 132 B.C., knew and used the version of the Hagiographa as well as of the Law and the Prophets[1]. This, it may be assumed, included the Psalter.

The character of the LXX varies greatly in different parts of the O.T. The work of pioneers in the task of translation, with no aids of grammar and lexicon to help them, naturally presents many imperfections. Yet not seldom it gives a valuable clue to the meaning of obscure words, or suggests certain corrections of the Massoretic Text. The version of the Psalter is on the whole fairly good, though it is often altogether at fault in difficult passages. It has a special interest for English readers, because, as will be seen presently, it has indirectly had considerable influence on the version most familiar to many of them.

Unfortunately the Septuagint has not come down to us in its original form. The text has suffered from numerous corruptions and alterations, partly through the carelessness of transcribers, partly through the introduction of fresh renderings intended to harmonise it with the Massoretic Text, or taken from other Greek Versions.

The most important MSS. of the LXX for the Psalter, to which reference will occasionally be made, are the following[2]:

The Vatican MS. (denoted by the letter B); a splendid copy of the Greek Bible, written in the fourth century A.D., and now preserved in the Vatican Library at Rome. Ten leaves of the Psalter, containing Pss. cv. 27—cxxxvii. 6, are unfortunately lost.

---

[1] See above, p. xii f.
[2] For fuller information see Dr Swete's edition of the LXX, published by the Camb. Univ. Press. The Psalter is to be had separately in a convenient form.

The equally splendid Sinaitic MS. (denoted by the letter א *Aleph*), also written in the fourth century, found by Tischendorf in the convent of St Catharine on Mt Sinai, and now at St Petersburg.

The Alexandrine MS. (denoted by the letter A), written in the middle of the fifth century, brought from Alexandria, and now the great treasure of the British Museum. Nine leaves are wanting in the Psalter (Ps. xlix. 19--lxxix. 10).

The Septuagint, with all its defects, is of the greatest interest to all students of the O.T.

(1) It preserves evidence for the text far more ancient than the oldest Hebrew MS., and often represents a text differing from the Massoretic recension.

(2) It is one of the most ancient helps for ascertaining the meaning of the language of the O.T., and is a valuable supplement to Jewish tradition.

(3) It was the means by which the Greek language was wedded to Hebrew thought, and the way prepared for the use of that language in the New Testament.

(4) The great majority of the quotations made from the O.T. by the writers of the N.T. are taken from the LXX.

(5) It is the version in which the O.T. was studied by the Fathers of the Eastern Church, and indirectly, in the old Latin Versions made from it, by those of the Western, until Jerome's new translation from the Hebrew came into use. In the Psalter its influence was permanent, for as will be seen below (p. lv), the new version never superseded the old.

(ii) *The Targum.* After the return from the Babylonian exile, Aramaic, sometimes inaccurately called Chaldee, began to take the place of Hebrew in Palestine. As Hebrew died out, the needs of the people were met by oral translations or paraphrases in Aramaic. Hence arose the Aramaic Versions commonly called the TARGUMS[1]. The Targum of the Psalter is on the whole a fairly good version, though it often assumes the character of a paraphrastic interpretation. In its present form it appears to contain elements as late as the ninth century, but in the main

[1] *Targum* means *interpretation* or *translation*. Cp. *dragoman*, lit. *interpreter*.

it belongs to a much earlier date. As a rule it represents the Massoretic recension, and is not of much value for textual criticism. It is interesting as preserving interpretations current in the ancient Jewish Church, in particular, for the reference of several passages in the Psalter to the Messiah[1].

(iii) *The Syriac Version*, known as the *Peschito* (*simple* or *literal* version), probably originated at Edessa, about the second century A.D. It was made from the Hebrew, with the help of Jewish converts or actual Jews. But the present text in some parts of the O.T. agrees with the LXX in such a way as to make it evident that either the original translators consulted that version, or subsequent revisers introduced renderings from it. This is largely the case in the Psalms.

(iv) *The later Greek Versions* require only a brief mention. That of AQUILA of Pontus, a Jewish proselyte from heathenism, was made in the beginning of the second century A.D., when the breach between Church and Synagogue was complete, and the Jews desired an accurate version for purposes of controversy with Christians. It is characterised by a slavish but ingenious literalism.

That of THEODOTION, made towards the end of the second century, or possibly earlier[2], was little more than a revision of the LXX.

That of SYMMACHUS, made probably a little later than that of Theodotion, was also based on the LXX. It aimed at combining accuracy and perspicuity, and was by far the best of the three.

These versions were collected in the gigantic work of ORIGEN (A.D. 185—254) called the HEXAPLA, which contained in six parallel columns, (1) the Hebrew Text, (2) the Hebrew transliterated into Greek letters, (3) Aquila, (4) Symmachus, (5) the LXX, (6) Theodotion. In the Psalter the Hexapla became the Octapla by the addition of two columns containing two more Greek versions known as the 'Fifth' (*Quinta*) and 'Sixth' (*Sexta*).

[1] See e.g. Ps. xxi. 1, 7; xlv. 2, 7; lxi. 6, 8; lxxii. 1; lxxx. 15.
[2] See Schürer's *Hist. of the Jewish People &c.*, Div. ii. § 33 (Vol. iii. p. 173, E. T.).

Unfortunately only fragments of these versions are extant[1]. Generally, though not always, they agree with the Massoretic Text.

(v) *The Latin Versions.* The earliest Latin Version of the O.T., the VETUS LATINA or OLD LATIN, was made in North Africa from the LXX. This version, of which various recensions appear to have been current, was twice revised by ST JEROME (Hieronymus). The first revision, made about A.D. 383, is known as the *Roman Psalter*, probably because it was made at Rome and for the use of the Roman Church at the request of Pope Damasus; the second, made about A.D. 387, is called the *Gallican Psalter*, because the Gallican Churches were the first to adopt it.

Shortly afterwards, about A.D. 389, Jerome commenced his memorable work of translating the O.T. directly from the Hebrew, which occupied him for fourteen years. After bitter opposition and many vicissitudes, it won its way by its intrinsic excellence to be the Bible of the Latin Church, and came to be known as THE VULGATE.

But long familiarity with the Old Latin Version of the Psalter made it impossible to displace it, and the Gallican Psalter is incorporated in the Vulgate in place of Jerome's new translation. That new translation, "iuxta Hebraicam veritatem," never came into general use. It is of great value for the interpretation of the text, and shews that the Hebrew text known to Jerome was in the main the same as the present Massoretic Text.

Accordingly, the student must remember that in the Psalter the Vulgate is an echo of the LXX, and not an independent witness to text or interpretation: while Jerome's translation (referred to as *Jer.*) occupies the place which the Vulgate does in the other books of the O.T.[2]

iii. *The English Versions.* It would be impossible to give here even a sketch of the history of the English Bible. But as the Version with which many readers are most familiar is not

---

[1] Collected with exhaustive completeness in F. Field's *Origenis Hexaplorum quae supersunt.* 1875.

[2] The best edition of Jerome's Psalter with critical apparatus is that by P. de Lagarde, *Psalterium iuxta Hebraeos Hieronymi,* 1874.

that in the Bible, but that in the Prayer-Book, it seems worth while to give a brief account of its origin and characteristics.

As the Old Latin Version held its ground against Jerome's more accurate translation, because constant liturgical use had established it too firmly for it to be displaced, so the older English Version of the Psalter taken from the Great Bible has kept its place in the Prayer-Book, and has never been superseded for devotional use.

The 'Great Bible,' sometimes known as Cromwell's, because the first edition (1539) appeared under his auspices, sometimes as Cranmer's, because he wrote the preface to the second edition (1540), was a revision of Matthew's Bible (1537), executed by Coverdale with the help of Sebastian Münster's Latin version, published in 1534—5.

Matthew's Bible was a composite work. The Pentateuch and N.T. were taken from Tyndale's published translation; the books from Ezra to Malachi and the Apocrypha from Coverdale's version; the remaining books from Joshua to 2 Chron. from a translation which there is little reason to doubt was made by Tyndale.

The Psalter in Matthew's Bible was therefore Coverdale's work: and Coverdale's Version (1535) lays no claim to independence. He tells us in the *Epistle unto the Kynges hyghnesse* prefixed to the work, that he had "with a cleare conscience purely and faythfully translated this out of fyve sundry interpreters," and the original title-page described the book as "faithfully and truly translated out of Douche and Latyn into Englishe."

The 'Douche' was doubtless the Swiss-German version known as the Zurich Bible: the 'Latyn' was of course the Vulgate: and it is worth while thus to trace the pedigree of the Prayer-Book Version, for in spite of successive revisions, it retains many marks of its origin. Many of its peculiar renderings, and in particular the additions which it contains, are derived from the LXX through the Vulgate.

The A.V. of 1611, though more accurate, is less melodious, and when, at the revision of the Prayer-Book in 1662, the version of 1611 was substituted in the Epistles and Gospels, the old Psalter was left untouched. "The choirs and congregations had grown familiar with it, and it was felt to be smoother and more easy to sing."[1]

The Revised Version of 1885 has made a great advance upon the A.V. in respect of accuracy of rendering. The changes made by the Revisers will, as a rule, be quoted in this commentary, but the translation must be read and studied as a whole in order properly to appreciate their force and value. Even with the help which the R.V. now supplies to the English reader, it does not seem superfluous to endeavour by more exact renderings to bring the student closer to the sense of the original.

It is well known that the A.V. frequently creates artificial distinctions by different renderings of the same word, and ignores real distinctions by giving the same rendering for different words: and this, though to a far less extent, is still the case in the R.V.[2] Rigid uniformity of rendering may be misleading, but it is well that attention should be called to distinctions where they exist. Again, the precise force of a tense, or the exact emphasis of the original, cannot always be given without some circumlocution which would be clumsy in a version intended for general use: but it is worth while to attempt to express finer shades of meaning in a commentary.

The best translation cannot always adequately represent the original: and it is well that the English reader should be reminded that the sense cannot always be determined with precision, and may often best be realised by approaching it from different sides.

[1] See Bp Westcott's *History of the English Bible*, chap. iii.
[2] See, for example, iii. 2, 7, 8, where the connexion is obscured by the rendering of the same word *help* in *v.* 2, and *salvation* in *v.* 8. Two entirely different words are rendered *blessed* in xli. 1, 13. The first expresses congratulation, (*Happy:* cp. *be made happy* in *v.* 2): the second expresses the tribute of human reverence to the divine majesty. The word rendered *trust* or *put trust in* in vii. 1, xi. 1 is quite distinct from the word similarly rendered in xiii. 5. It means *to take refuge in*, and the sense gains remarkably by the correct rendering. The exact rendering of a tense may be sufficient to draw a forcible picture, as in vii. 15.

CHAPTER VIII.

THE MESSIANIC HOPE.

Poetry was the handmaid of Prophecy in preparing the way for the coming of Christ. Prophetic ideas are taken up, developed, pressed to their full consequences, with the boldness and enthusiasm of inspired imagination. The constant use of the Psalms for devotion and worship familiarised the people with them. Expectation was aroused and kept alive. Hope became part of the national life. Even Psalms, which were not felt beforehand to speak of Him Who was to come, contributed to mould the temper of mind which was prepared to receive Him when He came in form and fashion far other than that which popular hopes had anticipated; and they were recognised in the event as pointing forward to Him.

This work of preparation went forward along several distinct lines, some of which are seen to converge or meet even in the O.T., while others were only harmonised by the fulfilment. Thus (1) some Psalms pointed forward to the Messiah as Son of God and King and Priest: others (2) prepared the way for the suffering Redeemer: others (3) only find their full meaning in the perfect Son of Man: others (4) foretell the Advent of Jehovah Himself to judge and redeem.

All these different lines of thought combined to prepare the way for Christ; but it must be remembered that the preparation was in great measure silent and unconscious. It is difficult for us who read the O.T. in the light of its fulfilment to realise how dim and vague and incomplete the Messianic Hope must have been until the Coming of Christ revealed the divine purpose, and enabled men to recognise how through long ages God had been preparing for its consummation.

(1) *The Royal Messiah* (Psalms ii. xviii. xx. xxi. xlv. lxi. lxxii. lxxxix. cx. cxxxii).

The Kingdom of Israel was at once the expression of God's purpose to establish an universal kingdom upon earth, and the means for the accomplishment of that purpose. The people of Israel was Jehovah's son, His firstborn (Ex. iv. 22, 23; Deut. xxxii.

6; Hos. xi. 1), and His servant (Is. xli. 8); and the Davidic king as the representative of the nation was Jehovah's son, His firstborn (2 Sam. vii. 14; Ps. ii. 7; lxxxix. 26, 27), and His servant (2 Sam. vii. 5 ff.). He was no absolute despot, reigning in His own right, but the 'Anointed of Jehovah' who was the true King of Israel, appointed by Him as His viceroy and representative (Ps. ii. 6). He was said to "sit upon the throne of the kingdom of the LORD over Israel" (1 Chr. xxviii. 5), or even "on the throne of the LORD" (1 Chr. xxix. 23).

Thus he was at once the representative of the people before Jehovah, and the representative of Jehovah before the people, and before the nations. To Him as Jehovah's viceroy was promised the sovereignty over the nations. Nathan's message to David (2 Sam. vii) was the Davidic king's patent of adoption and title deed of inheritance. It was the proclamation of "the everlasting covenant" which God made with the house of David (2 Sam. xxiii. 5). Upon the divine choice of David and his house, and in particular upon this great prophecy, are based a series of what may be called *Royal Psalms*. Critical events in the life of David or later kings, or in the history of the kingdom, gave occasion to David himself, or other poet-seers, to declare the full significance and extent of that promise. Successive kings might fail to realise their rightful prerogatives, but the divine promise remained unrevoked, waiting for one who could claim its fulfilment in all its grandeur.

Different aspects of the promise are presented in different Psalms. They can only be briefly summarised here: for fuller explanation reference must be made to the introductions and notes to each Psalm.

In Ps. ii the prominent thought is the divine sonship of the anointed king and its significance. The nations are mustering with intent to renounce their allegiance to the king recently enthroned in Zion. But their purpose is vain, for the king is none other than Jehovah's Son and representative. In rebelling against him they are rebelling against Jehovah, and if they persist, will do it to their own destruction.

In David's great thanksgiving (Ps. xviii) he celebrates Jehovah as the giver of victory, and recognises that his position as "the head of the nations" (*v.* 43) has been given him in order that he may proclaim Jehovah's glory among them (*v.* 49).

The relation of the king to Jehovah as His anointed representative is the ground of intercession and confidence in Ps. xx. 6; and the thanksgiving for victory which follows in Ps. xxi naturally dwells upon the high dignity which belongs to him in virtue of that relation, and anticipates his future triumphs. The same thought is repeated in Ps. lxi. 6 f.

Ps. xlv is a marriage song for Solomon or some later king of the house of David. In lofty language the poet sets before him the ideal of his office (cp. 2 Sam. xxiii. 3 ff.), and claims for him the fulness of the promise of eternal dominion. The union with a foreign princess suggests the hope of the peaceful union of all nations in harmonious fellowship with Israel.

Ps. lxxii is an intercession for Solomon or some other king on his accession. In glowing colours it depicts the ideal of his office, and prays that he may fulfil it as the righteous sovereign who redresses wrong, and may rule over a world-wide empire, receiving the willing homage of the nations to his virtue, and proving himself the heir of the patriarchal promise.

In some crisis of national disaster the author of Ps. lxxxix recites the promise to David, and contrasting its brilliant hopes with the disappointment which it was his trial to witness, pleads for the renewal of God's favour.

Ps. cx is a kind of solemn oracle. It describes David as king, priest, and conqueror. Jehovah adopts him as His assessor, placing him in the seat of honour at His side. Though not of Aaron's line he is invested with a priestly dignity. The new king of Zion must inherit all the privileges of the ancient king of Salem, and enter upon the religious as well as the civil memories of his capital.

Once more, in Ps. cxxxii, possibly in days when the kingdom had ceased to exist, and the representative of the house of David was only a governor appointed by a foreign conqueror, the ancient promise is pleaded in confidence that it must still find fulfilment.

These Psalms refer primarily to the circumstances of the

time. The revolt of the nations, the royal marriage, the accession of a prince of unique promise, the installation of the king, gave the inspired poets opportunity for dwelling on the promises and hopes connected with the Davidic kingdom. But successive princes of David's line failed to fulfil their high destiny, to subdue the nations, to rule the world in righteousness, to establish a permanent dynasty. The kingdom ceased to exist; yet it was felt that the divine promise could not fail; and hope was directed to the future. Men were led to see that the divine promise had not been frustrated but postponed, and to look for the coming of One who should 'fulfil' the utmost that had been spoken of Israel's king[1].

(2) *The suffering Messiah* (Pss. xxii. lxix. cix. xxxv. xli. lv.). Men's minds had to be prepared not only for a triumphant King, but for a suffering Saviour. The great prophecy of Is. lii, liii finds preludes and echoes in the Psalter in what may be called the *Passion Psalms*. The sufferings of David and other saints of the old dispensation were typical: they helped to familiarise men with the thought of the righteous suffering for God's sake, of suffering as the path to victory, of glory to be won for God and deliverance for man through suffering. They were the anticipation, as the sufferings of the members of the Christian Church are the supplement (Col. i. 24), of the afflictions of Christ.

But not only were these sufferings in themselves typical, but the records of them were so moulded by the Spirit of God as to prefigure the sufferings of Christ even in circumstantial details. These details are not the most important part of the type or prophecy; but they serve to arrest attention, and direct it to the essential idea.

These Psalms do not appear to have been applied to the Messiah in the Jewish Church as the Royal Psalms were. It was Christ Himself who first shewed His disciples that He must gather up into Himself and fulfil the manifold experiences of the people of God, in suffering as well as in triumph, and taught them to recognise that those sufferings had been foreor-

[1] For references to the Messianic interpretations of the Targums see note on p. liv.

dained in the divine purpose, and how they had been foreshadowed throughout the Old Testament.

Ps. xxii stands by itself among these Psalms. In its description of the Psalmist's sufferings, and in its joyous anticipation of the coming extension of Jehovah's kingdom, it foreshadows the Passion of Christ and its glorious fruits: and our Lord's use of the opening words (and probably of the whole Psalm) upon the Cross, stamps it as applicable to and fulfilled in Him.

Ps. lxix records the sufferings of one who was persecuted for God's sake (*vv.* 7 ff.). In his consuming zeal for God's house, in his suffering as the victim of causeless hatred (cp. xxxv. 19; cix. 3 ff.), in his endurance of reproach for his faithfulness to God, he was the prototype of Christ. The contemptuous mockery (*vv.* 12, 20) and maltreatment (*vv.* 21, 26) to which he was exposed, prefigured the actual sufferings of Christ. The curse which falls upon his persecutors (*v.* 25; cp. cix. 8) becomes the doom of the arch-traitor (Acts i. 20); and the judgment invoked upon his enemies (*vv.* 22—24) finds its fulfilment in the rejection of apostate Israel (Rom. xi. 9, 10).

The treachery of the faithless friend described in xli. 9 (cp. lv. 12 ff.) anticipates the treachery of the false disciple.

(3) *The Son of Man* (Pss. viii. xvi. xl). Psalms which describe the true destiny of man, the issue of perfect fellowship with God, the ideal of complete obedience, unmistakably point forward to Him who as the representative of man triumphed where man had failed.

Ps. viii looks away from the Fall and its fatal consequences to man's nature, position, and destiny in the purpose of God. Christ's perfect humanity answered to that ideal, and is seen to be the pledge of the fulfilment of the divine purpose for the whole race of mankind (Heb. ii. 6 ff.).

In Ps. xvi faith and hope triumph over the fear of death in the consciousness of fellowship with God. Yet the Psalmist did not escape death; his words looked forward, and first found their adequate realisation in the Resurrection of Christ (Acts ii. 25 ff.; xiii. 35).

In Ps. xl the Psalmist professes his desire to prove his gratitude to God by offering the sacrifice of obedience. But that obedience was at best imperfect. His words must wait to receive their full accomplishment in the perfect obedience of Christ (Heb. x. 5 ff.).

Christ as the perfect Teacher adopted and 'fulfilled' the methods of the teachers of the old dispensation (Ps. lxxviii. 1).

(4) *The coming of God.* Another series of Psalms describes or anticipates the Advent of Jehovah Himself to judge and to redeem. Such are xviii. 7 ff. l. lxviii. xcvi—xcviii. They correspond to the prophetic idea of 'the day of Jehovah,' which culminates in Mal. iii. 1 ff. They do not indeed predict the Incarnation, but they served to prepare men's minds for the direct personal intervention of God which was to be realised in the Incarnation. We find passages originally spoken of Jehovah applied in the N.T. to Christ[1]. The words of Ps. lxviii. 18, which describe the triumphant ascent of Jehovah to His throne after the subjugation of the world, are adapted and applied to the triumphant return of Christ to heaven and His distribution of the gifts of grace (Eph. iv. 8).

The words of cii. 25, 26, contrasting the immutability of the Creator with the mutability of created things, originally addressed to Jehovah by the exile who appealed to Him to intervene on behalf of Sion, are applied to the Son through whom the worlds were made (Hebr. i. 10).

Thus the inspired poetry of the Psalter, viewing the Davidic kingdom in the light of the prophetic promises attached to it, played its part in preparing men's minds for a King who should be God's Son and representative, as it came to be interpreted in the course of history through failure and disappointment. The record of the Psalmists' own sufferings helped to give some insight into the part which suffering must perform in the redemption of the world. Their ideals of man's destiny and duty implied the hope of the coming of One who should perfectly fulfil them. The expectation of Jehovah's advent to judge and redeem anticipated a direct divine interposition for the establishment of the divine kingdom in the world.

It is not to be supposed that the relation of these various elements of the preparation could be recognised, or that they

[1] See Bp Westcott's *Hebrews*, p. 89.

could be harmonised into one consistent picture beforehand. It was reserved for the event to shew that the various lines of hope and teaching were not parallel but convergent, meeting in the Person and Work of Him Who is at once God and Man, Son and Servant, Priest and King, Sufferer and Victor.

It has been assumed thus far that these Psalms refer primarily to the circumstances under which they were written. Many commentators however regard some of the 'Royal Psalms,' in particular Pss. ii. xlv. lxxii. cx. as direct prophecies of the Messianic King: some because they are unable to discover the precise historical occasion in existing records: others, because the language seems to reach beyond what could be predicated of any earthly king, and the N. T. application of these Psalms to Christ appears to them to require that they should be referred to Him alone.

The particular historical reference of each of these Psalms will be discussed in the introduction to it: here it must suffice to observe that such Psalms as ii and xlv produce the decided impression that they were written in view of contemporary events. Lofty as is the language used, it is no more than is warranted by the grandeur of the divine promises to the house of David; and if the words are applied to Christ with a fulness and directness which seems to exclude any lower meaning, it must be remembered that it was through the institution of the kingdom that men were taught to look for Him, and their fulfilment in Him presumes rather than excludes the view that they had a true, if partial, meaning for the time at which they were written.

Similarly in the case of the 'Passion Psalms' it has been thought that, at least in Ps. xxii, the Psalmist is speaking in the person of Christ. Yet even this Psalm plainly springs out of personal suffering; though it is equally plain that the character of that suffering was providentially moulded to be a type, and the record of it inspired by the Holy Spirit to be a prophecy, of the sufferings of Christ. That Ps. lxix cannot as a whole be placed in the mouth of Christ is evident, if for no other reason, from the confession of sin in *v*. 5.

Have then these Psalms, has prophecy in general, a 'double

sense?' a primary historical sense in relation to the circumstances under which they were written, and a secondary typical or prophetical sense, in which they came to be understood by the Jewish and afterwards by the Christian Church? We may no doubt legitimately talk of a 'double sense,' if what we mean is that Psalmist and Prophet did not realise the full meaning of their words, and that that meaning only came to be understood as it was unfolded by the course of history. But is it not a truer view to regard both senses as essentially one? The institutions of Israel and the discipline of the saints of old were designed to express the divine purpose as the age and the people were able to receive it. The divine purpose is eternally one and the same, though it must be gradually revealed to man, and man's apprehension of it changes. And it is involved in any worthy conception of inspiration that inspired words should express divine ideas with a fulness which cannot at once be intelligible, but only comes to be understood as it is interpreted by the course of history or illuminated by the light of fuller revelation.

Inspired words are "springing and germinant" in their very nature: they grow with the growing mind of man. They are 'fulfilled,' not in the sense that their meaning is exhausted and their function accomplished, but in the sense that they are enlarged, expanded, ennobled. What is temporary and accidental falls away, and the eternal truth shines forth in its inexhaustible freshness and grandeur.

For us the Psalms which were designed to prepare the way for the coming of Christ bear witness to the unity of the divine plan which is being wrought out through successive ages of the world.

(5) *The nations.* Under the head of Messianic Hope in the Psalter must be included the view which is presented of the relation of the nations to Jehovah and to Israel. Few features are more striking than the constant anticipation of the inclusion of all nations in Jehovah's kingdom.

On the one hand indeed the nations appear as the deadly enemies of Jehovah's people, leagued together for its destruction (ii. lxxxiii), but doomed themselves to be destroyed if they persist in their unhallowed purpose (ii. 9; ix. 17 ff.; xxxiii. 10; xlvi. 6 ff.; lix. 5, 8).

But concurrently with this view of the relation of the nations to Jehovah and Israel, another and more hopeful view is constantly presented. The nations as well as Israel belong to Jehovah, and are the objects of His care; they will eventually render Him homage; and Israel is to be the instrument for accomplishing this purpose and establishing the universal divine kingdom.

(*a*) The earth and all its inhabitants belong to Jehovah as their Creator (xxiv. 1; cp. viii. 1); they are under His observation (lxvi. 7), and subservient to His purposes (xxxiii. 14); He disciplines and teaches them (xciv. 10); they are addressed as being capable of moral instruction (xlix. 1).

He is the supreme and universal King and Judge (xxii. 28; xlvi. 10; xlvii. 2, 8, 9; xcvi. 13; xcviii. 9; xcix. 2; cxix. 4); the nations are constantly exhorted to render Him homage (ii. 8 ff.), to fear Him (xxxiii. 8), to praise Him (lxvi. 1 f.; cxvii. 1; cxlv. 21), and even to worship Him in His temple (xcvi. 7 ff.; c. 1, 2).

(*b*) The time will come when all nations will acknowledge His sovereignty (xxii. 27; lxvi. 4; lxviii. 29 ff.; lxxxvi. 9; cii. 22). The kings of the earth will render homage to their sovereign (cii. 15; cxxxviii. 4). To Him as the hearer of prayer shall "all flesh" come (lxv. 2); He is the confidence of all the ends of the earth (lxv. 5); and the Psalter ends with the chorus of universal praise from every living thing (cl. 6).

(*c*) Israel is Jehovah's instrument for accomplishing the world-wide extension of His kingdom.

In the early days of the kingdom it may have seemed that Israel's destiny was to subjugate the nations and include them in the kingdom of Jehovah by conquest (ii; xviii. 43; xlvii); yet the thought is never far distant that the object of Israel's victories is to make Jehovah known (xviii. 49; lvii. 9), and to lead to the harmonious union of the nations with His people (xlvii. 9). Ps. xlv suggests the hope of peaceful alliance, Ps. lxxii of conquest by moral supremacy (*vv.* 8 ff.). If to the last the thought of actual conquests survived (cxlix. 6 ff.), a more spiritual conception of Israel's relation to the nations grew up side by side with it. The Psalmist's gratitude for personal deliverance widens out into the prospect of the universal worship of Jehovah (xxii). Ps. lxvii expresses Israel's consciousness of its calling to be a blessing to the world, and the final purpose of its prosperity is the conversion of the nations. Zion becomes the spiritual metropolis in which nations once hostile are enrolled as citizens (lxxxvii); and Israel's deliverance from captivity is seen to lead to the universal worship of her Deliverer, and the gathering of the nations to Zion to serve Him (cii. 15, 21 ff.; cp. xcvi—xcviii).

Thus, even under the limitations of the old Covenant, were formed the hopes which are in part fulfilled, and in part still await fulfilment, in the Christian Church.

CHAPTER IX.

ON SOME POINTS IN THE THEOLOGY OF THE PSALMS.

A thorough examination of the Theology of the Psalms would exceed the limits of the present work. It would include an investigation whether any progress and development of doctrine can be traced in the Psalms of different periods. All that can be attempted here is a few brief notes on some points which require the student's attention or present special difficulties.

(i) *The relation of the Psalms to the Ordinances of Worship.* The Psalms represent the inward and spiritual side of the religion of Israel. They are the manifold expression of the intense devotion of pious souls to God, of the feelings of trust and hope and love which reach a climax in such Psalms as xxiii. xlii—xliii. lxiii. lxxxiv. They are the many-toned voice of prayer in the widest sense, as the soul's address to God in confession, petition, intercession, meditation, thanksgiving, praise, both in public and private. They offer the most complete proof, if proof were needed, how utterly false is the notion that the religion of Israel was a formal system of external rites and ceremonies. In such a book frequent reference to the external ordinances of worship is scarcely to be expected: but they are presumed, and the experience of God's favour is constantly connected with the Sanctuary and its acts of worship[1].

There are frequent references to *the Temple* as the central place of worship, where men appear before God, and where He specially reveals His power glory and goodness, and interprets the ways of His Providence (xlii. 2; xlviii. 9; lxiii. 2; lxv. 4; lxviii. 29; lxxiii. 17; xcvi. 6 ff.; &c.).

The impressive splendour of the priestly array is alluded to (xxix. 2, note; xcvi. 9; cx. 3).

The delight of the festal pilgrimages to Zion is vividly described (xlii. xliii. lxxxiv. cp. lv. 14). Consuming zeal for God's house in a corrupt age characterised the saint and exposed him to persecution (lxix. 9).

The joyous character of the O. T. worship is so striking a feature of the Psalter as scarcely to need special notice. The Psalter as the hymn-book of the Second Temple was entitled 'The Book of Praises.' We hear the jubilant songs of the troops of pilgrims (xlii. 4; cp. Is. xxx. 29): we see the processions to the Temple with minstrels and singers (lxviii. 24, 25): we hear its courts resound with shouts of praise (xcv. 1 ff.; c. 1, 4), and music of harp and psaltery, timbrel and trumpet, cymbals and pipe.

Sacrifice is referred to as the sanction of the covenant between God and His people (l. 5; cp. Ex. xxiv. 5 ff.); as the regular accompaniment of approach to God (xx. 3; l. 8 ff.; lxvi. 13, 15; xcvi. 8); as the natural expression of worship and thanksgiving (xliii. 4; li. 19; liv. 6; cvii. 22; cxviii. 27), especially in connexion with vows (lvi. 12; lxvi. 13 ff.), which are frequently mentioned (xxii. 25; lxi. 5, 8; lxv. 1; lxxvi. 11; cxvi. 14, 18). The Levitical ceremonies of purification are alluded to as symbols of the inward cleansing which must be effected by God Himself (li. 7).

But the great prophetic doctrine[2] of the intrinsic worthlessness of sacrifice apart from the disposition of the worshipper is emphatically laid down. It is not sacrifice but obedience that

---

[1] Cp. Oehler, *O. T. Theology*, § 201.
[2] From 1 Sam. xv. 22 onwards. See Amos v. 21 ff.; Hos. vi. 6: Is. i. 11 ff.; Mic. vi. 6 ff.; Jer. vi. 20; vii. 21 ff.; xiv. 12.

God desires (xl. 6 ff.); it is not thank-offering, but a thankful heart which finds acceptance with Him (l. 14, 23; cp. lxix. 30, 31); it is not sacrifice, but contrition which is the condition of forgiveness (li. 16 ff.). Penitence and prayer are true sacrifices (li. 17; cxli. 2): and the moral conditions which can alone make sacrifice acceptable and are requisite for approach to God are constantly insisted upon (iv. 5; xv. 1 ff.; xxiv. 3 ff.; xxvi. 6; lxvi. 18).

It is God Himself who 'purges away' iniquity (lxv. 3; lxxviii. 38; lxxix. 9; lxxxv. 2).

(ii) *The self-righteousness of the Psalmists.* Readers of the Psalms are sometimes startled by assertions of integrity and innocence which appear to indicate a spirit of self-righteousness and self-satisfaction approximating to that of the Pharisee (Luke xviii. 9). Thus David appeals to be judged according to his righteousness and his integrity (vii. 8; cp. xxvi. 1 ff.), and regards his deliverance from his enemies as the reward of his righteousness and innocence (xviii. 20 ff.); sincerity and innocence are urged as grounds of answer to prayer (xvii. 1 ff.), and God's most searching scrutiny is invited (xxvi. 2 ff.).

Some of these utterances are no more than asseverations that the speaker is innocent of particular crimes laid to his charge by his enemies (vii. 3 ff.); others are general professions of purity of purpose and single-hearted devotion to God (xvii. 1 ff.). They are not to be compared with the self-complacency of the Pharisee, who prides himself on his superiority to the rest of the world, but to St Paul's assertions of conscious rectitude (Acts xx. 26 ff.; xxiii. 1). They breathe the spirit of simple faith and childlike trust, which throws itself unreservedly on God. Those who make them do not profess to be absolutely sinless, but they do claim to belong to the class of the righteous who may expect God's favour, and they do disclaim all fellowship with the wicked, from whom they expect to be distinguished in the course of His Providence.

And if God's present favour is expected as the reward of right conduct, it must be remembered that the Israelite looked for the visible manifestation of the divine government of the world in the reward of the godly and the punishment of the evildoer in this present life (1 Kings viii. 32, 39). He felt that he had a right to be treated according to the rectitude of which he was conscious.

Further, it was commonly supposed that there was a proportion between sin and suffering; that exceptional suffering was an evidence of exceptional guilt. This idea throws light upon the assertions of national innocence in xliv. 17 ff., and of personal innocence in lix. 3. They are clearly relative, as much as to say, 'We know of no national apostasy which can account for this defeat as a well-merited judgment:' 'I am not conscious of any personal transgression for which this persecution is a fitting chastisement.' So Job repeatedly acknowledges the sinfulness of man, but denies that he has been guilty of any special sin to account for his extraordinary afflictions.

Some however of these utterances undoubtedly belong to the O. T. and not to the N.T. They are the partial expression of an eternal truth (Matt. xvi. 27), in a form which belongs to the age in which they were spoken. The N. T. has brought a new revelation of the nature of sin, and a more thorough self-knowledge: it teaches the inadmissibility of any plea of merit on man's part (Luke xvii. 10). But the docile spirit which fearlessly submits itself to the divine scrutiny and desires to be instructed (cxxxix. 23, 24) has nothing in common with the Pharisaism which is by its very nature incapable of improvement.

And side by side with these assertions of integrity we find in the Psalms the fullest recognition of personal sinfulness (li. 5; lxix. 5), of man's inability to justify himself before God (cxxx. 3 ff., cxliii. 2), of his need of pardon cleansing and renewal (xxxii. li. lxv. 3), of his dependence on God for preservation from sin (xix. 12 ff.), of the barrier which sin erects between him and God (lxvi. 18, l. 16 ff.); as well as the strongest expressions of absolute self-surrender and dependence on God and entire trust in His mercy (xxv. 4 ff., lxxiii. 25 ff.).

(iii) The so-called *Imprecatory Psalms* have long been felt to constitute one of the 'moral difficulties' of the O.T. We are startled to find the most lofty and spiritual meditations interrupted by passionate prayers for vengeance upon enemies, or ending in triumphant exultation at their destruction. How, we ask, can such utterances be part of a divine revelation? How can the men who penned them have been in any sense inspired by the Holy Spirit?

These imprecations cannot be explained away, as some have thought, by rendering the verbs as futures, and regarding them as authoritative *declarations* of the certain fate of the wicked. Of these there are many, but in not a few cases the form of the verb is that which specifically expresses a wish or prayer, and it cannot be rendered as a simple future.

Nor again can the difficulty be removed by regarding the imprecations of Pss. lxix and cix as the curses not of the Psalmist himself but of his enemies. Even if this view were exegetically tenable for these two Psalms, which is doubtful, expressions of the same kind are scattered throughout the Psalter. Moreover the Book of Jeremiah contains prayers for vengeance on the prophet's enemies, which are at least as terrible as those of Pss. lxix and cix.

In what light then are these utterances to be regarded? They must be viewed as belonging to the dispensation of the Old Testament; they must be estimated from the standpoint of the Law, which was based upon the rule of retaliation, and not of the Gospel, which is animated by the principle of love; they belong to the spirit of Elijah, not of Christ; they use the language of the age which was taught to love its neighbour and hate its enemy (Matt. v. 43)[1].

Our Lord explicitly declared that the old dispensation, though not contrary to the new, was inferior to it; that modes of thought and actions were permitted or even enjoined which would not be allowable for His followers; that He had come to 'fulfil' the Law and the Prophets by raising all to a higher moral and spiritual level, expanding and completing what was rudimentary and imperfect (Matt. v. 43; xix. 8; Luke ix. 55).

It is essential then to endeavour to understand the ruling

---

[1] It is well to remember, on the other hand, that the Law inculcates service to an enemy (Ex. xxiii. 4, 5), and forbids hatred, vengeance and bearing of grudges (Lev. xix. 17, 18): and the Book of Proverbs bids men leave vengeance to God (xx. 22), and control their exultation at an enemy's misfortune (xxiv. 17; cp. Job xxxi. 29); and teaches that kindness is the best revenge (xxv. 21, 22). We have here the germ of Christian ethics.

ideas and the circumstances of the age in which these Psalms were composed, in order to realise how, from the point of view of that age, such prayers for vengeance and expressions of triumph as they contain could be regarded as justifiable.

In the first place it is important to observe that they are not dictated merely by private vindictiveness and personal thirst for revenge. While it would perhaps be too much to say that they contain no tinge of human passion (for the Psalmists were men of infirmity, and inspiration does not obliterate personal character), they rise to a far higher level. They spring ultimately from zeal for God's cause, and they express a willingness to leave vengeance in the hands of Him to whom it belongs. Retribution is desired and welcomed as part of the divine order (lviii. 11; civ. 35).

This was a great advance upon the ruder stage of society, in which each man claimed to be his own avenger. David's first impulse when he was insulted by Nabal was to wreak a terrible vengeance upon him and all that belonged to him. It was the natural instinct of the time. But his final resolve to leave vengeance to God indicated the better feeling that was being learnt (1 Sam. xxv. 21 ff., 39).

Though their form belongs to the circumstances and limitations of the age, these invocations of vengeance are the feeling after a truth of the divine government of the world. For it is the teaching of the N.T. not less than of the O.T. that the kingdom of God must come in judgment as well as in grace. Love no less than justice demands that there should be an ultimate distinction between the good and the evil, that those who will not submit to the laws of the kingdom should be banished from it (Matt. xiii. 49, 50; xvi. 27; John v. 29).

But while the Gospel proclaims the law of universal love, and bids men pray without ceasing for the establishment of the kingdom of God by the repentance and reformation even of the most hardened offenders, and leave the issue to the future judgment of God, the Law with its stern principle of retribution and its limitation of view to the present life, allowed men to pray for the establishment of the kingdom of God through the destruction of the wicked.

INTRODUCTION. lxxiii

The Prophets and Psalmists of the O.T. had a keen sense of the great conflict constantly going on between good and evil, between God and His enemies[1]. That conflict was being waged in the world at large between Israel as the people of God and the nations which threatened to destroy Israel. The enemies of Israel were the enemies of Israel's God; Israel's defeat was a reproach to His Name; the cause at stake was not merely the existence of the nation, but the cause of divine truth and righteousness. This aspect of the conflict is most completely expressed in Ps. lxxxiii, and prayers for vengeance such as those of lxxix. 10, 12 and cxxxvii. 8 express the national desire for the vindication of a just cause, and the punishment of cruel insults.

Within the nation of Israel this same conflict was being waged on a smaller scale between the godly and the ungodly. When the righteous were oppressed and the wicked triumphant, it seemed as though God's rule were being set at nought, as though God's cause were losing. It was not only allowable but a duty to pray for its triumph, and that involved the destruction of the wicked who persisted in their wickedness. There must be no half-heartedness or compromise. In hatred as well as in love the man who fears God must be wholly on His side (cxxxix. 19—22). The perfect ruler resolves not only to choose the faithful in the land for his servants, but "morning by morning" to "destroy all the wicked of the land; to cut off all the workers of iniquity from the city of the LORD" (ci. 6—8); and it seemed only right and natural to pray that the Divine Ruler would do the same.

Further light is thrown on the Imprecatory Psalms by the consideration that there was as yet no revelation of a final judgment in which evil will receive its entire condemnation, or of a future state of rewards and punishments (see p. lxxv ff.). Men expected and desired to see a present and visible distinction between the righteous and the wicked, according to the law of the divine government (cxxv. 4, 5; cxlv. 20). It was part of God's lovingkindness not less than of His omnipotence to "reward

---

[1] See Rainy's *Development of Christian Doctrine*, p. 346, where there is a helpful treatment of the whole question.

every man according to his work" (lxii. 12). The sufferings of the godly and the prosperity of the ungodly formed one of the severest trials of faith and patience to those whose view was limited to the present life (Ps. xxxvii. lxxiii). Although God's sentence upon evil is constantly being executed in this world, it is often deferred and not immediately visible; and those who longed for the vindication of righteousness desired to have it executed promptly before their eyes. Hence the righteous could rejoice when he saw the wicked destroyed, for it was a manifest proof of the righteous government of Jehovah (lii. 5 ff.; liv. 7; lviii. 10, 11; xcii. 11).

Again, it must be remembered that we have been taught to distinguish between the evil man and evil: to love the sinner while we hate his sin. But Hebrew modes of thought were concrete. The man was identified with his wickedness; the one was a part of the other; they were inseparable. Clearly it was desirable that wickedness should be extirpated. How could this be done except by the destruction of the wicked man? What right had he to exist, if he persisted obstinately in his wickedness and refused to reform (l. 16 ff.)?

The imprecations which appear most terrible to us are those which include a man's kith and kin in his doom (lxix. 25; cix. 9 ff.). In order to estimate them rightly it must be borne in mind that a man's family was regarded as part of him. He lived on in his posterity: the sin of the parent was entailed upon the children: if the offence had been monstrous and abnormal, so ought the punishment to be. The defective conception of the rights of the individual, so justly insisted upon by Professor Mozley as one of the chief 'ruling ideas in early ages,' helps us to understand how not only the guilty man, but all his family, could be devoted to destruction[1].

Let it be noted too that what seems the most awful of all anathemas (lxix. 28) would not have been understood in the extreme sense which we attach to it: and some of the expressions which shock us most by their ferocity are metaphors derived from times of wild and savage warfare (lviii. 10; lxviii. 21 ff.). The noblest thoughts may coexist side by side with

[1] See Mozley's *Lectures on the Old Testament*, pp. 87 ff., 198 ff.

much that to a later age seems wholly barbarous and revolting.

These utterances then belong to the spirit of the O.T. and not of the N.T., and by it they must be judged. They belong to the age in which the martyr's dying prayer was not, "Lord, lay not this sin to their charge" (Acts vii. 60), but, "The Lord look upon it, and require it" (2 Chron. xxiv. 22). It is impossible that such language should be repeated in its old and literal sense by any follower of Him Who has bidden us to love our enemies and pray for them that persecute us.

Yet these utterances still have their lesson. On the one hand they may make us thankful that we live in the light of the Gospel and under the law of Love: on the other hand they testify to the punishment which the impenitent sinner deserves and must finally receive (Rom. vi. 23). They set an example of moral earnestness, of righteous indignation, of burning zeal for the cause of God. Men have need to beware lest in pity for the sinner they condone the sin, or relax the struggle against evil. The underlying truth is still true, that "the cause of sin shall go down, in the persons of those who maintain it, in such a manner as to throw back on them all the evil they have sought to do....This was waited for with inexpressible longing. It was fit it should be....This is not the only truth bearing on the point; but it is truth, and it was then the present truth[1]". It is in virtue of the truth which they contain that these Psalms can be regarded as 'inspired,' and their position in the records of divine revelation justified. Their fundamental motive and idea is the religious passion for justice; and it was by the Holy Spirit that their writers were taught to discern and grasp this essential truth; but the form in which they clothed their desire for its realisation belonged to the limitations and modes of thought of their particular age.

(iv) *The Future Life.* Death is never regarded in the O.T. as annihilation or the end of personal existence. But it is for the most part contemplated as the end of all that deserves to be called life. Existence continues, but all the joy and vigour of vitality are gone for ever (Is. xiv. 10; Ps. cxliii. 3 = Lam. iii. 6).

[1] Rainy, p. 348.

Communion with God is at an end: the dead can no longer "see" Him: they cannot serve or praise Him in the silence of Sheol: His lovingkindness, faithfulness, and righteousness can no longer be experienced there. See Ps. vi. 5; xxx. 9; lxxxviii. 4, 5, 10—12; cxv. 17; Is. xxxviii. 11, 18: and numerous passages in Job, e.g. vii. 9; x. 21 ff.; xiv.

Death is the common lot of all, which none can escape (xlix. 7 ff.; lxxxix. 48), but the righteous and the wicked are distinguished by the manner of their death (lxxiii. 19). When death comes to a man in a good old age, and he leaves his children behind him to keep his name in remembrance, it may be borne with equanimity; but premature death is usually regarded as the sign of God's displeasure and the penal doom of the wicked (xxvi. 9), and childlessness is little better than annihilation.

To the oppressed and persecuted indeed Sheol is a welcome rest (Job iii. 17 ff.), and death may even be a gracious removal from coming evil (Is. lvii. 1, 2); but as a rule death is dreaded as the passage into the monotonous and hopeless gloom of the under-world.

The continuance of existence after death has no moral or religious element in it. It is practically non-existence. The dead man 'is not' (xxxix. 13). It offers neither encouragement nor warning. It brings no solution of the enigmas of the present life. There is no hope of happiness or fear of punishment in the world beyond.

This world was regarded as the scene of recompence and retribution. If reward and punishment did not come to the individual, they might be expected to come to his posterity. For the man lived on in his children: this was his real continuance in life, not the shadowy existence of Sheol: hence the bitterness of childlessness.

Nowhere in the Psalter do we find the hope of a Resurrection from the dead. The prophets speak of a national, and finally of a personal resurrection (Hos. vi. 1 ff.; Is. xxvi. 19; Ezek. xxxvii. 1 ff.; Dan. xii. 2), and predict the final destruction of death (Is. xxv. 8). But just where we should have expected to find such a hope as the ground of consolation, it is conspicuously absent[1].

[1] lvi. 13; lxviii. 20; xc. 3; cxli. 7, which are sometimes referred to,

INTRODUCTION. lxxvii

Indeed it is set on one side as incredible (lxxxviii. 10). It is evident that there was as yet no revelation of a resurrection upon which men could rest; it was no article of the common religious belief to which the faithful naturally turned for comfort[1].

But do we not find that strong souls, at least in rare moments of exultant faith and hope, broke through the veil, and anticipated, not indeed the resurrection of the body, but translation through death into a true life of unending fellowship with God, like Enoch or Elijah?

Do not Pss. xvi, xvii, xlix, lxxiii, plainly speak of the hope of the righteous in his death?

The answer to this question is one of the most difficult problems of the theology of the Psalter. It can only be satisfactorily treated in the detailed exposition of the passages as they stand in their context. Some of the expressions which appear at first sight to imply a sure hope of deliverance from Sheol and of reception into the more immediate presence of God (e.g. xlix. 15, lxxiii. 24) are used elsewhere of temporal deliverance from death or protection from danger, and may mean no more than this (ix. 13, xviii. 16, xxx. 3, lxxxvi. 13, ciii. 4, cxxxviii. 7). Reading these passages in the light of fuller revelation we may easily assign to them a deeper and more precise meaning than their original authors and hearers understood. They adapt themselves so readily to Christian hope that we are easily led to believe that it was there from the first.

Unquestionably these Psalms (xvi, xvii, xlix, lxxiii) do contain the germ and principle of the doctrine of eternal life. It was present to the mind of the Spirit Who inspired their authors. The intimate fellowship with God of which they speak as man's highest good and truest happiness could not, in view of the nature and destiny of man and his relation to God, continue to be regarded as limited to this life and liable to sudden and final interruption. (See Matt. xxii. 31 ff.). It re-

cannot be interpreted of a resurrection. The text of xlviii. 14 is very uncertain; lxxxvi. 13 is a thanksgiving for deliverance from death; cxviii. 17 expresses the hope of such a deliverance.

[1] Contrast the precise statements in the *Psalms of Solomon*, quoted on p. xxxviii, where however it is only a resurrection of the righteous which is anticipated.

quired but a step forward to realise the truth of its permanence, but whether the Psalmists took this step is doubtful.

But even if they did, there was still no clear and explicit revelation on which the doctrine of a future life or of a resurrection could be based. It was but a 'postulate of faith,' a splendid hope, a personal and individual conclusion.

What was the meaning and purpose of this reserve in the teaching of the O. T.? Mankind had to be trained through long ages by this stern discipline to know the bitterness of death as the punishment of sin, and to trust God utterly in spite of all appearances. They had to be profoundly impressed with a sense of need and of the incompleteness of life here, in order that they might long for deliverance from this bondage and welcome it when it came (Heb. ii. 15). Nor could the revelation of the Resurrection and eternal life be made in fulness and certainty (so far as we can see) otherwise than through the victory of the second Adam who through death overcame death and opened unto us the gate of everlasting life (1 Cor. xv. 21 ff.).

Yet, as Delitzsch observes, there is nothing which comes to light in the New Testament which does not already exist in germ in the Psalms. The ideas of death and life are regarded by the Psalmists in their fundamental relation to the wrath and the love of God, in such a way that it is easy for Christian faith to appropriate and deepen, in the light of fuller revelation, all that is said of them in the Psalms. There is no contradiction of the Psalmist's thought, when the Christian as he prays substitutes hell for Hades in such a passage as vi. 5, for the Psalmist dreaded Hades only as the realm of wrath and separation from the love of God, which is the true life of man. Nor is there anything contrary to the mind of the authors in the application of xvii. 15 to the future vision of the face of God in all its glory, or of xlix. 14 to the Resurrection morning; for the hopes there expressed in moments of spiritual elevation can only find their full satisfaction in the world to come. The faint glimmerings of twilight in the eschatological darkness of the Old Testament are the first rays of the coming sunrise. And the Christian cannot refrain from passing beyond the limits of the Psalmists, and understanding the Psalms according to the mind of the Spirit, whose purpose in the gradual revelation of salvation was ever directed towards the final consummation. Thus understood, the Psalms belong to the Israel of the New Testament not less than of the Old Testament.

The Church, in using the Psalms for its prayers, recognises the unity of the two Testaments: and scholarship, in expounding the Psalms, gives full weight to the difference between them. Both are right; the former in regarding the Psalms in the light of the one unchanging salvation, the latter in distinguishing the different periods and steps in which that salvation was historically revealed[1].

The sacred poetry of heathen religions, in spite of all that it contains of noble aspiration and pathetic "feeling after God," has ceased to be a living power. But "the Psalms of those far distant days, the early utterances of their faith and love, still form the staple of the worship and devotion of the Christian Church"... "The Vedic hymns are dead remains, known in their real spirit and meaning to a few students. The Psalms are as living as when they were written.... They were composed in an age at least as immature as that of the singers of the Veda; but they are now what they have been for thirty centuries, the very life of spiritual religion—they suit the needs, they express, as nothing else can express, the deepest religious ideas of 'the foremost in the files of time.'[2]"

[1] Delitzsch, *The Psalms*, p. 63.
[2] Dean Church, *The Sacred Poetry of Early Religions*, pp. 12, 38.

In the Psalms the soul turns inward on itself, and their great feature is that they are the expression of a large spiritual experience. They come straight from " the heart within the heart," and the secret depths of the spirit. Where, in those rough cruel days, did they come from, those piercing, lightning-like gleams of strange spiritual truth, those magnificent outlooks over the kingdom of God, those raptures at His presence and His glory, those wonderful disclosures of self-knowledge, those pure outpourings of the love of God? Surely here is something more than the mere working of the mind of man. Surely they tell of higher guiding, prepared for all time; surely, as we believe, they hear "the word behind them saying, This is the way, walk ye in it," they repeat the whispers of the Spirit of God, they reflect the very light of the Eternal Wisdom. In that wild time there must have been men sheltered and hidden amid the tumult round them, humble and faithful and true, to whom the Holy Ghost could open by degrees the " wondrous things of His law," whom He taught, and whose mouths He opened, to teach their brethren by their own experience, and to do each their part in the great preparation.

DEAN CHURCH.

THE BOOK OF PSALMS.

PSALM I.

THIS Psalm is the development in poetical language and imagery of the thought repeated in so many forms in the Book of Proverbs (e.g. ii. 21, 22), that it is well with the righteous and ill with the wicked. The belief in Jehovah's righteous government of the world was a fundamental principle of Old Testament religion, and it is here asserted without any of those doubts and questionings which disturbed the minds of many Psalmists and Prophets, especially in the later stages of Old Testament revelation.

The Psalm forms an appropriate prologue to the Psalter, which records the manifold experiences of the godly. For it affirms the truth to which they clung, in spite of all appearances to the contrary, in spite of the sufferings of the righteous and the triumphs of the wicked, that the only sure and lasting happiness for man is to be found in fellowship with God.

The Psalm expresses a general truth, and does not appear to refer to any particular person or occasion. Hence date and authorship must remain uncertain. Some (without good reason) have assigned it to David, during his persecution by Saul, or during Absalom's rebellion: Dean (now Bp.) Perowne conjectures that it may have been written by Solomon as an introduction to a collection of David's poems: Prof. Cheyne thinks that it was a product of the fresh enthusiasm for the study of the Law in the time of Ezra.

Two considerations however limit the period to which it may be assigned.

(1) It is earlier than Jeremiah, who paraphrases and expands part of it in ch. xvii. 5—8 with reference to Jehoiakim or Jehoiachin.

(2) The most striking parallels in thought and language are to be found in the middle section of the Book of Proverbs (x—xxiv), which dates from a comparatively early period in the history of Judah, if not from the reign of Solomon himself. The 'scorner' is a character hardly mentioned outside of the Book of Proverbs: the contrast of the righteous and the wicked, and the belief that prosperity is the reward of piety, and adversity of ungodliness, are especially conspicuous in the middle section of that book: and further striking coincidences in detail of thought and language will easily be found.

The absence of a title distinguishes it from the mass of Psalms in Book I., and points to its having been derived from a different source. It may have been composed or selected as a preface to the original 'Davidic' collection (*Introd.* p. xliii), or, though this is less probable, placed here by the final editor of the Psalter.

The Psalm consists of two equal divisions:
  i. The enduring prosperity of the righteous (1—3),
  ii. contrasted with the speedy ruin of the wicked (4—6).

Observe the affinity of this Psalm to xxvi; and still more to cxii, which celebrates the blessedness of the righteous, and begins and ends with the same words (*Blessed...perish*): and contrast with its simple confidence the questionings of xxxvii and lxxiii, in which the problem of the prosperity of the wicked is treated as a trial of faith.

1 BLESSED *is* the man
That walketh not in the counsel of the ungodly,
Nor standeth in the way of sinners,
Nor sitteth in the seat of the scornful.

1—3. The happiness of the righteous.

1. More exactly:
   Happy the man who hath not walked in the counsel of wicked men,
   Nor stood in the way of sinners,
   Nor sat in the session of scorners.

Blessed] Or, happy: LXX μακάριος. Cp. Matt. v. 3 ff. The righteous man is first described negatively and retrospectively. All his life he has observed the precept, 'depart from evil' (xxxiv. 14).

the ungodly] Rather, wicked men: and so in *vv*. 4, 5, 6. It is the most general term in the O. T. for the ungodly in contrast to the righteous. If the primary notion of the Hebrew word *rāshā* is *unrest* (cp. Job iii. 17; Is. lvii. 20, 21), the word well expresses the disharmony which sin has brought into human nature, affecting man's relation to God, to man, to self.

sinners] Those who miss the mark, or go astray from the path of right. The intensive form of the word shews that habitual offenders are meant. Cp. Prov. i. 10 ff.

the scornful] Better, as the word is rendered in Proverbs, scorners: those who make what is good and holy the object of their ridicule. With the exception of the present passage and Is. xxix. 20 (cp. however Is. xxviii. 14, 22, R.V.; Hos. vii. 5) the term is peculiar to the Book of Proverbs. There 'the scorners' appear as a class of defiant and cynical freethinkers, in contrast and antagonism to 'the wise.' The root-principle of their character is a spirit of proud self-sufficiency, a contemptuous disregard for God and man (Prov. xxi. 24). It is impossible to reform them, for they hate reproof, and will not seek instruction (xiii. 1; xv. 12). If they seek for wisdom they will not find it (xiv. 6). It is folly to argue with them (ix. 7, 8).

But his delight *is* in the law of the LORD; 2
And in his law doth he meditate day and night.

They are generally detested (xxiv. 9), and in the interests of peace must be banished from society (xxii. 10). Divine judgments are in store for them, and their fate is a warning to the simple (iii. 34; xix. 25, 29; xxi. 11).

The three clauses of the verse with their threefold parallelism (walk, stand, sit: counsel, way, session: wicked, sinners, scorners) emphasise the godly man's entire avoidance of association with evil and evil-doers in every form and degree. They denote successive steps in a career of evil, and form a climax:—(1) adoption of the principles of the wicked as a rule of life: (2) persistence in the practices of notorious offenders: (3) deliberate association with those who openly mock at religion. With the first clause and for the phrase *counsel of the wicked* cp. Mic. vi. 16; Jer. vii. 24; Job x. 3; xxi. 16; xxii. 18: for *stood* &c., cp. Ps. xxxvi. 4. For both clauses cp. the concrete example in 2 Chron. xxii. 3—5. With the third clause cp. Ps. xxvi. 4, 5.

2. The positive principle and source of the righteous man's life. The law of the Lord is his rule of conduct. It is no irksome restriction of his liberty but the object of his love and constant study (Deut. vi. 6—9). True happiness is to be found not in ways of man's own devising, but in the revealed will of God. "The purpose of the Law was to make men happy." Kay. Cp. Deut. xxxiii. 29.

his delight] The religion of Israel was not an external formalism, but an obedience of the heart. Cp. xxxvii. 31; xl. 8; cxii. 1; cxix. 35, 97.

the law of the LORD] The Hebrew word *tôrâh* has a much wider range of meaning than *law*, by which it is always rendered in the A.V. It denotes (1) *teaching, instruction*, whether human (Prov. i. 8), or divine; (2) *a precept* or *law*; (3) *a body of laws*, and in particular *the Mosaic law*, and so finally *the Pentateuch*. The parallel to the second clause of the verse in Josh. i. 8 suggests a particular reference to Deuteronomy; but the meaning here must not be limited to the Pentateuch or any part of it. Rather as in passages where it is parallel to and synonymous with *the word of the* LORD (Is. i. 10; ii. 3) it should be taken to include all Divine revelation as the guide of life.

meditate] The Psalmists meditate on God Himself (lxiii. 6); on His works in nature and in history (lxxvii. 12; cxliii. 5).

3. The consequent prosperity of the godly man is emblematically described. As a tree is nourished by constant supplies of water, without which under the burning Eastern sun it would wither and die, so the life of the godly man is maintained by the supplies of grace drawn from constant communion with God through His revelation. Cp. lii. 8; xcii. 12; cxxviii. 3; Num. xxiv. 6. If a special tree is meant, it is probably not the oleander (Stanley, *Sinai and Palestine*, p. 146), which bears no fruit; nor the vine (Ezek. xix. 10); nor the pomegranate; but the palm. Its love of water, its stately growth, its evergreen foliage, its valuable fruit, combine to suggest that it is here referred to. Cp. Ecclus. xxiv. 14; and see Thomson's *Land and the Book*, p. 48 f.

3 And he shall be like a tree planted by the rivers of water,
That bringeth forth his fruit in his season;
His leaf also shall not wither;
And whatsoever he doeth shall prosper.
4 The ungodly *are* not so:
But *are* like the chaff which the wind driveth away.
5 Therefore the ungodly shall not stand in the judgment,
Nor sinners in the congregation of the righteous.

the rivers of water] Better, **streams of water**: either natural watercourses (Is. xliv. 4): or more probably artificial channels for irrigating the land. Cp. Prov. xxi. 1; Eccl. ii. 5, 6.

and whatsoever &c.] Or, as R.V. marg., *in whatsoever he doeth he shall prosper.* The figure of the tree is dropped, and the words refer directly to the godly man. The literal meaning of the word rendered *prosper* is *to carry through* to a successful result. Cp. Josh. i. 8; and for illustration, Gen. xxxix. 3, 23.

4—6. The character and destiny of the wicked.

4. In sharp contrast to the firmly-rooted, flourishing, fruitful tree is the chaff on the threshing-floor, worthless in itself, and liable to be swept away by every passing breeze.

The scattering of chaff by the wind is a common figure in the O.T. for the sudden destruction of the wicked. Cp. xxxv. 5; Job xxi. 18; Is. xxix. 5; Hos. xiii. 3. Here it describes their character as well as their fate. It would be vividly suggestive to those who were familiar with the sight of the threshing-floors, usually placed on high ground to take advantage of every breeze, on which the corn was threshed out and winnowed by throwing it up against the wind with shovels, the grain falling on the floor to be carefully gathered up, the chaff left to be carried away by the wind and vanish.

The P.B.V. following the LXX and Vulg. adds *from the face of the earth.* Cp. Am. ix. 8; Zeph. i. 2, 3.

5. *Therefore*] The real character of the wicked will be manifested in the judgment. Since they are thus worthless and unstable, destitute of root and fruit, the wicked will not hold their ground in the judgment, in which Jehovah separates the chaff from the wheat (Matt. iii. 12).

stand] So Lat. *causa stare*, and the opposite *causa cadere*. Cp. v. 5; cxxx. 3; Nah. i. 6; Mal. iii. 2; Wisd. v. 1.

in the judgment] Not, before a human tribunal: nor merely in the last judgment, (as the Targum and many interpreters understand it): but in every act of judgment by which Jehovah separates between the righteous and the wicked, and vindicates His righteous government of the world. Cp. as an illustration Num. xvi. Each such 'day of the LORD' is a type and pledge of the great day of judgment. Cp. Is. i. 24 ff., ii. 12 ff.; Mal. iii. 5; Eccl. xii. 14.

in the congregation of the righteous] The 'congregation of Israel,' which is the 'congregation of Jehovah,' is in its true idea and ultimate

For the LORD knoweth the way of the righteous:
But the way of the ungodly shall perish.

destination, the 'congregation of the righteous' (cxi. 1). It is the aim of each successive judgment to purify it, until at last the complete and final separation shall be effected (Matt. xiii. 41—43).

6. The teaching of the Psalm is grounded on the doctrine of divine Providence. Each clause of the verse implies the supplement of its antithesis to the other clause. 'The LORD knows the way of the righteous,' and under His care it is a 'way of life' (xvi. 11; Prov. xii. 28); 'a way of peace' (Is. lix. 8); 'a way eternal' (cxxxix. 24). Equally He knows the way of the wicked, and by the unalterable laws of His government it can lead only to destruction; it is a way of death (Prov. xiv. 12).

knoweth] Divine knowledge cannot be abstract or ineffectual. It involves approval, care, guidance; or abandonment, judgment. The righteous man's course of life leads to God Himself; and He takes care that it does not fail of its end (Nah. i. 7; 2 Tim. ii. 19).

PSALM II.

The circumstances which called forth this Psalm stand out clearly. A king of Israel, recently placed upon the throne, and consecrated by the solemn rite of anointing to be Jehovah's representative in the government of His people, is menaced by a confederacy of subject nations, threatening to revolt and cast off their allegiance. The moment is critical: but his cause is Jehovah's; their endeavour is futile. He asserts his high claims; and the nations are exhorted to yield a willing submission, and avoid the destruction which awaits rebels against the authority of Jehovah.

Who then was the king? and what was the occasion referred to? The king's consciousness of his high calling, and the confidence with which he appeals to the divine promise, point to a time when that promise was still recent, and the lofty ideal of the theocratic kingdom had not been blurred and defaced by failure and defeat. For such a time we must go back to the reigns of David and Solomon.

(1) The language of Acts iv. 25 does not decide the question, for 'David' in the N.T. may mean no more than 'the Psalter' (Heb. iv. 7) or 'a Psalmist.' The older commentators however attribute the Psalm to David, and suppose the occasion to have been the attack of the Philistines shortly after he was anointed king over all Israel (2 Sam. v. 17 ff.), or of the confederacy of Ammonites and Syrians described in 2 Sam. x. But the Psalm speaks plainly (*v.* 3) of *subject* nations, while the Philistines certainly were not David's subjects at the time, and it is doubtful if the Syrians were. See note on 2 Sam. x.

(2) On the other hand there is good reason for supposing that Solomon was the king referred to. He was anointed at Gihon, and solemnly enthroned on Zion (1 Kings i. 45). Zion was already 'Jehovah's holy mountain' in virtue of the presence of the Ark there. So strongly was the theocratic character of the kingdom then realised that he is said to have sat 'on the throne of Jehovah' (1 Chr. xxix. 23; cp. xxviii. 5).

The Psalm is based upon the great promise in 2 Sam. vii. 12 ff., which, although not limited to Solomon, would naturally be claimed by him with special confidence. Solomon succeeded to the great kingdom which his father had built up. But he was young. The succession was disputed. What more likely than that some of the subject nations should threaten to revolt upon his accession? Hadad's request (1 Kings xi. 21) shews that his enemies thought that their opportunity was come. It is true that we have no account of any such revolt in the Historical Books. But their records are incomplete and fragmentary; and the language of the Psalm implies that the revolt was only threatened, and had not as yet broken out into open war. There was still hope that wiser counsels might prevail (*vv.* 10 ff.); and if they did, we should hardly expect to find any reference in Kings and Chron. to a mere threat of rebellion. Moreover, though Solomon's reign was on the whole peaceful, there are incidental notices which make it plain that it was not uniformly and universally so. He made great military preparations (1 Kings iv. 26; ix. 15 ff.; xi. 27: 2 Chron. viii. 5 ff.), and engaged in wars (2 Chron. viii. 3); and Hadad and Rezon succeeded in 'doing him mischief' (1 Kings xi. 21—25).

(3) The conjectures which refer the Psalm to a later occasion have but little probability. The confederacy of Pekah and Rezin against Ahaz (Is. vii.); and the invasion of Judah by the Moabites and their allies (2 Chr. xx.) have been suggested: but neither of these was a *revolt* of subject nations.

The question still remains whether Solomon was himself the writer. The king and the poet appear to be identified in *vv.* 7 ff.; but in such a highly dramatic Psalm, it is at least possible that the poet might introduce the king as a speaker, as he introduces the nations (*v.* 3), and Jehovah (*v.* 6).

The particular historical reference is however of relatively small moment compared with the typical application of the Psalm to the Kingdom of Christ. To understand this, it is necessary to realise the peculiar position of the Israelite king. Israel was Jehovah's son, His firstborn (Ex. iv. 22; Deut. xxxii. 6); and Israel's king, as the ruler and representative of the people, was adopted by Jehovah as His son, His firstborn (2 Sam. vii. 13 ff.; Ps. lxxxix. 26, 27). It was a moral relationship, sharply distinguished from the supposed descent of kings and heroes from gods in the heathen world in virtue of which they styled themselves *Zeus-born*, *sons of Zeus*, and the like. It involved on the one side fatherly love and protection, on the other filial obedience and devotion.

The king moreover was not an absolute monarch in his own right. He was the Anointed of Jehovah, His viceroy and earthly representative. To him therefore was given not only the sovereignty over Israel, but the sovereignty over the nations. Rebellion against him was rebellion against Jehovah.

Thus, as the adopted son of Jehovah and His Anointed King, he was the type of the eternal Son of God, the 'Lord's Christ.' Then, as successive kings of David's line failed to realise their high destiny, men were taught to look for the coming of One who should fulfil the Divine words of promise, giving them a meaning and a reality beyond hope and imagination. See *Introd.* p. lviii ff.

This Psalm then is typical and prophetic of the rebellion of the kingdoms of the world against the kingdom of Christ, and of the final triumph of the kingdom of Christ. To Him all nations are given for an inheritance; if they will not submit He must judge them. This typical meaning does not however exclude (as some commentators think), but rather requires, a historic foundation for the Psalm.

In connexion with this Psalm should be studied 2 Sam. vii.; Ps. lxxxix.; and Pss. xxi., xlv., lxxii. and cx.

The references to this Psalm in the N.T. should be carefully examined.

(1) In Acts iv. 25—28, *vv.* 1, 2 are applied to the confederate hostility of Jews and Gentiles against Christ.

(2) *v.* 7 was quoted by St Paul at Antioch (Acts xiii. 33) as fulfilled in the Resurrection of Christ (cp. Rom. i. 4): and in the Epistle to the Hebrews the words are cited (the Messianic reference of the Psalm being evidently generally admitted) to describe the superiority of the Son to angels (i. 5): and as a declaration of the Divine sonship of Christ, in connexion with the proof of the Divine origin of His high-priesthood (v. 5).[1]

(3) It contains the title 'my Son' (Matt. iii. 17); and 'the Lord's Christ' (Luke ii. 26) which describe the nature and office of the Messiah. Comp. Matt. xvi. 16: John xx. 31.

(4) Its language is repeatedly borrowed in the Revelation, the great epic of the conflict and triumph of Christ's kingdom. He 'rules the nations with a rod of iron' (Rev. xii. 5, xix. 15); and delegates the same power to His servants (ii. 26, 27). 'Kings of the earth' occurs no less than nine times in this book (i. 5, &c.). 'He that sitteth in the heavens' is the central figure there (iv. 2 and frequently).

These quotations sufficiently explain the choice of the Psalm as one of the Proper Psalms for Easter Day.

In a few Heb. MSS. the Second Psalm is reckoned as the First, the First being treated as an independent prologue to the whole book; in a few other MSS. the two are united. Origen says that this was the case in one of two copies he had seen (*Op.* ii. 537): and there was an ancient Jewish saying, "The first Psalm begins with blessing (i. 1), and ends with blessing" (ii. 12). Some recensions of the LXX appear to have followed this arrangement, though Origen speaks as if all the Greek copies with which he was acquainted divided the two Psalms. Justin Martyr in his Apology (i. 40) cites Pss. i and ii as a continuous prophecy, and in Acts xiii. 33 D and cognate authorities representing the 'Western' text, read, 'in the *first* Psalm.'

But though there are points of contact in phraseology (*blessed*, i. 1, ii. 12; *meditate*, i. 2, ii. 1; *perish* connected with *way*, i. 6; ii. 12); they are clearly distinct in style and character. Ps. i is the calm expression of a general truth; Ps. ii springs out of a special occasion; it is full of movement, and has a correspondingly vigorous

---

[1] In D and cognate authorities the words, "Thou art my son, this day have I begotten thee" are substituted for "Thou art my beloved son, in thee I am well pleased," in Luke iii. 22. This was also the reading of the Ebionite Gospel.

rhythm. Probably the absence of a title to Ps. ii (contrary to the usual practice of Book I.) accounts for its having been joined to Ps. i.

The Psalm is dramatic in form. The scene changes. Different persons are introduced as speakers. Its structure is definite and artistic. It consists of four stanzas, each (except the second) of seven lines.

i. The poet contemplates with astonishment the tumult of the nations, mustering with the vain idea of revolt from their allegiance (1—3).

ii. But looking from earth to heaven he beholds Jehovah enthroned in majesty. He mocks their puny efforts. He has but to speak, and they are paralysed (4—6).

iii. The king speaks, and recites the solemn decree by which Jehovah has adopted him for His son, and given him the nations for his inheritance, with authority to subdue all opposition (7—9).

iv. The poet concludes with an exhortation to the nations to yield willing submission, instead of resisting to their own destruction (10—12).

2 Why do the heathen rage,
And the people imagine a vain *thing?*
2 The kings of the earth set themselves,
And the rulers take counsel together,

1—3. The muster of the nations and its design.

1. *Why*] The Psalmist gazes on the great tumult of the nations mustering for war, till the sight forces from him this question of mingled astonishment and indignation. Their insurrection is at once causeless and hopeless.

the heathen] Better, as R.V., **the nations.** *Gōyim*, variously rendered in A.V. *nations, heathen, Gentiles,* denotes the non-Israelite nations as distinguished from and often in antagonism to the people of Jehovah. Sometimes the word has a moral significance and may rightly be rendered *heathen.*

rage] Rather, as in marg., *tumultuously assemble;* or, *throng together.* Cp. the cognate subst. in Ps. lxiv. 2, *insurrection,* R.V. *tumult,* marg. *throng.*

the people] R.V. rightly, **peoples.** Comp. xliv. 2, 14.

imagine] Or, *meditate:* the same word as in i. 2; but in a bad sense, as in xxxviii. 12.

2. *The kings of the earth*] In contrast to 'my king,' *v.* 6. Cp. the use of the phrase in striking contexts, lxxvi. 12; lxxxix. 27; cii. 15; cxxxviii. 4; cxlviii. 11; Is. xxiv. 21.

set themselves] The tenses of the original in *vv.* 1, 2 give a vividness and variety to the picture which can hardly be reproduced in translation. *Rage* and *take counsel* are perfects, representing the throng as already gathered, and the chiefs seated in divan together: *imagine* and *set themselves* are imperfects (the graphic, pictorial tense of Hebrew poetry), representing their plot in process of development. The rapid

Against the LORD, and against his anointed, *saying*,
Let us break their bands asunder, 3
And cast away their cords from us.
He that sitteth in the heavens shall laugh : 4
The LORD shall have them in derision.
Then shall he speak unto them in his wrath, 5
And vex them in his sore displeasure.
Yet have I set my king 6

lively rhythm moreover well suggests the stir and tumult of the gathering host.

against the LORD] They would not deny that in making war upon Israel they were making war upon Israel's God (2 Kings xviii. 32 ff.); but they little knew Whom they were defying (2 Kings xix. 22 ff.).

3. The words of the kings and rulers exhorting one another to cast off *the yoke* of subjection. Bands are the fastenings by which the yoke was secured upon the neck (Jer. xxvii. 2; xxx. 8; Nah. i. 13; &c.): cords are perhaps merely synonymous with *bands:* but as the language of the previous clause is derived from the figure of an ox yoked for ploughing, *cords* may naturally be understood to mean the reins by which the animal was guided and kept under control. Cp. Job xxxix. 10; Hos. xi. 4.

4—6. The poet-seer draws aside the veil, and bids us look from earth to heaven. There the supreme Ruler of the world sits enthroned in majesty. With sovereign contempt He surveys these petty plottings, and when the moment comes confounds them with a word.

4. *He that sitteth in the heavens*] Enthroned in majesty (cxxiii. 1), but withal watching and controlling the course of events upon the earth (xi. 4; ciii. 19; cxiii. 4 ff.; Rev. v. 13; vi. 16).

shall laugh...shall have them in derision] Or, *laugheth...mocketh at them.* Cp. xxxvii. 13; lix. 8; Prov. i. 26. The O.T. uses human language of God without fear of lowering Him to a human level.

the LORD] This is the reading of 1611, restored by Dr Scrivener. Most editions, and R.V., have *the Lord*, in accordance with the Massoretic Text, which reads *Adonai*, not JEHOVAH. The variation is perhaps significant. God is spoken of as the sovereign ruler of the world, rather than as the covenant God of Israel.

5. *Then*] There is a limit to the divine patience. He will not always look on in silence. If they persist in their folly He must speak, and His word (like that of His representative, Is. xi. 4) is power.

vex] Trouble, confound, dismay, with panic terror, paralysing their efforts. Cp. xlviii. 5; lxxxiii. 15, 17.

in his sore displeasure] Lit. *fiery wrath* (Ex. xv. 7), a word used almost exclusively of divine anger.

6. *Yet have I set*] R.V., **Yet I have set.** The first stanza ended with the defiant words of the rebels: the second stanza ends with the answer of Jehovah. The sentence is elliptical, and the pronoun is

Upon my holy hill of Zion.
7 I will declare the decree:
The LORD hath said unto me, Thou *art* my Son;
This day have I begotten thee.
8 Ask of me,
And I shall give *thee* the heathen *for* thine inheritance,
And the uttermost parts of the earth *for* thy possession.

emphatic: 'Why this uproar, when it is *I* Who have set up My king'
&c. The meaning of the word rendered *set* has been much disputed,
but it certainly means *set up*, or *appointed*, not, as A.V. marg., *anointed*.
Cp. Prov. viii. 23.

my king] A king appointed by Me, to rule over My people, as My
representative. Cp. 1 Sam. xvi. 1.

my holy hill of Zion] Zion, the name of the ancient strong-hold
which became the city of David (2 Sam. v. 7), consecrated by the
presence of the Ark until the Temple was built, is the poetical and prophetical name for Jerusalem in its character as the holy city, the earthly
dwelling-place of Jehovah, and the seat of the kingdom which He had
established. For a discussion of the topographical difficulties connected with the site of Zion see Comm. on 2 Samuel, p. 239.

7—9. Jehovah has acknowledged the king as His own: and now
the king takes up Jehovah's declaration, and appeals to the Divine decree
of sonship, and the promise of world-wide dominion.

7. *the decree*] The solemn and authoritative edict, promulgated in
the promise made to David and his house through Nathan (2 Sam. vii.
12 ff.).

hath said unto me] Better, **said unto me** (R.V.), or, **said of me**.

this day] The day when he was anointed king. If Nathan was (as
is commonly supposed) Solomon's tutor, he had no doubt trained him
to a consciousness of his high calling; and when in concert with Zadok
he anointed him (1 Kings i. 34), he would not fail to impress upon him
the significance of the rite. Comp. David's charge to him in 1 Chr. xxii.
6 ff.

have I begotten thee] *I* is the emphatic word in the clause, contrasting
the new sonship by adoption with the existing sonship by natural relation.
The recognition of Christ's eternal sonship in the Resurrection corresponds to the recognition of the king's adoptive sonship in the rite of
anointing (Acts xiii. 33; Rom. i. 4).

8. *Ask of me*] Inheritance is the natural right of sonship. Yet
even the son must plead the promise and claim its fulfilment. Dominion
over the nations is not expressly mentioned in 2 Sam. vii.; but cp. Ps.
lxxxix. 27.

inheritance...possession] Words frequently applied to the gift of
Canaan to Israel (Gen. xvii. 8; Deut. iv. 21, xxxii. 49). Now the
world shall be his with equal right. Jehovah is king of the world, and

Thou shalt break them with a rod of iron; 9
Thou shalt dash them in pieces like a potter's vessel.
Be wise now therefore, O ye kings: 10
Be instructed, ye judges of the earth.
Serve the LORD with fear, 11
And rejoice with trembling.
Kiss the Son, lest he be angry, 12

He offers His representative a world-wide dominion. Cp. lxxii. 8; Zech. ix. 9, 10.

9. *Thou shalt break them with a rod of iron*] A figure for the severity of the chastisement that awaits rebels. Or perhaps, 'an iron sceptre' (xlv. 6), symbol of a stern and irresistible rule. But the word rendered *break them*, if read with different vowels, may mean *rule* (lit. *shepherd*) *them*: so the LXX (and after it Rev. ii. 27; xii. 5), Syriac, and Jerome. In this case *rod* will mean a shepherd's *staff* (Mic. vii. 14), and the phrase will be an oxymoron.

a potter's vessel] An emblem of easy, complete, irreparable destruction. The confederacy is shattered into fragments which cannot be reunited. Cp. Jer. xix. 11; Is. xxx. 11; Prov. vi. 15.

10—12. The poet speaks, drawing the lesson from the great truths which have been set forth. There is a better way. Submission may avert destruction. The leaders of the nations are exhorted to be wise in time, and accept the suzerainty of Jehovah instead of resisting until His wrath is kindled.

10. *Be wise now therefore*] *Now therefore* should stand first, as in R.V., emphatically introducing the conclusion to be drawn from the statements of the preceding verses.

kings...judges of the earth] Not the rebel leaders of *v.* 2 exclusively, though the warning has a special significance for them, but all world-rulers. *Judges* = rulers generally, administration of justice being one of the most important functions of the king in early times. Cp. cxlviii. 11; Prov. viii. 16.

11. *Serve*] The context indicates that political submission to Jehovah in the person of His representative is primarily intended. Cp. xviii. 43; lxxii. 11. But the wider meaning must not be excluded. *Serve* and *fear* are words constantly used with a religious meaning; and political submission to Israel is only the prelude to that spiritual submission of the nations to Jehovah, which is a constant element in the Messianic expectation of the O.T. Cp. xxii. 27, 28; lxvii. 7; c. 1 ff.; cii. 15; &c.

rejoice with trembling] There is no need to alter the reading to *tremble* (xcvi. 9) or to look for this meaning in the word rendered *rejoice*. Joyfulness tempered with reverent awe befits those who approach One so gracious yet so terrible. Cp. xcvii. 1; c. 2; Hos. iii. 5; xi. 10, 11; Heb. xii. 28. P.B.V. adds *unto him* with LXX and Vulg.

12. *Kiss the Son*] According to this rendering the exhortation to serve Jehovah is followed by an exhortation to pay homage to His

And ye perish *from* the way,

representative. For the *kiss* of homage cp. 1 Sam. x. 1; 1 Kings xix. 18; Job xxxi. 27; Hos. xiii. 2. But this rendering must certainly be abandoned. (1) Not to mention some minor difficulties, it assumes that the Psalmist has used the Aramaic word *bar* for son (cp. *Bar-jona, Bar-jesus*) instead of the usual Hebrew word *ben*. The only example of its use in the *Hebrew* of the O.T. (it is of course found in the *Aramaic* of Ezra and Daniel) is in Prov. xxxi. 2, a passage which contains other marked Aramaisms. No satisfactory reason has been suggested for its introduction here. We should not expect a poet to borrow a foreign word for *son* either for 'emphasis' or for 'euphony.'

(2) None of the ancient Versions, with the exception of the Syriac, give this sense to the words. They represent two views as to the meaning. (*a*) The LXX, and of course the Versions dependent on it, render, *Lay hold of instruction:* and similarly the Targum, *Receive instruction*. (*b*) Symmachus and Jerome render, *Worship purely;* and to the same effect, but with his usual bald literalism, Aquila gives, *Kiss choicely*.

The Syriac gives the meaning *Kiss the son:* but its rendering is merely a transcription of the Hebrew words. The reading of the Ambrosian MS., which agrees with the rendering of the LXX, is a correction by a later hand to the reading of the Hexaplar Syriac.

Jerome was acquainted with the translation *Worship the son*, but rejected it as doubtful. The passage in his treatise *against Ruffinus* (i. 19) deserves quotation. He had been charged with inconsistency for translating *Worship purely* (adorate pure) in his Psalter, though he had given *Worship the son* (adorate filium) in his Commentary. After discussing the possible meanings of the words he concludes thus: "Why am I to blame, if I have given different translations of an ambiguous word? and while in my short commentary where there is opportunity for discussion I had said *Worship the Son*, in the text itself, to avoid all appearance of forced interpretation, and to leave no opening for Jewish cavils, I have said, *Worship purely*, or *choicely;* as Aquila also and Symmachus have translated it."

It is however easier to shew that the rendering *Kiss the Son* is untenable, than to decide what rendering should be adopted. *Bar* (beside other senses inapplicable here) may mean *choice*, or, *pure*. Hence some commentators have adopted the renderings *Worship the chosen one;* or, *Worship in purity* (cp. xviii. 20, 24; xxiv. 3—5). But the substantial agreement of the LXX and Targum points to the existence of a widely-spread early tradition as to the sense, and on the whole it seems best to follow their general direction and render, *Embrace instruction*, or perhaps, *obedience*. No rendering is free from difficulty, and it may be doubted whether the text is sound. But an exaggerated importance has frequently been attached to the words. The uncertainty as to their meaning does not affect the general drift of the Psalm, or its Messianic interpretation.

lest he be angry] The subject of the verb is Jehovah Himself. The verb is applied to God in all the thirteen passages where it occurs.

When his wrath is kindled but a little :
Blessed *are* all they that put their trust in him.

perish from *the way*] Rather, as R.V., **perish in the way**: find that your expedition leads only to ruin. Cp. i. 6. P.B.V. adds *right* from the LXX (ἐξ ὁδοῦ δικαίας).

when his wrath is kindled but a little] Better, **For quickly** (or *easily*) **may his anger blaze forth**. *Kindled* fails to give the idea of the Divine wrath blazing up to *consume* all adversaries. Cp. lxxxiii. 14 f.; Is. xxx. 27.

Blessed are *all they that put their trust in him*] Rather, **Happy are all they that take refuge in him**: lit. seek asylum or shelter: cp. Jud. ix. 15; Ruth ii. 12 (R.V.); Ps. vii. 1; lvii. 1. Here primarily, those are congratulated who place themselves under His protectorate by accepting the suzerainty of His king; but as in the preceding verse, the deeper spiritual sense must not be excluded. Cp. xxxiv. 8. Nah. i. 7 combines the thought with that of i. 6 *a*.

PSALM III.

The third and fourth Psalms are closely connected and should be studied together. The one is a morning hymn, after a night spent safely in the midst of danger (iii. 5); the other an evening hymn, when the danger, though less imminent, has not passed away (iv. 8). The spirit and the circumstances are the same : there are resemblances of language and of structure. Compare iii. 1 ("they that distress me") with iv. 1 ("in distress"); iii. 2 with iv. 6 ("there be many that say" is an expression peculiar to these two Psalms); iii. 3 with iv. 2 ; iii. 5 with iv. 8; and on the structure of Ps. iv see below. They are clearly the work of the same author, in the same crisis of his life. That author is in high position (iii. 6) and speaks with a tone of authority (iv. 2 ff.); he is attacked by enemies, not apparently foreigners (iii. 1, 6), whose project is profane and unprincipled (iv. 2, 4, 5) : his cause is pronounced desperate (iii. 2), but with unshaken faith he appeals to the experience of past deliverances, and with absolute confidence casts himself upon Jehovah for protection and deliverance.

We can hardly be wrong in accepting the title which states that the third Psalm was written by David when he fled from Absalom his son, and the third Psalm carries the fourth with it. Of that flight a singularly graphic account is preserved in 2 Sam. xv—xviii. Read in the light of it, these Psalms gain in point and force and vividness. The peril of his position and the ingratitude of the people must be realised in order to estimate duly the strength of the faith and the generosity of feeling, to which these Psalms give expression. The absence of any reference to Absalom himself is thoroughly natural. Comp. 2 Sam. xviii. 33.

It has been suggested that the precise occasion of Ps. iii was the morning after the first night following upon David's flight from Jerusalem. That night however was spent in the passage of the Jordan, in consequence of Hushai's urgent message (2 Sam. xvii. 15—22), and we must rather think of the morning after some night later on, perhaps the next, which had been marked by unexpected rest, in contrast to the sudden alarms of the previous night.

The fourth Psalm was written somewhat later, when David had had time to reflect on the true character of the rebellion; perhaps at Mahanaim, which was his head-quarters for some time.

The second Psalm describes the Kingdom of the Lord's Anointed threatened by enemies from without: the third and fourth tell of a time when it was in danger from intestine foes. All three alike are inspired by the conviction that human schemes are impotent to frustrate the Divine purpose.

The Psalm is divided into four stanzas, each, with the exception of the third, closed by a *Selah*.

i. The present distress, *vv.* 1, 2.
ii. God the source of help and protection, *vv.* 3, 4.
iii. Confidence in the midst of danger, *vv.* 5, 6.
iv. Prayer for deliverance, and blessing on the people, *vv.* 7, 8.

A Psalm of David, when he fled from Absalom his son.

3 LORD, how are they increased that trouble me!
Many *are* they that rise up against me.
2 Many *there be* which say of my soul,
There is no help for him in God. Selah.

1, 2. David lays his need before Jehovah. He is threatened by a rebellion which hourly gathers fresh adherents. His cause is pronounced utterly desperate.

1. *they...that trouble me*] R.V. **mine adversaries**: lit. *they that distress me*. Cp. iv. 1.

increased...many] "The conspiracy was strong; for the people *increased* continually with Absalom. And there came a messenger to David, saying, The hearts of the men of Israel are after Absalom" (2 Sam. xv. 12, 13; cp. xvi. 15).

many are *they that rise up against me*] lit. *many are rising up against me*. The rebellion is in full progress and gathering strength. The phrase is used of enemies in general, but is specially appropriate to *insurgents* against the established government. Cp. 2 Sam. xviii. 31, 32.

2. Faint-hearted friends may be meant, as well as insolent enemies like Shimei, who professed to regard the king's calamities as the divine punishment for his past crimes (2 Sam. xvi. 8 ff.).

of my soul] The 'soul' in O. T. language is a man's 'self;' it represents him as a living, thinking, conscious individual.

help] Or, *salvation*, as in *v.* 8; where see note. Cp. 'save me' in *v.* 7. But the words 'soul' and 'salvation' are not primarily to be understood in a spiritual sense.

in God] As distinguished from men. All help, divine as well as human, fails him in his need. Hence the general term *God* is used.

But thou, O LORD, *art* a shield for me;　　　　　3
My glory, and the lifter up of mine head.
I cried unto the LORD *with* my voice,　　　　　4
And he heard me out of his holy hill.　Selah.
I laid me down and slept;　　　　　　　　　　　5
I awaked; for the LORD sustained me.
I will not be afraid of ten thousands of people,　6

But where David expresses his own confident assurance (*v.* 8) or pleads for help (*v.* 4), he uses the covenant name Jehovah. The LXX however, which P.B.V. follows, reads, *in his God*.

3, 4. Men may say that God has forsaken him, but he knows that it is not so.

3. *a shield for me*] More significantly the original, **a shield about me**. A natural metaphor for a warrior-poet. Cp. God's promise to Abraham, Gen. xv. 1; Deut. xxxiii. 29; Ps. xviii. 2, &c.

my glory] The honour of the Israelite king was derived from Jehovah, whose representative he was. Cp. xxi. 5; lxii. 7; and see note on iv. 2. *My worship* (P.B.V.)=*my honour* or *glory*.

the lifter up of mine head] A general truth. David is still confident that as Jehovah raised him from low estate to royal dignity, and brought him up from depths of trouble in times past, He can even now save him and restore him to the throne. Cp. 2 Sam. xv. 25.

4. An appeal to past experiences of answered prayer. 'As often as I **called**,'—the imperfect tense in the Heb. denotes repeated action or habit—'he **answered** me.' Cp. iv. 1; xci. 15.

out of his holy hill] Cp. ii. 6. Zion, the seat of the Ark of the covenant, which was the symbol and pledge of Jehovah's presence, is as it were the centre from which He exercises His earthly sovereignty. Cp. xiv. 7; xx. 2; Am. i. 2. There is possibly a tacit reference to the sending back of the Ark (2 Sam. xv. 25), which may have discouraged some of his followers. He would assure them that its absence does not diminish Jehovah's power to help.

5, 6. Not only past but present experience justifies this confidence.

5. The pronoun is emphatic:—*I*, pursued by enemies, despaired of by friends:—and the words refer to the actual experience of the past night. The calmness which could thus repose in the face of danger was a practical proof of faith.

sustained] R.V. **sustaineth**. The tense suggests the unceasing, ever active care by which he is upheld. The same word is used in xxxvii. 17, 24; lxxi. 6; cxlv. 14. Contrast xxvii. 2.

6. Cp. xxvii. 3. Numbers were on the side of Absalom, and but for the divinely sent infatuation which made him reject Ahithophel's clever advice, in all probability David's handful of followers would have been overwhelmed without effort (2 Sam. xvii. 1 ff.).

That have set *themselves* against me round about.
7 Arise, O LORD; save me, O my God:
For thou hast smitten all mine enemies *upon* the cheek bone;
Thou hast broken the teeth of the ungodly.
8 Salvation *belongeth* unto the LORD:
Thy blessing *is* upon thy people. Selah.

set themselves *against me*] A private individual could hardly speak thus; and we are reminded of Ahithophel's counsel to strike one blow at the king, and save a civil war.

7, 8. The Psalm concludes with a prayer for deliverance as in times past, and for a blessing on the people.

7. *Arise, O LORD*] The opening words of the ancient marching-shout of Israel, rich in memories of deliverance and victory. See Num. x. 35. Cp. lxviii. 1.

for thou hast smitten] Again, as in *v.* 4, appeal is made to the experience of the past as the ground of prayer. Hitherto Jehovah has put His enemies to shame, and destroyed their power for mischief. The buffet on the cheek was a climax of insult which shewed that all spirit and power of resistance were gone. Cp. 1 Kings xxii. 24; Job xvi. 10; Lam. iii. 30; Mic. v. 1. Then, by a natural figure (how appropriate in David's mouth! cp. 1 Sam. xvii. 34), the wicked are pictured as ferocious wild beasts, rushing upon their prey, but suddenly deprived of their power to hurt. Cp. lviii. 6.

8. *Salvation*] R. V. marg. *victory* unduly limits the thought, though no doubt it is the particular form in which David desires to see Jehovah's saving power manifested. 'Save' is the constant prayer, 'salvation' the constant desire, of the Psalmists. The Hebrew words thus rendered denote primarily enlargement, liberation from a state of confinement and distress, power to move freely and at will, and so deliverance generally. Such deliverance comes from Jehovah alone: it is eagerly sought as the proof of His favour. It is, mainly at least, temporal and material, and is looked for in this life; for in the O. T. this life is the sphere of God's dealings with His people. But the word grows with the growth of revelation, till it gains an inexhaustible fulness of spiritual meaning in the N. T.

thy blessing is *upon thy people*] Rather as R.V., **thy blessing be upon thy people.** This prayer reveals the noble heart of the true king, to whom the welfare of his people is more than his own personal safety. Like Him of whom he was the type, he intercedes on behalf of the rebels, for 'thy people' cannot be limited to the loyal few. The whole nation is still Jehovah's people, though they have been misled into revolt against His king. As the sequel shewed, the revolt was the work of a party, not of the nation (2 Sam. xix. 9).

PSALM IV.

The occasion of this Psalm has already been discussed in the introduction to Ps. iii. Some days at least have elapsed. The immediate personal peril is past. Reflection has deepened David's consciousness of his own integrity, and his sense of the rebels' guilt. The Psalm breathes a spirit of righteous indignation, which rises completely above mere personal vindictiveness.

Its structure, if the indications afforded by the *Selah* at the end of *v.* 2 and *v.* 4 are to be followed, is similar to that of its companion Psalm.
  i. Appeal to God, and remonstrance with the rebels, *vv.* 1, 2.
  ii. The true character of the rebellion exposed, *vv.* 3, 4.
  iii. The better way indicated, *vv.* 5, 6.
  iv. The supreme joy of perfect trust, *vv.* 7, 8.

Most commentators however divide the Psalm thus: i. Appeal to God, *v.* 1; ii. Remonstrance with enemies, *vv.* 2—5; iii. The superiority of God-given joy to all earthly grounds of rejoicing, *vv.* 6—8. This division however neglects the Selah, which serves to emphasise the important thought of *v.* 3, and after *v.* 4 prepares the way for repentance following on reflection: it ignores the parallelism of structure with Ps. iii, and though at first sight attractive, fails to bring out the true connexion and sequence of the thoughts.

To the chief Musician on Neginoth, A Psalm of David.

**Hear me when I call, O God of my righteousness: 4
Thou hast enlarged me** *when I was* **in distress;**

The title should be rendered as in R.V., **For the Chief Musician; on stringed instruments.** See Introd. pp. xix f., xxii.

1, 2. An appeal to God, and an expostulation with men.

1. *Hear me* &c.] **When I call, answer me.** Cp. *v.* 3 and iii. 4. The LXX and Vulg. represent a different vocalisation and render, "when I called, the God of my righteousness answered me." This reading agrees well with the second clause of the verse, but on the whole the rhythm of the sentence is in favour of the Massoretic text.

O God of my righteousness] David is confident of the integrity of his heart and the justice of his cause. To God alone he looks to help him to his right, and vindicate his righteousness openly in the sight of men by making that cause triumphant. Cp. vii. 8 ff.; 1 Kings viii. 32.

thou hast enlarged me] R.V., **Thou hast set me at large.** But the words are perhaps best taken as a relative clause, *thou who hast set me at large;* giving a second reason for his appeal to God in the experience of past deliverances, possibly with particular reference to the events of the last few days. This natural figure for liberation from distress may be derived from the idea of an army which has been hemmed in by

 Have mercy upon me, and hear my prayer.
2 O ye sons of men, how long *will ye turn* my glory into shame?
How long will ye love vanity, *and* seek after leasing? Selah.
3 But know that the LORD hath set apart *him that is* godly
 for himself:

enemies in some narrow pass escaping into the open plain. Cp. 1 Sam. xxiii. 26 for an illustration.

Have mercy upon me] Rather, as marg., **be gracious unto me**. The word suggests the free bestowal of favour rather than the exercise of forgiving clemency. It is connected with the word rendered 'gracious' in the fundamental passage Ex. xxxiv. 6. Cp. Ps. lxxxvi. 15.

2. *O ye sons of men*] From appealing to God he turns to remonstrate with the rebels, and singles out the leaders from the general mass. The phrase used is *bnē îsh*, which in xlix. 2 is rendered 'high,' and in lxii. 9, 'men of high degree,' in opposition to *bnē ādām*, rendered 'low' and 'men of low degree.' At the same time by calling them 'sons of men' he contrasts them with God, the defender of his cause.

my glory] There is no need to inquire whether David's personal honour or his royal dignity is meant. Both are included, for both were defamed and insulted. But it was an aggravation of the rebels' offence that the king had a special 'glory' as the representative of Jehovah. Cp. iii. 3, note.

vanity...leasing] The rebellion is *a vain thing*, destined to end in failure, like the threatened uprising of the nations (ii. 1): it is *a lie*, for it is based on the false principle of personal ambition setting itself up against the divinely appointed king. Cp. Is. xxviii. 15, 17. Another possible interpretation would refer the words to the false imputations and underhand intrigues by which Absalom and his confederates sought to tarnish David's reputation and undermine his authority. Cp. 2 Sam. xv. 2 ff. But the verbs used (*love...seek*) point rather to the end desired than to the means employed.

leasing] R.V. **falsehood**. *Leasing* (v. 6) is an obsolete word for a lie: from A.S. *leás*, empty, and so false: used by Chaucer, Spenser, and Shakespeare. Cp. *Faerie Queene*, II. 11. 10:
  "Slaunderous reproches, and fowle infamies,
   Leasinges, backbytinges."

3, 4. The reason why the attempt is doomed to failure. Warning to reflect before it is too late.

3. *hath set apart*] *Hath distinguished*. The verb combines the idea of *marvellous dealing* with that of choice and separation. Cp. xvii. 7; cxxxix. 14; Is. xxix. 14.

him that is godly] The word *chāsîd* which is thus rendered is one of the characteristic words of the Psalter. It is derived from *chesed*, 'mercy' or 'lovingkindness,' and denotes either (1) one who is characterised by dutiful love to God and to his fellow-men; the 'godly,' or 'merciful' man, xviii. 25; or (2) 'one who is the object of Jehovah's lovingkind-

PSALM IV. 4—6.

The LORD will hear when I call unto him.
Stand in awe, and sin not: 4
Commune with your own heart upon your bed, and be still.
  Selah.
Offer the sacrifices of righteousness, 5
And put your trust in the LORD.
There be many that say, Who will shew us *any* good? 6
LORD, lift thou up the light of thy countenance upon us.

---

ness,' as R.V. margin 'one that He favoureth': cp. A.V. marg., lxxxvi. 2. See Additional Note i., p. 221, for a further discussion of its meaning.

4. Let wholesome fear, continues David, deter you from persisting in this course of action, which is nothing less than sinful. R.V. marg. gives the rendering of the LXX, "Be ye angry," i.e. If you must needs be angry and discontented with my government, do not be carried away by passion into open rebellion. The rendering is possible, for the word is used of the perturbation of wrath as well as of fear. But it gives a less obvious and suitable sense. The words are adopted (but not as an express quotation) by St Paul in his warning against resentment, Eph. iv. 26.

commune &c.] Lit. *speak in your heart*. The voice of conscience, unheeded in the turmoil and excitement of the day, or silenced by fear of men and evil example, may make itself heard in the calm solitude of the night, and convince you of the truth. Comp., though the turn of thought is different, lxiii. 6; cxlix. 5.

be still] Desist from your mad endeavour.

5, 6. After an interval for reflection indicated by the interlude (Selah) David points the malcontents among the people to the true source of prosperity.

5. *sacrifices of righteousness*] Sacrifices offered in a right spirit, cp. Deut. xxxiii. 19; Ps. li. 19. The rebels are still addressed. The sacrifices with which they pretended to hallow their cause (2 Sam. xv. 12) were a wretched hypocrisy, inasmuch as they were acting in opposition to the will of God. Let them approach Him in a right spirit, and instead of impatiently trying to remedy evils by revolution, rely entirely upon His guidance.

6. David knows well that there are plenty of discontented grumblers among his subjects, ready to follow anyone who makes them fair promises. His answer to them is a prayer for a blessing upon himself and his people (*us*), which recalls the great Aaronic benediction of Num. vi. 24—26, fusing into one the two petitions, "The LORD make His face to shine upon thee," "the LORD lift up His countenance upon thee." Cp. Ps. xxxi. 16; lxxx. 3, 7, 19.

The 'many', as in iii. 2, are chiefly the wavering mass of the people, who had not yet taken a side; but some at least of Absalom's partisans, and some of David's half-hearted followers are included.

7 Thou hast put gladness in my heart,
More than *in* the time *that* their corn and their wine increased.
8 I will both lay me down in peace, and sleep:
For thou, LORD, only makest me dwell in safety.

7, 8. A joy and peace which are independent of outward circumstances.

7. *more than* &c.] Lit. *more than* (the joy of) *the time of their corn and wine when they were increased:* i.e. more than their rejoicings for harvest and vintage even when they were most abundant: well expressed in R.V., **more than they have when their corn and their wine are increased.** The persons referred to may be either the malcontents, or men in general. The boisterous mirth of harvest and vintage rejoicings (Is. ix. 3; Jer. xlviii. 33) is the highest form of joy which they know whose desires are limited to earthly things; but deeper far is that inward joy which is the gift of God, for it is one of the fruits of the Spirit, Gal. v. 22; cp. Rom. xiv. 17.

The words gain fresh point when it is remembered that David was reduced to straits for the bare necessaries of life till he reached his hospitable friends at Mahanaim (2 Sam. xvii. 27—29).

8. In peace will I lay me down and sleep at once: no fears or anxieties delaying slumber. In iii. 5 he recorded his experience: here he gives expression to the trust which sprang from it.

for thou LORD, only] **For it is thou, LORD, alone, who** &c. This exquisite expression of absolute confidence, the rhythm of which in the original is as reposeful as the thought, gives an excellent sense in connexion with the context. 'Many' had declared that he was abandoned by God as well as man (iii. 2), but in unshaken faith he claims Jehovah as his sole protector, beside whom he needs no other.

But the word rendered 'alone' elsewhere means *apart*, when joined with verbs denoting dwelling. Thus it is used of Israel, isolated and separate from the nations, in Num. xxiii. 9; and in Deut. xxxiii. 28; Jer. xlix. 31, it is combined with the word here rendered 'in safety'. So probably the meaning is, 'It is Thou, LORD, who makest me dwell *apart* in safety:' isolated from my foes in Thy safe keeping. Hence R.V. marg. gives, *in solitude.*

PSALM V.

Another morning prayer, uttered by one who is exposed to danger from the machinations of unscrupulous and hypocritical enemies. The title assigns it to David, and he might have written thus when he was in the court of Saul, or shortly before the outbreak of Absalom's rebellion.

It has been urged that *v.* 7 assumes the existence of the Temple, and is therefore decisive against the Davidic authorship. This however is not certain. The term "house of the LORD" presents no difficulty.

It is used of the Tabernacle (Ex. xxiii. 19, xxxiv. 26; Deut. xxiii. 18; Josh. vi. 24; 1 Sam. i. 24, iii. 15), and also of the tent which David pitched for the ark on Mount Zion (2 Sam. xii. 20). But could this ark-tent be called a *temple*? The Heb. word *hêycāl* denotes a spacious building, whether temple or palace (Ps. xlv. 8, 15), and would not be a strictly appropriate designation for it. It is however applied to the sanctuary at Shiloh (1 Sam. i. 9, iii. 3), and may have remained in use, and been applied to the ark-tent in David's time. It should at any rate be noticed that in xxvii. 4, 6, 'house of the LORD,' 'temple,' and 'tent' (A.V. tabernacle) are all used in close juxtaposition.

It is moreover at least possible that here, as in xi. 4, xviii. 6, xxix. 9 (?), the temple is heaven, the dwelling-place of God, of which the earthly temple is but the symbol.

The Psalm opens with an urgent cry for a favourable hearing (1—3). Jehovah will not tolerate the wicked (4—6); but the Psalmist, through His lovingkindness, is admitted to His presence. He prays that he may be preserved from falling into the snares of his insidious foes (7—9); and that their just condemnation and punishment may exhibit a proof of God's righteous government which will cheer the hearts of His servants (10—12).

To the chief Musician upon Nehiloth, A Psalm of David.

Give ear to my words, O LORD, 5
Consider my meditation.
Hearken unto the voice of my cry, my King, and my God: 2
For unto thee will I pray.
My voice shalt thou hear *in* the morning, O LORD; 3

The title may be rendered with R.V., **For the Chief Musician; with the Nehiloth,** or, (marg.) *wind instruments.* See Introd. pp. xix, xxii.

1—3. Introductory petitions for a favourable hearing.

1. *my meditation*] The Heb. word, which occurs again only in xxxix. 3, may denote either the unspoken prayer of the heart (cp. the cognate verb in i. 2); or the low, murmuring utterance of brooding sorrow. Cp. Is. xxxviii. 14. So Jerome, *murmur meum.*

2. *my cry*] A word specially used of an imploring cry to God for help (xxii. 24; xxviii. 2; &c.).

my King, and my God] Cp. lxxxiv. 3. The language is all the more significant, if the petitioner was David. He appeals to Him, Whose chosen representative he was.

**3. O LORD, in the morning shalt thou hear my voice;
In the morning will I order** *my prayer* **unto thee, and will keep watch.** (R.V.)

'In the morning' is repeated with emphasis. The first thought of the day is prayer. Cp. lv. 17, lxxxviii. 13; lix. 16, xcii. 2, lvii. 8.

In the morning will I direct *my prayer* unto thee, and will look up.
4 For thou *art* not a God that hath pleasure in wickedness: Neither shall evil dwell *with* thee.
5 The foolish shall not stand in thy sight:

will I direct] Better, as R.V., **will I order**. The word means *to arrange*, and is used of setting in order the pieces of wood (Gen. xxii. 9; Lev. i. 7), or the parts of the sacrifice (Lev. i. 8), upon the altar. One of the first duties of the priests in the morning was to prepare the wood for the morning sacrifice, which was offered at sunrise (Lev. vi. 12; Num. xxviii. 4). Hence some commentators think that the Psalmist intends to compare his daily morning prayer to the daily morning sacrifice. Cp. cxli. 2. But the word 'order' has no exclusive or even predominant sacrificial reference; and we should probably rather compare the expressions 'to order one's words' or 'one's cause' in Job xxxii. 14, xxiii. 4, and the more closely parallel use of the word without an object in Job xxxiii. 5, xxxvii. 19.

and will look up] Rather, as R.V., **will keep watch**, for an answer, like a sentinel on the look out (2 Sam. xviii. 24). Cp. Micah vii. 7; Hab. ii. 1.

4—6. The ground of the Psalmist's confident expectation of an answer is the holiness of God, who will tolerate no evil. Comp. the ideal of an earthly king's court in Ps. ci.

4. *a God*] *El*, not *Elohim*. If the fundamental idea of this name for God is that of *power*[1], its use here is significant. Power without goodness is the fetishistic conception of deity, to which human nature is prone (l. 21).

neither shall evil dwell with *thee*] Rather, as R.V. marg., with the LXX, Vulg. and Jerome, **The evil man shall not sojourn with thee**. He cannot be (so to speak) God's guest, and enjoy the hospitality and protection which Oriental custom prescribes. See on xv. 1, and cp. lxi. 4. To sinners the divine holiness is a consuming fire which they cannot endure (Is. xxxiii. 14).

5, 6. Various classes of evil doers. *The foolish*, or rather **the arrogant**, a word denoting boastful blustering presumption rather than folly; cp. lxxiii. 3, lxxv. 4: *workers of iniquity*, the standing expression in the Psalms for those who make a practice of what is morally worthless (cp. John iii. 20, v. 29); those 'that speak **lies**' (for *leasing* see on iv. 2); cp. lviii. 3, vii. 14: **men of bloodshed and deceit**, who do not shrink from murder and that by treachery, in fact the Shimeis and Doegs and Ahithophels and Joabs of David's time.

shall not stand in thy sight] This may simply mean that they cannot impose upon God. He passes judgment on their hollow pretensions (cp. i. 5), and they shrink away condemned. But the idea is

---

[1] Attractive but questionable is Lagarde's explanation of the name *El* as 'the Being to Whom man turns,' the aim and end of all human longing and effort.

Thou hatest all workers of iniquity.
Thou shalt destroy them that speak leasing: 6
The LORD will abhor the bloody and deceitful man.
But *as for* me, I will come *into* thy house in the multitude 7
of thy mercy:
And in thy fear will I worship toward thy holy temple.
Lead me, O LORD, in thy righteousness because of mine 8
enemies;

probably rather of courtiers standing in the presence of a monarch. Cp. Prov. xxii. 29; Ps. ci. 7; and the picture of the heavenly council in Job i. 6, ii. 1.

will abhor] **Abhorreth**; a strong word: abominates, as something wholly unnatural and detestable.

7—9. In sharp contrast to the banishment of the wicked from God's presence is the Psalmist's freedom of access. He prays for the special guidance needed by one who is surrounded by insidious enemies.

7. *I will come* &c.] Better, as R.V., following the order of the original: **in the multitude** [or, *abundance*] **of thy lovingkindness will I come into thy house**. Cp. lxix. 13, 16, cvi. 7, 45. The wicked are excluded from Jehovah's presence by their own act; the godly man is admitted to it by Jehovah's grace. Note the contrast between "the multitude of thy lovingkindness," and "the multitude of their transgressions," *v.* 10.

and *in thy fear*] Omit *and*. Fear, reverent awe, is the right spirit for approach to a holy God. Cp. ii. 11; Heb. xii. 28, 29.

will I worship] The Heb. word means *to prostrate one's self*, the Oriental attitude of reverence to a superior or supplication (Gen. xviii. 2); hence in general, of the corresponding disposition of mind, *to worship*. The Psalmist worships facing the sanctuary which was the outward sign of Jehovah's presence among His people. Or is the heavenly temple meant? (1 Kings viii. 22).

8. The prayer for guidance which is the main object and central thought of the Psalm.

Lead me...in thy righteousness] i.e. because Thou art righteous. A comparison of xxiii. 3; Prov. viii. 20; xii. 28; might incline us to understand the meaning to be, 'Lead me in the path of right conduct which Thou hast marked out for me:' but the true parallels are xxxi. 1, lxxi. 2, cxix. 40, cxliii. 1, 11; which shew clearly that God's own righteousness is meant. One element of that righteousness is faithfulness to His saints in the fulfilment of covenant promises, and to this the Psalmist appeals.

because of mine enemies] A peculiar word found only in xxvii. 11, liv. 5, lvi. 2, lix. 10. Render, as in R.V. margin, **them that lie in wait for me**, like fowlers (Jer. v. 26, R.V.), or a leopard for its prey (Hos. xiii. 7). He prays that he may be preserved from falling into their snares.

Make thy way straight before my face.
9 For *there is* no faithfulness in their mouth;
Their inward *part is* very wickedness;
Their throat *is* an open sepulchre;
They flatter with their tongue.
10 Destroy thou them, O God;
Let them fall by their own counsels;
Cast them out in the multitude of their transgressions;
For they have rebelled against thee.
11 But let all those that put their trust in thee rejoice:

make thy way straight] Or, as P.B.V. and R.V., **plain**. The word means both *level* and *straight*. The godly man's life is a path marked out for him by God (xvii. 5, lxxiii. 24, lxxxvi. 11). He prays that it may be such that he may be in no danger of stumbling or losing his way. 'Bring us not into temptation.'

9. The reason for the Psalmist's special need of guidance is the treacherous character of his enemies. There is **no stedfastness**, nothing upon which he can depend, in their talk: their inmost heart is bent on destruction (lit. *is destructions*, or perhaps, as R.V. marg., *a yawning gulf*): their throat, the instrument of speech (cxv. 7, cxlix. 6), threatens death like an open grave, though their words are so smooth and specious.

10—12. As he calls to mind their malice he can no longer refrain, but breaks out into urgent prayer that sentence may be passed upon them as guilty of high treason against God; that so, in the triumph of the right, the godly may rejoice in God's favour and protection. On such prayers see Introduction, p. lxx ff.

10. *Destroy thou them, O God*] R.V., **Hold them guilty**; punish them; for it is by visible failure and disaster that their condemnation is to be made known.

let them fall by their own counsels] Let their own machinations recoil on their heads and bring them to ruin. Cp. 2 Sam. xv. 31. Better so than as margin, *fall from*, i.e. *fail in*, *their counsels*. Cp. lxiv. 8.

cast them out] As no longer worthy to dwell in the land: or, **thrust them down** from the position which they occupy. Cp. lxii. 4; xxxvi. 12.

for they have rebelled against thee] Rebellion against the king was in a special way rebellion against Jehovah, whose representative he was. But it may refer quite generally to their defiance of divine authority, and their persecution of God's servant.

11. We may render more exactly:
So shall all those that take refuge in thee rejoice,
They shall ever shout for joy while thou protectest them,
And they that love thy name shall exult in thee.

Let them ever shout for joy, because thou defendest them:
Let them also that love thy name be joyful in thee.
For thou, LORD, wilt bless the righteous;
With favour wilt thou compass him as *with* a shield.

12

The punishment of the wicked according to their deeds is an occasion for the universal rejoicing of the godly. Not only do they sympathise with their fellow-saint in his deliverance, but they see in it a vindication of Jehovah's righteous government, and an assurance that those who have put themselves under His protection will not find their confidence misplaced.

that love thy name] Cp. lxix. 36, cxix. 132. 'The Name of Jehovah' is the compendious expression for His character and attributes as He has revealed them to men. See Oehler's *O.T. Theology*, § 56. Needs must those who love Him as He has revealed Himself rejoice when He proves Himself true to His promises.

defendest them] **Protectest**, or **shelterest them**; in Thy secret pavilion (xxvii. 5, xxxi. 20); or, under Thy outspread wings (xci. 4).

12. The R.V. follows the Massoretic punctuation in transferring LORD to the second half of the verse:

O LORD, thou wilt compass him with favour as with a shield.

a shield] **A buckler**, or large shield to protect the whole body. Cp. xxxv. 2, xci. 4; 1 Sam. xvii. 7. From 1 Kings x. 16, 17 it would seem that the 'buckler' (A.V. 'target') was about double the size of the 'shield.'

PSALM VI.

The Psalmist has been suffering from severe and long-continued sickness, which has brought him to the brink of the grave. The most bitter part of his trial is that he feels it to be a token of God's displeasure; and malicious enemies aggravate his suffering by taunting him with being forsaken by God.

This is the natural view of the Psalmist's situation. Many however think that the attacks of enemies are his chief and primary ground of complaint, though these have wrought upon him until mental anxiety has produced actual sickness. But it is plain from *vv.* 1—3 that he is suffering from a *direct* divine visitation, and that the persecution of which he complains (*v.* 7) is a consequence and aggravation of it. Suffering and misfortune were popularly regarded (as we learn from the Book of Job) as evidences of commensurate guilt on the part of the sufferer. Hence when the godly suffered, he became a butt for the scornful taunts of the godless. Cp. Ps. xli.

The title assigns the Psalm to David. Some, wrongly supposing that the hostility of enemies is the chief ground of complaint, would refer it to the time when he was persecuted by Saul: others think that this and some other Psalms were the outcome of a dangerous illness from which he suffered in the interval between his sin with Bathsheba and Absalom's rebellion. The fact is that here, as in many other Psalms, there is little or nothing to fix the author or even the period to which the Psalm belongs. This however is clear, that the Psalm is the record of a personal experience, not the utterance of the nation in a time of calamity, personified as a sick and persecuted sufferer. Comp. Ps. xxx, which is a corresponding thanksgiving.

This Psalm is the first of the seven known from ancient times in the Christian Church as 'the Penitential Psalms' (vi, xxxii, xxxviii, li, cii, cxxx, cxliii). They are all prescribed for use on Ash Wednesday, the 51st in the Commination Service, and the remaining six as Proper Psalms.

The Psalm falls into three divisions:
  i. The cry of anguish for relief in suffering, 1—3.
  ii. Earnest yet calmer pleading for deliverance, 4—7.
  iii. Triumphant assurance of answered prayer and restoration to God's favour, 8—10.

To the chief Musician on Neginoth upon Sheminith, A Psalm of David.

6 O LORD, rebuke me not in thine anger,
   Neither chasten me in thy hot displeasure.
2 Have mercy upon me, O LORD; for I *am* weak:
   O LORD, heal me; for my bones are vexed.

The title should be rendered as in R.V., **For the Chief Musician; on stringed instruments, set to the Sheminith** (or, *the eighth*). See Introd. pp. xix, xxii f.

1—3. The Psalmist pleads for mercy, deprecating the severity of God's visitation.

1. The emphasis in the original lies on the words *not in Thine anger, neither in Thy hot displeasure.* The Psalmist pleads that his present suffering exceeds the measure of loving correction (Job v. 17; Prov. iii. 11, 12; Jer. x. 24; Rev. iii. 19). He can only interpret it as a sign that the wrath of God is resting upon him. Perhaps, like Job, he can detect no special sin to account for it. At least it is noteworthy that the Psalm contains no explicit confession of sin, and in this respect it is a remarkable contrast to the kindred Ps. xxxviii, which opens with the same words.

2. *Have mercy upon me*] **Be gracious unto me.** See note on iv. 1.
I am weak] R.V., **I am withered away**, retaining the primary meaning of the word. Cp. Nah. i. 4, where it is rendered *languisheth*.

heal me] So Jeremiah prays (xvii. 14), combining this petition with that of *v.* 4. Cp. Job v. 18; Ps. xxx. 2; xli. 4; cxlvii. 3.

for my bones are vexed] Even the solid framework of the body, the seat of its strength and solidity, is racked and shaken well nigh to dissolution. Cp. xxii. 14. 'The bones,' in the language of Hebrew poetry, denote the whole physical organism of the living man, as being the fundamental part of it. Hence they are the seat of health (Prov. xvi. 24), or of pain, as here. In some passages, 'the bones' come to be identified with the man himself, as a living agent. Cp. xxxv. 10. On the word 'vexed,' see note on ii. 5.

My soul is also sore vexed : 3
But thou, O LORD, how long?
Return, O LORD, deliver my soul : 4
O save me for thy mercy's sake.
For in death *there is* no remembrance of thee : 5
In the grave who shall give thee thanks?

3. Mind as well as body, the inner self as well as its outer organism, is dismayed. Our Lord appropriates these words, in view of His approaching Passion (John xii. 27), using the Greek word (ταράσσειν) employed by the LXX.

how long?] Cp. xc. 13. How pregnant is the aposiopesis! How long wilt Thou be angry? How long wilt Thou hide Thy face and refuse to hear me? Cp. xiii. 1.

It is recorded of Calvin in his last painful illness that he uttered no word of complaint unworthy of a Christian man; only raising his eyes to heaven he would say *Usquequo Domine* (Lord, how long?) for even when he was in health, this was a kind of watchword with him, in reference to the troubles of the brethren (*Vita: Opp.* Tom. 1).

4—7. He renews his prayer, and in a calmer tone, reasons with God.

4. *Return*] For Jehovah seems to have abandoned him. Cp. xc. 13.

O save me for thy mercy's sake] R.V., **save me for thy lovingkindness' sake**. Jehovah declares Himself to be "a God...plenteous in *lovingkindness* and truth, who keeps *lovingkindness* for thousands" (Ex. xxxiv. 7, 8), and the Psalmist intreats Him to be true to this central attribute in His own revelation of His character.

5. A further plea. There can be no gain in his death. Nay, Jehovah will be the loser by it. For man is created to praise God, and God delights in his praise. But in the state to which man passes at death, he can no longer gratefully call to mind His goodness (cxlv. 7), or celebrate His praise.

Here, as in xxx. 9, lxxxviii. 10—12, cxv. 17 (cp. Is. xxxviii. 18 ff.; the Book of Job; Eccles. ix. 5, vi. 10); we meet with that dreary despairing view of the state after death, which the Hebrews shared with the rest of the ancient world. They did not look forward to annihilation, but to a dreamy, shadowy, existence which did not deserve the name of life. The dead, they thought, were cut off from all activity and enjoyment, and worst of all, from the consciousness of God's presence, and from that communion with Him, which is the essence of 'life' (xxx. 5). It is hardly possible for us who live in the light of Christ's Resurrection (2 Tim. i. 10), to realise what the lifelong slavery to the fear of death (Heb. ii. 15) meant to the faithful Israelite, and the bold struggles of his faith to break the fetters. See Introd. p. lxxv ff.

in the grave] It is far better, with the R.V., to retain the Hebrew word **Shĕôl** to denote the abode of the departed. It is the O.T. equivalent of *Hades*, by which it is rendered in the LXX. It was thought

6 I am weary with my groaning;
All the night make I my bed to swim;
I water my couch with my tears.
7 Mine eye is consumed because of grief;
It waxeth old because of all mine enemies.
8 Depart from me, all ye workers of iniquity;
For the LORD hath heard the voice of my weeping.
9 The LORD hath heard my supplication;
The LORD will receive my prayer.
10 Let all mine enemies be ashamed and sore vexed:
Let them return *and* be ashamed suddenly.

of as a vast subterranean abyss, where all alike were gathered; a place of gloom and silence, but withal of rest, however joyless, for its shadowy denizens have no more power to do harm than good. "There the wicked cease from troubling; and there the weary be at rest." Cp. Job iii. 13—19; Is. xiv. 9 ff. See Oehler's *O.T. Theology*, § 78.

6. *I am weary with my groaning*] So Baruch complained, Jer. xlv. 3, R. V. Cp. Ps. lxix. 3.

all the night] Rather, **every night**. His sorrow is of long continuance, and knows no respite.

7. **Mine eye is wasted away because of provocation;**
It is waxed old because of all mine adversaries.
With the first clause comp. xxxi. 9. The look of the eye is a sure indication of the state of health, mental and bodily. The word rendered *adversaries* means literally *them that distress me*. Cp. vii. 4, 6; and the cognate words in iii. 1, iv. 1.

8—10. The cloud breaks. Heaviness is turned to joy. With a sudden inspiration of faith the Psalmist realises that his prayer is heard, and predicts the speedy confusion of his enemies.

8. *Depart from me, all ye workers of iniquity*] Words used by our Lord, Matt. vii. 23.

9. Twice he repeats the confident assertion of faith, that Jehovah has heard his prayer, and with equal confidence adds the assurance that He will accept it favourably, and not reject it. Cp. 1 John v. 14, 15.

10. It is better to render the verbs as future:
All mine enemies shall be ashamed and sore vexed;
They shall turn back, they shall be ashamed in a moment.
The 'dismay', which he had felt to be a token of divine displeasure (*vv.* 2, 3), is now retorted upon those who took a malicious delight in his misfortunes. When God returns to His servant, his assailants are repulsed in sudden and ignominious defeat. Cp. xxxv. 4, 26, lvi. 9, lxxxiii. 17.

PSALM VII.

The Psalmist is assailed by ruthless enemies who are bent upon taking his life, charging him with heinous crimes. He solemnly protests entire innocence, and appeals to God as the supreme Judge to vindicate his cause.

The title gives a clue to the circumstances under which the Psalm was written. It is called "*Shiggaion of David, which he sang unto the* LORD, *concerning the words of Cush a Benjamite.*" *Shiggaion* (see Introd. p. xix) probably denotes a poem of passionate ecstatic character, written under the influence of strong emotion, and reflecting its origin in its form.

Cush is not mentioned elsewhere. It is plain however that he was one of those fellow tribesmen and close adherents of Saul, who insinuated that David was intriguing against the king's life (1 Sam. xxii. 8) and by their baseless calumnies further inflamed his already irritated mind. Of such slanderers David complains in 1 Sam. xxiv. 9, xxvi. 19. Cush is simply a proper name not otherwise known to us. There is no reason for taking it to mean *a Cushite* or *Ethiopian* (*super verba Aethiopis*, Jerome); or as a by-name for Saul himself as *a black-hearted man* (though the identification of Cush with Saul is as old as the Targum); still less for identifying Cush with Shimei.

The fact that Cush is not elsewhere mentioned shews that the title is of great antiquity. It comes, if not from David himself, at least from an editor who possessed fuller information about David's history, either in still living tradition, or in writings such as those mentioned in 1 Chr. xxix. 29.

The Psalm belongs then to that period of David's life, when he was hunted from place to place by Saul; and it strikingly reflects the characteristic feelings of that time as they are portrayed in the Book of Samuel. 1 Sam. xxi—xxvi, especially xxiv and xxvi, should be read in illustration of it. Compare particularly the reference to slanders in the title with 1 Sam. xxiv. 9, xxvi. 19: the virulence of persecution described in *vv.* 1, 2 with 1 Sam. xx. 1, 31, xxiii. 15, &c.: the protestations of innocence in *vv.* 3, 4 with 1 Sam. xx. 1, xxiv. 10, 11, 17, xxvi. 18, 23, 24: the appeal to God as Judge in *vv.* 6, 8 with 1 Sam. xxiv. 12, 15.

The energy and vigour of the Psalm correspond to the circumstances. Pressing danger, the rankling sense of injustice, a strong faith in the judicial righteousness of God, are its inspiring motives.

Ancient Jewish tradition prescribes it for use on the feast of Purim.

The Psalm falls into two principal divisions, the first mainly personal, the second general:

i. David's prayer for God's intervention on his behalf, *vv.* 1—10.

After an appeal setting forth the urgency of his need (1, 2) and a solemn protestation of his innocence of the crimes laid to his charge (3—5), David prays God to appear as Judge, and publicly do him justice (6—8). A prayer for the triumph of righteousness, and a confident expression of trust in God, (9, 10) close the first part, and form the transition to the second part.

ii. The judicial activity of God, vv. 11—17.

God unceasingly executes vengeance on the wicked (11—13); and wickedness works its own punishment (14—16). Concluding ascription of praise to Jehovah for this manifestation of His righteousness (17).

Shiggaion of David, which he sang unto the LORD, concerning the words of Cush the Benjamite.

7 O LORD my God, in thee do I put my trust:
Save me from all them that persecute me, and deliver me:
2 Lest he tear my soul like a lion,
Rending *it* in pieces, while *there is* none to deliver.
3 O LORD my God, if I have done this;
If there be iniquity in my hands;
4 If I have rewarded evil *unto* him that was at peace with me;

1, 2. The Psalmist's cry for help, based on Jehovah's relation to him.

1. *in thee do I put my trust*] **In thee have I taken refuge.** See note on ii. 12, and comp. the opening words of Pss. xi, xvi, xxxi, lvii, lxxi; and cxli. 8. David has put himself under Jehovah's protection, and appeals to Him on the ground of this covenant relationship between them. *In thee* is emphatic.

all them that persecute me] R.V., **all them that pursue me.** Saul and his followers. Cp. 1 Sam. xxiii. 28, xxiv. 14, xxv. 29, xxvi. 18.

2. His enemies are many, but one is conspicuous above all for merciless ferocity. Cush, or perhaps Saul himself, is meant (1 Sam. xx. 1). For the simile cp. x. 9, xvii. 12, xxii. 13, 21.

my soul] My life: me, regarded as a living individual.

3—5. The appeal for help is supported by a solemn protestation of innocence. If he is guilty of the crimes laid to his charge, may he be surrendered to the utmost fury of his enemies.

3. *if I have done this*] 'This' refers to the crimes of which he was falsely accused by Cush, and is further explained in the two following lines.

if there be iniquity in my hands] **Wrong** as the opposite of right: what is crooked and distorted: a different word from that used in *v.* 14 and in *v.* 5. Compare the closely similar language of David's protest in 1 Sam. xxiv. 11, "Know thou and see that there is neither evil nor transgression in mine hand:" and 1 Sam. xxvi. 18, "What have I done? or what evil is in mine hand?"

4. *If I have rewarded evil* &c.] If I have been guilty of unprovoked outrage, such, it is perhaps implied, as that of which Saul is guilty toward me (1 Sam. xxiv. 17). This is probably right; but another possible rendering deserves mention: *If I have requited him*

(Yea, I have delivered him that without cause is mine enemy:)
Let the enemy persecute my soul, and take *it*; 5
Yea, let him tread down my life upon the earth,
And lay mine honour in the dust. Selah.
Arise, O LORD, in thine anger, 6

that rewarded me evil; i.e. taken revenge into my own hands. Cp. David's solemn disclaimer of such conduct in 1 Sam. xxiv. 12.
Yea, I have delivered him that without cause is mine enemy] R.V., **him that without cause was mine adversary**, as in v. 6. See on vi. 7. The clause is a parenthesis, asserting that his conduct had been the very opposite of that which was attributed to him. Far from committing unprovoked outrages, he had saved the life of his enemy, and that though the enemy's hostility to him was causeless. The words refer to the occasions in the cave and in the camp, when David prevented his followers from taking Saul's life (1 Sam. xxiv. 4 ff.; xxvi. 8 ff.). The construction is bold, but it is thoroughly in keeping with the style of the Psalm, with its passionate protestations of innocence; and there is no need to adopt an unsupported meaning of the word for 'deliver,' and render, not as a parenthesis but in direct continuation of the preceding clause, *and have spoiled him that without cause was mine adversary*, with a supposed reference to 1 Sam. xxiv. 4, 5, or xxvi. 11: or to alter the text by transposing two letters, so as to mean: *and oppressed mine adversary without cause.*

5. Render:
   Let an enemy pursue my soul and overtake it;
   Yea, trample my life to the ground,
   And make my glory to dwell in the dust.

With the first line comp. Ex. xv. 9, echoed again in Ps. xviii. 37. The last line might mean only, 'degrade my dignity, treat me with insult and ignominy;' but the parallelism of 'my soul,' 'my life,' 'my glory,' is decisive in favour of interpreting 'my glory' to mean 'my soul,' as in xvi. 9; xxx. 12; lvii. 8. The 'soul' is so designated either as the noblest part of man, or as the image of the divine glory. 'The dust' will then be 'the dust of death.' Cp. xxii. 15; and the exact parallel 'dwellers in the dust,' Is. xxvi. 19. David then invokes death by an enemy's hand if he is guilty, and death, as the language implies, with every circumstance of violence and disgrace.

6—8. Conscious of his integrity, David appeals to Jehovah, as the Judge of the world, to hold an assize, and vindicate his innocence.

6. *Arise...lift up thyself...awake*] Cp. iii. 7, ix. 19, x. 12, xliv. 23, xciv. 2, and many similar invocations; couched in human language, as though God could be an otiose spectator, or even like a sentinel negligently slumbering on his watch, though the Psalmists well knew that Israel's watchman neither slumbered nor slept (cxxi. 3, 4).

in thine anger] Cp. vi. 1. Holiness and Justice can only be manifested as anger in their judicial relation to sin and wrong.

Lift up thyself because of the rage of mine enemies:
And awake for me *to* the judgment *that* thou hast commanded.
7 So shall the congregation of the people compass thee about:
For their sakes therefore return thou on high.
8 The LORD shall judge the people:
Judge me, O LORD, according to my righteousness,

because of the rage of mine enemies] Or, **against the ragings of mine adversaries.**

and awake for me to *the judgment* that *thou hast commanded*] The R.V., **and awake for me; thou hast commanded judgment,** represents the abruptness of the original. The exact turn of the thought is obscure. Perhaps, with a sudden intuition of faith, David realises that his prayer for God's interposition is answered, and, so to speak, the commission issued for holding the assize which he proceeds to describe in *vv.* 7, 8. Or the words may give the ground of his prayer: 'arise, inasmuch as judgment is Thy ordinance and function' (Gen. xviii. 25).

7. Render:
**And let the assembly of peoples come round about thee:
And over it return thou on high.**

The judgment scene. The Psalmist prays that 'the peoples' may be summoned to stand round the tribunal. It is a general summons. No distinction is made between Israel and other nations. Jehovah is exercising His judicial functions in their fullest extent as the Judge of all the earth.

The second line is difficult. There is much authority in favour of the interpretation, 'Return to heaven, when the judgment is finished, soaring away above the vast throng and vanishing to Thy abode on high, thus proving that Thou art the supreme Judge of all.'

This explanation no doubt presents a grand poetic picture; but it is clearly untenable, for no mention has yet been made of the judgment, and *v.* 8 goes on to speak of it as in progress. It is best (if the Massoretic text is retained) to explain: 'once more occupy the throne of judgment above the assembly, resume the judicial functions which seem for a time to have been abandoned.' But it is doubtful if the word 'return' fairly yields this sense, and it is probable that we should change the vowel points, and read *sit* instead of *return*. 'Over it take Thy seat on high' upon the throne of judgment, gives precisely the sense needed by the context. Comp. the parallels in the closely related Ps. ix., *vv.* 4, 7.

8. Render as R.V.:
The LORD ministereth judgment to the peoples.

Jehovah has taken His seat and opened the assize (cp. the exactly similar sequence of ideas in ix. 7, 8: and see Is. iii. 13, 14, R.V.): and the Psalmist comes forward with a plea to have justice done him.

judge me] Here as elsewhere, of a judgment favourable to the petitioner (xxvi. 1, xxxv. 24, xliii. 1, lxxxii. 3): 'do me justice.' David

And according to mine integrity *that is* in me.
O let the wickedness of the wicked come to an end; but 9
establish the just:
For the righteous God trieth the hearts and reins.
My defence *is* of God, 10
Which saveth the upright in heart.
God judgeth the righteous, 11

challenges a decision according to his righteousness and his integrity; not that he would claim to be perfect and sinless, but he has "a conscience void of offence toward God and toward men," and protests his innocence of the charges of treachery which have been brought against him. See Introduction, p. lxix ff. Comp. 1 Sam. xxvi. 23 (R.V.).

that is *in me*] The marg. alternative of R.V., *be it unto me*, is suggested to meet a difficulty in the usage of the preposition, which commonly means *upon*. But the rendering of the text can be defended as a well, established idiom, of which examples will be found in xlii. 6, 11; or we may render *upon me*, and regard righteousness and integrity as a cloak which envelopes the Psalmist. Cp. Job xxix. 14.

9, 10. His own personal need is but one small part of the great cause, and he passes on to pray for the larger hope of the universal destruction of evil and triumph of the righteous.

9. More exactly:
O that the evil of wicked men might come to an end, and that thou wouldest establish the righteous;
For a trier of hearts and reins is God the righteous.

The last clause adds the ground upon which the hope and prayer of the first clause is based. God is righteous, and He is a discerner of hearts; there can therefore be no doubt of His will and His ability to distinguish between the righteous and the wicked by an impartial judgment. Cp. 1 Sam. xvi. 7; Is. xi. 3, 4. According to the ancient exegetical tradition represented by the Hebrew accents (Wickes' *Treatise on the Accentuation* &c., p. 43), the first clause should be rendered, *O let evil make an end of the wicked*, and it is certainly a striking truth that the punishment of the wicked springs out of their own misdeeds: comp. *vv.* 14 ff., and perhaps xxxiv. 21: but the sense given by the LXX, Jerome, and the English Versions is probably right.

trieth the hearts and reins] A favourite thought with Jeremiah: see ch. xi. 20, xvii. 10, xx. 12; cp. Rev. ii. 23. The heart is regarded in the O.T. as the organ of thought and will, which determines the man's moral and religious character, the reins (kidneys) as the seat of the emotions: see Delitzsch, *Biblical Psychology*, § xiii.; and Oehler, *Old Testament Theology*, § 71.

10. *My defence* is *of God*] R.V., **my shield is with God**. Lit. *my shield is upon God;* it rests with God to defend me. Cp. lxii. 7.

11—13. The theme of the judicial righteousness of God, in all its certainty and terribleness, is further developed.

And God is angry *with the wicked* every day.
12 If he turn not, he will whet his sword;
He hath bent his bow, and made it ready.
13 He hath also prepared for him the instruments of death;
He ordaineth his arrows against the persecutors.
14 Behold, he travaileth with iniquity,
And hath conceived mischief,
And brought forth falsehood.

> 11. Render with R. V.;
> **God (*Elohim*) is a righteous judge,**
> **Yea, a God (*El*) that hath indignation every day.**

Whatever men may think (x. 4, 11, 13), God's judicial wrath against evil never rests. The addition *strong and patient* in P.B.V. is derived from the LXX through the Vulgate, *strong* being a rendering of *El*, and *patient* a gloss.

12. **If a man turn not** from his evil way and repent, God 'will whet his sword:' nay, He has already strung His bow and made it ready to discharge the arrow of punishment. God is described under the figure of a warrior, armed with sword and bow to execute vengeance on the wicked. Cp. Deut. xxxii. 41, 42. The tenses of the first clause represent the judgment as in process of preparation from time to time; those of the second clause as ready to be launched against the offender at any moment. The wicked aim their arrows at the upright in heart (xi. 2), but 'the saviour of the upright in heart' aims *His* arrows at them and frustrates their plots.

R.V. marg. *Surely he will again whet his sword* is a possible but less satisfactory rendering. *vv.* 12, 13 may then be referred either to God, or to the enemy intending to renew his attack.

13. Render:
> **Yea at him hath he aimed deadly missiles;**
> **Making his arrows fiery.**

Or, *Yea, for him hath he prepared* &c.

The description of the warrior-judge is continued. God's arrows are His lightnings (xviii. 14; Zech. ix. 14), which He aims at the impenitent sinner. There may be a reference to the fire-darts of ancient warfare (Lat. *malleoli*), arrows with tow, pitch, and other inflammable materials attached to them, lighted and discharged into a besieged town with the object of setting it on fire. Cp. 'the fire-charged darts of the evil one,' Eph. vi. 16.

14—16. The punishment of the wicked described from another point of view as the natural result of his own actions. He falls into the snare which he laid for others.

14. Render the second line,
> **Yea he conceiveth mischief and bringeth forth falsehood.**

Words of studied ambiguity are chosen, ironically describing the action of the wicked man in its intention and its result. The 'iniquity'

He made a pit, and digged it, 15
And is fallen into the ditch *which* he made.
His mischief shall return upon his own head, 16
And his violent dealing shall come down upon his own pate.
I will praise the LORD according to his righteousness: 17
And will sing *praise* to the name of the LORD most High.

(lit. *worthlessness*: see on v. 5) which he laboriously plans is destined to prove vanity and failure: the 'mischief' which he conceives for others issues in calamity for himself: the resultant 'falsehood' deceives not others but himself. Cp. for the figure, Job xv. 35; Is. xxxiii. 11, lix. 4.

15. More exactly:
He hath dug a pit and delved it deep,
And is fallen into the ditch he was making.
Another picture of the destruction of the wicked. He 'is snared in the work of his own hands' (ix. 16). The figure is taken from the pitfalls used by hunters. See Ezek. xix. 4; and cp. lvii. 6; Eccl. x. 8. Observe the graphic force of the tense in the last line. His schemes for the destruction of others prove his own ruin even before he has completed them.

16. The certain recoil of evil upon the evil-doer. Cp. 1 Sam. xxv. 39: and the figures in Prov. xxvi. 27, and Ecclus. xxvii. 25, "Whoso casteth a stone on high casteth it on his own head."

17. A closing doxology.
I will praise the LORD] R.V., **I will give thanks unto the LORD.** The idea conveyed by this word, so characteristic of the Psalter, is that of the *acknowledgement* due from man to God for His goodness. Hence the rendering of the LXX, ἐξομολογήσομαι, and of the Vulg., *confitebor*.

according to his righteousness] Manifested and vindicated in the judgment of the wicked.

the name of the LORD Most High] Since He has thus revealed Himself in His character of Supreme Governor of the world. On the title *Most High* see Additional Note ii, p. 222.

PSALM VIII.

It is the marvel of God's choice of man to be the chief revelation of Himself and His representative on earth that is the theme of this Psalm. Although God's glory is so conspicuously stamped upon the heavens, He makes infants the defenders of His cause (1, 2). The infinite vastness of the heavens would seem to make a puny creature like man beneath God's notice (3, 4). Not so, for He has made him in His own image, and appointed him His viceroy over creation (5, 6), in all its varied forms of life (7, 8).

Man then, not Nature, is the central thought in the poet's mind. It is indeed the contemplation of the heavens with all their wealth of mystery and magnificence which by the law of contrast has turned his gaze to man. Nature is wonderful as the reflection of God's glory, but man is more wonderful still. Mere atom as he seems to be compared with those starry depths (and what force modern astronomical discovery adds to the contrast), he is in truth more mysterious and wonderful than they, for he is by nature scarce less than God, and appointed to be His viceroy in the world. Man's dignity is the true marvel of the universe.

The Psalmist looks away from the Fall with its heritage of woe, from the sin and failure and rebellion of mankind, to man's nature and position and destiny in the original purpose of God. And was he not justified in doing so? The image of God in man is defaced but not destroyed (1 Cor. xi. 7; St James iii. 9); the grant of dominion is not abrogated (Gen. ix. 2 ff.), though its conditions are modified. Prophets and Apostles look steadily forward to the restoration of man's destined relation to God and to creation (Is. xi. 1—9; Rom. viii. 18—22). God's purposes are not frustrated by man's sin, and the Psalm is virtually a prophecy. It finds 'fulfilment' in the Incarnation.

The writer of the Epistle to the Hebrews (ii. 6 ff.) quotes vv. 4—6, and contrasts man's failure with this his lofty destiny. "We see not yet all things subjected to him." "But," as he goes on to say, applying the Psalmist's words to the condescension of the Incarnation, "we behold him who hath been made a little lower than the angels, even Jesus, because of the suffering of death crowned with glory and honour." The Son of Man, the representative of the race, receives as the reward of His obedience unto death the honour designed for man, and in His exaltation we see "the pledge that the Divine counsel of love will not fail of fulfilment" (Bp. Westcott, *Christus Consummator*, p. 21).

St Paul too quotes the last half of v. 6 as an assurance of the final triumph of Christ (1 Cor. xv. 27; cp. Eph. i. 22). If all things were subjected to the first Adam who failed through sin, not less must they be subjected to the second Adam who triumphs through obedience, and fulfils the destiny of the race.

The title attributes the Psalm to David, and it may well be his. The fact that the author of the Book of Job was familiar with the Psalm (cp. Job vii. 17 ff. with v. 4) would be a strong confirmation of the accuracy of the title, if that book could be assigned with certainty to the time of Solomon; but the uncertainty as to its date prevents any argument being drawn from the allusion. It has been suggested that David composed the Psalm as a shepherd on the plains of Bethlehem. With all its marvellous depth of meaning, it certainly possesses a striking freshness and simplicity; but would it not be more natural to regard it as the later fruit of seeds of thought sown then and gradually brought to maturity?

The appropriateness of this Psalm as one of the Proper Psalms for Ascension Day is obvious. It is in the Ascension of Christ that we see man, in the person of his perfect representative, "crowned with glory and honour."

To the chief Musician upon Gittith, A Psalm of David.

O LORD our Lord,
How excellent *is* thy name in all the earth!
Who hast set thy glory above the heavens.

On the title, **For the Chief Musician; set to the Gittith** (R.V.), see Introd. p. xxiii.

1, 2. The fundamental thought and motive of the Psalm:—the revelation of JEHOVAH's majesty on earth.

1. *O LORD, our Lord*] **Jehovah, our Lord.** Coverdale rightly felt the need of some audible distinction between LORD (=JEHOVAH) and *Lord* (=Adonai), when he rendered *O Lorde oure Governoure*. Cp. Jerome's *Domine dominator noster*. How fitting is this acknowledgment of Jehovah's sovereignty for the opening of a Psalm in which man's delegated dominion over the world is brought into such prominence. Here, for the first time in the Psalter, the Psalmist associates others with himself in addressing Jehovah (*"our* Lord"). He speaks on behalf of the covenant people, hardly as yet (at any rate consciously) on behalf of all mankind. Cp. Neh. x. 29; viii. 10; Ps. cxxxv. 5; cxlvii. 5; Is. xxvi. 13.

how excellent] Or, **majestic**. The word is related to that rendered *honour* in *v.* 5, and *majesty* in civ. 1. It suggests the ideas of amplitude, splendour, magnificence. Cp. lxxvi. 4; xciii. 4 (A.V. *mighty*).

thy name] That expression of Thyself in the works of Creation and Providence by which Thy character may be recognised. Cp. v. 11.

Who hast set] "The Hebrew," as the margin of the R.V. candidly notes, "is obscure." The word, as vocalised in the Massoretic Text, is imperative, 'set thou': but the construction would be unparalleled, and a prayer for the manifestation of God's glory in the heavens would be out of place, for it is already manifested there. No satisfactory explanation can be offered without some alteration of the text. Changing the vowels we may render, 'Thou whose glory is spread over the heavens,' (cp. Hab. iii. 3): or, 'Thou whose glory is celebrated above the heavens.' Cp. the LXX, 'Thy magnificence is exalted above the heavens' (ἐπήρθη ἡ μεγαλοπρεπία σου ὑπεράνω τῶν οὐρανῶν). But it seems best to make the slight change of consonants required for the rendering of the A.V., which gives an excellent sense, and is supported by the Targum, Syriac, Symmachus, **and** Jerome, among the ancient versions. Jehovah has set His glory **upon the heavens** (so R.V. rightly, though retaining *above* in the marg.), clothed them with a glory which is the reflection and manifestation of His own (civ. 1). Cp. the uses of the phrase in Num. xxvii. 20; 1 Chr. xxix. 25; Dan. xi. 21; and a similar phrase in Ps. xxi. 5.

The connexion of the clause has still to be considered. It may be joined with the preceding invocation, and a full stop placed at the end of the verse as in A.V.: or it may be taken in close connexion with *v.* 2:

> Thou who hast set thy glory upon the heavens,
> Out of the mouth of children and sucklings hast thou founded strength.

2 **Out of the mouth of babes and sucklings hast thou ordained strength**
Because of thine enemies,
That *thou* mightest still the enemy and the avenger.

This construction seems preferable; for it leaves the opening invocation to stand by itself as it does at the close of the Psalm (*v.* 9): it emphasises the contrast between Jehovah's revelation of Himself in the splendour of the heavens, and His revelation of Himself in the weakest specimens of humanity, which, paradox as it may seem, is not less but more significant and convincing; and thus it brings out the parallelism between the last clause of *v.* 1 and *v.* 3, and between *v.* 2 and *v.* 4 ff. But however we punctuate, *v.* 2 must not be disconnected from *v.* 1.

2. Render:
> Out of the mouth of children and sucklings hast thou founded strength,
> Because of thine adversaries,
> To quell the enemy and the avenger.

Instead of *founded strength*, we might render, *founded a stronghold*, established a defence: but the more general sense is preferable. The LXX gives a free version, 'Thou hast perfected praise,' and in this form the words are quoted in Matt. xxi. 16.

The general sense is plain. Jehovah has ordained that even the feeblest representatives of humanity should be His champions to confound and silence those who oppose His kingdom and deny His goodness and providential government. The mystery of man, of a being made in the image of God to know God, is greater than the mystery of the heavens, with all their immensity and majesty, as truly as the spiritual and eternal is greater than the material and temporal. Man therefore, even in the weakness of childhood, is a witness of the existence and character of God. But *how* is the testimony uttered? The words must not be prosaically defined and limited. The inarticulate, unspoken testimony to its Creator borne by the mere existence of the infant with its wonderful instincts and capacities for development; the powers of reason and thought and speech; the exercise of these powers in the praise of God with the simple faith of childhood; all are included. Nor is it mere poetic fancy to say that

> "Trailing clouds of glory do we come,
> From God, who is our home,"

and that

> "Heaven lies about us in our infancy."

This truth was illustrated in the Hosannas of the children who welcomed the Lord on His triumphal entry into Jerusalem, while the chief priests and scribes hardened their hearts in contemptuous hostility, (Matt. xxi. 15 ff.); but it has a wider scope than that particular instance.

The interpretation of 'children and sucklings' as 'weak and humble

When I consider thy heavens, the work of thy fingers,   3
The moon and the stars, which thou hast ordained;
What *is* man, that thou art mindful of him?   4
And the son of man, that thou visitest him?

believers' (Matt. xi. 25), does not take account of the context. It may be a justifiable application of the words, but there is no hint that they are used figuratively, and it is of man as man that the Psalmist speaks here not less than in *vv*. 4 ff. Nor again must the words be understood in a general sense as the equivalent of 1 Cor. i. 26 ff., though a part of the truth they contain illustrates the principle of divine economy there asserted.

'Thine adversaries'...'the enemy and avenger' must not be limited to the enemies of the nation by a reference to xliv. 5, 16. These no doubt are among the enemies of Jehovah; but all within the nation who oppose God's purposes or question His Providence, the 'wicked,' the 'scorners,' (i. 1) the 'fools' (xiv. 1) are equally included. The 'avenger' in particular is one who usurps, in his own selfish interests, a judicial function which belongs to God alone (Deut. xxxii. 35; Nah. i. 2).

3, 4. The contemplation of the heavens in all their splendour forces the Psalmist to wonder that God should choose so insignificant a thing as man for the object of His special regard.

3. *thy heavens*] The heavens as created by God and manifesting His glory. Cp. lxxxix. 11; Job xxxvi. 29; xxxviii. 33; Is. xl. 26. It is of the sky at night that the Psalmist is thinking, for he does not mention the sun; and unquestionably the star-lit sky, especially in the transparent clearness of an Eastern atmosphere, is more suggestive of the vastness and variety and mystery of the universe. See the eloquent passage from Whewell's *Astronomy*, Book III. ch. 3, quoted by Bp. Perowne.

the work of thy fingers] The deft workmanship of a skilful artificer supplies a figure for the creative operations of God. Cp. xix. 1; cii. 25.

4. Then (so the ellipse may be filled up), the thought is forced upon me

What is frail man that thou shouldest be mindful of him?
And the son of man, that thou shouldest visit him?

The words for *man* are chosen to emphasise his weakness in contrast to the vast and (apparently) unchanging structure of the heavens. *Enosh* denotes man in his frailty, impotence, mortality (ciii. 15); hence it is used with special frequency in Job, where man is contrasted with God (e.g. Job iv. 17, where A.V. renders *mortal man*). *Ben-ādām* (son of man) denotes man according to his earthly origin. Cp. Job's 'man that is born of a woman' (xiv. 1).

God's 'visitation' of man is His constant, loving, providential, regard (Job x. 12). It is to God's present and continuous care that the verse refers. It is not until *v*. 5 that the Psalmist looks back to man's original creation.

There is an echo of these words in cxliv. 3, and Jer. xv. 15; and Job

5 For thou hast made him a little lower than the
    angels,
  And hast crowned him *with* glory and honour.
6 Thou madest him to have dominion over the works
    of thy hands;
  Thou hast put all *things* under his feet:
7 All sheep and oxen,
  Yea, and the beasts of the field;
8 The fowl of the air, and the fish of the sea,
  And whatsoever passeth *through* the paths of the seas.

parodies them, when he asks in the bitterness of his soul how man can be of such importance to God that He should think it worth while to persecute him (vii. 17 ff.).

On the quotation of *vv.* 4—6 in Hebr. ii. 6 ff., see above.

5, 6. The Psalmist looks back to man's creation. God's regard was exhibited in the nature with which man was endowed, and the position of sovereignty in which he was placed.

5. Render as R.V.:
   For thou hast made him but little lower than God,
   And crownest him with glory and honour.

In rendering *than the angels* the A.V. follows the LXX, Vulg., Targ. and Syriac. The later Greek versions (Aquila, Symmachus and Theodotion) and Jerome, rightly render *than God*. For though in some cases *Elohim* (God or gods) is applied to supernatural beings generally (1 Sam. xxviii. 13), angels are rather called 'sons of God;' and moreover there is a clear reference to the creation of man in the image of God, after His likeness (Gen. i. 26, 27).

'Glory' and 'honour' (or, **majesty**: *worship* in P.B.V. is an archaism for *honour*) are the attributes of royalty: of God Himself (cxlv. 5, 12), and of kings who are His representatives (xxi. 5; xlv. 3). Man is crowned king of creation.

6. Again a reference to Gen. i. 26, 28. 'Thou hast put all things under his feet' reads like a paraphrase of the word there rendered 'let them have dominion,' which means primarily 'to tread under foot,' and thence 'to rule.' On St Paul's application of the words in 1 Cor. xv. 27 see above.

7, 8. Man's subjects are as it were mustered and passed in review: domestic animals, and even the wild creatures that roam at large over the open country; the birds of the air (lit. *heaven*, as civ. 12), and the fish of the sea, and all the manifold inhabitants of the mysterious depths of ocean. See Gen. i. 21; ix. 2. Cp. Homer's ὑγρὰ κέλευθα (*Il.* i. 312); "the wet sea-paths," as Milton calls them in his version of the Psalm.

The living creatures here enumerated are only mentioned by way of example and illustration of "all things." In the Psalmist's day the

9 O LORD our Lord, how excellent *is* thy name in all the earth!

dominion of man over nature was most strikingly exercised in his mastery over the animal creation, which he tamed or caught and turned to his own use. "Man has become," says Darwin, "even in his rudest state, the most dominant animal that has ever appeared on this earth." In our own day it is by the investigation of the great laws of nature, and by the utilisation of the great forces of nature, that man asserts and extends his sovereignty.

9. How can the Psalmist better close than with the same exclamation of reverent wonder with which he began; repeated now with fuller significance, after meditation on the way in which the truth it asserts is most signally declared!

PSALM IX.

There is evidently a close relationship between the Ninth and Tenth Psalms. In the LXX, Vulg., and Jerome's Latin Version they are reckoned as a single Psalm: and the absence of a title to Ps. x, contrary to the general rule in Book I (Introd. p. xxxix), may indicate that in the Hebrew text also it was originally united to Psalm ix.[1]

They are connected by resemblances (a) of *form*, and (b) of *language*. (a) The same 'alphabetic' or 'acrostic' structure appears in both. In Ps. ix. the pairs of verses begin with successive letters of the alphabet, with the exceptions that the fourth letter (*Daleth*) is missing; the fifth letter (*Hē*) is obscured by a corruption of the text in *v.* 7; and the eleventh letter (*Kaph*) is represented by *Qōph*[2] in *v.* 19. Ps. x begins with the twelfth letter (*Lamed*); but the alphabetical arrangement is then dropped, and six letters are passed over. At *v.* 12 however the structure of Ps. ix reappears, and *vv.* 12, 14, 15, 17 begin with the last four letters of the alphabet in order. (b) *Language.* 'In times of trouble' (ix. 9, x. 1) is a peculiar phrase found nowhere else: the word for 'oppressed' or 'downtrodden' (ix. 9; x. 18) occurs elsewhere only in Ps. lxxiv. 21; Prov. xxvi. 28 (?): 'mortal man' is mentioned at the close of both Psalms in the same connexion (ix. 19, 20; x. 18). Comp. further ix. 12 *a* with x. 4, 13: ix. 12 *b* with x. 12, and ix. 18 with x. 11: 'for ever and ever,' ix. 5, x. 16: the appeal to 'arise' ix. 19, x. 12: and other points of thought and expression.

But while the resemblance in form and language is so marked, the difference in tone and subject is not less striking. The individuality of the writer, which is so prominent in Ps. ix. (*vv.* 1—4; 13, 14), disappears in Ps. x. Ps. ix is a triumphant thanksgiving, rarely passing into prayer (*vv.* 13, 19): its theme is the manifestation of God's sovereign righteousness in the defeat and destruction of *foreign enemies* of the nation. Ps. x is a plaintive expostulation and prayer, describing

---

[1] Comp. the analogous case of Pss. xlii, xliii.
[2] I.e. the hard guttural Semitic *k*, the 19th letter of the alphabet, takes the place of the soft *k*.

the tyrannous conduct of *godless men within the nation*[1], and pleading that God will no longer delay to vindicate His righteousness, and prove Himself the Defender of the helpless.

The two Psalms present an unsolved literary problem. The description of the wicked man (x. 3—11) may have been taken from another poem, for it is distinguished by other peculiarities, besides the absence of the alphabetic structure. We cannot tell whether verses beginning with the missing letters of the alphabet were displaced to make room for it, or whether it stood here from the first. The latter alternative seems most probable, for the concluding verses of the Psalm have links of connexion with *vv.* 3—11. Comp. 'helpless" in *v.* 14 with *vv.* 8, 10; *v.* 13 with *v.* 4; *v.* 14 with *v.* 11.

Ps. ix however appears to be complete in itself, and it seems preferable to regard Ps. x as a companion piece rather than as part of a continuous whole.

The connexion of thought is clear. The Psalmist has watched the great conflict between good and evil being waged in two fields: in the world, between Israel and the heathen nations; in the nation of Israel, between godless oppressors of the weak and their innocent victims. He has seen the sovereignty of God decisively vindicated in the world by the defeat of Israel's enemies: but when he surveys the conflict within the nation, wrong seems to be triumphant. So he prays for an equally significant demonstration of God's sovereignty within the nation by a signal punishment of the wicked who deny His power or will to interpose.

These Psalms have been assigned to widely differing dates. But the tradition of their Davidic origin may be right. The author of Ps. ix speaks as the representative of the nation, in language more natural to a king than to anyone else. The enemies of the nation are his enemies (*v.* 3); the national cause is his cause (*v.* 4).

This Psalm then may celebrate David's victories in general (2 Sam. viii); and x. 16 may refer in particular to the expulsion of the Philistines who occupied the north of Palestine for some time after the disaster of Gilboa (1 Sam. xxxi. 7), and to the subjugation of the Jebusites.

Nor is it difficult to understand how David might have to deplore the existence of domestic evils such as those described in Ps. x, without being able to remedy them[2]. The misgovernment of Saul's later years, and the contest between Ish-bosheth and David must have left a serious legacy of civil disorder (1 Sam. xxii. 1, 2; 2 Sam. iii. 1, 22, iv. 2); and we have indications that David was not in a position to control his powerful nobles and enforce the administration of justice (2 Sam. iii. 39; xv. 2 ff.).

The Davidic origin of Ps. ix is supported by its connexion with Ps. vii. The closing words of Ps. vii (cp. xviii. 49) are taken up and expanded in Ps. ix. 1, 2: both Psalms are inspired by a vivid sense of the judicial righteousness of Jehovah (vii. 6 ff., 11; ix. 4, 7, 8, 16, 19): in both we have the thought of evil recoiling upon its authors (vii. 14 ff.;

---

[1] The only reference to 'the nations' (in *v.* 16) is by way of illustration.
[2] Compare the account of Charlemain's reign in Dean Church's *Beginning of the Middle Ages*, p. 125.

PSALM IX. 43

ix. 15 ff.). The connexion of v. 11, vii. 17, viii. 1, 9, ix. 1, 10; should also be noted.

It may further be remarked that in Ps. x triumphant injustice is regarded in the simplest light as a wrong that calls for redress; not as in Ps. xxxvii, as a ground of discontent, or as in Ps. lxxiii, as a trial of faith.

The train of thought is as follows.

Ps. ix. The Psalmist resolves to celebrate Jehovah's praise for victory won by His help (1—4). He contrasts the transitoriness of the nations in their wickedness with the eternal sovereignty of the righteous Judge (5—8), Who never fails to defend the godly (9, 10). A renewed invitation to praise (11, 12) is succeeded by a prayer for help in the hour of need (13, 14); and the revelation of Jehovah's judicial righteousness in the discomfiture of the heathen is once more proclaimed (15, 16). After an interlude of music the Psalm concludes with a confident anticipation of the certainty of judgment and deliverance (17, 18), and a prayer that the nations may be taught to know their human impotence (19, 20).

Ps. x. From the conflict between Israel and the nations in which God's sovereignty has been victoriously manifested, the Psalmist turns to the triumph of might over right in Israel itself. He remonstrates with Jehovah for His apparent indifference (1, 2), and draws a graphic picture of the atheistic self-complacency and pitiless tyranny of 'the wicked man' (3—11). An urgent appeal to Jehovah to intervene and right these crying wrongs is followed by a confident expression of assurance that they are not unobserved or disregarded (12—14). The prayer for the extirpation of evil finds a pledge for its fulfilment in the eternal sovereignty of Jehovah and the extermination of the heathen from His land (15, 16). The prayer of faith cannot remain unanswered, and heaven-protected right will finally be triumphant over earthly might (17, 18).

The title should be rendered as in R.V., **For the Chief Musician; set to Muth-labben.** Probably (if the Massoretic text is sound) *Muth-labben* are the opening words of some well-known melody to which the Psalm was to be sung. Comp. the title of xxii: 'set to Ayyeleth hash-Shahar,' i.e. 'the hind of the morning'; and of lvi and lvii. The words are obscure, but may mean 'Die for the son,' or, 'Death to the son.'

The analogy of other titles is decisive against all the interpretations which explain these words to refer to the contents or occasion of the Psalm; 'upon the death of Ben,' or, 'Labben,' or 'the son;' by whom some unknown but formidable enemy of the nation, or Goliath, or even (as though David could possibly have written in this tone then) Absalom, is supposed to be intended. The tradition that it refers to Goliath is as old as the Targum, which paraphrases, "Concerning the death of the man who went forth between the camps," an allusion to 1 Sam. xvii. 4, where the Heb. word for 'champion' is 'man of the space between the camps.'

It is however possible that the present text is a corruption of the words 'upon Alamoth' which occur in the title of xlvi (cp. 1 Chr. xv. 20). So the LXX, Aquila, and Theodotion appear to have read, though they give wrong renderings. See Introd. p. xxii.

PSALM IX. 1—4.

To the chief Musician upon Muth-labben, A Psalm of David.

9 (א) I will praise *thee*, O LORD, with my whole heart;
I will shew forth all thy marvellous works.
2 I will be glad and rejoice in thee:
I will sing *praise* to thy name, O thou most High.
3 (ב) When mine enemies are turned back,
They shall fall and perish at thy presence.
4 For thou hast maintained my right and my cause;
Thou satest in the throne judging right.

1—4. The Psalmist's purpose to praise Jehovah for the recent manifestation of His righteous judgment in the defeat of His enemies. Each of the four lines in *vv.* 1, 2 begins with *Aleph*, the first letter of the alphabet.

1. *I will praise* thee, *O LORD*] R.V., **I will give thanks unto the LORD**, as in vii. 17.

with my whole heart] With the *heart*, not with the lips only (Is. xxix. 13): with the *whole* heart, acknowledging that all the honour is due to Jehovah. Cp. Deut. vi. 5. These conditions of true worship correspond to the divine attributes of omniscience (vii. 9), and 'jealousy' (Ex. xxxiv. 14).

thy marvellous works] A special term for the singular and conspicuous works of God, both in nature (Job v. 9), and in His dealings with His people (Ex. iii. 20), particularly in the great crises of their history (lxxviii. 4, 11, 32), which declare His power and love, and arouse the admiration of all who behold them. The word includes 'miracles' commonly so called, as one limited class of 'the wonderful works of God,' but is of much wider application. To recount and celebrate His marvellous works is the duty and delight of God's saints.

2. *rejoice*] R.V., **exult**; the same word as in v. 11 *c*. The closing words of Ps. vii are taken up and expanded in these two verses.

3, 4. Stanza of *Beth*. It is best to place a semicolon only at the end of *v.* 2, and render *v.* 3 in close connexion with it:
  Because mine enemies turn back,
  Stumble and perish at Thy presence.
The 'presence' or 'face' of God is to His enemies necessarily a manifestation of victorious wrath. Comp. xxi. 9 (R.V. marg.); xxxiv. 16; Ex. xiv. 24. The verse is a vivid picture of a panic rout: the foe turning to flee, stumbling in their precipitate haste, overtaken and annihilated. Cp. xxxv. 5, 6.

4. In the defeat of his enemies he sees God's judicial intervention on his behalf. God has pronounced and executed sentence in his favour. Cp. vii. 8, 9.

thou satest &c.] Better, **thou didst take thy seat on the throne, judging righteously.** *The throne* is that of judgment (*v.* 7; Prov. xx. 8). God has assumed this judicial character, in answer to the Psalmist's prayer in vii. 7.

(ג) Thou hast rebuked the heathen, thou hast destroyed the 5
wicked,
Thou hast put out their name for ever and ever.
(ה) O thou enemy, destructions are come to a perpetual 6
end :
And thou hast destroyed cities ;
Their memorial is perished *with* them.

5, 6. Stanza of *Gimel.* The utter destruction of the nations in their wickedness.

5. *Thou hast rebuked the heathen*] Or, as R.V. text, **the nations**, though here, where the word is parallel to *the wicked*, and denotes the nations in obstinate and sinful opposition to God's people, *heathen* (R.V. marg.) might stand. God's 'rebuke' is the effectual sentence of His wrath which carries its own execution with it (lxxvi. 6).

thou hast put out their name] R.V., **Thou hast blotted out their name.** Cp. Deut. ix. 14.

**6. The enemy are consumed, left desolate for ever;
And (their) cities thou didst uproot ; the very remembrance of
them is perished.**

An address to the enemy (P.B.V. and A.V.) would be out of place here ; and the word rendered *destructions* does not bear an active sense, but means *ruins* or *desolations.* It is best to regard the words as still addressed to Jehovah, continuing the description of His judgment on the enemies of Israel. The language of this and the preceding verse recalls that of the curse on Amalek: "I will utterly *blot out the remembrance* of Amalek from under heaven" (Ex. xvii. 14; cp. Deut. xxv. 19). 'Their memorial' or 'remembrance' refers grammatically to the enemy, not to the cities, and the pronoun is repeated in the original to emphasise the contrast between those who are thus destroyed and forgotten, and Jehovah who sits enthroned on high for ever.

Critical reasons however suggest a slight alteration of the text. If the emphatic pronoun is transferred from the end of *v.* 6 to the beginning of *v.* 7, and a verb supplied, we may render,

They are perished, but the LORD sitteth &c.

This emendation (approved by Delitzsch) marks the contrast still more strongly (cp. cii. 26), and moreover makes the pair of verses 7 and 8 begin, as they should, with the letter *Hē.* There is also much to be said in favour of transposing the clauses of *v.* 6 thus, as proposed by Nowack :

The enemy are consumed, the remembrance of them is perished:
And the cities thou didst uproot are desolate for ever.

7—10. A stanza of four verses, each (as the text stands) beginning with the letter *Vāv.* But *v.* 7 may originally have begun with *Hē.* [In Dr Scrivener's text *Hē* is prefixed to *v.* 6; but this verse should belong to the stanza of *Gimel*). The eternity of Jehovah's sovereignty is contrasted with the annihilation of His enemies: the righteousness of His rule with the injustice of the wicked.

7 (ו) But the LORD shall endure for ever :
He hath prepared his throne for judgment.
8 And he shall judge the world in righteousness,
He shall minister judgment to the people in uprightness.
9 The LORD also will be a refuge for the oppressed,
A refuge in times of trouble.
10 And they that know thy name will put their trust in thee:
For thou, LORD, hast not forsaken them that seek thee.

7. But the LORD, in contrast to the enemies of His people, **shall sit enthroned for ever**, as King and Judge. For this pregnant sense of *sit*, cp. xxix. 10; Exod. xviii. 14.

8. *And he shall judge*] *He* is emphatic. His administration, in contrast to that of so many human rulers, will be one of perfect justice and equity. And it will be universal. The vindication of his right which the Psalmist has just experienced is the earnest of a judgment which will embrace the whole world and all peoples. For *people* read **peoples**, and for *uprightness*, **equity**, as in xcviii. 9. Cp. vii. 8; xcvi. 10, 13; Acts xvii. 31.

The Heb. word *tēbhēl* rendered *world* denotes the fruitful, habitable part of the earth (cp. οἰκουμένη), here of course including its inhabitants. Cp. Prov. viii. 31.

9, 10. So may Jehovah be a high tower for the down-trodden,
A high tower in times of extremity;
And let them that know Thy name trust in Thee,
Because Thou hast not forsaken them that seek Thee, O Jehovah.

These verses express the result of Jehovah's judgment in the deliverance of those who are crushed and down-trodden (x. 18; Job v. 4) by the world's magnates, and the consequent encouragement of the faithful.

a refuge] **A high tower** or **fort**; in the Psalter always metaphorically of God. Cp. xviii. 2, &c., and the use of the cognate verb in xx. 1 and elsewhere. The figure may well be derived from the experience of David in his outlaw life. The down-trodden victim is lifted up far out of the reach of his tormentors. Cp. Prov. xviii. 10.

trouble] A word occurring elsewhere only in x. 1. It seems to mean the *extremity* of trouble in which all hope of deliverance is cut off. The idea may be that the precipice which apparently barred the fugitive's escape proves to be his retreat from his pursuers.

10. *they that know thy name*] Who recognise the character of God thus revealed in His Providence. Cp. "they that love thy name," v. 11; and viii. 1; xci. 14.

thou, LORD, hast not forsaken] Cp. the noble words of Ecclesiasticus ii. 10; "Look at the generations of old and see; did ever any trust in the Lord, and was confounded? or did any abide in his fear, and was forsaken? or whom did he ever despise, that called upon him?"—the "sentence" which "fell with weight" upon John Bunyan's spirit in the agony of his spiritual despair. "It was with such strength and comfort

(¶) Sing *praises* to the LORD, which dwelleth in Zion: 11
Declare among the people his doings.
When he maketh inquisition for blood, he remembereth 12
them:
He forgetteth not the cry of the humble.

on my spirit, that I was as if it talked with me." *Grace Abounding*, § 62 ff.
them that seek thee] See note on xxiv. 6.

11, 12. Stanza of *Zayin*. A call to praise.

11. *which dwelleth in Zion*] Or, (cp. *v*. 7) *sitteth enthroned*. Zion became the special abode of Jehovah from the time when the Ark, the symbol of His Presence, was placed there (lxxvi. 2; cxxxii. 13 f.). The cherubim which overshadowed the ark were the throne of His glory (lxxx. 1; xcix. 1). It was the earthly counterpart of heaven (ii. 4): from thence He manifested Himself for the help of His people (iii. 4; xx. 2).

the people] Rather, **the peoples**, as R.V. marg. Not Israel, but the nations around, are meant. Jehovah's *doings* (lxxvii. 12; lxxviii. 11; ciii. 7), i.e. His mighty works on behalf of His people, are to be proclaimed among them. The first step towards their conversion is that they should know the evidences of His power and love. Cp. xviii. 49; lvii. 9; xcvi. 3; cv. 1; Is. xii. 4.

12. **For he that maketh requisition for bloodshed hath remembered them:**
He hath not forgotten the cry of the humble.
The call to praise is based on a definite experience (*hath remembered, hath not forgotten*), rather than on a general truth (*remembereth, forgetteth not*). Jehovah is the Goel, the Avenger of blood, who investigates all offences against His sacred gift of human life, and demands satisfaction for them (Gen. ix. 5 f.). Such offences 'cry' to God for vengeance (Gen. iv. 10). 'Bloodshed' may include crimes of violence which fall short of actual murder, but rob men of the rightful use and enjoyment of their lives. Cf. Job xxiv. 2 ff.

them] The oppressed seekers of Jehovah mentioned in *vv*. 9, 10; the 'poor' of the next line.

the cry] For illustration comp. Ex. iii. 7, 9; 1 Sam. ix. 16; Job xxxiv. 28.

the humble] R.V. **the poor**, marg. **meek**. The traditional reading (*Qrî*) is '*anāvīm*, though the text (*K'thîbh*) has '*aniyyîm*. Both words are derived from the same root, meaning *to bend* or *bow down*. The first is intransitive in form, and denotes the character of one who bows himself down: *lowly, humble, meek* (LXX πραΰς). The second is passive in form, and denotes primarily the condition of one who is bowed down by external circumstances of poverty, trouble, or oppression: *poor, afflicted* (comp. the cognate substantive in *v*. 13, *my trouble*, R.V. *affliction*). But inasmuch as humility is learnt in the school of affliction and poverty (cp. Matt. v. 3 with Luke vi. 20), it often has

13 (ח) Have mercy upon me, O Lord;
Consider my trouble *which I suffer* of them that hate me,
Thou that liftest me up from the gates of death:
14 That I may shew forth all thy praise
In the gates of the daughter of Zion:

the secondary sense of *meek, humble* (LXX generally πτωχός, πένης, sometimes ταπεινός or πραΰς), and the distinction between the two words is lost. The second of the two words (but not the first) is often coupled or in parallelism with *ebhyōn* 'needy,' v. 18), or *dal* 'weak,' 'feeble' (lxxxii. 3, 4); and these words also, though primarily denoting condition, tend to acquire a moral significance.

The 'afflicted,' 'poor,' 'meek,' 'humble,' are a class that meet us frequently in the Psalms and Prophets. They are those whose condition specially calls for the special protection of Jehovah, and of righteous rulers who are His true representatives (Ps. lxxii. 2, 4, 12); and whose character for the most part fits them to be objects of the divine favour. They are contrasted with the proud, the scorners, the oppressors, whose contemptuous independence and high-handed violence will meet with due punishment (Prov. iii. 34).

13, 14. Stanza of *Cheth*. The connexion is difficult. The preceding and succeeding verses speak of deliverance granted, of victory won. Why then this abruptly introduced prayer for relief? To regard it as the 'cry of the afflicted' in their past distress seems inconsistent with the vigorous directness of the Psalm; and it is best to suppose that the recollection of dangers which still threaten prompts a prayer even in the moment of triumph. But it is possible that by a simple change in the vocalisation (Introd. p. li) the verbs should be read as perfects instead of imperatives:—'Jehovah *hath been gracious* unto me; he *hath seen* my affliction...lifting me up &c.' So the Greek version of Aquila; and so Jerome, according to the best reading (*misertus est mei...vidit afflictionem meam*).

13. *Have mercy upon me*] Rather, **Be gracious unto me.** See note on iv. 1.

consider my trouble &c.] **See the affliction which I suffer from them that hate me.** Cp. x. 14; xxxi. 7; Exod. iii. 7, 9; iv. 31.

thou that liftest me up from the gates of death] He had been brought down as it were to the very entrance of that mysterious place from which he knew of no possibility of return; to the gates which opened for entrance but not for exit. Cp. cvii. 18; Job xxxviii. 17; Is. xxxviii. 10, Matt. xvi. 18; and the Homeric Ἀΐδαο πύλαι (*Il.* v. 646, &c.). How different the Christian view of "the grave and gate of death" as the passage to "a joyful resurrection!"

14. *in the gates*] i.e. with the utmost publicity (cxvi. 14); for the city gates were the common place of concourse and business, corresponding to the agora or forum of Greece and Rome. Cp. Job xxix. 7; Prov. viii. 3; Jer. xvii. 19, 20. The implied contrast between "the

I will rejoice in thy salvation.
(ט) The heathen are sunk down in the pit *that* they made: 15
In the net which they hid is their own foot taken.
The LORD is known *by* the judgment *which* he executeth: 16
The wicked is snared in the work of his own hands.
Higgaion. Selah.
(י) The wicked shall be turned into hell, 17

cheerful ways of men" and the gloomy entrance to the nether world is obvious.

Ports (P.B.V.) is an obsolete word for *gates*, from Lat. *porta*.

the daughter of Zion] A poetical personification of the citizens or the city as an individual. Originally Zion was thought of as the mother, the citizens collectively as her daughter; but as terms for land and people are easily interchanged, the expression came to be applied to the city itself (Is. i. 8; Lam. ii. 15). 'Daughter of Zion' occurs nowhere else in the Psalter (see however 'daughter of Tyre,' xlv. 12; 'daughter of Babylon,' cxxxvii. 8), but together with the cognate phrases 'daughter of Jerusalem,' 'daughter of my people' &c. frequently in Isaiah, Jeremiah, Micah, Zephaniah, Zechariah, and is specially characteristic of the Lamentations.

salvation] R.V. marg., *saving help*. See note on iii. 8.

15, 16. Stanza of *Teth*, resuming the description of the judgment. Wickedness has been made to minister to its own discomfiture. Cp. vii. 15 f.

15. *The heathen*] **The nations,** as in *v.* 5. The figures are taken from the pitfalls and nets used in hunting. Cp. vii. 15, xxxv. 7, 8, lvii. 6.

16. **Jehovah hath made himself known, he hath executed judgment,**
Snaring the wicked in the work of his own hands.

For God's revelation of Himself in judgment comp. xlviii. 3 (R.V.): Ex. vii. 5; xiv. 4, 18; Ezek. xxxviii. 23.

Higgaion] A musical term, rendered *a solemn sound* in xcii. 3, and here in conjunction with *Selah* directing the introduction of a jubilant interlude, to celebrate the triumph of the divine righteousness.

17, 18. Stanza of *Yod*. Confident anticipation for the future, arising naturally out of the contemplation of Jehovah's recent judgment.

17. R.V. rightly:
The wicked shall return to Sheol,
Even all the nations that forget God.

Sheol is not hell as the place of torment. What is meant is that the career of the wicked in this world will be cut short by the judgment of God. Cp. lv. 15, lxiii. 9. But why '**return?**' Man must 'return' unto the ground from which he was taken, to the dust of which he was made, to his elementary atoms (Gen. iii. 19; Ps. civ. 29, xc. 3). A still closer parallel is to be found in the words of Job (xxx. 23) 'unto

PSALMS 4

And all the nations that forget God.
18 (כ) For the needy shall not alway be forgotten :
The expectation of the poor shall *not* perish for ever.
19 Arise, O Lord ; let not man prevail :
Let the heathen be judged in thy sight.
20 Put them in fear, O Lord :
That the nations may know themselves *to be but* men. Selah.

death wilt thou make me return.' Cp. too Job i. 21. The shadowy existence in Sheol to which man passes at death is comparable to the state of non-existence out of which he was called at birth. " From the great deep to the great deep he goes." There Job will have no more enjoyment of life, there 'the wicked' will have no more power for evil.

that forget God] Cp. Ps. l. 22; Job viii. 13, for the phrase, and Ps. x. 4 for the thought. Observe that it is *God*, not *Jehovah* ; the nations could not know Him in His character of the God of revelation, but even to them "he left not himself without witness" (Acts xiv. 17), but manifested to them what they could know concerning Himself (Rom. i. 18—23). Deliberate wickedness, especially as shewn in antagonism to God's chosen people, implied a culpable forgetfulness of God.

18. For the needy shall not perpetually be forgotten;
   Nor the hope of the afflicted be disappointed for ever.
Man forgets God ; but God does not forget man.

expectation] The patient **hope** which waits upon God in faith (LXX ὑπομονή: Vulg. patientia). Comp. the frequent use of the cognate verb generally rendered *wait*: xxv. 3, 5, 21, xxvii. 14, xxxvii. 9, 34, xl. 1, cxxx. 5; Is. xxv. 9, xxvi. 8: and elsewhere.

the poor] Here the traditional reading is '*aniyyīm*, 'afflicted,' though the text has '*anāvīm*, 'meek.' See note on *v.* 12.

19, 20. This stanza should begin with *Kaph*, but (if the text is sound) the similar letter *Qoph* is substituted for it. [*Kaph* is prefixed to *v.* 18 in Dr Scrivener's text; but this verse belongs to the stanza of *Yod*.] It is a prayer for further and still more complete judgment upon the nations, that they may be taught to know their human weakness.

Arise, O Jehovah ; let not mortal man wax strong :
Let the nations be judged in thy presence.
Ordain terror for them, O Jehovah,
Let the nations know they are but mortal.

The word for 'man' (*enōsh*) denotes man in his weakness as contrasted with God (2 Chr. xiv. 11; Job iv. 17; Is. li. 7, 12). 'Strength' is the prerogative of God (lxii. 11); though men and nations are apt to think that it is inherent in themselves (lii. 7); and therefore the Psalmist prays that the proud antagonism of the nations may receive a salutary lesson. They are to be summoned to Jehovah's presence and there judged.

20. *Put them in fear*] Lit. *set terror for them :* some awe-inspiring exhibition of power, such as were the wonders of the Exodus. (Deut.

(ל) Why standest thou afar off, O LORD? 10
Why hidest thou *thyself* in times of trouble?
The wicked in *his* pride doth persecute the poor: 2
Let them be taken in the devices that they have imagined.
For the wicked boasteth of his heart's desire, 3
And blesseth the covetous, *whom* the LORD abhorreth.

iv. 34, xxvi. 8, xxxiv. 12; Jer. xxxii. 21.) The rendering of LXX, Vulg., Syr., *appoint a lawgiver over them*, (reading *mōreh* for *mōrah*) is certainly wrong, though it is adopted by Luther and by some modern critics.

PSALM X.

1, 2. Stanza of *Lamed*. Expostulation with Jehovah for neglect of His persecuted people, and statement of the wrongs which call for redress.

1. *Why standest thou afar off*] As an indifferent or indolent spectator. Cp. xxxviii. 11 (of fair-weather friends); xxii. 1 (of God); Is. lix. 14; and the corresponding prayer in xxii. 11, 19, xxxv. 22, xxxviii. 21, lxxi. 12. Conversely, God is said to be 'near' when His power is manifested (lxxv. 1, xxxiv. 18).

why hidest thou thyself] Lit. *why mufflest thou?*—Thine eyes so that Thou dost not see (Is. i. 15); Thine ears so that Thou dost not hear (Lam. iii. 56). Cp. Ps. lv. 1.

in times of trouble] Or, of extremity. See note on ix. 9.

2. The general sense of the first clause is that given by R.V.:
 In the pride of the wicked the poor is hotly pursued;
or possibly, *is consumed*, by fear, anxiety, and distress.

In the second clause there is a double ambiguity. The verb *taken* may be rendered as a wish or as a statement of fact; and its subject may be the 'wicked' or the 'poor.' Hence either, as A.V.,
let them (the wicked) *be taken in the devices that they have imagined*:
or, as LXX, Vulg., R.V. marg.:
they (the poor) *are taken in the devices that they* (the wicked) *have imagined*.

With the first rendering comp. vii. 15, 16, ix. 16: but the second is on the whole preferable. It gives a good parallelism to the first line of the verse; and a further description of the wrongs of the poor suits the context better than a parenthetical cry for retribution.

3—11. The Psalmist justifies his complaint by a description of the reckless character (3—6) and the ruthless conduct (7—11) of the wicked man, and he traces them to their source in his virtual atheism. The alphabetic structure disappears in this section.

3. A difficult verse. *Boasteth of his heart's desire* may mean either, makes shameless boast of his selfish greed without any pretence at concealment; or, boasts that he obtains all that he desires, and that, as the

4 The wicked, through the pride of his countenance, will not
seek *after God:*
God *is* not *in* all his thoughts.
5 His ways are always grievous;
Thy judgments *are* far above out of his sight:
As for all his enemies, he puffeth at them.

next clause shews, without troubling himself about God. This clause may be rendered;
and in his rapacity renounceth, yea contemneth Jehovah.
The verb rendered *bless* in A.V. means also *to bid farewell to, to renounce* (Job i. 5, ii. 9, &c.; R.V.). *Covetous* is an inadequate rendering for a word which means *to appropriate by violence or injustice.* The wicked man's lawless plundering of the poor is a virtual renunciation of Jehovah; nay more, it indicates positive contempt for Him (*v.* 13; Is. i. 4, v. 24).

Another rendering however deserves consideration:
For the wicked singeth praise over his own soul's lust:
And in his rapacity blesseth, (but) contemneth Jehovah.
He gives thanks for his prosperity, and like the shepherds of Zech. xi. 5, blesses God, though his conduct is really the grossest contempt for Him.

Grammatically possible, but far less forcible, is the rendering of R.V. marg., *blesseth the covetous*, but *contemneth* &c.: and *v.* 13, which combines 3 *b* and 4 *a*, is decisive against the rendering of A.V., *whom the* LORD *abhorreth.*

4. The A.V. follows the Ancient Versions in rendering, '*the wicked...will not seek* after God:' but a comparison of *v.* 13, which clearly recapitulates *vv.* 3, 4, is decisive in favour of rendering as follows:
As for the wicked, according to the loftiness of his looks, he saith,
  He will not make requisition:
There is no God, is the sum of his devices.
The construction is abrupt and forcible. The wicked man's scornful countenance is the index of his character (ci. 5); all his **devices** (as *v.* 2) are planned on the assumption that God does not regard and punish (ix. 12); upon a virtual atheism, for such an epicurean deity, "careless of mankind," would be no 'living and true God.' Cp. xiv. 1.

5, 6. The security of the wicked. He fears neither God nor man.

5. *His ways* &c.] Rather, as R.V., **His ways are firm at all times.** His plans succeed: he is never harassed by vicissitudes of fortune. Cp. lv. 19, lxxiii. 3—5; Jer. xii. 1, 2.

thy judgments &c.] God, he thinks, is too far away in heaven to interfere. The possibility of retribution does not enter into his calculations or disturb his equanimity. Cp. Job xxii. 12 ff.; and contrast the spirit of Ps. xviii. 22.

enemies] R.V. **adversaries.** Cp. vi. 7, vii. 4, 6, viii. 2.

puffeth at them] Openly by his gestures expressing his scorn and contempt for them. Cp. 'snuff,' Mal. i. 13.

He hath said in his heart, I shall not be moved: 6
For *I shall* never *be* in adversity.
His mouth is full *of* cursing and deceit and fraud: 7
Under his tongue *is* mischief and vanity.

6. *He hath said*] R.V. **he saith**, and so in *vv.* 11, 13. He presumes in his carnal self-confidence to use language which the righteous man employs in faithful dependence upon God (xvi. 8, &c.).

for I shall *never* &c.] R.V., **To all generations I shall not be in adversity**. Hardly in the sense that "pride stifles reason," and "he expects to live for ever" (Cheyne); but rather that he identifies his descendants with himself, and looks forward to the uninterrupted continuance of their prosperity. Cp. xlix. 11; and the promise to the righteous man in xxxvii. 27—29.

7. His sins of tongue; *cursing*,—which may include both malicious imprecation (Job xxxi. 30, R.V.) and perjury (lix. 12: Hos. iv. 2): **deceits**, the plural, as in xxxviii. 12, expressing their abundance and variety: **oppression** (lv. 11, lxxii. 14), which he advocates, or abets by false witness (xxvii. 12, xxxv. 11; Ex. xxiii. 1).

Under his tongue, ready for immediate use, is a store of *mischief and* **iniquity** (vii. 14). This is the usual interpretation; but it seems strange to regard 'under the tongue' as synonymous with 'upon the tongue,' and the use of the phrase in Job xx. 12 suggests another explanation. Wickedness is there spoken of as a delicious morsel which is kept in the mouth to be enjoyed. (See Prof. Davidson's note.) And similarly here the mention of the mouth as the organ of speech leads up to the thought of the tongue as the organ of taste. Mischief and iniquity are thoroughly to the wicked man's taste. Cp. Prov. xix. 28, which speaks of iniquity as the wicked man's favourite food: and Job xv. 16.

The first half of the verse (according to the LXX) is woven by St Paul into his description of human corruption in Rom. iii. 14.

8—11. The wicked man's crimes. He is described as a brigand, lying in wait to rob; as a lion lurking for its prey; as a hunter snaring his game. His victims are the innocent and defenceless poor.

The reference is probably to the bands of freebooters which, in the absence of a system of police, have always been common in the East. At no time was the country entirely free from them, and in periods of anarchy they would multiply rapidly. See Jud. xi. 3; 1 Sam. xxii. 2; 2 Sam. iv. 2; Hos. vi. 9; St Luke x. 30. The emphatic warning of the wise man to his disciple in Prov. i. 10—18 (a passage which should be studied in illustration of this Psalm) shews that such a life was common, and had strong attractions for young men.

But in all probability the Psalmist has also in view the powerful nobles who plundered their poorer neighbours, and made their lives intolerable by oppressive exactions. They were no better than the professed brigands, and no doubt did not shrink from actual murder.

8 He sitteth in the lurking places of the villages:
In the secret places doth he murder the innocent:
His eyes are privily set against the poor.
9 He lieth in wait secretly as a lion in his den:
He lieth in wait to catch the poor:
He doth catch the poor, when he draweth him into his net.
10 He croucheth, *and* humbleth himself,
That the poor may fall by his strong *ones*.
11 He hath said in his heart, God hath forgotten:
He hideth his face; he will never see *it*.

See the prophets generally, and in particular Micah's bitter invective, ii. 1—11; iii. 1—3. Cp. Ecclus. xiii. 18, 19.

8. He coucheth in ambush in the villages:
In the secret places doth he murder the innocent,
His eyes watch privily for the helpless.

The unwalled villages would be most exposed to the raids of marauders; and the country-folk, as Micah shews, suffered most from the oppression of the nobles.

Helpless (R.V.) or *hapless* (R.V. marg.) are good renderings of an obscure word peculiar to this psalm (*vv.* 10, 14).

9. Render:
He lieth in ambush in the secret place as a lion in his lair:
He lieth in ambush to catch the poor:
He catcheth the poor, dragging him off with his net.

The wicked man is now described as a lion, lurking in his lair in the forest till his prey comes near. In the third clause the figure is changed for that of a hunter: probably the victim is dragged off to be sold for a slave.

10. We may render with R.V.
He croucheth, he boweth down,
And the helpless fall by his strong ones.

An obscure verse. According to the rendering of the R.V., which follows the traditional reading (*Qrî*), the figure of the lion is resumed. The word rendered *boweth down* is used of a lion *couching* in Job xxxviii. 40, the whole of which verse should be compared with *vv.* 9, 10. *His strong ones* is explained to mean *his claws*.

But it seems preferable to regard the poor as the subject, and, neglecting the Massoretic accents, to render: **He is crushed, he boweth down and falleth; (yea) the helpless (fall) by his strong ones:** i.e. the ruffians of the wicked man's retinue. The R.V. marg., *And being crushed*, follows the reading of the text (*Kthîbh*), and gives the same sense.

11. He saith in his heart, God (*El*) hath forgotten:
He hath hidden his face; he hath not seen nor ever will.

Experience, he thinks, confirms the assumption from which he started (*v.* 4), that God will not trouble Himself to interfere: the exact opposite

(ק) Arise, O LORD; O God, lift up thine hand: 12
Forget not the humble.
Wherefore doth the wicked contemn God? 13
He hath said in his heart, Thou wilt not require *it*.
(ר) Thou hast seen *it*; for thou beholdest mischief and spite, 14
To requite *it* with thy hand:
The poor committeth *himself* unto thee;

of the faith of the saints (ix. 12, 18). The last clause means literally, *He hath not seen for ever:* i.e. hath not seen hitherto nor will hereafter.

12—18. An urgent plea that Jehovah will vindicate His own character by action, grounded upon a confident assurance of the present reality of His government. The alphabetical arrangement is here resumed.

12, 13. Stanza of *Qōph*.

12. *Arise*] The usual summons to action. Cp. iii. 7, vii. 6 (notes); ix. 19.

O God] *El*, as in v. 11.

lift up thine hand] The attitude of action. Cp. similar phrases in cxxxviii. 7; Ex. vii. 5; Mic. v. 9; and contrast Ps. lxxiv. 11.

forget not the humble] Disprove the calumny of the wicked (*v.* 11). The Qrī '*anavīm*, 'humble' or 'meek,' is preferable to the Kthībh '*aniyyīm*, 'afflicted' or 'poor.' The spirit in which sufferings have been borne is urged as a plea. Cp. *v.* 17.

13. Why, urges the Psalmist in support of his appeal, has God so long tolerated the blasphemies of the wicked man (*vv.* 3, 4), and by inaction let Himself be misunderstood? The verbs are in the perfect tense, expressing what long has been and still is the case.

he hath said] R.V. **and say.**

14. Stanza of *Resh*, consisting of one long verse. Originally in all probability there were two verses, as in the other alphabetic stanzas.

Thou hast seen it] Whatever the wicked may imagine to the contrary, arguing from his own limited experience (*v.* 11). Faith triumphs over appearances, for it rests on the unchanging character of God, Who never ceases to 'behold,' to observe all that goes on upon the earth. Cp. xxxiii. 13; xxxv. 22; xciv. 9.

mischief and spite] The words may be understood thus, of the wrong done; or, as in R.V. marg., of the suffering endured, *travail and grief*. The first word inclines rather to the objective, the second to the subjective sense. Perhaps we might render: *mischief and vexation*.

to requite it with thy hand] More exactly as R.V., **to take it into thy hand.** God's observation cannot fail to lead to action. In His own time He will take the matter in hand. Cp. P.B.V., which however, in opposition to the Hebrew accents, connects the words with the following clause, 'That thou mayest take the matter into thine hand: the poor &c.'

the poor] **The helpless** (*vv.* 8, 10) *abandons* (such is the literal sense

Thou art the helper of the fatherless.
15 (ש) Break thou the arm of the wicked and the evil *man*:
Seek out his wickedness *till* thou find none.
16 The LORD *is* King for ever and ever:
The heathen are perished out of his land.

of the word) himself and his cause to God, Who will never abandon him (ix. 10).

thou art] Rather as R.V., **thou hast been**. It is an appeal to experience. The 'fatherless' (or 'orphan') is mentioned as a typical example of the friendless and unprotected, who are under God's special guardianship. Cp. the primitive law of Ex. xxii. 22 ff., reechoed in the latest utterance of prophecy, Mal. iii. 5.

15, 16. Stanza of *Shin*. Prayer for the extermination of evil, based on the facts of faith and history.

15. *Break* &c.] Paralyse his power to do mischief. Cp. xxxvii. 17; Job xxxviii. 15.

of the wicked and the evil man] So the ancient versions, taking the most obvious division of the words. R.V. follows the accentuation of the Hebrew text in rendering, **and as for the evil man, seek out** &c.

seek out &c.] Lit. *when thou requirest his wickedness, thou shalt not find*. The word is the same as that used in ix. 12 and in *vv.* 4, 13. The Psalmist looks forward to a time when the wicked will be powerless to do harm. When God 'makes inquisition' and holds His assize, He will find no crime to punish, cp. xvii. 3. There may be an allusion to the proverbial phrase 'to seek and not find,' used in reference to what has utterly disappeared (xxxvii. 36), but a special word for 'seek' is chosen for the sake of the allusion indicated.

16. The second clause has been variously explained to refer (1) to the past, or (2) to the future (prophetic perfect). If (1) it refers to the past, the Psalmist finds the guarantee for the fulfilment of his prayers and hopes in the extermination of the Canaanites, or, it may be, in the repulse of 'the nations' referred to in ix. 5, 6, 15 ff. As the nations have been driven out before God's people, so the wicked must ultimately give place to the godly, and Jehovah's land will become in fact what it is in name, the Holy Land. Cp. the frequent warnings to Israel that the fate of the Canaanites might be theirs (Deut. viii. 19, 20, &c.). If (2) the clause refers to the future, it is a confident anticipation (expressed as though it were already realised) of the ultimate destruction of the foreign oppressors of Israel, including, it may be supposed, all the godless of whom they are typical.

The first explanation suits the context best. The complaint and prayer of the psalm are directed against wicked oppressors within the nation of Israel, not against foreign enemies. An anticipation of the destruction of such external enemies is foreign to the line of thought. But an appeal to history as the ground of hope for the future is quite in place.

his land] Cp. Lev. xxv. 23; Joel ii. 18.

(ת) LORD, thou hast heard the desire of the humble: 17
Thou wilt prepare their heart, thou wilt cause thine ear to hear:
To judge the fatherless and the oppressed, 18
That the man of the earth may no more oppress.

17, 18. Stanza of *Tav*. God has 'seen' (*v*. 14); He has also 'heard'; the prayer of faith cannot remain unanswered.

17. 'The desire of the **meek**' is contrasted with 'the desire of the wicked' (*v*. 3), which in spite of his boasting is doomed to end in disappointment (cxii. 10).
The second half of the verse may be taken as an explanatory parenthesis: *thou didst prepare* (or *direct*) *their heart* to pray (1 Sam. vii. 3), *thou didst cause thine ear to attend:* or as expressing the further anticipation, *thou wilt establish* (*encourage, comfort*) *their heart: thou wilt* &c.

18. So justice will be done to the orphan (*v*. 14) and the downtrodden (ix. 9); **that mortal man which is of the earth may be terrible no more**: may no more insolently defy God, and do violence to men. Cp. ix. 19, 20; xxxvii. 35, note.

PSALM XI.

The Psalmist's situation is desperate. His life is in peril. Fainthearted friends counsel flight. Wickedness is in the ascendant and irresistible. Indignantly he repudiates their suggestion. Jehovah is his protector. It would be the act of unbelief as well as cowardice to seek any other refuge. Triumphantly he proclaims his faith that Jehovah is the righteous Governor of the world, Who will destroy the wicked and welcome the righteous into His Presence.

The points of connexion between this Psalm and Pss. v, vii, x, xvii, should be studied. If they are David's, so may this be. It is strikingly appropriate to the circumstances of his life at the court of Saul, and to this period it should be referred, rather than to the time when Absalom's conspiracy was hatching. David was in a position of responsibility (1 Sam. xviii. 13, 16, 30) which he could not abandon without clear indication that it was his duty to do so; the jealousy of the mad king grew daily, until at last he plainly expressed his wish to be rid of David (1 Sam. xix. 1). Doubtless many of his rivals at the court were ready enough to take his life; but so popular a leader could not be openly murdered. They must wait for an opportunity of despatching him secretly. Meanwhile his friends advised him to secure his safety by flight, and argued that it was hopeless to continue an unequal struggle, when right was subverted by the action of the central authority of the state. But the time for flight had not come, and conscious of his rectitude, David resolves to face the danger in confident assurance that Jehovah will protect him.

The Psalm consists of two equal stanzas of three verses each, with a concluding verse.

i. The suggestions of faint-hearted friends (1—3).
ii. The true ground of confidence (4—6).
iii. The outlook of faith (7).

To the chief Musician, *A Psalm* of David.

11 In the LORD put I my trust:
How say ye to my soul,
Flee *as* a bird *to* your mountain?
2 For lo, the wicked bend *their* bow,
They make ready their arrow upon the string,
That *they* may privily shoot at the upright in heart.
3 If the foundations be destroyed,
What can the righteous do?

1—3. Faith's indignant repudiation of faint-hearted counsel in the hour of danger.

1. *put I my trust*] Rather, **have I taken refuge** (cp. vii. 1): and therefore it would be an act of unbelief as well as cowardice to seek another asylum in the mountain.

to my soul] To me, as one whose very life is in danger. Cp. iii. 2, note.

Flee as *a bird*] Or, as R.V. marg., *flee ye birds*. David and his companions are addressed, and exhorted to flee to their obvious or accustomed place of refuge in the mountain. But the pronoun *your* should probably be omitted. See Note iii, p. 222. Timorous and defenceless birds supply a graphic figure for the victims of persecution who have no resource but flight. Cp. 1 Sam. xxvi. 20; Lam. iii. 52. The 'mountain' or 'hill-country' with its caves and strongholds was the natural place of retreat for fugitives. See 1 Sam. xiv. 22; xxiii. 14; xxvi. 1; 1 Macc. ii. 28. Possibly 'to flee to the mountain' may have been a proverbial phrase, taken from the narrative of Gen. xix. 17 ff., for the last resource in extremity of peril.

2. The words of the faint-hearted friends continued. They justify their advice by pointing to the treacherous intentions of remorseless enemies. Similar language is used figuratively of slander in lxiv. 3, 4; Jer. ix. 3; but here it may be taken literally of intent to murder. Cp. 1 Sam. xix. 1 ff. For the language cp. vii. 12, 10.

privily] Lit. as R.V., **in darkness**. LXX, *in a moonless night*.

3. The state, or society, is compared to a building. The foundations upon which it rests (or **the pillars** which support it) are the fundamental principles of law and order and justice. The figure sometimes denotes nobles, or chief men, as in Is. xix. 10 (R.V.), but the more general explanation is preferable here. Cp. lxxv. 3; lxxxii. 5; Ezek. xxx. 4. When these principles are being subverted, 'what,' asks the voice of despair, 'can the righteous do?' and the form of the question

The LORD *is* in his holy temple, 4
The LORD's throne *is* in heaven:
His eyes behold,
His eyelids try, the children of men.
The LORD trieth the righteous: 5
But the wicked and him that loveth violence his soul hateth.

in the original seems to be intended to exclude the possibility of an encouraging answer.

But the verse should probably be rendered (cp. R.V. marg.), *For the foundations are being overthrown; what hath the righteous wrought?* The efforts of the righteous have availed nothing to avert the general anarchy. What then, it is implied, can he hope to effect by remaining in the midst of it at the peril of his life?

4—6. David's answer, justifying his rejection of his friends' advice. They look to earth alone; he looks up to heaven. They judge by the appearance of the moment; his faith beholds the righteous Governor of the world exercising His sovereignty. On earth justice may be suspended or subverted; but the Eternal Judge has not quitted His throne in heaven.

4. More exactly:
Jehovah in his holy temple, Jehovah, whose throne is in heaven, His eyes behold &c.

The last clause is the predicate on which the emphasis falls. The temple is here heaven, as in xviii. 6; xxix. 9; Mic. i. 2; Hab. ii. 20. There Jehovah sits enthroned in Majesty as King and Judge (ix. 4, 7), surveying the course of human affairs. Cp. x. 14; xiv. 2; cii. 19 ff. The epithet 'holy' emphasises the contrast with earth. The confusions and mistakes and prejudices of earth cannot enter there.

behold] The Heb. word suggests the idea of a discerning, penetrating gaze. The P.B.V., *His eyes consider the poor*, is derived through the Vulg. from the LXX[1].

his eyelids try] The eyelids are contracted when we wish to examine an object closely. 'Try' is a metaphor from refining. He distinguishes at a glance between dross and gold. Cp. vii. 9.

5. Each half of the verse is to be completed from the other. God proves and approves the righteous: He proves and rejects the wicked.

trieth] *Alloweth* in P.B.V. means 'approveth after trial.' Cp. Rom. xiv. 22; 1 Thess. ii. 4.

his soul hateth] Cp. Is. i. 14. God's *soul* is a bold expression for His innermost, essential nature, which cannot do otherwise than hate evil, and of necessity also the evil man, in so far as he surrenders himself to 'love violence,' deliberately choosing evil for his good. Cp. Mic. iii. 2; Rom. i. 32.

---

[1] The consonants of the word for *poor* (עֲנִי) resemble those of the word for *his eyes* (עֵינָיו), and this word appears to have been doubly read and translated by the LXX.

6 Upon the wicked he shall rain snares, fire and brimstone,
And a horrible tempest: *this shall be* the portion of their cup.
7 For the righteous LORD loveth righteousness;
His countenance doth behold the upright.

> 6. Literally:
> Let him rain snares upon the wicked!
> Fire and brimstone and scorching blast be the portion of their cup!

A wish takes the place of the simple statement (*he shall rain*) which might have been expected. Cp. xii. 3. May the wicked meet the fate of Sodom, so often alluded to as the typical example of signal judgment upon gross and defiant sin. The language is borrowed from Gen. xix. 24. Cp. Deut. xxix. 23; Ezek. xxxviii. 22. The 'snares' are to entangle them so that they cannot escape from the fire which consumes, and the fatal simoom which suffocates. But possibly we should follow the version of Symmachus in reading *coals of fire* for *snares*. So Cheyne and others. Cp. xviii. 12; and cxl. 10 (a psalm containing other allusions to this psalm).

> 7. For Jehovah is righteous; he loveth righteous deeds;
> The upright shall behold his face.

The character of Jehovah is the ground of the judgment which has been described; and the reward of the upright is contrasted with the punishment of the wicked.

Righteous deeds may denote the manifestations of Jehovah's righteousness (Jud. v. 11; 1 Sam. xii. 7), as well as the righteous acts of men (Is. xxxiii. 15); but the context points to the latter meaning here.

The A.V. rendering of the second line gives a good sense:—He beholds the upright with favour. The P.B.V. follows the ancient versions in its rendering, 'will behold *the thing that is just*.' But usage and parallel passages are decisive in favour of the rendering of R.V. given above. The wicked are banished and destroyed; but the upright are admitted to the presence of Jehovah, as trusted courtiers to the presence of their sovereign (cp. v. 4, 5; xv. 1; xvii. 15; cxl. 13); they gaze upon that Face which is the source of light and joy and salvation (iv. 6; xvi. 11; xliv. 3). It is one of the 'golden sayings' of the Psalter, 'fulfilled' in the revelation of the Gospel. See Matt. v. 8; 1 John iii. 2; Rev. xxii. 4.

PSALM XII.

A prayer for help in an age of apparently universal hypocrisy, dissimulation, and untrustworthiness. The title assigns it to David, who might have written it while he was at the court of Saul, or during his outlaw life. Men like Doeg were in positions of authority. Unscrupulous enemies were poisoning Saul's mind against him (1 Sam. xxvi. 19). The ungrateful citizens of Keilah were ready to betray their deliverer (1 Sam. xxiii. 11). The Ziphites deliberately meditated treachery (1 Sam. xxiii. 19 ff.).

The situation of the writer resembles that described in Ps. v. (*vv.* 5, 6, 9, 10); *v.* 5 should be compared with ix. 18 and x. 5; 'I will arise' (*v.* 5) is the answer to the prayer of iii. 7, vii. 6, ix. 19, x. 12.

But the language is general, and the Psalm might belong to almost any age. Similar complaints are found in Hosea, Isaiah, Micah, Jeremiah. In every period of the Church's history there have been godly men who, separated from friends and persecuted by enemies, have been tempted to say with Elijah, "I, even I only, am left; and they seek my life to take it away."

In this psalm prophecy and psalmody meet. The Psalmist speaks to God, and God answers through the Psalmist (*v.* 5). It is no doubt possible that he is quoting some prophetic utterance (cp. lxxxix. 19 ff.), but there is no need of the supposition. He can himself hear God speak, and deliver His word as an authoritative message. Cp. ii. 6, 7 ff., l. 1 ff., lx. 6 ff., lxxxi. 6 ff., lxxxii. 2 ff., xci. 14 ff.

The Psalm falls into two equal divisions, each consisting of two equal stanzas.

i. Prayer for help amid prevailing faithlessness (1, 2). O that insolent braggarts might be exterminated! (3, 4).

ii. Jehovah's promise of help; its purity and preciousness (5, 6). The Psalmist's confidence in the divine guardianship in the midst of unrestrained wickedness (7, 8).

To the chief Musician upon Sheminith, A Psalm of David.

Help, LORD; for the godly *man* ceaseth;   **12**
For the faithful fail from among the children of men.
They speak vanity every one with his neighbour: 2
With flattering lips *and* with a double heart do they speak.

On the title, **For the Chief Musician, set to the Sheminith** (R.V.), see Introd. pp. xix, xxiii.

1, 2. A cry for help in the midst of prevailing faithlessness.

1. *Help*] Render **save**, as in iii. 7, vi. 4, vii. 1, and elsewhere; and note the connexion with *in safety, v.* 5.

for the godly man ceaseth &c.] Godly, or kindly, men are no more: the faithful fail (or as R.V. marg., *faithfulness faileth*) from among the sons of men. Mercy and truth, lovingkindness and trustworthiness, seem to have become extinct. Similar complaints are common in the prophets. See Hos. iv. 1; Mic. vii. 2; Is. lvii. 1, lix. 14 ff.; Jer. v. 1 ff., vii. 28, ix. 2 ff. For the meaning of *godly* see note on iv. 3 and Additional Note i, p. 221. Here it means 'one who practises lovingkindness towards his fellow-men as a religious duty.'

2. Hypocrisy and duplicity are universal. Men's words are *vanity*, or *falsehood*, hollow and unreal. Their flatteries come from 'a double heart,' lit. *a heart and a heart*, which thinks one thing and utters another, and has no constancy or consistency, but thinks one thing to-day and another thing to-morrow. Cp. Prov. xxvi. 24 ff. For the opposite see 1 Chr. xii. 33, 38.

3 The LORD shall cut off all flattering lips,
  And the tongue that speaketh proud *things:*
4 Who have said, With our tongue will we prevail;
  Our lips *are* our own: who *is* lord over us?
5 For the oppression of the poor, for the sighing of the needy,
  Now will I arise, saith the LORD;
  I will set *him* in safety *from him that* puffeth at him.
6 The words of the LORD *are* pure words:
  As silver tried in a furnace of earth, purified seven times.

3, 4. The prayer for help passes into a prayer for the excision of these false-hearted braggarts. Cp. v. 10.

3. Render: **May Jehovah cut off** &c. Cp. xxxi. 17, 18.
proud things] Lit. as R.V., **great things**; further defined in *v.* 4.

4. *Who*] Namely, the owners of the flattering lips and boastful tongues. '*Our tongue*,' they say, '*we will make mighty: our lips are with us*,' under our own control, at command as faithful allies; *who is lord over us?* No one can call us to account for our use of them (x. 4). Unscrupulous courtiers appear to be meant, who deliberately propose to obtain their own ends by reckless disregard of truth, e.g. by flattery, slander, false witness, and the like.

5, 6. The Psalmist hears God's answer, and affirms its trustworthiness.

5. Render: **Because of the spoiling of the poor, because of the groaning of the needy.** Cp. Ex. ii. 24.
Now will I arise &c.] Cp. Is. xxxiii. 10. The moment for action has at length come.
I will set him &c.] An obscure clause. Either (1) as R.V., **I will set him in safety at whom they puff.** Cp. x. 5. The despised victim will be put beyond the reach of his tormentors. Or (2) as R.V. marg., *I will set him in the safety he panteth for.* Or perhaps (3) *I will set him in safety when they pant for him;* i.e. pursue him like wild beasts with gaping jaws ready to devour him. Cp. lvi. 1, 2; Am. viii. 4.

6. A general truth with direct application to the promise of the preceding verse. In Jehovah's words there is no dross of flattery or insincerity or falsehood. Unlike the words of men, they are wholly to be relied on.
as *silver tried*] Omit *as*. Silver is a natural emblem of purity and preciousness. The metaphor underlies the language of xviii. 30, cxix. 140, Prov. xxx. 5.
in a furnace of earth] The precise meaning is doubtful. Either (1) **in a furnace on the earth** (R.V.), i.e. a furnace built on the ground, the point of which is not obvious: or (2) *silver refined in a furnace* (*flowing down*) **to the earth** may be meant to picture the bright stream of pure metal flowing from the furnace, shewing that the process of refining has done its work.

Thou shalt keep them, O LORD,
Thou shalt preserve them from this generation for ever.
The wicked walk on every side,
When the vilest men are exalted.

purified seven times] Again and again till no trace of dross is left. Seven is the number of completeness and perfection. Cp. lxxix. 12; Prov. vi. 31; Is. xxx. 26.

7, 8. Concluding expression of confidence in Jehovah's protection, which is sorely needed when wickedness prevails unchecked.

7. More exactly:
Thou, O Jehovah, wilt preserve them (as xvi. 1);
Thou wilt guard him &c.
The first **Thou** is emphatic: **them** refers to the poor and needy of *v.* 5: **him** in the second line singles out *each one* of the victims of persecution as the object of divine care. Comp. the similar change from plur. (*poor and needy*) to sing. in *v.* 5. But possibly we should follow the LXX and read **us**, instead of *them* and *him*, or at any rate in place of *him*.

this generation] As the men of one age are commonly distinguished by special characteristics, *generation* acquires an ethical significance, and denotes *kind, class*, in good or bad sense. Comp. xiv. 5; Prov. xxx. 11—14; Matt. xvii. 17.

8. Jehovah will preserve the righteous; although **when vileness is exalted among the sons of men**, when worthless or profligate men are raised to positions of authority, the wicked stalk insolently everywhere, unabashed and unrestrained. Cp. xi. 1—3. The Psalmist returns to the thought of the prevailing corruption, from which he started.

PSALM XIII.

From the darkness of despair (*vv.* 1, 2) the Psalmist wins his way through prayer (3, 4) to a joyous hope of ultimate deliverance (5, 6).

His power of endurance is well-nigh spent. Jehovah seems to have forgotten or forsaken him. His own resources are exhausted. If Jehovah does not come to his help, he must succumb, and his enemies will triumph. But past reliance on Jehovah has not been vain; and he ends with a full assurance that he will live to praise Him for renewed deliverance.

Such may have been David's feelings when he had been for some time a hunted fugitive (1 Sam. xxvii. 1). The language is general, but one foe in particular stands out (*vv.* 2, 4) above the rest of his 'adversaries' as specially powerful and relentless (1 Sam. xviii. 29, xxiv. 4, xxvi. 8). If the Psalm is David's, it belongs to a somewhat later time than Ps. vii.

To the chief Musician, A Psalm of David.

13 How long wilt thou forget me, O LORD? for ever?
  How long wilt thou hide thy face from me?
2 How long shall I take counsel in my soul,
  Having sorrow in my heart daily?
  How long shall mine enemy be exalted over me?
3 Consider *and* hear me, O LORD my God:
  Lighten mine eyes, lest I sleep the *sleep of* death;
4 Lest mine enemy say, I have prevailed against him;
  And those that trouble me rejoice when I am moved.

1, 2. A reproachful expostulation in the hour of despair.

1. How long, O Lord, wilt thou forget me for ever? (R.V.) Feeling, not logic, shapes the sentence, combining two questions into a self-contradictory expression. He is tempted to deny faith's confession (ix. 18), and assent to the sneer of the godless (x. 11). He is ready to ask, 'Wilt thou forget me for ever?' but he thrusts the thought away with 'How long?' which implies a termination. In the words of Luther, 'hope despairs and yet despair hopes.' Cp. lxxix. 5, lxxxix. 46.

wilt thou hide thy face] In anger or indifference. Cp. x. 1, 11; and contrast iv. 6, xi. 7.

2. Lit. **How long shall I set counsels in my soul?** devising one plan after another in vain.

daily] The Heb. word means *by day* in contrast to *by night* (xxii. 2). We must either supply *by night* in the preceding line (it is added in some MSS. of the LXX): at night he revolves his plans, in the day his sorrow returns with crushing force as he realises their futility:—or with R.V. render **all the day**, which however is hardly justified by usage. But an easy emendation gives the sense *daily*, which seems to be required by the context.

be exalted] Be in authority and have the upper hand. Cp. xii. 8.

3, 4. A prayer, in calmer tone.

3. Behold (x. 14), instead of hiding Thy face, **answer me** (iii. 4) instead of forgetting my need.

Lighten mine eyes] Revive and quicken me. The eyes are the index of vital energy. They 'waste away,' they lose their light, they 'are darkened,' by sickness or sorrow (vi. 7, xxxviii. 10; Lam. v. 17). They are 'enlightened' when strength and spirits are restored (1 Sam. xiv. 27, 29; Ezr. ix. 8). It is the light of God's face, the illumination of His love and favour, which is the source of life (iv. 6; xxxi. 16; xxxvi. 9).

4. and *those* &c.] R.V., **Lest mine adversaries rejoice when I am moved.** Cp. xxxviii. 16. And by their triumph, as the emphatic contrast of the following verse implies, the honour of God Whom he trusts will suffer.

But I have trusted in thy mercy; 5
My heart shall rejoice in thy salvation.
I will sing unto the LORD, because he hath dealt bountifully 6
with me.

5, 6. The joy of deliverance.
5. More exactly:
But as for me, in thy lovingkindness do I trust. Cp. v. 7.
My heart shall rejoice...I will sing] Better: **let my heart rejoice...let me sing.** Faith has triumphed. He can look forward with confidence. But humility transforms his resolution to give thanks into a prayer.
Because he hath dealt bountifully with me] He looks back from the stand-point of deliverance granted. P.B.V. follows the LXX in adding from vii. 17, *Yea, I will praise the Name of the Lord most Highest.*

PSALM XIV.

The deep and universal corruption of mankind is traced to its source in their failure to seek after God (1—3). This corruption is illustrated by the cruel treatment to which 'the people of Jehovah' have been subjected (4). But He proves Himself their defender (5, 6); and the Psalm concludes with a prayer that He will gladden Israel with a full deliverance (7).

It is commonly supposed that the Psalmist is describing the depravity of his own age and his own country. But at least in *vv.* 1—3 it is of mankind at large (*the sons of men, v.* 2) that he is speaking. His words recall the great examples of corruption in the primeval world; in the days before the Flood, at Babel, in Sodom.

The reference of *vv.* 4—6 is less clear. It depends on the meaning assigned to 'my people' in *v.* 4. (1) 'My people' may mean the faithful few in Israel, the godly poor, who were devoured by heartless oppressors. In this case *vv.* 5, 6 must refer to the future, prophetically anticipating the judgment which will overtake these godless tyrants. (2) If however 'my people' means the nation of Israel, *vv.* 4—6 must refer either to some present oppression by foreign enemies and their anticipated discomfiture; or to a typical example of oppression and deliverance in the past, such as that of Israel in Egypt. If we are right in supposing that *vv.* 1—3 refer to the primitive history of mankind, the latter interpretation seems preferable. The Psalmist naturally passes on to the oppression of Israel in Egypt as the next great instance of defiant antagonism to Jehovah. *Vv.* 5, 6 are then to be explained as a historical allusion to the destruction of the Egyptians at the Red Sea: and the memory of that great national deliverance leads up to the concluding prayer of *v.* 7.

The Psalm recurs in Book ii as Ps. liii, with some variations. *Elohim* (God) is substituted for Jehovah (LORD) in accordance with the general practice of the editor of that book (see Introd. p. xlf.): and *v.* 5 differs widely from xiv. 5, 6. Is this difference due to corruption of text or intentional change? The curious similarity of the letters is in favour of the view that the text of liii. 5 is a restoration of characters which had become partially obliterated: but it is equally possible that the editor of the collection intentionally altered the text in order to introduce a fresh historical reference, probably to the overthrow of Sennacherib.

The structure of the Psalm resembles that of Ps. xi: two equal stanzas of three verses each, with a concluding verse.

The title of Ps. liii runs "For the Chief Musician; set to Mahalath. Maschil of David." *Mahalath* (cp. title of Ps. lxxxviii) may mean *sickness*, and is best explained as the initial word of some well-known song, to the melody of which the Psalm was set; rather than as denoting a mournful style of music, or some kind of instrument. On *Maschil* see Introd. p. xviii.

To the chief Musician, *A Psalm* of David.

14 The fool hath said in his heart, *There is* no God.
They are corrupt, they have done abominable works,
There is none that doeth good.

1—3. The universal depravity of mankind, and its cause.

1. *The fool*] A class of men, not a particular individual. The word *nâbâl* here used for *fool* denotes moral perversity, not mere ignorance or weakness of reason. 'Folly' is the opposite of 'wisdom' in its highest sense. It may be predicated of forgetfulness of God or impious opposition to His will (Deut. xxxii. 6, 21; Job ii. 10; xlii. 8; Ps. lxxiv. 18, 22): of gross offences against morality (2 Sam. xiii. 12, 13): of sacrilege (Josh. vii. 15): of ungenerous churlishness (1 Sam. xxv. 25). For a description of the 'fool' in his 'folly' see Is. xxxii. 5, 6 (A.V. *vile person, villainy*).

hath said in his heart] It is his deliberate conclusion, upon which he acts. Cp. x. 6, 11, 13.

There is no God] Cp. x. 4. This is hardly to be understood of a speculative denial of the existence of God; but rather of a practical disbelief in His moral government. Cp. lxxiii. 11; Jer. v. 12; Zeph. i. 12; Rom. i. 28 ff.

They are corrupt &c.] More emphatically the original: **They corrupted their doings, they made them abominable, there was none doing good.** Mankind in general are the subject of the sentence. Abandoning belief in God, they depraved their nature, and gave themselves up to practices which God 'abhors' (v. 6). 'Corrupted' describes the self-degradation of their better nature; 'made abominable' the character of their conduct in the sight of God. Such was the condition of the world before the Flood. See Gen. vi. 11, 12; and with the last line of this verse, cp. Gen. vi. 5. P.B.V. follows LXX and Vulg. in adding *no not one* as in *v.* 5. For *doings* Ps. liii has *iniquity*:—'they did abominable iniquity.'

2. For a while Jehovah as it were overlooked the growing corruption. At length He 'looked down' (xxxiii. 13, 14). So in the yet simpler

The LORD looked down from heaven upon the children of 2
men,
To see if there were *any* that did understand, and
seek God.
They are all gone aside, they are *all* together be- 3
come filthy:
There is none that doeth good, no, not one.
Have all the workers of iniquity no knowledge? 4

language of the Pentateuch He is said to have 'come down to see' the wickedness of Babel and Sodom (Gen. xi. 5; xviii. 21; and note the use of 'look down' in the latter narrative though in a different connexion, xviii. 16). Are not these typical examples of human corruption in the Psalmist's mind? 'Jehovah looked down...to see if there were any that did understand (or *deal wisely*, R.V. marg., for the verb often denotes right action as well as right purpose), **that did seek God.**' Cp. ix. 10. The use of *God*, not *Jehovah*, is significant. It is of mankind in general, not of Israel, that the Psalmist is speaking. God made Himself known through the voice of conscience, and in the works of creation, but men would not follow the light of conscience, or read the book of nature. See Acts xiv. 17; xvii. 27; Rom. i. 19 ff.

3. The result of the investigation. **All were turned aside** from the path of right (Ex. xxxii. 8; Judg. ii. 17): **together had they become tainted**, a word which in Arabic means *to go bad* or *turn sour*, but in Hebr. is used only in a moral sense, here and in Job xv. 16.

Three verses follow here in the P.B.V. which are not in the Hebrew text, and are rightly omitted in the A.V. The first three verses of the Psalm are quoted by St Paul in Rom. iii. 10—12, in proof of the universal depravity of mankind. He supplements them by further quotations from Ps. v. 9; cxl. 3; x. 7; Is. lix. 7, 8; Ps. xxxvi. 1: and this cento of passages was at an early date interpolated in the LXX, from which it passed to the Vulgate, and thence to the P.B.V. The addition is found in the Vatican and Sinaitic MSS. (B and א), and other MSS. which represent the older unrevised text; but was rightly obelized by Origen, and has disappeared from the Alexandrian MS. (A) and the mass of later MSS.

4—6. The corruption of men exemplified in their oppression of Jehovah's people. Its condign punishment.

4. Jehovah Himself speaks. The first clause may be taken as in A.V., 'Have all the workers of iniquity no knowledge?' Are they so ignorant that they cannot distinguish between right and wrong? Cp. *v*. 2 and lxxxii. 5. But a much better connexion with *v*. 5 is gained by rendering, *Were not all the workers of iniquity made to know?* (or, following the ancient versions in a change of the vocalisation, *shall not...be made to know?*) i.e. taught by sharp experience to know their error. Then *v*. 5 follows as the answer to the question. 'Yes, indeed! there

Who eat up my people *as* they eat bread,
And call not upon the LORD.
5 There were they in great fear:
For God *is* in the generation of the righteous.
6 You have shamed the counsel of the poor,
Because the LORD *is* his refuge.

&c.' For this pregnant sense of *know*, cp. Hos. ix. 7; Judg. viii. 16 (*taught*, lit. *made to know*).

who eat up &c.] Lit. *eating my people they eat bread.* The A.V. follows the ancient versions in understanding this to mean, 'they devour my people as naturally as they take their daily food.' But the words seem rather to mean, 'they live by devouring my people.' Cp. Mic. iii. 1—3; Is. iii. 14 f. And this they do without regard to Jehovah.

But who are meant by *my people* and the *workers of iniquity*? Possibly the godly few who alone deserve the name of Jehovah's people (Micah ii. 9; iii. 3, 5; and often in the prophets), and the nobles who oppress them. But it is more natural to explain 'my people' of the nation of Israel; and in this case 'the workers of iniquity' must be foreign oppressors, or, if we assume a reference to past history as in *vv.* 1—3, the Egyptians. In favour of this view it should be noted that Israel is constantly called 'my people' in Ex. iii—x; and the last clause of the verse is illustrated by Ex. v. 2. Cp. also Jer. ii. 3.

5. This verse is commonly explained to refer to the future, the perfect tense expressing the certain assurance of the Psalmist that judgment will be executed. Cp. xxxvi. 12. But it is more natural to refer it to the past. 'There' points emphatically to some signal instance in which panic terror and overwhelming calamity overtook 'the workers of iniquity.' If *v.* 4 may be understood of the oppression of Israel in Egypt, *v.* 5 will refer to the overthrow of the Egyptians in the Red Sea (Ex. xiv. 24, 25). Ps. liii. 5 adds *where no fear was*, no natural cause for alarm.

for God &c.] Present among them to defend them. 'The generation' (see on xii. 7) 'of the righteous' is synonymous with 'my people;' either the nation, which might be so described in respect of its calling, and in contrast to its oppressors: or the godly part of it.

6. *You have shamed*] R.V., **Ye put to shame.** You deride the resort of the afflicted to Jehovah as mere folly. But the word usually means to *frustrate* or *confound:* and the line may be explained, 'Would ye frustrate the counsel of the poor! Nay! for Jehovah' &c. Cp. R.V. marg., which gives *But* for *Because.*

the poor] Or, **afflicted.** Cp. ix. 12: and Ex. iii. 7, 17; iv. 31.

In Ps. liii the equivalent of *vv.* 5, 6 reads thus:

" For God hath scattered the bones of him that encampeth against thee;
Thou hast put them to shame, because God hath rejected them."

The bones of Israel's enemies lie bleaching upon the field of battle, where their bodies were left unburied (Ezek. vi. 5). This can hardly be an anticipation of some future defeat. It must rather be an allusion to some historic event; and it at once suggests the miraculous annihila-

O that the salvation of Israel *were come* out of Zion! 7
When the LORD bringeth back the captivity of his people,
Jacob shall rejoice, *and* Israel shall be glad.

tion of Sennacherib's great army. The text appears to have been altered by the editor of Book II to introduce a reference to the most famous example in later times of the discomfiture of worldly arrogance venturing to measure its strength with Jehovah. With this reading it is clear that *v.* 4 must refer to the nation and its enemies, not to oppressors and their victims within the nation.

7. Concluding prayer for the deliverance of Israel.
out of Zion] The dwelling-place of Jehovah. See note on iii. 4.
When the LORD *bringeth back* &c.] Or, as R.V. marg., *when the* LORD *returneth to the captivity of his people.* At first sight these words appear to fix the date of the Psalm in the period of the Exile (cxxvi. 1). Nor does the first line of the verse exclude such a view. For the exiled turned to Zion even in her desolation (Dan. vi. 10; 1 Kings viii. 44), and from thence Jehovah might be expected to restore His people. But (1) it is very probable that the phrase rendered *bring back the captivity* means rather *restore the fortunes.* This meaning suits all the passages in which it occurs, while *turn the captivity* does not, except in the figurative sense of *restoring prosperity.* See e.g. Job xlii. 10; Ezek. xvi. 53; Zeph. ii. 7. And (2) even if *turn the captivity* is the true meaning, the phrase is used by Amos (ix. 14) and Hosea (vi. 11) long before the Babylonish Captivity.

v. 7 is frequently regarded as a later liturgical addition; and certainly it does not cohere very closely with the rest of the Psalm. But some conclusion is needed. The Psalm can hardly have ended abruptly with *v.* 6.

Jacob shall rejoice, &c.] Properly a wish or prayer (cp. xiii. 5, 6): **let Jacob rejoice, and Israel be glad.**

PSALM XV.

Who is worthy to be a citizen of Zion, to dwell in the immediate presence of Jehovah, to enjoy His protection and blessing (*v.* 1)? The question is first answered in general terms (*v.* 2). None but the man of integrity, justice, and truthfulness. Then, in *vv.* 3—5, special instances are given, illustrating the way in which his conduct has been governed by these principles. The Psalm concludes with a promise of blessing.

The fulfilment of man's duty to his neighbour is a primary condition of fellowship with God. It is in this that his 'integrity' (see on *v.* 2) is tested and finds expression. Cp. Matt. xix. 16 ff.; Rom. xiii. 8—10; 1 John iv. 20, 21; and the Epistle of St James generally.

The Psalm is closely related to Ps. xxiv, which is generally thought to have been written for the translation of the Ark to the tent which David had prepared for it in Zion (2 Sam. vi. 17), and it may belong to the same period. The title *holy mountain* is no objection to this view.

It does not necessarily imply that the Ark had already long been there. Zion would at once be consecrated by Jehovah's Presence. And such a solemn occasion would be a most fitting opportunity for inquiring what kind of conduct was required of those into whose midst a Holy God had come or was about to come (Lev. xi. 44, 45).

Compare generally xxiv. 3—5; v. 4—7; ci; Is. xxxiii. 13—16.

This Psalm is fitly appointed as one of the Proper Psalms for Ascension Day. Christ entered into the Presence of God, after fulfilling all its requirements in a perfect human life.

A Psalm of David.

15 LORD, who shall abide in thy tabernacle?
Who shall dwell in thy holy hill?
2 He that walketh uprightly, and worketh righteousness,

> 1. More exactly:
> Jehovah, who shall sojourn in thy tent?
> Who shall dwell in thy holy mountain?
>
> Who is worthy to be received as Jehovah's guest, to enjoy His protection and hospitality, to dwell in the place which He has consecrated by His Presence? Cp. v. 4. It is not as a mere form of speech that the Psalmist addresses Jehovah. By this appeal he at once places himself and his readers in immediate relation to Jehovah. The question is asked of Him, and the answer is given as in His Presence.
>
> *In thy tent* might be wholly metaphorical and mean no more than *in thy abode*, but here where it stands in parallelism to *thy holy mountain*, it is natural to see a reference to 'the tent' which David pitched for the Ark on Mount Zion. Cp. xxvii. 5, 6. 'Sojourn' commonly denotes a temporary stay, but not necessarily so (lxi. 4); the special point here lies in the protection which the guest in Oriental countries claims from his host. "The Arabs give the title of *jār allāh* to one who resides in Mecca beside the Caaba." Robertson Smith's *Religion of the Semites*, p. 77.
>
> Not merely ministers at the sanctuary or even worshippers are meant, but all the inhabitants of Jerusalem, who were often too prone to assume that God's presence among them was a guarantee of security, instead of recognising that it demanded holiness on their part (Mic. iii. 11). Spiritually, the question concerns all who would draw near to God.
>
> 2. The conditions of access stated positively. The man must be 'integer vitae scelerisque purus.'
>
> *He that walketh uprightly*] Or, *perfectly*. *Integrity* is the rule of his life in relation to God as well as man. The word *tāmīm* means (1) *complete*, (2) *without blemish*, of sacrificial victims, (3) in a moral sense, *perfect, sincere, blameless*. It includes whole-hearted devotion to God, and complete integrity in dealing with men. Cp. Gen. xvii. 1; Deut. xviii. 13; Ps. xviii. 23, ci. 2, 6, cxix. 1; vii. 8, xxvi. 1, 11;

And speaketh the truth in his heart.
He that backbiteth not with his tongue,
Nor doeth evil to his neighbour,
Nor taketh up a reproach against his neighbour
In whose eyes a vile *person* is contemned;
But he honoureth them that fear the LORD.
He that sweareth to *his own* hurt, and changeth not.

Matt. v. 48. The Sept rendering is ἄμωμος, for which comp. Eph. i. 4; Col. i. 22, &c.
and worketh righteousness] Cp. Acts x. 35; 1 John iii. 7.
and speaketh the truth in his heart] Truth is the substance of his thoughts. But it is preferable to render **speaketh truth with his heart**. He speaks truth, and his whole heart goes along with it, unlike the double-hearted flatterers of xii. 2.

3. In the preceding verse the present participle is used; but here the perfect tense, describing how his actual behaviour has been governed by the principles of truth and justice.
**He that hath had no slander on his tongue,
Nor done evil to his fellow,
Nor taken up reproach against his neighbour.**
Neighbour in A.V. represents two different words. *Friend* (R.V.) however is somewhat too strong for the first, which denotes anyone with whom he is associated in the intercourse of life. The general sense of the last line is clear. He has not made his neighbour's faults or misfortunes the object of his ridicule or sarcasm (lxix. 20). The precise meaning is however not quite certain. Either (1) *uttered* reproach, or (2) *taken up*, and given currency to, what might otherwise have lain unheeded; or (3), as is most probable, *loaded* his neighbour with reproach, adding to the burden of his trouble (lxix. 7).

4. Render with R.V.,
In whose eyes a reprobate is despised.
The truthfulness of his character is shewn in his estimate of men. The world's false estimates are one of the evils which will disappear in the Messianic age (Is. xxxii. 5 ff.). *A reprobate*, one who is not good metal but worthless dross (Jer. vi. 30), he treats with well-merited contempt, while 'he honoureth those that fear Jehovah.'
By the Targum and some commentators, ancient and modern, the clause is rendered, *despised is he in his own eyes, rejected*, which is well paraphrased in P.B.V. "He that setteth not by himself, but is lowly in his own eyes;" cp. 2 Sam. vi. 22. But (1) the words 'despicable reprobate' are such as David could hardly use to express humility and self-abasement; and (2) the contrast required by the parallelism is not 'he despises himself and honours others,' but 'he abhors the base and honours the godly,' i.e. shews right discernment in his regard for men. Cp. xvi. 3; 1 Sam. ii. 30.

He that *sweareth* &c.] **Though he hath sworn to his own hurt, he changeth not.** He performs his oaths and vows without modification

5 *He that* putteth not out his money to usury,
Nor taketh reward against the innocent.
He that doeth these *things* shall never be moved.

or rebatement, even though they may have been rashly made and prove to be to his own disadvantage. Comp. the phrase in the Law for the expiation of rash oaths (Lev. v. 4), "if any one swear rashly with his lips *to do evil* or to do good." Any 'changing' of animals devoted by vows (which were of the nature of oaths) was expressly forbidden (Lev. xxvii. 10). Here the reference is quite general.

The LXX, Vulg., and Syr. render, by a slight change of vocalisation, *to his fellow* (cp. *v.* 3): and P.B.V. (as in lxxxiv. 7) combines both renderings in its paraphrase, 'He that sweareth *unto his neighbour* and disappointeth him not, *though it were to his own hindrance.*'

**5.   He that hath not put out his money for usury,
   Nor taken bribes against the innocent.**

Two of the most common and flagrant offences against justice. Cp. Is. xxxiii. 15; Ezek. xxii. 12. Taking interest was forbidden by the Law in dealing with a fellow-countryman as an unbrotherly act (Lev. xxv. 36, 37; cp. Ex. xxii. 25; Ezek. xviii. 17), but allowed in dealing with foreigners (Deut. xxiii. 19, 20). Cp. xxxvii. 26, cxii. 5. For a survey of opinion on the subject in the Christian Church see *Dict. of Christian Antiquities*, Art. *Usury*, or Cunningham's *Christian Opinion on Usury*. The positive rule of the O.T. has become obsolete under the circumstances of modern society, but the principle which underlies it is still of obligation.

Bribery has always been the curse of Oriental countries. For the laws against it see Deut. xxvii. 25; Ex. xxiii. 7, 8; Deut. xvi. 19; and comp. numerous passages in the prophets.

shall never be moved] The Psalmist's conclusion goes a step further than his opening question. Such a man as he has described will not only be admitted to fellowship with Jehovah, but under His protection will enjoy unshaken prosperity. Cp. xvi. 8.

PSALM XVI.

This Psalm is a joyous profession of faith and hope, springing from the sense of a living fellowship with Jehovah. The danger, if special danger there was, which prompted the prayer of *v.* 1, lies entirely in the background. The Psalmist's whole soul is possessed and kindled by the thought that Jehovah is his highest good.

It has been suggested that the Psalm was written by David during his outlaw life. He had been banished from his share in the inheritance of Jehovah, and exposed to the danger of apostasy (1 Sam. xxvi. 19, R.V. marg.). In this hour of trial he triumphs in the thought that Jehovah Himself is the portion of his inheritance, a fairer portion than the goodliest fields and vineyards which could have fallen to his lot (*vv.* 5, 6); and he energetically repudiates the idea of yielding to the temptation to serve another god (*v.* 4).

There are many links of connexion (see Introd. to Ps. xvii) between this Psalm and Ps. xvii, and they may with good reason be assigned to the same author. As Ps. xvii may with much probability be referred to the time of David's persecution by Saul, the presumption in favour of the Davidic authorship of Ps. xvi is strengthened.

Many critics however refer both Psalms to a much later period. Ewald groups together xvii, xvi, xlix (in this order), and on the ground of language and contents places them in the Exile.

If, as is often assumed to be the case, xvi. 9—11 and xvii. 15 explicitly declare the Psalmist's belief in a resurrection and a future life of blessedness, in sharp contrast to such passages as vi. 5, xxx. 9, lxxxviii. 10—12, these Psalms could hardly be placed earlier than the Exile. Delitzsch indeed, while admitting that the doctrine of a Resurrection does not appear in pre-exilic times as a truth of revelation, asks why it should not appear in Davidic Psalms as 'a bold postulate of faith.' But if the line of interpretation adopted below is correct, the Psalmist's thoughts are to be viewed from a different stand-point altogether. "His antithesis is not this world and the next, but life with God and life without God." (Cheyne.)

The Psalm falls into three divisions.

i. The Psalmist grounds his prayer for protection on his relation to Jehovah, Who alone is the source of happiness. His delight is in the society of the faithful; with apostates he will have no fellowship (1—4).

ii. The thought that Jehovah is his sole good, the source of all his weal, is taken up and developed (5—8).

iii. Secure in this faith he anticipates a life of true felicity in unbroken fellowship with Jehovah (9—11).

For a valuable exposition of this Psalm by Prof. W. Robertson Smith see *The Expositor*, 1876, Vol. IV. pp. 341 ff.

Michtam of David.

Preserve me, O God: for in thee do I put my trust.   **16**
O *my soul*, thou hast said unto the LORD, Thou *art* my Lord: 2

On the title *Michtam* see Introd. p. xviii.

1, 2. The Psalmist's prayer and profession of faith.

1. *Preserve me*] Not that he is at the moment in special danger; but only in God's keeping (xii. 7; xvii. 8) can soul and body be safe.
God] *El*, as in v. 4; xvii. 6.
for in thee &c.] **For in thee have I taken refuge.** God is responsible for protecting His liegeman. See note on vii. 1, and cp. xvii. 7.

2. The Massoretic Text reads *thou* (fem.) *hast said*, assuming that the poet holds colloquy with himself, and addresses his soul, as in xlii. 5; Lam. iii. 24 (a passage evidently based on this psalm). So the Targum. But an ellipse of *O my soul* cannot be grammatically justified; and R.V. is certainly right in reading **I have said**, with LXX, Vulg., Syr., Jer. Cp. xxxi. 14; xci. 2; cxl. 6.
my Lord] The confession of Jehovah's *servant* (cp. xxxv. 23), in

My goodness *extendeth* not to thee;
3 *But* to the saints that *are* in the earth,
And *to* the excellent, in whom *is* all my delight.

contrast to the self-asserting independence of xii. 4. R.V. marg. *the Lord* is possible, but less satisfactory.

my goodness extendeth *not to thee*] Render with R.V., **I have no good beyond thee.** "Not merely is God the source of all his weal, but everything which he recognises as a true good, God actually contains within Himself" (Robertson Smith). Cp. lxxiii. 25. The P.B.V. *my goods are nothing unto thee* (cp. l. 9 ff.) follows LXX and Vulg., τῶν ἀγαθῶν μου οὐ χρείαν ἔχεις: *bonorum meorum non eges.*

3, 4. The Psalmist's society.

3. A difficult verse, the text of which appears to be corrupt.

(1) The best rendering is that of R.V. It is true that it can only be wrung from the Massoretic text by some violence, but an easy emendation removes the grammatical difficulty.

As for the saints [lit. *holy ones*] **that are in the earth** [or, *land*] **They are the excellent** [*nobles*] **in whom is all my delight.**
From God in heaven the Psalmist turns to men on earth. The true 'nobles' (Judg. v. 13) in whose society he delights, are not the wealthy or powerful in the world's estimation, but 'the holy'; those in whom Israel's calling to be 'a holy nation' (Ex. xix. 6) has been actually realised. Cp. xv. 4. These he proceeds to contrast with apostates (*v.* 4). For them nothing but calamity is in store: with them and their worship he will have nothing to do.

(2) We may however (with R.V. marg.) connect *v.* 3 with *v.* 2, thus: (I have said) **unto** [or, *of*] **the saints** &c., **they are the excellent** &c. The general sense will remain the same as in (1).

(3) Combining the two alternatives in R.V. marg., we may connect *v.* 3 both with *v.* 2 and with *v.* 4 thus: (I have said) **unto the saints** &c., **and the excellent in whom is all my delight: their sorrows** &c. Secure in his own choice of Jehovah he warns others against the fatal consequences of apostasy, and repudiates the idea of it for himself. In this case it is possible that *saints* may mean *holy* by calling, though not necessarily in character; and *excellent* may mean *nobles* in rank only.

(4) Taking the second alternative of R.V. marg. only, we may render: **As for the saints...and the excellent in whom is all my delight: their sorrows** &c. So Ewald, who explains, "*This* seems most profoundly to distress him, that the very Israelites, who ought to be the saints and pass for such...the noble, princely men, whom he especially so intensely loves, even these begin to betake themselves increasingly to heathenism." But it is difficult to suppose that he would speak of men who were falling into idolatry in language such as this. (4) may safely be rejected; and (1) is simpler than (2) and (3), and deserves the preference.

(5) Of the host of conjectural emendations it will suffice to mention

Their sorrows shall be multiplied *that* hasten *after* another 4
god:
Their drink offerings of blood will I not offer,
Nor take up their names into my lips.
The LORD *is* the portion of mine inheritance and of my cup: 5
Thou maintainest my lot.

that of Baethgen, which is based on the LXX: '*Unto the saints which are in his land doth Jehovah shew honour: all his delight is in them.*' It gives a good contrast to v. 4, but is not convincing.

4. *Their sorrows*] This, and not *their idols* (Targ. Symm. Jer.), is the right rendering. Cp. xxxii. 10; 1 Tim. vi. 10.

that *hasten* after *another* god] The Heb. cannot be so rendered. Rightly R.V., **that exchange** *the* LORD **for another** *god*. Cp. cvi. 20; and the exact parallel in Jer. ii. 11. Less probable is R.V. marg., *give gifts for;* for though the verb is used of giving a dowry for a wife (Ex. xxii. 16), and marriage is a common figure for the relationship between God and His people, the wife in this figure always represents the people.

Their drink offerings of blood] Variously explained of libations accompanying human sacrifices, or libations of blood offered in idolatrous rituals instead of oil and wine, or libations offered with blood-stained hands and therefore abominable (Is. i. 15; lix. 3); but probably meaning that their libations are as detestable as though they were composed of blood. Cp. Is. lxvi. 3.

nor take up &c.] R.V., **nor take their names upon my lips**. Not the idolaters' names, but the names of their gods, which are the expression of their religion. "In Semitic antiquity the very name of a god included a predication of his power, dignity, or virtues; so that even to utter such names as Baal and Molech, that is *Lord* and *King*, was an act of homage." (Robertson Smith.) Cp. Ex. xxiii. 13; Hos. ii. 17; Zech. xiii. 2.

5, 6. Jehovah is the Psalmist's portion.

5. *the portion* &c.] Lit. *the portion of my share and my cup:* i.e. my allotted portion and cup. The word rendered *share* denotes *a portion assigned*, whether of land or property or food. The A.V., *portion of mine inheritance*, implies that Jehovah is compared to the share allotted him in the distribution of the land, a view supported by 5 *b*, 6; but *my cup* suggests rather the idea of a portion of food: Jehovah is all that he needs to satisfy hunger and thirst. Comp. xlii. 2; John vi. 35; and contrast xi. 6.

Thou maintainest my lot] Lit. *thou holdest fast my lot.* My welfare is in Thy hand; no man can rob me of it. But the form of the word rendered *maintainest* is anomalous; and context and parallelism seem to require a further statement of what God *is* for the Psalmist rather than what He *does* for him. Hence some critics render, *Thou art the possession of my lot.*

6 The lines are fallen unto me in pleasant *places;*
Yea, I have a goodly heritage.
7 I will bless the LORD, who hath given me counsel:
My reins also instruct me *in* the night seasons.
8 I have set the LORD always before me:
Because *he is* at my right hand, I shall not be moved.
9 Therefore my heart is glad, and my glory rejoiceth:
My flesh also shall rest in hope.

The language used here reminds us of the Levites, who had no portion or inheritance, but Jehovah was their portion (Num. xviii. 20; Deut. x. 9; xviii. 1). Israel was a nation of priests (Ex. xix. 6); and spiritually, Jehovah was the portion of Israel (Jer. x. 16), and of individual Israelites (lxxiii. 26; cxix. 57; cxlii. 5; Lam. iii. 24).

6. *The lines* &c.] Portions of land measured by line and distributed by lot. The language is still figurative. Jehovah is to him as the choicest of possessions in the goodly land. (*v.* 11; xxvii. 4; xc. 17; Prov. iii. 17; Jer. iii. 19.)

Yea &c.] The peculiar phrase in the original expresses his conscious sense of the beauty of his heritage.

7, 8. The mutual relation of the Psalmist and Jehovah.

7. *given me counsel*] Taught me to choose Him and to follow Him. Cp. xxxii. 8 (R.V.); lxxiii. 24.

my reins also &c.] This clause may be taken as still depending on *I will bless the LORD,* and rendered, **yea, that in the night seasons my reins have instructed me.** In the quiet hours of the night God admonishes and instructs him through the voice of conscience. Cp. iv. 4; xvii. 3. *The reins* stand for the organs of emotion, the feelings and conscience. 'Heart and reins' denote the whole innermost self, thought and will (vii. 9).

8. The true 'practice of the Presence of God' (cxix. 30; xviii. 22). The LXX has, *I beheld the Lord always before my face.*

at my right hand] As advocate (cix. 31), or champion (cx. 5; cxxi. 5). A warrior defending another person would naturally stand on his right.

9—11. The blessed outcome of this fellowship is joy, confidence, progress.

9. *my glory*] i.e. my soul. See note on vii. 5. The LXX renders freely *my tongue.*

my flesh also shall rest in hope] So the Vulg., *insuper et caro mea requiescet in spe.* Beautiful and suggestive as this rendering is, it is inaccurate and misleading, and must be replaced by that of R.V. **My flesh also shall dwell in safety** (marg. *securely*). Cp. Jer., *et caro mea habitavit* [v.l. *habitabit*] *confidenter.*

Dwell in safety is a phrase repeatedly used of a life of undisturbed security in the promised land. See Deut. xxxiii. 12, 28; Prov. i. 33;

For thou wilt not leave my soul in hell; 10
Neither wilt thou suffer thine Holy One to see corruption.
Thou wilt shew me the path of life: 11
In thy presence *is* fulness of joy;
At thy right hand *there are* pleasures for evermore.

Jer. xxiii. 6; xxxiii. 16. Fellowship with Jehovah guarantees outward security as well as inward joy. The words do not refer, primarily at least, to the rest of the body in the grave in the hope of a joyful resurrection. *Flesh* does not denote the dead corpse, but the living organism in and through which the soul works: together with heart and soul it makes up the whole man (lxiii. 1; lxxiii. 26; lxxxiv. 2; cp. 1 Thess. v. 23).

 10. Once more the translation must be revised;
  For thou wilt not abandon my soul to Sheol;
  Neither wilt thou suffer thy beloved one to see the pit.
Jehovah will not surrender him to the unseen world, which is like some monster gaping for its prey. He can plead, as one of Jehovah's *beloved ones* (*chasîd* see on iv. 3, and Addit. Note, p. 221) for the exercise of His lovingkindness (xvii. 7). The text (*Kthîbh*) has *thy loved ones* (plur.), but the traditional reading (*Qrî*) *thy loved one* (sing.) is supported by all the versions and required by the context.

The word *shachath*, rendered *corruption* by LXX, Vulg., and Jerome, probably means *the pit* (R.V. marg.) i.e. the grave. 'Pit' *must* be its meaning in many passages (e.g. vii. 15; xxx. 9; Prov. xxvi. 27), and *may* be its meaning always. *Shachath* might be derived from a root meaning *to destroy* (not properly *to decay*), but it is unnecessary to assume that the same form has two derivations and senses. 'To see the pit' (xlix. 9) = 'to see (i.e. experience) death,' lxxxix. 48.

 11. *Thou wilt shew me* &c.] Lit. **Thou wilt cause me to know** (cxliii. 8) **the path of life**: not only preserve me from death, but lead me onward in that fellowship with Thee which alone is worthy to be called LIFE. See Prov. x. 17; xv. 24; Matt. vii. 14; John xvii. 3. 'The path of life' is not merely a path which leads to life, but one in which life is to be found. It is 'the path of righteousness' (Prov. xii. 28). 'The way of life' is frequently contrasted in the Book of Proverbs with ways that lead to Sheol and death. Cp. too Deut. xxx. 15. It leads onward in the light of God's Presence; and in that Presence is *satisfying fulness of joys*. Cp. xvii. 15; xxi. 6; iv. 6, 7; Prov. xix. 23.

 at thy right hand] R.V. rightly, **in thy right hand**, as the sole Dispenser of all lasting good. Cp. Prov. iii. 16. The world's joys fade; God's joys alone are eternal.

 Comp. Hooker's noble words (*Eccl. Pol.* i. 11. 2): "Then are we happy when fully we enjoy God, as an object wherein the powers of our souls are satisfied even with everlasting delight; so that although we be men, yet by being unto God united we live as it were the life of God."

 Vv. 8—11 were quoted by St Peter on the day of Pentecost (Acts ii. 25—28), and *v.* 10*b* by St Paul at Antioch in Pisidia (Acts xiii. 35), as a prophecy of Christ's resurrection. The quotation is made from the LXX., which is a free rendering of the Hebrew. St. Peter shews that David's glowing words of faith and hope (the argument will be the same if the psalm was the work of some other writer) were not fully realised in himself. He did not finally escape from death. Were his words then a mere idle dream? No! Guided by the Holy Ghost he 'looked forward' to Christ. Over Him Whose fellowship with God was perfect and unbroken by sin, death could have no dominion (Acts ii. 24). In His Resurrection the words first found their adequate realisation, their fulfilment. But their prophetic character does not exclude their primary reference to the Psalmist's own faith and hope.

But the question must be asked, What was the meaning which the Psalmist's words had for himself? Does he speak of fellowship with God in this life only, or does he pierce the veil, and realise not only the possibility but the certainty of a continued life of conscious fellowship with God hereafter, and even of the resurrection of the body?

It is difficult to divest the words of the associations which have gathered round them, and impartially to weigh their original meaning. On the one hand, however, it is unquestionable that similar language is used elsewhere of deliverance from temporal death, and enjoyment of fellowship with God in this life; while in other psalms we find the gloomiest anticipations of death, and the dreariest pictures of the state of the departed. On the other hand it is clear that the words *admit* of reference to an unending life of fellowship with God.

The truth may be (as will be seen more clearly in Ps. xvii) that the antithesis is not between life here and life hereafter, but between life with and life without God; and for the moment, in the overpowering sense of the blessedness of fellowship with God, death fades entirely from the Psalmist's view.

The doctrine of a future life is however involved in the Psalmist's faith. He grounds his hope of deliverance on his relation to Jehovah; and such a relation could not be interrupted by death (Matt. xxii. 32). But this truth could only be apprehended gradually and through long struggles, and only fully realised when Christ "annulled death, and brought life and incorruption to light through the Gospel." (2 Tim. i. 10.)

For ourselves the words must bear the fuller meaning with which Christ's resurrection has illuminated them. To us they must speak of that 'eternal life' which is begun here, and is to be consummated hereafter (John vi. 47, 54; xiv. 19).

PSALM XVII.

The Psalmist and his companions (*v.* 11) are beset by proud and pitiless enemies, bent upon their destruction. One among them is conspicuous for the virulence of his hostility (*v.* 12). Such an occasion in David's life is described in 1 Sam. xxiii. 25 ff., when "Saul pursued after David in the wilderness of Maon...and David made haste to get away for fear of Saul; for Saul and his men compassed David and his men round about to take them." The thoughts and language of the Psalm find parallels in Davidic Psalms, especially vii and xi. Many critics however refer this Psalm as well as xvi to a much later period. Ewald places them in the Exile.

The links of connexion between this Psalm and Ps. xvi should be studied. Compare xvii. 3 with xvi. 7; xvii. 5 with xvi. 11, 8; xvii. 6 with xvi. 1 (*God*=El); xvii. 7 with xvi. 1, 10 (one who has taken refuge in Jehovah naturally appeals to the Saviour of those that take refuge in Him; Jehovah's beloved one (*chásid*) naturally pleads for the manifestation of His *chesed* or lovingkindness); xvii. 14 with xvi. 5 (the contrast between the portion of the worldly and that of the Psalmist). The ground of appeal in xvii is that integrity of devotion which inspires xvi; in both Psalms communion with Jehovah is set forth as the highest joy; xvii. 15 re-echoes xvi. 9—11. Cp. 'I shall be satisfied' (xvii. 15) with 'satisfying fulness' (xvi. 11). But the tone of the two Psalms presents a striking contrast, and points to the difference in the Psalmist's circumstances. In xvi danger is in the background: the Psalm breathes a spirit of calm repose and joyous serenity. In xvii danger is pressing, and help is urgently needed. The faith of calmer days is being put to the proof.

The Psalm may be divided thus:

i. Appeal to Jehovah for justice on the ground of the petitioner's integrity (1—5).

ii. Prayer for protection on the ground of Jehovah's relation to him, enforced by a description of the virulence of his enemies (6—12).

iii. Reiterated prayer for Jehovah's help, and contrast between the contentment of these men with their material blessings and his own longing for the closest communion with God (13—15).

A prayer of David is a fitting title for this Psalm. Cp. *v.* 1, and Introd. p. xiv.

A Prayer of David.

Hear the right, O LORD, attend unto my cry,   17
Give ear unto my prayer, *that goeth* not out of feigned lips.
Let my sentence come forth from thy presence;   2

1, 2. An appeal for justice.

1. *the right*] Lit. *righteousness* or *justice*. With a righteous cause and a just appeal (vii. 8) the Psalmist appears before the righteous Judge (vii. 17; ix. 4, 8), confident in the integrity of his motives towards God and man. A good conscience is the indispensable condition of earnest prayer.

my cry] The word denotes a shrill piercing cry, frequently of joy, sometimes as here of entreaty, "expressive of emotional excitement such as an Eastern scruples not to use in prayer" (Cheyne). Cp. lxi. 1; Jer. vii. 16.

that goeth not out of feigned lips] Uttered *by no deceitful lips.* Cp. v. 6; x. 7. There is no hypocrisy in this prayer.

2. The petition. *Let* **my judgment** *come forth from thy presence.*

Let thine eyes behold the things that are equal.
3 Thou hast proved mine heart; thou hast visited *me* in the night;
Thou hast tried me, *and* shalt find nothing;
I am purposed *that* my mouth shall not transgress.
4 Concerning the works of men, by the word of thy lips
I have kept *me from* the paths of the destroyer.
5 Hold up my goings in thy paths,
That my footsteps slip not.

Cp. xxxvii. 6; Is. xlii. 1, 3, 4; Hab. i. 4. Pronounce sentence for me; publish it; give effect to it, and vindicate the justice of my cause.

Let thine eyes &c.] Better, **Thine eyes behold equity**, or, **with equity**. The prayer is based on the known character of Jehovah. His discernment is complete and impartial. Cp. xi. 4; ix. 8.

3—5. The bold language of a good conscience. See Introd. p. lxix. Cp. Acts xxiii. 1; xxiv. 16.

3. *Thou hast tried mine heart* (vii. 9; xi. 4, 5); *thou hast visited me in the night*, when men's thoughts range unrestrainedly, and they appear in their true colours (xxxvi. 4); *thou hast* **proved** or refined me (lxvi. 10), *and* **findest** *nothing*, no dross of evil purpose. But see next note.

I am purposed &c.] A difficult and much disputed clause. The A.V., retained in R.V. text, follows the Massoretic accents. It is however better to connect this and the preceding clause thus:
Thou hast proved me, and findest no evil purpose in me;
My mouth doth not transgress.

In thought, word, and deed (*v.* 4), he has nothing to fear from the Divine scrutiny.

4. As for the works of men, by the word of thy lips
I have shunned the paths of the violent.

In regard to his behaviour as a man among men, he has obeyed the Divine precepts, and marked and shunned the ways of violent men, avoiding their example and society. God's commandments have been his preservation, supplying the rule and the strength for his conduct. 'The paths of the violent' are the opposite of the 'path of life,' xvi. 11. (Prov. i. 19; ii. 11—19, &c.). Robbery with violence is mentioned as the commonest form of wrong-doing to neighbours (Jer. vii. 11; Ezek. xviii. 10). For illustration of the verse from David's life see 1 Sam. xxv. 32 ff.; xxiv. 10 ff.; cp. Ps. vii. 3 ff.

The P.B.V., *Because of men's works, that are done against the words of thy lips*, is untenable.

5. My steps have held fast to thy tracks,
My feet have not slipped.

The A.V. is grammatically untenable. He describes his conduct positively. *Paths*, a different word from that in *v.* 4, denotes the

PSALM XVII. 6—9.

I have called upon thee, for thou wilt hear me, O God: 6
Incline thine ear unto me, *and* hear my speech.
Shew thy marvellous lovingkindness, O thou that savest by 7
 thy right hand them which put their trust *in thee*
From those that rise up *against them.*
Keep me as the apple of the eye, 8
Hide me under the shadow of thy wings,
From the wicked that oppress me, 9
From my deadly enemies, *who* compass me about.

beaten tracks made by wheeled vehicles. *Slipped* (the same word as *moved* in xv. 5, xvi. 8), of moral 'slips' and 'falls.'

6—9. After protesting his integrity he resumes his prayer.

6. *I have called upon thee*] I is emphatic. Being such an one as I am, I have called upon Thee, in full confidence that Thou wilt **answer** me.
O God] *El*, as in xvi. 1. See note on v. 4.
hear] Wrongly printed in italics in many editions.

7. *Shew thy marvellous lovingkindness*] Lit., *Make marvellous thy lovingkindnesses*: Vulg. *mirifica misericordias tuas*. Cp. xxxi. 21, and note on ix. 1. The word implies a signal intervention on his behalf. The need is great, but God's power is greater.

Parallel passages decide in favour of connecting *O thou that savest by thy right hand* (lx. 5; xx. 6). R.V. follows the original in transferring *by thy right hand* to the end of the verse for emphasis. But the balanced brevity of the Hebrew (the whole verse contains but six words) defies translation. For *put their trust*, cp. xvi. 1; for *those that rise up against thee*, cp. lix. 1, xviii. 48. Grammatically possible, but unsupported by analogy, is the rendering of R.V. marg., *from those that rise up against thy right hand;* cp. P.B.V., *from such as resist thy right hand*, which follows the LXX, Vulg., and Jer. (*a resistentibus dexterae tuae*).

8. *Keep me* &c.] Or, **Preserve me** (the same word as in xvi. 1) *as the apple* or *pupil of the eye*, an emblem of that which is tenderest and dearest, and therefore guarded with the most jealous care. Cp. Deut. xxxii. 10; Prov. vii. 2; Zech. ii. 8.

Hide me &c.] A favourite figure, taken from the care of the mother-bird for her young, not however specially from the hen (Matt. xxiii. 37), for there is no trace in the O. T. of the practice of keeping domestic fowls. Cp. xxxvi. 7; lvii. 1; lxi. 4; lxiii. 7; xci. 4. As the first half of the verse may refer to Deut. xxxii. 10, the figure may have been suggested by the reference to the eagle in *v*. 11; but the figure there is quite different. God's leading of His people is compared with the eagle teaching its young to fly.

9. *that oppress me*] R.V., **that spoil me.** Cp. xii. 5. (R.V.).
my deadly enemies] Nothing but his life will satisfy them. Cp. 1 Sam. xxiv. 11. This is the sense, whether the exact meaning is *enemies*

10 They are inclosed *in* their own fat:
With their mouth they speak proudly.
11 They have now compassed us *in* our steps:
They have set their eyes bowing down to the earth;
12 Like as a lion *that* is greedy of his prey,
And as it were a young lion lurking in secret places.
13 Arise, O LORD, disappoint him, cast him down:
Deliver my soul from the wicked, *which is* thy sword:
14 From men *which are* thy hand, O LORD,
From men of the world, *which have* their portion in *this* life,

in soul, i.e. with murderous intent (xxvii. 12; xli. 2), or *enemies against* (my) *soul*.

10—12. The character of his enemies.

10. Prosperity has resulted in obtuse self-complacency and contemptuous arrogance. Cp. lxxiii. 7, 8; Job xv. 27. The right rendering of 10 a is however probably (cp. R.V. marg.) **Their heart** (lit. *midriff*) **have they shut up.** They have closed it against every influence for good and all sympathy. Cp. 1 John iii. 17. See for this explanation Prof. Robertson Smith's *Religion of the Semites*, p. 360.

they speak proudly] Cp. xii. 3 ff.; x. 2; xxxi. 18; lxxiii. 6.

11. It has come to this that they beset the Psalmist and his adherents at every step. See 1 Sam. xxiii. 26.

They have set &c.] R.V., **They set their eyes to cast us down to the earth.** They watch intently for an opportunity of overthrowing us. Cp. xxxvii. 32, 14; x. 8.

12. *Like as a lion* &c.] Lit., **He is like a lion that is greedy to raven.** (xxii. 13). One of the pursuers (Saul, if the singer is David) is conspicuous for ferocity and craftiness. Cp. vii. 2; x. 8, 9.

13. *Arise, O LORD* (iii. 7), **confront him,** meet him face to face as he prepares to spring (or, as R.V. marg., *forestall him*), **make him bow down,** crouching in abject submission (xviii. 39). The same word is used of the lion in repose, Gen. xlix. 9; Num. xxiv. 9.

13, 14. *from the wicked*, which is *thy sword: from men* which are *thy hand*] This rendering, which is in part that of Jerome, is retained in R.V. marg. For the thought that God uses even the wicked as His instruments see Is. x. 5, where the Assyrian is called the rod of Jehovah's anger. But R.V. text is preferable: **from the wicked by thy sword; from men, by thy hand.** Cp. vii. 12.

14. *from men of the world*] Men whose aims and pleasures belong to the 'world that passeth away': those who in N.T. language are 'of the world' (John xv. 19), 'sons of this age' (Luke xvi. 8; xx. 34, 35), 'who mind earthly things' (Phil. iii. 19). They are further described as those **whose portion is in** [this] **life.** Jehovah Himself is the portion of the godly (xvi. 5); these men are content with a portion of material and transitory things. See xlix. 6 ff.; lxxiii. 3 ff.; Wisdom ii. 6 ff.

And whose belly thou fillest *with* thy hid *treasure:*
They are full *of* children,
And leave the rest of their *substance* to their babes.
As for me, I will behold thy face in righteousness :   15
I shall be satisfied, when *I* awake, *with* thy likeness.

The sense is still better given by the rendering of R.V. marg., **From men whose portion in life is of the world.** God deals with them according to their own base desires. They care only for the satisfaction of their lower appetites (Phil. iii. 19), and so He "who maketh His sun to rise on the evil and the good" fills their belly with His store of blessings, gratifies the animal part of their nature (Job xxii. 18; Luke xvi. 25).

They are full of *children*] Better, **They are satisfied with sons**, the universal desire of men in Oriental countries being to see a family perpetuating their name (Job xxi. 8, 11); and **leave their superabundance to their children**; their prosperity continues through life, they have enough for themselves and to spare for their families.

15. **As for me, in righteousness let me behold thy face: Let me be satisfied, when I awake, with thy likeness.**
With the low desires of worldly men the Psalmist contrasts his own spiritual aspirations. He does not complain of their prosperity; it does not present itself to him as a trial of patience and a moral enigma, as it does to the authors of Pss. xxxvii. and lxxiii. Their blessings are not for an instant to be compared with his. 'To behold Jehovah's face' is to enjoy communion with Him and all the blessings that flow from it; it is the inward reality which corresponds to 'appearing before Him' in the sanctuary. Cp. xvi. 11. 'Righteousness' is the condition of that 'beholding'; for it is sin that separates from God. Cp. xi. 7 note; xv. 1 ff.; Matt. v. 8; Heb. xii. 14.

He concludes with a yet bolder prayer, that he may be admitted to that highest degree of privilege which Moses enjoyed, and *be satisfied* with *the likeness* or *form of Jehovah*. See Num. xii. 6—8. Worldly men are satisfied if they see themselves reflected in their sons: nothing less than the sight of the form of God will satisfy the Psalmist. Cp. xvi. 11.

But what is meant by *when I awake*? Not 'when the night of calamity is at an end'; a sense which the word will not bear. What he desires is (1) the *daily* renewal of this communion (cp. cxxxix. 18; Prov. vi. 22); and (2) as the passage in Numbers suggests, a *waking sight* of God, as distinguished from a dream or vision.

The words are commonly explained of awaking from the sleep of death to behold the face of God in the world beyond, and to be transfigured into His likeness. Death is no doubt spoken of as sleep (xiii. 3), and resurrection as awakening (Is. xxvi. 19; Dan. xii. 2). But elsewhere the context makes the meaning unambiguous. Here, however, this reference is excluded by the context. The Psalmist does not anticipate death, but prays to be delivered from it (*vv.* 8 ff.). The contrast present to his mind is not between 'this world' and 'another world,' the 'present life' and the 'future life,' but between the false life and the true life in this present world, between 'the flesh' and 'the spirit,' between the 'natural man' with his sensuous desires, and the 'spiritual man' with his Godward desires. Here, as in xvi. 9—11, death fades from the Psalmist's view. He is absorbed with the thought of the blessedness of fellowship with God[1].

But the doctrine of life eternal is implicitly contained in the words. For it is inconceivable that communion with God thus begun and daily renewed should be abruptly terminated by death. It is possible that the Psalmist and those for whom he sung may have had some glimmering of this larger hope, though how or when it was to be realised was not yet revealed. But whether they drew the inference must remain doubtful. In the economy of revelation "heaven is first a temper and then a place."

It is indeed impossible for us to read the words now without thinking of their 'fulfilment' in the light of the Gospel: of the more profound revelation of righteousness (Rom. i. 17); of the sight of the Father in the Incarnate Son (John xiv. 9); of the hope of transfiguration into His likeness here and hereafter, and of the Beatific Vision (2 Cor. iii. 18; Phil. iii. 21; 1 John iii. 2; Rev. xxii. 4).

It may be remarked that none of the ancient versions render as though they definitely referred the passage to the Resurrection. Targ., Aq., Symm., Jer., all give a literal version. The LXX, *I shall be satisfied when Thy glory appears:* Syr., *when Thy faithfulness appears:* Theod., *when Thy right hand appears:* seem to have had a different text. *Thy glory* is substituted for *thy form* in LXX as in Num. xii. 18.

PSALM XVIII.

At length the warrior-king was at peace. The hairbreadth escapes of his flight from Saul, when his life was in hourly peril and he knew not whither to turn for safety; the miseries and bitterness of civil strife, through which though chosen by Jehovah to rule His people he had to fight his way to the throne; the wars with surrounding nations, which, jealous of Israel's rising power, had leagued together to crush the scarcely consolidated kingdom;—all were past and over. David had been preserved through every danger; victory had accompanied his arms; he was the accepted king of an united people; the nations around acknowledged his supremacy. To crown all, Jehovah's message communicated by Nathan had opened out the prospect of a splendid future for his posterity.

In this hour of his highest prosperity and happiness David composed this magnificent hymn of thanksgiving. He surveys the course of an

---

[1] Comp. Delitzsch: "The contrast is not so much here and hereafter, as world (life) and God. We see here into the inmost nature of the O.T. belief. All the blessedness and glory of the future life which the N.T. unfolds is for the O.T. faith contained in Jehovah. Jehovah is its highest good; in the possession of Him it is raised above heaven and earth, life and death; to surrender itself blindly to Him, without any explicit knowledge of a future life of blessedness, to be satisfied with Him, to rest in Him, to take refuge in Him in view of death, is characteristic of the O.T. faith." *The Psalms,* p. 181.

eventful life; he traces the hand of Jehovah in every step; and his heart overflows with joyous gratitude. The inspiring thought of the whole Psalm is that Jehovah has made him what he is. To His loving care and unfailing faithfulness he owes it that he has been preserved and guided and raised to his present height of power.

By expressive metaphors he describes what Jehovah had proved Himself to be to him (1—3); and then depicting in forcible figures the extremity of peril to which he had been brought (4—6), he tells how in answer to his prayer Jehovah manifested His power (7—15), and delivered him from the enemies who were too strong for him (16—19). In strong and simple consciousness of his own integrity (20—23), he delights to trace in this deliverance a proof of Jehovah's faithfulness to those who are faithful to Him, in accordance with the general law of His dealings (24—27). To Him alone he owes all that he is (28—30); He, the unique and incomparable God, has given him strength and skill for war (31—34); He it is who has made him victorious over his enemies (35—42); He it is who has made him king over his people and supreme among surrounding nations (43—45). It is Jehovah alone; and His praise shall be celebrated throughout the world. Nor is His lovingkindness limited to David only; the promise reaches forward, and embraces his posterity for evermore (46—50).

That David was the author of this Psalm is generally admitted, except by critics who question the existence of Davidic Psalms at all. Not only does it stand in the Psalter as David's, but the compiler of 2 Samuel embodied it in his work as at once the best illustration of David's life and character, and the noblest specimen of his poetry.

The internal evidence of its contents corroborates the external tradition. The Psalmist is a distinguished and successful warrior, general, and king (*vv.* 29, 33, 34, 37 ff., 43): he has had to contend with domestic as well as foreign enemies (43 ff.), and has received the submission of surrounding nations (44). He looks back upon a life of extraordinary trials and dangers to which he has been exposed from enemies among whom one was conspicuous for his ferocity (4 ff., 17, 48). He appeals to his own integrity of purpose, and sees in his deliverance God's recognition of that integrity (20 ff.); yet throughout he shews a singular humility and the clearest sense that he owes to Jehovah's grace whatever he has or is. These characteristics, taken together, point to David, and to no one else of whom we have any knowledge: and the intense personality and directness of the Psalm are a strong argument against the hypothesis that it is a composition put into his mouth by some later poet.

At what period of David's life the Psalm was written has been much debated. But title and contents both point unmistakably to the middle period of his reign, when he was in the zenith of his prosperity and power, rather than to the close of his life. His triumphs over his enemies at home and abroad are still recent; the perils of his flight from Saul are still fresh in his memory. On the other hand there is not a trace of the sins and sorrows which clouded the later years of his reign. The free and joyous tone of the Psalm, and its bold assertions of integrity, point to a time before his sin with Bath-sheba, and

Absalom's rebellion. The composition of the Psalm may therefore most naturally and fitly be assigned to the interval of peace mentioned in 2 Sam. vii. 1, which may (see notes there) have been subsequent to some at least of the wars described in ch. viii, for the arrangement of the book does not appear to be strictly chronological. But it must be placed after the visit of Nathan recorded in 2 Sam. vii, as *v.* 50 clearly refers to the promise then given: unless indeed *v.* 50 is to be regarded as a later addition to the Psalm. In that time of tranquillity David reviewed the mercies of Jehovah in this sublime ode of thanksgiving, and planned to raise a monument of his gratitude in the scheme for building the Temple, which he was not allowed to carry out.

The title of the Psalm is composite. The first part of it, *For the Chief Musician. A Psalm of David the servant of the* LORD, is analogous to the titles of other psalms in this collection: the second part is taken from 2 Sam. xxii. 1, or from the older history which the compiler of Samuel made use of.

Comp. the similar titles in Ex. xv. 1; Deut. xxxi. 30.

Here, as in the title of Ps. xxxvi, David is styled *Jehovah's servant.* Cp. 2 Sam. iii. 18; vii. 5, 8; 1 Kings viii. 24; Ps. lxxviii. 70; lxxxix. 3, 20; cxxxii. 10. Any Israelite might profess himself Jehovah's servant in addressing Him, but only a few who were raised up to do special service or who stood in a special relation to Jehovah, such as Abraham, Moses, Joshua, David, Job, are honoured with this distinctive title.

Saul is mentioned by name as the most bitter and implacable of David's enemies. (For the form of expression cp. Ex. xviii. 10.) David's preservation in that fierce persecution which was aimed at his very life was the most signal instance of the providence which had watched over him. Much of the language of this Psalm reflects the experience of that time of anxiety and peril.

THE TWO RECENSIONS OF PSALM XVIII.

The existence of this Psalm in two forms or recensions, in the Psalter and in 2 Sam., is a fact of the highest interest and importance in its bearing on the history and character of the Massoretic text of the O. T. Two questions obviously arise: (1) how are the variations to be accounted for? and (2) which text is to be preferred as on the whole nearest to the original?

Defenders of the integrity of the Massoretic text have maintained that both recensions proceeded from the poet himself, and are both equally authentic. That in Samuel is supposed to be the original form; that in the Psalter is supposed to be a revision prepared by David himself, probably towards the close of his life, for public use. This hypothesis can neither be proved nor disproved, but few will now maintain it. It is certain that many of the variations are due to errors of transcription (see on *vv.* 4, 10, 41, 42, 50); and the great probability is that those which appear to be due to intentional alteration were the work of a later reviser (see on *vv.* 11, 32, 45).

Critics differ widely as to the relative value of the two texts. Both texts have unquestionably been affected by errors of transcription, and the text in 2 Sam. has suffered most from this cause, less care having been bestowed on the preservation of the historical books. On the other hand the text in the Psalter appears to the present editor to have been subjected to a literary revision at a later date, in which peculiar forms, which were possibly "licences of popular usage" have been replaced by the forms in ordinary use; unusual constructions simplified; archaisms and obscure expressions explained. If this view is correct, the text in Samuel best preserves the original features of the poem, while at the same time it frequently needs correction from the text in the Psalter.

To the chief Musician, *A Psalm* of David the servant of the LORD, who spake unto the LORD the words of this song in the day *that* the LORD delivered him from the hand of all his enemies, and from the hand of Saul: And he said,

I will love thee, O LORD, my strength. 18
The LORD *is* my rock, and my fortress, and my deliverer; 2
My God, my strength, in whom I will trust;
My buckler, and the horn of my salvation, *and* my high tower.

1—3. Introductory prelude, in which one title is heaped upon another to express all that experience had proved Jehovah to be to David.

1. *I will love thee*] **Fervently do I love thee**, a word occurring nowhere else in this form, and denoting tender and intimate affection. This verse is omitted in 2 Sam.

2. The imagery which David uses is derived from the features of a country abounding in cliffs and caves and natural strongholds, with which he had become familiar in his flight from Saul. *The rock*, or **cliff** (*sela*) where he had been so unexpectedly delivered from Saul (1 Sam. xxiii. 25—28): *the fortress* or **stronghold** in the wilderness of Judah or the fastnesses of En-gedi (1 Sam. xxii. 4, xxiii. 14, 19, 29, xxiv. 22); "the rocks of the wild goats" (1 Sam. xxiv. 2; 1 Chr. xi. 15); were all emblems of Him who had been throughout his true Refuge and Deliverer.

my God] *El*, and so in *vv.* 30, 32, 47. See note on v. 4.

my strength &c.] Lit., **my rock in whom I take refuge.** Here first in the Psalter occurs the title **Rock**, so frequently used to describe the strength, faithfulness, and unchangeableness of Jehovah. See *vv.* 31, 46; Deut. xxxii. 4, 15, 18, 30, 31; 1 Sam. ii. 2; Ps. xix. 14; xxviii. 1; &c. Here, as the relative clause shews, the special idea is that of an asylum in danger. Cp. xciv. 22; Deut. xxxii. 37.

my buckler &c.] As **my shield** He defends me: as *the horn of my salvation* He drives my enemies before Him and gives me the victory. The horn is a common symbol of irresistible strength, derived from horned animals, especially wild oxen. See Deut. xxxiii. 17; and note the use of the phrase in Lk. i. 69. Cp. Ps. xxviii. 7, 8.

my high tower] See note on ix. 9. 2 Sam. adds, "and my retreat, my saviour, who savest me from violence,"

3 I will call upon the LORD, who is *worthy* to be praised:
So shall I be saved from mine enemies.
4 The sorrows of death compassed me,
And the floods of ungodly men made me afraid.
5 The sorrows of hell compassed me about:
The snares of death prevented me.

3. Not merely a resolution or expression of confidence for the future (*I will call...so shall I be saved*); but the expression of a general conviction of God's faithfulness to answer prayer; **whensoever I call... then am I saved** &c. Cp. lvi. 9. This conviction is based on experience, and illustrated by what follows (*v*. 6).

worthy *to be praised*] Cp. xlviii. 1, xcvi. 4, cxiii. 3, cxlv. 3. Jehovah is the one object of Israel's praise (Deut. x. 21), and on Israel's praises He sits enthroned (Ps. xxii. 3). The keynote of worship is *Hallelujah*, 'praise ye Jah,' and the Hebrew title of the Psalter is *Tehillim*, i.e. *Praises*.

4—6. In forcible figures David pictures the extremity of need in which he cried for help, and not in vain. Again and again there had been 'but a step between him and death.' (1 Sam. xx. 3.) The perils to which he had been exposed are described as waves and torrents which threatened to engulf him or sweep him away: Sheol and Death are represented as hunters laying wait for his life with nets and snares.

4. *The sorrows of death*] Rather, as R.V., **The cords of death**. But the word has been wrongly introduced here from *v*. 5, and the true reading should be restored from 2 Sam.: **the waves** (lit. *breakers*) **of death**. This gives a proper parallelism to *floods* in the next line. But the reading *cords* must be very ancient, for Ps. cxvi. 3 appears to recognise it.

floods of ungodly men] More graphically the original, **torrents of destruction**, or, **ungodliness**. Destruction threatened him like a torrent swollen by a sudden storm, and sweeping all before it (Jud. v. 21). The Heb. word *belial*, lit. *worthlessness*, may mean *destruction*, physical mischief, as well as *wickedness*, moral mischief: and the context points rather to the former sense here. Death, Destruction, and Sheol, are indeed almost personified, as conspiring for his ruin.

5. Render with R.V.,
The cords of Sheol were round about me:
The snares of death came upon me.

The Heb. word rendered *sorrows* in the A.V. may no doubt have the meaning *pangs*, and is so rendered by the LXX (ὠδῖνες θανάτου... ὠ. ᾅδου, cp. Acts ii. 24). But the parallelism decides in favour of the rendering *cords*. Death and Sheol, the mysterious unseen world (see on vi. 5), are like hunters lying in wait for their prey with nooses and nets.

prevented] i.e. came before, confronted me (xvii. 13) with hostile intention. See note on *v*. 18.

In my distress I called upon the LORD,
And cried unto my God:
He heard my voice out of his temple,
And my cry came before him, *even* into his ears.
Then the earth shook and trembled;
The foundations also of the hills moved

6. *called...cried*] The tense in the original denotes *frequent* and *repeated* prayer. The text of 2 Sam. has *called* twice, no doubt by an error of transcription.

out of his temple] The palace-temple of heaven, where He sits enthroned. See on xi. 4. Cp. *v.* 16.

and my cry &c.] R.V., **and my cry before him came into his ears.** But the terse vigour of the text in 2 Sam. is preferable: "and my cry was in his ears." An alternative reading or an explanatory gloss has crept into the text here, to the detriment of the rhythm.

7—15. Forthwith David's prayer is answered by the Advent of Jehovah for the discomfiture of his enemies. He manifests Himself in earthquake and storm. The majestic though terrible phenomena of nature are the expression of His presence. Nature in its stern and awful aspect is a revelation of His judicial wrath. We may call this an 'ideal' description of a Theophany; for though it is possible that David refers to some occasion when his enemies were scattered by the breaking of a terrible storm (cp. Josh. x. 11; Jud. v. 20 f.; 1 Sam. vii. 10), we have no record of such an event having actually happened in his life; and in any case the picture is intended to serve as a description of God's providential interposition for his deliverance in general, and not upon any single occasion. His power was exerted as really and truly as if all these extraordinary natural phenomena had visibly attested His Advent. Compare the accounts of the Exodus and the Giving of the Law. See Ex. xix. 16—18; Jud. v. 4, 5; Ps. lxviii. 7, 8, lxxvii. 16—18: and cp. l. 2 ff., xcvii. 2 ff., cxiv; Is. xxix. 6, xxx. 27 ff., lxiv. 1 ff; Hab. iii. 3 ff.

Ps. xxix should be compared as illustrating David's sense of the grandeur and significance of natural phenomena.

The earthquake (*v.* 7); the distant lightnings (*v.* 8); the gathering darkness of the storm (*vv.* 9—11); the final outburst of its full fury (*vv.* 12—15); are pictured in regular succession.

7. The paronomasia of the original in the first line might be preserved by rendering, **Then the earth did shake and quake.**

the foundations &c.] Render: **And the foundations of the mountains trembled.** The strong mountains were shaken to their very bases. Cp. Is. xxiv. 18; Hab. iii. 6. The text in 2 Sam. has "the foundations of heaven;" heaven as well as earth trembled. Its 'foundations' may be the mountains on which the vault of heaven seems to rest: cp. "the pillars of heaven" (Job xxvi. 11): or more probably the universe is spoken of as a vast building, without any idea of applying the details of the metaphor precisely.

And were shaken, because he was wroth.
8 There went up a smoke out of his nostrils,
And fire out of his mouth devoured:
Coals were kindled by it.
9 He bowed the heavens also, and came down:
And darkness *was* under his feet.
10 And he rode upon a cherub, and did fly:

because he was wroth] The coming of Jehovah for the deliverance of His servant is necessarily a coming for the judgment of His enemies; and 'wrath' is that attribute of God's character which moves Him to judgment. Cp. Rev. vi. 16, 17.

8. The startling boldness of the language will be intelligible if the distinctive character of Hebrew symbolism is borne in mind. It is no "gross anthropomorphism," for the poet did not intend that the mind's eye should shape his figures into a concrete form. His aim is vividly to express the awfulness of this manifestation of God's wrath, and he does it by using figures which are intended to remain as purely mental conceptions, not to be realised as though God appeared in any visible shape. See some excellent remarks in Archbishop Trench's *Comm. on the Epistles to the Seven Churches*, p. 43.

a smoke] The outward sign of the pent-up fires of wrath. So anger is said *to smoke* (Ps. lxxiv. 1; lxxx. 4 *marg.*). This bold figure is suggested by the panting and snorting of an infuriated animal. See the description of the crocodile in Job xli. 19—21.

out of his nostrils] Cp. v. 15. *In his wrath* (R.V. marg.) is a possible rendering, but the context and parallelism are against it.

fire] The constant emblem of the consuming wrath of God. See Ex. xv. 7; Deut. xxxii. 22; Ps. xcvii. 3; Heb. xii. 29.

coals &c.] Or, **hot burning coals came out of it**: the fiery messengers of vengeance (cxl. 10).

9. The dark canopy of storm clouds, which is the pavement under His feet (Nah. i. 3), lowers as He descends to judgment. God is said to *come down* when He manifests His power in the world (Gen. xi. 7, xviii. 21; Is. lxiv. 1). The *darkness*, or better as R.V., **thick darkness**, in which He conceals Himself from human view, symbolises the mystery and awfulness of His Advent (Ex. xix. 16; xx. 21: 1 Kings viii. 12; Ps. xcvii. 2).

10. As the Shechinah, or mystic Presence of Jehovah in the cloud of glory, rested over the cherubim which were upon the "Mercy-seat" or covering of the ark (2 Sam. vi. 2; Ps. lxxx. 1; Heb. ix. 5), so here Jehovah is represented "riding upon a cherub," as the living throne on which He traverses space.

The Cherubim appear in Scripture (*a*) as the guardians of Paradise (Gen. iii. 24): (*b*) as sculptured or wrought figures in the Tabernacle and Temple (Ex. xxv. 17—22, xxvi. 1; 1 Kings vi. 23 ff.; vii. 29, 36): (*c*) in prophetic visions as the attendants of God (Ezek. x. 1 ff.; cp. Ezek. i; Is. vi; Rev. iv). The Cherubim of the Tabernacle and Temple

Yea, he did fly upon the wings of the wind.
He made darkness his secret place; 11
His pavilion round about him
Were dark waters *and* thick clouds of the skies.
At the brightness *that was* before him his thick clouds passed, 12
Hail-*stones* and coals of fire.
The LORD also thundered in the heavens, 13
And the Highest gave his voice;
Hail-*stones* and coals of fire.
Yea, he sent out his arrows, and scattered them; 14

seem to have been winged human figures, representing the angelic attendants who minister in God's Presence: those of Ezekiel's vision appear as composite figures (Ez. x. 20, 21), symbolical perhaps of all the powers of nature, which wait upon God and fulfil His Will.

yea, he did fly] R.V. **yea, he flew swiftly.** The Heb. word is a peculiar one, used of the *swooping* of birds of prey (Deut. xxviii. 49; Jer. xlviii. 40, xlix. 22). The reading "yea, he was seen" in 2 Sam. is an obvious corruption. The consonants of the two words are so nearly alike (וידא—וירא), that the rarer word would easily be altered into the more common one. For "the wings of the wind" cp. civ. 3.

11. R.V. **He made darkness his hiding-place, his pavilion round about him;**
Darkness of waters, thick clouds of the skies.
The darkness of the rain-charged storm-cloud is the tent in which Jehovah shrouds His Majesty. Cp. Job xxxvi. 29; Ps. xcvii. 2. The rhythm gains by the omission of *his hiding-place*, as in 2 Sam.; and the text there may be right in reading *gathering of waters* for *darkness of waters*.

12. The best rendering of this obscure verse seems to be:
From the brightness before him there passed through his thick clouds hailstones and coals of fire.
The flashes of lightning, accompanied by hail (Ex. ix. 23, 24), are as it were rays of the "unapproachable light" in which He dwells, piercing through the dense clouds which conceal Him. The text in 2 Sam. which has only, "at the brightness before him coals of fire were kindled," is evidently mutilated.

13. *and the Highest* &c.] R.V., **and the Most High uttered his voice.** *The Most High* is the title of God as the Supreme Ruler of the Universe. See vii. 17; and Additional Note II, p. 222. Thunder is the voice of God. See xxix. 3; Job xxxvii. 2—5. The words *hailstones and coals of fire* have no proper grammatical construction, and are wanting in the LXX and in 2 Sam. They seem to have been added here from *v.* 12 by an error of transcription.

14. And he sent out &c. (R.V.) gives the connexion better than *Yea*. Lightnings are Jehovah's arrows. Cp. lxxvii. 17; Hab. iii. 11.
Scattered them clearly refers to the enemies whose destruction was the object of this Divine interposition (*v.* 3).

And he shot out lightnings, and discomfited them.
15 Then the channels of waters were seen,
And the foundations of the world were discovered
At thy rebuke, O Lord,
At the blast of the breath of thy nostrils.
16 He sent from above, he took me,
He drew me out of many waters.
17 He delivered me from my strong enemy,
And from them which hated me: for they were too strong for me.
18 They prevented me in the day of my calamity:

and he shot out lightnings] Better, **yea, lightnings in abundance**; or, as R.V., **lightnings manifold**.
discomfited] A word denoting the confusion of a sudden panic, and used especially of supernatural defeat. Cp. Ex. xiv. 24 (R.V.); Josh. x. 10; Jud. iv. 15; 1 Sam. vii. 10. Ps. cxliv. 6, 7 is based on *vv.* 14, 16.

15. The waters of the sea retreat, its bed is seen, and the hidden bases of the world are laid bare, owning their Lord and Master, as of old at the Exodus when "He rebuked the Red Sea, and it was dried up." See Ex. xv. 8; Ps. cvi. 9; Nah. i. 4. Cp. too Matt. viii. 26. *Channels of* **the sea** (2 Sam.) is the preferable reading.
were discovered] i.e. as R.V., **were laid bare**, the original meaning of the word *discover*, which it generally retains in the A.V. Cp. xxix. 9.
at the blast &c.] Cp. *v.* 8.

16—19. The deliverance which was the object of Jehovah's manifestation of His power.

16. *He sent from above*] R.V., **He sent from on high**: but it seems better to render, **He reached forth from on high**, as the writer of Ps. cxliv. 7 understood the words. He stretched out His hand and caught hold of the sinking man, and drew him out of the floods of calamity which were overwhelming him (*v.* 4).
drew me] The word is found elsewhere only in Ex. ii. 10, to which there may be an allusion. 'He drew me out of the great waters of distress, as He drew Moses out of the waters of the Nile, to be the deliverer of His people.' For *many* or *great waters* as an emblem of danger, cp. xxxii. 6, lxvi. 12, lxix. 2, 3.

17. Figures are dropped, and David refers explicitly to his deliverance from his 'strong' or 'fierce' enemy Saul, and Saul's partisans who hated him, from whom but for this Divine intervention he could not have escaped, for **they were too mighty** for him.

18. *They prevented me*] **They came upon me** (R.V.), or, **encountered me**. *Prevent* is used in a sense which illustrates the transition from its original meaning *to go before* to its modern meaning *to hinder*. Cp. Milton's *Paradise Lost*, VI. 129:

But the LORD was my stay.
He brought me forth also into a large place;   19
He delivered me, because he delighted in me.
The LORD rewarded me according to my righteousness;   20
According to the cleanness of my hands hath he recompensed me.
For I have kept the ways of the LORD,   21
And have not wickedly departed from my God.
For all his judgments *were* before me,   22
And I did not put away his statutes from me.

      Half way he met
    His daring foe, at this prevention more
     Incens'd.

See Mr Aldis Wright's *Bible Word-Book*.
 my stay] My staff (xxiii. 4) and support. Cp. Is. x. 20.
 19. From the straits of peril he is brought forth into the freedom of safety. Cp. iv. 1, xxxi. 8.
 because he delighted in me] This was the ground of God's deliverance, and it now becomes the leading thought of the Psalm. Cp. xxii. 8, xli. 11; 2 Sam. xv. 26; and also Matt. iii. 17. The latter reference gains fresh significance if it is remembered that the theocratic king was called Jehovah's son (ii. 7; 2 Sam. vii. 14).
 20—23. The language is inspired by the courage of a childlike simplicity. It is no vainglorious boasting of his own merits, but a testimony to the faithfulness of Jehovah to guard and reward His faithful servants. David does not lay claim to a sinless righteousness, but to single-hearted sincerity in his devotion to God. Compare his own testimony (1 Sam. xxvi. 23), God's testimony (1 Kings xiv. 8), and the testimony of history (1 Kings xi. 4, xv. 5), to his essential integrity. Cp. vii. 8, xvii. 3, 4; and see Introd. p. lxix f.
 Is not this conscious rectitude, this "princely heart of innocence," a clear indication that the Psalm was written before his great fall?
 20. *rewarded me*] Or, **dealt with me**, for the primary idea of the word is not that of recompence, although this lies in the context. Cp. xiii. 6.
 the cleanness of my hands]=the innocence of my conduct. Cp. xxiv. 4, xxvi. 6.
 21. He goes on to substantiate the assertion of the preceding verse. Cp. the prayer of v. 8. Sin is in its nature a separation from God. Cp. Heb. iii. 12.
 22. God's commandments were continually present to his mind as the rule of his life. Cp. Deut. vi. 6—9; Ps. cxix. 30, 102; and contrast the spirit of the ungodly man in Ps. x. 5.
 and I did not put away &c.] In order to sin without compunction. This reading suits the parallelism best, and is preferable to that in 2 Sam., "and as for his statutes, I did not depart from them."

23 I was also upright before him,
And I kept myself from mine iniquity.
24 Therefore hath the LORD recompensed me according to my righteousness,
According to the cleanness of my hands in his eyesight.
25 With the merciful thou wilt shew thyself merciful;
With an upright man thou wilt shew thyself upright;
26 With the pure thou wilt shew thyself pure;
And with the froward thou wilt shew thyself froward.

23. *upright before him*] R.V., **perfect with him**, living in the fellowship of a sincere devotion. See note on xv. 2.

I kept myself from mine iniquity] I have watched over myself that I might not transgress, lest I should cherish any sin till it became a part of me. There is no reference to indwelling corruption or a besetting sin.

24—27. The law of God's dealings with men. The assertion of *v.* 20 is repeated as the conclusion to be drawn from the review of David's conduct in *vv.* 21—23, and is confirmed in *vv.* 25—27 by a statement of the general laws of God's moral government. His attitude towards men is and must be conditioned by their attitude towards Him. Cp. 1 Sam. ii. 30; xv. 23. There must be some moral correspondence in a man's character to enable God to reveal Himself to Him as 'merciful,' 'perfect,' 'pure.'

25. *With the merciful* &c.] The man whose conduct in life is governed by the spirit of lovingkindness will himself experience the lovingkindness of Jehovah. Cp. Matt. v. 7; vi. 12, 14, 15; and for the meaning of *merciful* see notes on iv. 3, xii. 1, and Additional Note I, p. 221.

with an upright man &c.] Rather as R.V., **with the perfect man thou wilt shew thyself perfect**. Singlehearted devotion will find a response of unswerving faithfulness.

The text in 2 Sam. has "the perfect hero," the man who is valiant in maintaining his own integrity. But the reading is questionable.

26. *With the pure* &c.] Lit. *one who purifies himself*, cp. 1 John iii. 3. Cp. xxiv. 4, lxxiii. 1. Matt. v. 8 is the N.T. commentary on the words.

and with the froward &c.] Better, as R.V., **and with the perverse thou wilt shew thyself froward**. The 'perverse' man, whose character is morally distorted, is given over by God to follow his own crooked ways, till they bring him to destruction. God must needs be at cross purposes with the wicked, frustrating their plans, and punishing their wickedness. See Lev. xxvi. 23, 24; Job v. 12, 13; Is. xxix. 9 ff.; Prov. iii. 34; Rom. i. 28; Rev. xxii. 11; and for an illustration comp. the history of Balaam (Num. xxii. 20).

For thou wilt save the afflicted people; 27
But wilt bring down high looks.
For thou wilt light my candle: 28
The LORD my God will enlighten my darkness.
For by thee I have run *through* a troop; 29
And by my God have I leaped over a wall.
As for God, his way *is* perfect: 30
The word of the LORD is tried:
He *is* a buckler to all those that trust in him.

27. *For thou wilt save* &c.] 2 Sam. has the better reading, "and the afflicted people thou wilt save."

the afflicted people] Or, **lowly**: those who have learnt humility in the school of suffering. See note on ix. 12, and cp. Zeph. iii. 12.

but wilt bring down &c.] **But haughty eyes wilt thou bring low.** "Haughty eyes" are one of the seven things which are an abomination to Jehovah (Prov. vi. 17). Cp. Is. ii. 11, 12, 17.

The parallel text in 2 Sam. has, "Thine eyes are upon the haughty, whom thou wilt bring low."

28—30. These general principles of God's dealing with men are confirmed by David's own experience.

28. **For thou dost light my lamp,**
    Jehovah my God maketh my darkness bright.

The burning lamp is a natural metaphor for the continuance of life and prosperity, derived, it is said, from the Oriental practice of keeping a light constantly burning in the tent or house, which symbolised the maintenance of the life and prosperity of the family. Cp. Job xviii. 6; Prov. xiii. 9. The second line of the verse indicates that the figure here refers to the preservation of David's own life, rather than to the permanence of his dynasty, as in cxxxii. 17; 1 Kings xi. 36, xv. 4.

The text of 2 Sam. has "For thou art my lamp, O LORD." Cp. Ps. xxvii. 1.

29. **For by thee I run after a troop,**
    And by my God I leap over a wall.

The language is general, but it seems to contain a reminiscence of two memorable events in David's life: the successful pursuit of the predatory 'troop' of Amalekites which had sacked Ziklag (1 Sam. xxx; in *vv.* 8, 15, 23 the same word *troop* is used of the Amalekites): and the capture of Zion, effected with such unexpected ease that he seemed to have leapt over the walls which its defenders boasted were impregnable (2 Sam. v. 6—8).

The rendering *run after* is preferable to *break* (A.V. marg.). The point is the speed of the pursuit, not the completeness of the defeat.

30. *As for God* (El), *his way is perfect*, flawless and without blemish, like His work (Deut. xxxii. 4), and His law (Ps. xix. 7): *the word*, or promise, *of the LORD is tried*, refined like pure gold, without dross of uncertainty or insincerity (Ps. xii. 6, cxix. 140): **he is a**

31 For who *is* God save the LORD?
  Or who *is* a rock save our God?
32 *It is* God that girdeth me *with* strength,
  And maketh my way perfect.
33 He maketh my feet like hinds' *feet*,
  And setteth me upon my high places.
34 He teacheth my hands to war,

shield to all them that take refuge in him (*v.* 2). The last two lines are quoted in Prov. xxx. 5.

31—34. The unique character of Jehovah, to whom alone David owes all that he is. Observe how he recognises that the advantages of physical strength and energy, important qualifications in times when the king was himself the leader of the people in battle, were gifts of God; yet that it was not these which saved him and made him victorious, but Jehovah's care and help (*vv.* 35 ff.). Cp. 1 Sam. xvii. 34—36.

**31. For who is a God save Jehovah?
And who is a Rock beside our God?**

Jehovah alone is *Elōah*, a God to be feared and reverenced. The singular *Elōah* is found instead of the usual plural *Elohim* elsewhere in the Psalter only in l. 22; cxiv. 7; cxxxix. 19. It is used frequently in Job; in Deut. xxxii. 15, 17; Is. xliv. 8; Hab. i. 11, iii. 3; and in a few other passages.

For *Rock* see note on *v.* 2; and for similar declarations of the unique character of Jehovah cp. Deut. xxxii. 31; 1 Sam. ii. 2; 2 Sam. vii. 22.

32. It is *God*] R.V., **The God** [*El*] **that girdeth me with strength.** Cp. *v.* 39; xciii. 1; 1 Sam. ii. 4.

maketh my way perfect] Removing the obstacles which might have hindered me from the complete accomplishment of the career He has marked out for me. Observe the analogy between the perfection of God's way (*v.* 30) and His servant's. Cp. Matt. v. 48 for a higher development of the same thought.

The traditional reading (*Qrî*) in 2 Sam. is, "God is my strong fortress, and guideth my way in perfectness"; while the written text (*Kthībh*) has, "he guideth the perfect in his way": but the exact meaning is obscure. A simpler word has apparently been substituted in the text of the Psalm.

33. *like hinds' feet*] The hind, like the gazelle, was a type of the agility, swiftness, and sure-footedness which were indispensable qualifications in ancient warfare. Cp. 2 Sam. ii. 18; 1 Chron. xii. 8.

setteth me upon my high places] The metaphor of the hind, bounding freely over the hills, is continued. David's high places are the mountain strongholds, the occupation of which secured him in the possession of the country. Cp. Deut. xxxii. 13; and Hab. iii. 19, which is a reminiscence of this passage and Deut. xxxiii. 29.

34. The first line is borrowed in cxliv. 1.

So that a bow of steel is broken *by* mine arms.
Thou hast also given me the shield of thy salvation : 35
And thy right hand hath holden me up,
And thy gentleness hath made me great.
Thou hast enlarged my steps under me, 36
That my feet did not slip.
I have pursued mine enemies, and overtaken them : 37
Neither did I turn again till they were consumed.
I have wounded them that they were not able to rise : 38
They are fallen under my feet.
For thou hast girded me *with* strength unto the battle : 39
Thou hast subdued under me those that rose up against me.

so that a bow of steel &c.] R.V., **so that mine arms do bend a bow of brass**. The ability to bend a metal bow (cp. Job xx. 24) was a sign of supereminent strength. Readers of the *Odyssey* will recall Ulysses' bow, which no one but himself could bend (Hom. *Od.* XXI. 409).

35—38. But it is not to his own valour that his successes are to be ascribed.

35. Jehovah's saving help has been his defence—cp. *vv.* 2, 3, 46, and Eph. vi. 17:—Jehovah's right hand supports him that his foot should not slip (xx. 2; xciv. 18): Jehovah's **condescension**—lit. *meekness* or *lowliness*—makes him great. The word is a bold one to apply to God, but its meaning is explained by cxiii. 5, 6; Is. lvii. 15; and the choice of the humble shepherd boy to be the king of Israel was a signal example of this characteristic of the Divine action.
Loving correction (P.B.V.) is a conflate rendering combining παιδεία (*discipline*) from the LXX, and mansuetudo (*gentleness*) from Jerome. The second line of the verse is omitted in 2 Sam.; and *thine answering* (i.e. of prayer) is read in place of *thy condescension*.

36. *enlarged my steps* &c.] Given me free space for unobstructed movement (cp. *v.* 19; Prov. iv. 12), and the power to advance with firm, unwavering steps.

37. Cp. Ex. xv. 9. 2 Sam. reads *destroyed* for *overtaken*.

38. *I have wounded them*] Rather, **I have smitten them through** (Deut. xxxiii. 11; Job xxvi. 12). 2 Sam. has "Yea I consumed them, and smote them through," the first verb being probably a gloss.

The R.V. renders the verbs in *vv.* 37, 38 as futures (*I will pursue*, &c.), but it is best to regard these verses, like those which precede and those which follow, as a retrospect. See Additional Note IV, p. 223.

39—42. Thus God gave him victory over all his enemies.

39. Cp. *v.* 32 *a*.
those that rose up against me] Enemies in general (Ex. xv. 7; Deut. xxxiii. 11), not necessarily rebellious subjects, though the word is specially applicable to them (iii. 1).

40 Thou hast also given me the necks of mine enemies;
That I might destroy them that hate me.
41 They cried, but *there was* none to save *them:*
Even unto the LORD, but he answered them not.
42 Then did I beat them small as the dust before the wind:
I did cast them out as the dirt in the streets.
43 Thou hast delivered me from the strivings of the people;
And thou hast made me the head of the heathen:
A people *whom* I have not known shall serve me.

40. Yea mine enemies hast thou made to turn their backs unto me,
And as for them that hated me, I cut them off.
The first line means that his enemies were put to flight before him (Ex. xxiii. 27), not (as the A.V. seems to imply) that he planted his foot on their necks in token of triumph (Josh. x. 24).

41. *They cried*] Cp. *v.* 6. The Heb. text in 2 Sam. has *they looked* for help (Is. xvii. 7, 8), but the LXX supports the reading *cried*, which is certainly right. There is only the difference of one letter in the consonants of the two words (ישויעו–ישעו).

Even *unto the LORD*] At first sight this might seem to indicate that the foes referred to were Israelites. But it is better to understand it of the heathen. After vainly seeking help from their own gods, in the extremity of their despair they cry to Jehovah. Cp. 1 Sam. v. 12; Jonah iii. 7 ff.

42. Two figures are combined to express the annihilation of David's enemies. They were, as it were, pounded to dust (2 Kings xiii. 7), and then scattered like that dust driven before the wind. Cp. Is. xxix. 5; xli. 2. 2 Sam. reads only "as the dust of the earth."

I did cast them out &c.] Flung them away as worthless refuse (Zeph. i. 17). But **the mire of the streets** is usually spoken of as trampled under foot (Is. x. 6; Mic. vii. 10; Zech. x. 5), and it suits the parallelism better to read with the LXX and 2 Sam., *I did stamp them* (Mic. iv. 13). The variation is again due to the confusion of similar letters (ארקם–אדקם). The addition at the end of the verse in 2 Sam., "and did spread them abroad," is probably a gloss.

43—45. The establishment of David's dominion at home and abroad.

43. *from the strivings of the people*] 2 Sam. has "from the strivings of my people," and the reference seems to be to the civil war and internal dissension which disturbed the early years of David's reign, while Saul's house still endeavoured to maintain its position. See 2 Sam. iii. 1. Through all these conflicts he had been safely brought, and made **the head of the nations,** supreme among surrounding peoples. See 2 Sam. viii. 1—14; Ps. ii. 8.

thou hast made me] In 2 Sam. "thou hast preserved me to be the head of the nations."

a people whom *I have not known shall serve me*] Rather, **a people**

As soon as they hear *of me*, they shall obey me: 44
The strangers shall submit themselves unto me.
The strangers shall fade away, 45
And be afraid out of their close places.
The LORD liveth; and blessed *be* my rock; 46
And let the God of my salvation be exalted.
It is God that avengeth me, 47

whom I knew not did serve me. There is no reason for the sudden transition of the A.V. to the future here and in the two following verses. David is still thankfully recounting how God had raised him to his present eminence. There may be a special reference to the subjugation of the Syrians and their allies, whom he might well describe as "a people whom he had not known." See 2 Sam. viii. 6; x. 19.

**44. As soon as they heard of me they offered me obedience,
Strangers came cringing unto me.**

At the mere report of David's victories foreign nations offered their allegiance, as for example Toi of Hamath. See 2 Sam. viii. 9 ff. The word rendered *submit themselves*, marg. *yield feigned obedience*, denotes originally the unwilling homage paid by the vanquished to their conqueror. Cp. Deut. xxxiii. 29; Ps. lxvi. 3; lxxxi. 15.

In 2 Sam. the order of the clauses is inverted.

**45. The strangers faded away,
And came trembling out of their fastnesses.**

Their strength and courage failed like a withering leaf or a fading flower (Is. xxviii. 1, 4), and they surrendered at discretion to the triumphant invader. Cp. Mic. vii. 17; 1 Sam. xiv. 11. The obscure reading in 2 Sam. may mean "came limping out of their fastnesses"; a picture of the exhausted defenders of the fortress dragging themselves along with difficulty and reluctant to lay down their arms before the conqueror. The LXX gives this rendering (ἐχώλαναν) in the Psalm.

46—50. Concluding thanksgiving and doxology.

46. *The LORD liveth*] Life is the essential attribute of Jehovah. He is the Living God in contrast to the dead idols of the heathen. The experience of David's life is summed up in these words. It had been to him a certain proof that God is the living, active Ruler of the world. Cp. Josh. iii. 10.

and let &c.] R.V., **and exalted be the God of my salvation.** Cp. xxiv. 5. 2 Sam. reads, "the God of the rock of my salvation."

47. Render:
**Even the God that executed vengeance for me,
And subdued peoples under me.**

Vengeance is the prerogative of God (xciv. 1); it is His vindication of the righteousness and integrity of His servants. Such a thanksgiving as this does not shew a spirit of vindictiveness in David, but is a recognition that God had 'pleaded his cause,' and maintained the right. God had avenged him for the cruel injustice of Saul (1 Sam.

And subdueth the people under me.
48 He delivereth me from mine enemies:
Yea, thou liftest me up above those that rise up against me:
Thou hast delivered me from the violent man.
49 Therefore will I give thanks unto thee, O LORD, among the heathen,
And sing *praises* unto thy name.
50 Great deliverance giveth he to his king;

xxiv. 12); for the contemptuous insults of Nabal (1 Sam. xxv. 39); for the factious opposition of those who refused to acknowledge him as king in spite of his Divine call (2 Sam. iv. 8).

The second line of the verse refers, like *v*. 43, to success in overcoming internal as well as external opposition to his rule. Cp. cxliv. 2. It is not, however, the boast of a triumphant despot, but the thanksgiving of a ruler who recognised the vital importance of union for the prosperity of Israel, and knew that the task of reconciling the discordant elements in the nation was beyond his own unaided powers.

For *subdueth* 2 Sam. has ' bringeth down.'

48. My deliverer from mine enemies;
Yea, thou didst set me on high from them that rose up against me,
From the man of violence didst thou rescue me.

My deliverer, as in *v*. 2. 2 Sam. has "that bringeth me forth." **The man of violence** might mean men of violence in general, but it is more natural to regard it as a reference to Saul. Cp. cxl. 1, 4, 11.

49. The celebration of Jehovah's faithfulness to His servant is not to be confined within the narrow limits of Israel. His praise is to be proclaimed among the nations, which, as they are brought under the dominion of His people, may eventually be brought to the knowledge of Jehovah. Cp. xcvi. 3, 10. This verse is quoted by St. Paul in Rom. xv. 9 (together with Deut. xxxii. 43; Ps. cxvii. 1; Is. xi. 10), in proof that the Old Testament anticipated the admission of the Gentiles to the blessings of salvation.

50. These closing words may be due to a later poet, who thus sums up the lessons of the Psalm. But they may well be David's own. He drops the first person, and surveys his own life from without, in the light of the great promise of 2 Sam. vii. 12—16. These are the deliverances Jehovah has wrought for the king of His choice; this is a sample of the lovingkindness which He has shewn to His Anointed, and will shew to his seed for evermore. The words reach forward to the perfect life, and the world-wide victories, of the Christ, the Son of David.

Great deliverance &c.] Lit. *He magnifieth the salvations of his king*. Cp. xx. 6. The *K'thîbh* and the Versions in 2 Sam. have the same reading: but the *Qrî*, which the A.V. follows, has "He is a tower of deliverance for his king." Cp. Ps. lxi. 3; Prov. xviii. 10.

And sheweth mercy to his anointed,
To David, and to his seed for evermore.

The consonants of the two words, as originally written defectively and without vowels, are identical.
mercy] **lovingkindness.** Cp. xvii. 7; 2 Sam. vii. 15.

PSALM XIX.

This Psalm consists of two distinct parts. The first part celebrates the revelation of the Power and Majesty of God in Nature, the universal and unceasing testimony of the heavens to their Creator (*vv.* 1—6). The second part celebrates the moral beauty and beneficent power of Jehovah's 'Law' in its manifold elements and aspects (*vv.* 7—11); and the Psalmist, viewing his own life in the sight of this holy Law, concludes with a prayer for pardon, preservation, and acceptance (*vv.* 12—14).

The identity of the Lawgiver of Israel with the Creator of the Universe was a fundamental principle of Old Testament religion (Amos iv. 13; v. 7, 8): and the Psalm is certainly intended to suggest a comparison between the universal revelation of God's majesty in creation, manifest to all mankind (Rom. i. 19, 20), and the special revelation of His moral character and of man's duty in His 'Law,' given to Israel only. The use of the Divine names is significant. In the first part God is styled *El*, as the God of power, the Creator: in the second part He is styled Jehovah (seven times repeated), the Name by which He made Himself known as the covenant God of Israel, the God of grace and redemption.

Were the two parts the work of one poet? Form, style, and tone point to a negative answer. No doubt the same poet might have adopted a fresh rhythm to correspond to the change of subject; and the abruptness of the transition from one part to the other cannot be pressed as an argument against unity of authorship, for it is quite in accordance with the spirit of Hebrew poetry to place two thoughts side by side, and leave the reader to draw the intended inference. But the closest parallel to the first part is Ps. viii: to the second, Ps. cxix.

We know from the example of Ps. cviii that no scruples were felt in combining parts of different poems into a new whole; and it seems most probable that the second part of the Psalm was written as a supplement to part of an already existing poem, or that portions of two poems were combined, with a view of suggesting the comparison between God's two great volumes of Nature and the Scriptures.

Each of these volumes has its special lessons. Rightly interpreted, they can never be in conflict. "It is written," says Lord Bacon, "*Coeli enarrant gloriam Dei;* but it is not written *coeli enarrant voluntatem Dei:* but of that it is said, *ad legem et testimonium: si non fecerint secundum verbum istud &c.*" (*Advancement of Learning*, II. 25, 3).

"The starry sky above me," said Kant, "and the moral law in me,... are two things which fill the soul with ever new and increasing admiration and reverence." Wallace's *Kant*, p. 53.

What does the Psalmist mean by "the law of Jehovah," which he describes in different aspects as testimony, precepts, commandment, fear, judgments? It is the moral law embodied in the Pentateuch, but not this exclusively, but all the priestly and prophetic teaching by which Jehovah's will was made known. The "Law" is to the writer no burdensome and vexatious restriction of liberty, but a gracious reflection of the holiness of God, designed to lead man in the way of life and peace. Yet already in the closing verse we have a hint of the sterner function of the Law as an instrument for teaching man to know his own sinfulness (Rom. iii. 20), and to feel the need of an effectual atonement (Rom. viii. 3).

Ps. xix is one of the Proper Psalms for Christmas Day. The Revelation of God in Nature, and the Revelation of God in His Word, prepared the way for the crowning Revelation of God in the Incarnation (Bp. Perowne).

To the chief Musician, A Psalm of David.

19 The heavens declare the glory of God;
And the firmament sheweth his handywork.
2 Day unto day uttereth speech,
And night unto night sheweth knowledge.

1—6. The universal revelation of God in Nature.

1. "The glory of the LORD" denotes (1) that visible manifestation of His Presence by which He was wont to reveal Himself to Israel, the *Shechinah* as it was called in later times (Ex. xvi. 7, 10; xxxiii. 22; Rom. ix. 4): and (2) in a wider sense, as here, the glory of God is the unique majesty of His Being as it is revealed to man, that manifestation of His Deity which the creature should recognise with reverent adoration. All creation is a revelation of God, but the heavens in their vastness, splendour, order, and mystery are the most impressive reflection of His greatness and majesty. The simplest observer can read the message; but how much more emphatic and significant has it become through the discoveries of modern astronomy!

the firmament] Lit. *the expanse:* the vault of heaven, spread out over the earth (Gen. i. 6 ff.; Job xxxvii. 18), proclaims what He has done and can do.

2. This proclamation is continuous and unceasing. "Dies diem docet." Each day, each night, hands on the message to its successor in an unbroken tradition. Day and night are mentioned separately, for each has a special message entrusted to it: the day tells of splendour, power, beneficence; the night tells of vastness, order, mystery, beauty, repose. They are "like the two parts of a choir, chanting forth alternately the praises of God." (Bp. Horne.)

uttereth] Lit. *pours out*, in copious abundance.

sheweth] Or, *proclaimeth*, a different word from that of *v.* 1. *Knowledge* is "that which may be known of God" (Rom. i. 19). "Aristotle

There is no speech nor language, 3
Where their voice is not heard.
Their line is gone out through all the earth, 4

says[1], that should a man live under ground, and there converse with works of art and mechanism, and should afterwards be brought up into the open day, and see the several glories of the heaven and earth, he would immediately pronounce them the works of such a being as we define God to be." Addison in *The Spectator*, No. 465.
    3. (*a*) The rendering of A.V. means that the message of the heavens reaches all nations of every language alike, and is intelligible to them. But the Heb. words rendered *speech* and *language* will not bear this explanation.
    (*b*) The rendering
              It is not a speech or words
              Whose voice is unintelligible,
is that of most of the ancient versions (LXX, Aq., Symm., Theod., Vulg., Jer.). But it does not satisfy the parallelism, and it is unnatural to refer *their voice* to 'speech and words' rather than to 'the heavens.'
    (*c*) It is best to render (cp. R.V.)
        There is neither speech nor words,
        Unheard is their voice.
Their message though real is inarticulate. Thus understood, the verse qualifies *v*. 2, and is in close connexion with *v*. 4. Theirs is a silent eloquence, yet it reaches from one end of the world to the other. Comp. Addison's paraphrase:
        "What though in solemn silence all
        Move round the dark terrestrial ball?
        What though nor real voice nor sound
        Amid their radiant orbs be found?
        In reason's ear they all rejoice,
        And utter forth a glorious voice,
        For ever singing, as they shine,
        'The hand that made us is divine'."
    4. This proclamation is universal. The phrase *Their line is gone out* &c., is to be explained by Jer. xxxi. 39; Zech. i. 16. The measuring line marks the limits of possession. The whole earth is the sphere throughout which the heavens have to proclaim their message. The rendering of P.B.V. *their sound* follows LXX, Vulg., Symm., Jer., Syr., but it is not justifiable as a rendering of the present text, though it may be got by an easy emendation.
    A wider application is given to these words by St Paul in Rom. x. 18. But his use of them is not merely the adoption of a convenient phrase. It implies a comparison of the universality of the proclamation of the Gospel with the universality of the proclamation of God's glory in Nature.

---

[1] The passage is a fragment of Aristotle's *Dialogue on Philosophy* quoted by Cicero *De Natura Deorum*, ii. 37. 95, and is well worth referring to.

And their words to the end of the world.
In them hath he set a tabernacle for the sun,
5 Which *is* as a bridegroom coming out of his chamber,
And rejoiceth as a strong *man* to run a race.
6 His going forth *is* from the end of the heaven,
And his circuit unto the ends of it:
And there is nothing hid from the heat thereof.

7 The law of the LORD *is* perfect, converting the soul:
The testimony of the LORD *is* sure, making wise the simple.

In them &c.] How naturally the poet singles out the Sun as the chief witness to God's glory, and personifies it as though it were a king or hero, for whose abode the Creator has fixed a tent in the heavens.

5. Thence he comes forth morning by morning like the bridegroom in all the splendour of his bridal attire, in all the freshness of youthful vigour and buoyant happiness (Is. lxi. 10; lxii. 5): like the hero exulting in the consciousness of strength, and eager to put it to the proof. Cp. Jud. v. 31.

6. The beneficent influences of his light and heat are universally felt.

7—11. Yet more wonderful than this declaration of God's glory, more beneficent than the sun's life-giving light and heat, is Jehovah's revelation of His will, which quickens and educates man's moral nature. Its essential characteristics and its beneficent influences are described with an enthusiastic and loving admiration.

Note the peculiar rhythm of *vv.* 7—9, in which each line is divided by a well-marked caesura. Cp. Lam. i. 1 ff.

7. *The law of the LORD*] Instruction, teaching, doctrine, are the ideas connected with the word *torah*, rendered *law*. See on i. 2. Like Jehovah's work (Deut. xxxii. 4), and His way (Ps. xviii. 30), it is *perfect*, complete, flawless; without defect or error; a guide which can neither mislead nor fail. Observe that the name JEHOVAH now takes the place of *God* (*v.* 1); for we have entered the sphere of the special revelation to Israel.

converting the soul] Rather, as R.V., **restoring the soul**; refreshing and invigorating man's true self (cp. xxiii. 3); like food to the hungry (Lam. i. 11, 19); like comfort to the sorrowful and afflicted (Lam. i. 16; Ruth iv. 15).

the testimony] The 'law,' regarded as bearing witness to Jehovah's will, and man's duty (Ex. xxv. 16, 21). It is *sure*, not variable or uncertain. Cp. xciii. 5, cxi. 7.

the simple] A character often mentioned in Proverbs (i. 4, &c.): the man whose mind is *open* to the entrance of good or evil. He has not closed his heart against instruction, but he has no fixed principle to repel temptation. He needs to be made wise. Cp. cxix. 130; 2 Tim. iii. 15.

The statutes of the LORD *are* right, rejoicing the heart: 8
The commandment of the LORD *is* pure, enlightening the eyes.
The fear of the LORD *is* clean, enduring for ever: 9
The judgments of the LORD *are* true *and* righteous altogether.
More to be desired *are they* than gold, yea, than much fine 10
gold:
Sweeter also than honey and the honeycomb.
Moreover by them *is* thy servant warned: 11
And in keeping of them *there is* great reward.
Who can understand *his* errors? 12
Cleanse thou me from secret *faults*.
Keep back thy servant also from presumptuous *sins;* 13

8. *The statutes*] Rather, as R.V., **the precepts**, the various special injunctions in which man's obligations are set forth. These *make glad the heart* with the joy of moral satisfaction.
pure] An epithet applied to the sun, Cant. vi. 10. "The law is light" (Prov. vi. 23), and light-giving. Cp. cxix. 105, 130; Eph. i. 18.
9. *The fear of the LORD*] Another synonym for the 'law,' inasmuch as its aim and object is to implant the fear of God in men's hearts. (Deut. iv. 10). It is *clean* or *pure* (xii. 6), in contrast to the immoralities of heathenism. It is like Jehovah Himself (Hab. i. 13), and like Him, it *stands fast for ever* (cii. 26); for "righteousness is immortal" (Wisd. i. 15).
The judgments] Decisions, ordinances. These *are truth* (John xvii. 17); one and all they are in accordance with the standard of absolute justice (Deut. iv. 8).
10. Such is the law in all its parts; a treasure to be coveted; the sweetest of enjoyments when received into the heart. Cp. cxix. 72, 103, 127.
the honeycomb] Lit. *the droppings of the honeycomb*, the purest honey which drops naturally from the comb.
11. The Psalmist, as Jehovah's servant, *lets himself be warned* by the law. Cp. Ezek. xxxiii. 4 ff.
great reward] Cp. Prov. xxii. 4; 1 Tim. iv. 8, vi. 6.

12—14. The contemplation of this holy law leads the Psalmist to express his personal need of preservation and guidance.
12. More exactly:
   Errors who can discern?
   From hidden (faults) clear thou me.
Who can be aware of the manifold lapses of ignorance or inadvertence? Acquit me, do not hold me guilty in respect of them.
13. For sins committed 'in error,' (A.V. *through ignorance*) and for 'hidden' offences, the ceremonial law provided an atonement (Lev. iv. 1 ff., 13 ff., v. 2 ff.; Num. xv. 22 ff.); but for sins committed 'with a

Let them not have dominion over me :
Then shall I be upright,
And I shall be innocent from *the* great transgression.
14 Let the words of my mouth,
And the meditation of my heart, be acceptable in thy sight,
O LORD, my strength, and my redeemer.

high hand,' in a spirit of proud defiance, there was no atonement (Num. xv. 30, 31). From such *presumptuous sins* he prays to be restrained, as David was once restrained from a desperate act of revenge (1 Sam. xxv. 39). Such sins soon become a man's masters, and he becomes their slave (John viii. 34). They *rule over him*, instead of his ruling over them (Gen. iv. 7). For *presumptuous*, lit. *proud*, cp. *presumptuously*, lit. *in pride*, Ex. xxi. 14; Deut. xvii. 12, 13.

Then (he continues) if Thou dost grant me this grace, **shall I be perfect**, heart-whole with Thee (xviii. 23), **and I shall be clear from great transgression**, innocent of the deadly sin of rebellion (Is. i. 2) and apostasy from Jehovah.

But the word rendered '*presumptuous* sins' everywhere else means '*proud* men,' and this may be its meaning here. The Psalmist prays to be saved from the oppression of the proud and godless, lest he should be tempted even to deny God. Cp. Ps. cxix. 121, 122; and note how often "the proud" are mentioned in that Psalm, and how the thought of faithfulness to the Law in the teeth of mockery and persecution is emphasised (*vv*. 51, 69, 78, 85—87).

14. *be acceptable*] An expression borrowed from the laws of sacrifice. See Lev. i. 3, 4 (R.V.); cp. Ex. xxviii. 38. Prayer, "uttered or unexpressed," is a spiritual sacrifice. Cp. cxli. 2; Hos. xiv. 2.

The P.B.V., *be always acceptable*, is from the LXX. The Heb. for *always* would be *tāmīd*. If this word may be restored to the text on the authority of the LXX, it would suggest a reference to the daily sacrifice which was to be offered *continually* (Ex. xxix. 38 ff.), and in later times was called the *Tāmīd*.

my strength &c.] **My rock** (see on xviii. 2), and *my redeemer*, delivering me from the tyranny of enemies and the bondage of sin, as He delivered Israel from the bondage of Egypt. Cp. Ex. xv. 13; Is. lxiii. 9.

PSALM XX.

The 20th and 21st Psalms are closely related in structure and contents. Both are liturgical Psalms: the first is an intercession, the second a thanksgiving. In both the king, the representative of Jehovah and the representative of the people, is the prominent figure; and the salvation or victory which Jehovah bestows upon him is the leading thought.

In Ps. xx the king is preparing to go out to battle against formidable enemies. Before starting he offers solemn sacrifices, and commits his cause to Jehovah, the sole Giver of victory. The Psalm was apparently intended to be sung while the sacrifice was being offered. It breathes a spirit of simple faith in Jehovah's aid. Israel's enemies rely upon their material forces: Israel trusts in Jehovah alone.

In Psalm xxi the campaign is over. The victory is won. The people with their king are again assembled to give thanks for the salvation which Jehovah has wrought for them; and in the flush of victory they anticipate with confidence the future triumphs of their king.

There is little to determine the particular occasion of these Psalms. The title of Ps. xx in the Syriac Version refers it to David's war with the Ammonites: and some commentators see in xx. 7 an allusion to the chariots and horses of the Syrians who were in alliance with the Ammonites (2 Sam. viii. 4, x. 18); and in xxi. 3, 9 allusions to the circumstances of the capture of Rabbah (2 Sam. xii. 30, 31). Others think that the king may have been Asa (2 Chr. xiv. 9), or Uzziah (2 Chr. xxvi). The personal importance of the king as the leader of the army, and the spirit of simple trust in Jehovah, not in material forces, point to an early rather than a late date. If the Psalms refer to David, it is natural to suppose that they were written by some poet other than the king himself.

Ps. xx consists of two stanzas with a concluding verse.

i. The people's intercession for the king, sung by the congregation, or by the Levites on their behalf, while the sacrifice was being offered (1—5).

ii. A priest or prophet (or possibly the king himself) declares the acceptance of the sacrifice, and confidently anticipates victory (6—8).

iii. Concluding prayer of the whole congregation (9).

To the chief Musician, A Psalm of David.

The LORD hear thee in the day of trouble; **20**
The name of the God of Jacob defend thee;
Send thee help from the sanctuary,   2

1—5. The people's prayer for their king's success.

1. *hear thee*] R.V., **answer thee**, and so in *vv*. 6, 9.

the day of trouble] Or *distress*, when *adversaries* (a cognate word) press him hard. The impending campaign is specially, though not exclusively, meant. Cp. xlvi. 1; Num. x. 9.

The name &c.] May the God of Jacob prove Himself to be all that His Name implies (see on v. 11): may He Who is a tower of refuge (ix. 9, xviii. 2) **set thee up on high** in safety from thy enemies. Cp. Prov. xviii. 10. *God of Jacob* is often synonymous with *God of Israel* (xlvi. 7, 11); yet the choice of this name cannot but suggest the thought of Jehovah's providential care for the great ancestor of the nation. Cp. the exactly similar language of Gen. xxxv. 3: "God, who *answered me in the day of my distress;*" and the references to Jacob's history in Hos. xii. 4, 5.

2. *the sanctuary*] Here, as the parallel *out of Zion* shews, the earthly sanctuary is meant. See notes on iii. 4, xiv. 7; and cp. *v*. 6.

And strengthen thee out of Zion;
3 Remember all thy offerings,
And accept thy burnt sacrifice.   Selah.
4 Grant thee according to thine own heart,
And fulfil all thy counsel.
5 We will rejoice in thy salvation,
And in the name of our God we will set up *our* banners:
The LORD fulfil all thy petitions.
6 Now know I that the LORD saveth his anointed;

strengthen]   Lit. *support;* the same word as *hath holden me up* in xviii. 35.

3.   May He remember all the offerings by which in past time the king has expressed his self-devotion and his dependence on Jehovah, and accept those by which he is now consecrating the present expedition. For sacrifice before a war see 1 Sam. vii. 9, 10, xiii. 9—12; and cp. the phrase *to sanctify a war* (Jer. vi. 4, R.V. marg.).   *Offering* properly denotes the so-called *meal-offering*, which accompanied the *burnt-offering*.

Remember]   Possibly an allusion to the *memorial*, or part of the meal-offering which was burnt by the priest on the altar, as it were bringing the worshippers for whom it was offered to God's remembrance (Lev. ii. 2, 9, 16; Acts x. 4).

accept]   Lit., *regard as fat*.   The fat, as the choicest part, was Jehovah's portion, and was always to be burnt (Lev. iii. 3 ff. 16).   Less probable is the alternative in A.V. marg., *turn to ashes*, by fire from heaven (Lev. ix. 24).

4.   *according to thine own heart*]   The literal rendering of the Heb. The R.V. restores the more graceful rendering of P.B.V., *thy heart's desire;* but the expression is a different one from that in xxi. 2.

counsel]   In the war.   Cp. 2 Sam. xvi. 20; 2 Kings xviii. 20.

5.   The prayer is still continued.   *Let us* (or, *That we may*) *shout for joy at thy salvation;* Jehovah Himself was Israel's Saviour (xxi. 1; 1 Sam. x. 19), and the king was His chosen instrument for saving His people (2 Sam. iii. 18).

set up our *banners*]   Rather, **wave** them in token of triumph, than set them up as a memorial of the victory.   The cognate substantive is specially used of the *standards* of the tribes (Num. i. 52, ii 2 ff.).   Cp. Cant. vi. 4, 10.

The LXX however has, *we shall be magnified*.

petitions]   Cp. xxi. 2.

6—8.   The sacrifice has been offered.   Faith regards it as accepted, and in its acceptance sees the pledge of victory.   The voice of a priest, or prophet, or possibly of the king himself, is now heard proclaiming this confidence (*v.* 6), and professing for himself and the people their trust in Jehovah alone (*vv.* 7, 8).

6.   *Now know I*]   Cp. lvi. 9, cxxxv. 5.

He will hear him from his holy heaven
With the saving strength of his right hand.
Some *trust* in chariots, and some in horses:
But we will remember the name of the LORD our God.
They are brought down and fallen:
But we are risen, and stand upright.
Save, LORD:
Let the king hear us when we call.

saveth] Lit., *hath saved:* i.e. *will surely save.* To faith the victory is already won. Cp. the tenses in *v.* 8, and see Additional Note IV, p. 223.

his anointed] The title which expresses the king's consecration to Jehovah is the pledge of his right to expect Jehovah's help (Hab. iii. 13).

he will hear him] R.V., **he will answer him** (as in *vv.* 1, 9) **from his holy heaven**, of which the holy place in Zion (*v.* 2) is but the earthly type.

with the saving strength &c.] Lit., *with mighty acts of salvation of his right hand:* the mighty acts of deliverance (cvi. 2, cl. 2) wrought by the right hand of the Most High (xvii. 7, lx. 5). Cp. xxi. 13.

7. *Some*] The heathen enemy, like Pharaoh (Ex. xiv), and Sennacherib (2 Kings xix. 23); not here heathenish Israelites, as in Is. xxxi. 1—3.

But we will remember the name] R.V., **But we will make mention of the name** &c. This shall be our watchword and our strength. Cp. Jud. vii. 18; 1 Sam. xvii. 45; 2 Chr. xvi. 8, 9; Ps. xxxiii. 16 f.; Is. xxvi. 13; Hos. i. 7.

8. *They are brought down*] R.V., **They are bowed down**; the same word as in xviii. 39. It is still the language of faith, anticipating the entire subjugation of the enemy, and the triumph of Israel.

9. Concluding prayer of the people.

The rendering of A.V. and R.V. follows the punctuation of the Massoretic text. The prayer *for* the earthly king is addressed *to* the heavenly King whose representative he is. But Jehovah is not elsewhere styled absolutely *the King* (cxlv. 1 and Is. vi. 5 are not complete parallels); and the verse appears to correspond to *v.* 6. It seems best to follow the LXX and Vulg. in reading *O LORD, save the king; and answer us* &c. The rendering of the Vulg. *Domine salvum fac regem* is the origin of the familiar *God save the king.* See note on 1 Sam. x. 24. The P.B.V., *Save Lord, and hear us, O King of heaven, when we call upon thee,* is a free combination of the Heb. and Vulg. (LXX).

PSALM XXI.

Thanksgiving for victory is the leading motive of this Psalm, which is, as has already been remarked, a companion to Ps. xx. Its occasion need not be looked for in a coronation festival (*v.* 3), or a royal birthday (*v.* 4). It is quite natural that thanksgiving for victory should lead the poet to speak of the high dignity of the king, and to anticipate his future victories (*vv.* 8—12).

The exalted language of *vv.* 4—6 has led some interpreters to deny the historical reference of the Psalm, and to regard it as a prophecy of the Messianic King. The Targ. paraphrases *king* in *vv.* 1 and 7 by *king Messiah*. Such an interpretation is excluded by the general sense of the Psalm. The language applied to the king is not without parallel in the O. T.; and it is illustrated by expressions in the Assyrian royal Psalms: e. g. "Distant days, everlasting years, a strong weapon, a long life, many days of honour, supremacy among the kings, grant to the king, the lord, who made this offering to his gods" (quoted by Prof. Cheyne). Israel was not uninfluenced by the thoughts and language common to Oriental nations: and if other nations believed that their kings were reflections of the divinity, Israel believed that its king was the representative of Jehovah. Language which startles us by its boldness was used of him: language which was adopted and adapted by the Holy Spirit with a prophetic purpose, and only receives its 'fulfilment' in Christ. The Psalm then has a prophetic aspect, and looks forward through the earthly king of whom it spoke in the first instance, to Him who "must reign, till he hath put all his enemies under his feet" (1 Cor. xv. 25).

Hence its selection as one of the Proper Psalms for Ascension Day. The structure of the Psalm is similar to that of Ps. xx.

i. A thanksgiving on behalf of the king for the victory granted to him: addressed to Jehovah and probably sung by the congregation or the Levites (1—7).

ii. Anticipation of future triumphs, addressed to the king, and perhaps sung by a priest (8—12).

iii. Concluding prayer of the congregation (13).

To the chief Musician, A Psalm of David.

21 The king shall joy in thy strength, O LORD;
And in thy salvation how greatly shall he rejoice!
2 Thou hast given him his heart's desire,
And hast not withholden the request of his lips. Selah.
3 For thou preventest him *with* the blessings of goodness:

1—7. The people's thanksgiving for Jehovah's favour to their king.

1. The prayers of Ps. xx have been answered. The victory is won, and the king rejoices. He has trusted in Jehovah, and now the ground of his rejoicing is the strength which Jehovah has put forth on his behalf, the deliverance which Jehovah has wrought for him. Cp. ix. 14; Ex. xv. 2.

2. This verse refers chiefly, but not exclusively, to the prayers for the success of the expedition referred to in xx. 3—5.

3. *thou preventest him* &c.] For *prevent*, see note on xviii. 18. Jehovah, as it were, *goes to meet* the king and bless him with success

Thou settest a crown of pure gold on his head.
He asked life of thee, *and* thou gavest *it* him, 4
Even length of days for ever and ever.
His glory *is* great in thy salvation: 5
Honour and majesty hast thou laid upon him.
For thou hast made him most blessed for ever: 6
Thou hast made him exceeding glad with thy countenance.
For the king trusteth in the LORD, 7
And through the mercy of the most High he shall not be moved.
Thine hand shall find out all thine enemies: 8
Thy right hand shall find out those that hate thee.
Thou shalt make them as a fiery oven in the time of thine 9
    anger:

(*goodness*=good things, Prov. xxiv. 25): and once more crowns him king. The victory is a Divine confirmation of his sovereignty (1 Sam. xi. 13 ff.). There may possibly be an allusion to the crown of the Ammonite king (2 Sam. xii. 30).

4. *He asked...thou gavest*] Cp. ii. 8. Long life was one of Jehovah's special blessings under the old covenant. It was a natural object of desire when the hope of a future life was all but a blank. See Ex. xxiii. 26; 1 Kings iii. 11; Prov. iii. 2. But how can *length of days for ever and ever* be said of a mortal king? Partly in the same way as the salutation "Let the king live for ever" was used (1 Kings i. 31; Neh. ii. 3); partly because he was regarded as living on in his posterity (2 Sam. vii. 29). Cp. xlv. 2, 6; lxi. 6; lxxii. 5, 17.

5. Glory, honour, majesty, are Divine attributes (viii. 1, 5; civ. 1); and the victorious king shines with a reflection of them.

hast thou laid] Rather as R.V., **dost thou lay.** Cp. lxxxix. 19 for the same word used of Divine endowment.

6. R.V. **For thou makest him most blessed for ever:**
    Thou makest him glad with joy in thy presence.
Lit. *thou makest him blessings*, the possessor and the medium of blessing. Cp. Gen. xii. 2. The victory is a pledge of Divine favour and fellowship, an evidence that the king walks in the light of Jehovah's countenance. Cp. iv. 6; xvi. 11; lxxxix. 15; cxl. 13.

7. The grounds of this blessing: on the king's side, trust; on God's side, **lovingkindness** (xviii. 50). This verse forms the transition to the second division of the Psalm.

8—12. The king, who must be supposed to be present, is now addressed. This victory is an earnest of future victories. The total destruction of all his enemies is confidently anticipated.

8. *shall find out*] Reach them and get them into thy power (1 Sam. xxiii. 17).

9. *Thou shalt make them as a fiery oven*] R.V., **as a fiery furnace.**

The LORD shall swallow them up in his wrath, and the fire
shall devour them.
10 Their fruit shalt thou destroy from the earth,
And their seed from among the children of men.
11 For they intended evil against thee:
They imagined a mischievous device, *which* they are not
able *to perform*.
12 Therefore shalt thou make them turn their back,
When thou shalt make ready *thine arrows* upon thy strings
against the face of them.
13 Be thou exalted, LORD, in thine own strength:
So will we sing and praise thy power.

The comparison is condensed, and inexact in form; but the sense is clear: thou wilt consume them as fuel in a furnace. The phrase is figurative (Mal. iv. 1): yet there may be an allusion to the terrible vengeance inflicted on the Ammonites (2 Sam. xii. 31).

in the time of thine anger] Lit. *in the time of thy countenance*, or *presence:* when Thou appearest in person. Cp. 2 Sam. xvii. 11. 'The face of Jehovah' is the manifestation of His Presence in wrath as well as in mercy (xxxiv. 16); and the king is His representative.

10. Even their posterity shall be utterly destroyed. Cp. ix. 5; xxxvii. 28. *Fruit* = children, 'the fruit of the womb' (Lam. ii. 20).

11, 12. **Though they threaten thee with evil,**
Though they devise a mischievous plan, they shall avail naught,
For thou shalt make them turn their backs,
Aiming with thy bowstrings against their faces.

13. The congregation's concluding prayer (as in xx. 9), returning to the thought of *v.* 1. Jehovah is exalted when He manifests His strength (vii. 6; xlvi. 10; lvii. 5, 11). R.V., **in thy strength**, for *in thine own strength*.

thy power] **Thy might**, made known in mighty acts of salvation (xx. 6).

PSALM XXII.

The first and greatest of the 'Passion Psalms,' consecrated for us by our Lord's appropriation of it to Himself. His utterance of the opening words of it upon the Cross has been thought with much probability to indicate that the whole Psalm was the subject of His meditations during those hours of agony. But this application and fulfilment does not exclude a primary and historical reference.

A. i. The Psalm opens with the agonised cry of a persecuted saint, who feels himself deserted by God (*vv.* 1, 2). He appeals to the character of God (*v.* 3) and to the experience of His mercy in past ages (*vv.* 4, 5), whereas he is the butt and victim of scornful persecutors

PSALM XXII.

(*vv.* 6—8), though from his birth he has been dependent upon God (*vv.* 9, 10).

ii. He urges his plea for help (*v.* 11), describing alternately the virulence of his foes (*vv.* 12, 13, 16, 18), and the pitiable plight to which he is reduced (*vv.* 14, 15, 17). Still more earnestly he repeats his prayer (*vv.* 19—21), till in an instant the certainty of deliverance flashes upon him (21 *b*).

B. i. The darkness of despair is past. He can look forward with confidence to the future. He avows his purpose to proclaim God's goodness in a public act of thanksgiving (*v.* 22), calling upon all that fear Jehovah to join him in adoration (*vv.* 23, 24), and to share the blessings of the eucharistic feast (*vv.* 25, 26).

ii. And now a yet sublimer prospect opens to his view. Jehovah's sovereignty will one day be universally recognised (*vv.* 27—29); and His gracious Providence will be celebrated by all succeeding generations (*vv.* 30, 31).

The Psalm thus falls into two divisions, each of which is subdivided into two nearly equal parts.

A. Present needs. i. Plaintive expostulation (1—10). ii. Prayer for deliverance (11—21).

B. Future hopes. i. Thanksgiving for answered prayer (22—26). ii. The extension of Jehovah's kingdom (27—31).

Commentators differ widely in their views of the scope, occasion, and date of the Psalm. The chief lines of interpretation may be termed the personal, the ideal, the national, and the predictive.

(1) The first impression produced by the Psalm is that it is a record of personal experience. The title ascribes it to David, and it has been variously supposed to reflect the circumstances of Saul's persecution, or Absalom's rebellion, or perhaps to gather into one focus all the vicissitudes of a life of much trial, or possibly to describe the fate he feared at some crisis rather than actual experiences. Delitzsch, who maintains the Davidic authorship, supposes it to have been written with reference to David's narrow escape from Saul in the wilderness of Maon (1 Sam. xxiii. 25 f.). But he admits that the history gives us no ground for supposing that David actually underwent such sufferings as are here described. There is, he thinks, an element of poetic hyperbole in the picture, which has been used by the Spirit of God with a prophetic purpose. The Psalm has its roots in David's own experience, but its language reaches far beyond it to the sufferings of Christ.

Others have thought of Hezekiah, whose deliverance and recovery made an impression upon foreign nations (2 Chr. xxxii. 23); others, with more probability, of Jeremiah, with special reference perhaps to the situation described in ch. xxxvii. 11 ff.; others of some unknown poet of the Exile.

(2) But many features in the Psalm appear to transcend the limits of an individual experience. Hence some have seen in the speaker the ideal person of the righteous sufferer. The Psalm describes how the righteous must suffer in the world; how Jehovah delivers him in his extremity; how that deliverance redounds to His glory and the extension of His kingdom.

(3) From a somewhat similar point of view others have regarded the speaker as a personification of the Jewish nation in exile, persecuted by the heathen, apparently forsaken by Jehovah.

(4) Others again, concentrating their attention upon the striking agreement of the Psalm, even in minute details, with the facts of Christ's Passion, have regarded it as wholly predictive.

Each of these lines of interpretation contains some truth; none is complete by itself. The intensely personal character of the Psalm bears witness that it springs from the experience of an individual life; yet it goes beyond an individual experience; the Psalmist is a representative character; he has absorbed into himself a real sense of the sufferings of others like himself, perhaps even of Israel as a nation; he interprets their thoughts; to some extent, secondarily at any rate, he is the mouthpiece of the nation. But the Psalm goes further. It is prophetic. These sufferings were so ordered by the Providence of God, as to be typical of the sufferings of Christ; the record of them was so shaped by the Spirit of God, as to foreshadow, even in detail, many of the circumstances of the Crucifixion; while the glorious hopes for the future anticipate most marvellously the blessed consequences of the Passion; *ut non tam prophetia quam historia videatur* (Cassiodorus). But the fulfilment far transcends the prophetic outline, and reveals (what in the Psalm is but hinted at, if so much as hinted at) the connexion of redemption with suffering.

It is impossible to speak definitely about the date and authorship of the Psalm. It is certainly difficult to connect it with what we know of David's life; and we seem rather to be within the circle of prophetic thought out of which sprang the portrait of the suffering servant of Jehovah in the second book of Isaiah. The parallels with that book should be carefully studied. Yet the portrait there is more fully developed. The redemptive purpose of suffering is more explicitly realised. Here, though a glorious future succeeds the night of suffering, there is no organic connexion shewn between them.

The Psalm should be studied in the light of its fulfilment in regard both to its general drift and to particular allusions. The opening words were uttered by Christ upon the Cross (Matt. xxvii. 46; Mark xv. 34). St John (xix. 24) expressly speaks of the partition of Christ's garments by the soldiers as a fulfilment of *v.* 18 (cp. Matt. xxvii. 35, where however the quotation is interpolated). *vv.* 14 ff. are a startlingly graphic anticipation of the agonies of crucifixion, even to the piercing of the hands and feet. The mockery of the bystanders is described in the language of the Psalm, and the chief priests borrow it for their scoffing (*vv.* 7 ff., cp. Matt. xxvii. 39—44; Mark xv. 29 ff.; Luke xxiii. 35 ff.). The words of thanksgiving (*v.* 22) are applied to Christ by the author of the Epistle to the Hebrews (ii. 12). The application of the concluding verses is obvious, though no actual reference is made to them in the N.T.

Yet it should be observed in how many points the type falls short of the fulfilment. It could not be otherwise. It is but one of many fragments of truth revealed beforehand which were to be summed up and receive their explanation in Christ.

Two points deserve special notice in connexion with the Messianic application of the Psalm. It contains no confession of sin; and it has none of the terrible imprecations which startle us in the kindred Psalms lxix and cix.

The choice of the Psalm as a Proper Psalm for Good Friday needs no comment.

> To the chief Musician upon Aijeleth Shahar, A Psalm of David.
>
> **My God, my God, why hast thou forsaken me? 22
> *Why art thou so* far from helping me, *and from* the words of my roaring?**

upon Aijeleth Shahar] Rather, **set to Ayyéleth hash-Shahar**, i.e. *the hind of the morning*, the title of some song to the melody of which the Psalm was to be sung, so called either from its opening words or from its subject. Cp. the title of Ps. ix. It is useless to speculate whether 'the hind of the morning' in this song meant literally the hind bestirring itself, or hunted, in the early morning, or figuratively, the morning dawn. The phrase is used in the Talmud for the first rays of the dawn, "like two horns of light ascending from the east," but this later use can hardly determine its meaning here.

Explanations which regard the phrase as descriptive of the contents of the Psalm:—e.g. the hind as an emblem of persecuted innocence, the dawn as an emblem of deliverance:—must be rejected as contrary to the analogy of other titles.

The LXX renders, *concerning the help that cometh in the morning*, explaining *ayyéleth* by the similar word *eyālūth* (*strength* or *succour*) in *v.* 19. The Targum connects it with the morning sacrifice, and paraphrases *concerning the virtue of the continual morning sacrifice*.

1—10. The pleading cry of the forsaken and persecuted servant of God.

1. The expostulation of astonishment and perplexity, not a demand for explanation. Faith and despair are wrestling in the Psalmist's mind. Faith can still claim God as 'my God,' and does not cease its prayers; despair thinks itself forsaken. So Zion in her exile said, "Jehovah hath forsaken me, and the Lord hath forgotten me" (Is. xlix. 14). Cp. xiii. 1, lxxxviii. 14. *God* is *El*, and so in *v.* 10. Cp. lxiii. 1, and note on v. 4.

Christ upon the Cross used the Aramaic version of these words, for Aramaic was His mother tongue. *Eli* (Matt. xxvii. 46) is the Hebrew word, retained in the present text of the Targum: *Eloi* (Mark xv. 34) the Aramaic. The best MSS. have *Eloi* in Matt. also.

Why art thou so far &c.] The alternative rendering in R.V. marg., *far from my help are the words of my roaring*, follows the construction adopted by the LXX, Vulg., and Jer. But it is harsh, even if *my help* (or *my salvation*) is taken to mean God Himself (xxxv. 3); and the rendering in the text appears to give the sense correctly. Cp. x. 1; and see *vv.* 11, 19.

my roaring] The groaning of the sufferer in his distress is compared to the lion's roar. Cp. xxxii. 3; xxxviii. 8.

8—2

2 O my God, I cry in the daytime, but thou hearest not;
And in the night season, and am not silent.
3 But thou *art* holy, O thou that inhabitest the praises of Israel.
4 Our fathers trusted in thee:
They trusted, and thou didst deliver them.
5 They cried unto thee, and were delivered:
They trusted in thee, and were not confounded.
6 But I *am* a worm, and no man;

2. *thou hearest not*] R.V., **thou answerest not**.
and am not silent] Better as R.V. marg., **but find no rest**: no answer comes to bring me respite.

3. An appeal to God's moral character, as the Holy One of Israel. The Heb. word for *holy* is derived from a root signifying *separation*. It characterises God negatively, as separate from the limitations and imperfections of the world and man; and positively, it comes to express the essential nature of God in its moral aspect, as pure, righteous, faithful, supremely exalted. In virtue of His holiness he cannot be false to His covenant. Cp. Habakkuk's plea (i. 12); and for another side of the truth, Is. v. 16.

O thou that inhabitest the praises of Israel] Rather as R.V. marg., **O thou that art enthroned upon the praises of Israel**: a bold adaptation of the phrase *that sittest enthroned upon the cherubim* (2 Sam. vi. 2; 2 Kings xix. 15; Ps. lxxx. 1; xcix. 1). The praises of Israel, ascending like clouds of incense, form as it were the throne upon which Jehovah sits. They are a perpetual memorial of His mighty acts in times past (Ex. xv. 11; Ps. lxxviii. 4; Is. lxiii. 7); and surely He cannot have ceased to give occasion for those praises (*v*. 25)! The P.B.V. is based on an untenable construction of the words, in its rendering, *And thou continuest holy, O thou worship of Israel*, and it takes *praises of Israel* to mean God Himself as the object of Israel's praises.

4, 5. The thought of the preceding line is developed in an appeal to the past history of the nation. Cp. xliv. 1, lxxviii. 3, ix. 10. 'Thou didst deliver them: why then am I deserted?' The emphasis is throughout on **thee**.

In thee did our fathers trust:
They trusted, and thou didst deliver them.
Unto thee did they cry, and escaped:
In thee did they trust, and were not put to shame.

6, 7. The contrast of his own lot.

6. *a worm*] Trampled under foot, despised, defenceless. Almost every word of this verse finds a parallel in the second part of Isaiah. Jehovah's servant Israel is there called a worm (xli. 14); and the ideal representative of Israel is one whom men despise (xlix. 7, liii. 3); from whom they shrink with horror as scarcely human (lii. 14, liii. 2, 3). Comp. too li. 7.

A reproach of men, and despised of the people.
All they that see me laugh me to scorn: 7
They shoot out the lip, they shake the head, *saying*,
He trusted on the LORD *that* he would deliver him: 8
Let him deliver him, seeing he delighted in him.
But thou *art* he that took me out of the womb: 9
Thou didst make me hope *when I was* upon my mother's breasts.
I was cast upon thee from the womb: 10
Thou *art* my God from my mother's belly.

the people] Or, **people**, generally; those with whom he is brought in contact.
  7. *laugh me to scorn*] LXX. ἐξεμυκτήρισαν, the word used by St Luke (xxiii. 35) of the rulers scoffing at Christ. **They gape with their lips** (Job xvi. 10; Ps. xxxv. 21); **they shake the head** (cix. 25; Lam. ii. 15; Job xvi. 4), gestures partly of contempt, partly of feigned abhorrence. Comp. Matt. xxvii. 39.
  8.   'Roll it upon Jehovah! let him deliver him:
    Let him rescue him, for he delighteth in him.'
Ironically they bid the sufferer 'roll' i.e. commit his cause to Jehovah. The verb is certainly imperative, as in xxxvii. 5; Prov. xvi. 3; though the Versions all give the perfect tense, and the words are quoted in that form in Matt. xxvii. 43. Usage makes it certain that the subject in the last clause is Jehovah, as in xviii. 19.
  There is a remarkable parallel to this passage in Wisdom ii. 16 ff. The ungodly say of the righteous man: "He maketh his boast that God is his Father. Let us see if his words be true, and let us prove what shall happen in the end of him. For if the just man be the son of God, he will help him, and deliver him from the hand of his enemies." The whole passage is worth comparing.
  9. *But thou* art *he*] Rather, **Yea, thou art he.** The mocking words of his enemies are true, and he turns them into a plea. All his past life has proved Jehovah's love. Cp. lxxi. 5, 6.
  thou didst make me hope] Rather, **that didst make me trust,** (cp. *vv.* 4, 5). The marg., *keptest me in safety,* lit. *didst make me lie securely upon my mother's breasts,* is a less probable rendering. The P.B.V. *my hope* follows LXX, Vulg., Jer., which represent a slightly different reading.
  10. Upon thee have I been cast &c. *Upon thee* stands first emphatically. Cp. *vv.* 4, 5. To THY care have I been entrusted from my birth. Cp. lv. 22; lxxi. 6. There does not seem to be any reference to the practice of placing a new-born infant upon its father's knees, as much as to say, Thou didst adopt me.

  11—21. The Psalmist pleads for help with intenser earnestness. The virulence of his foes increases. Strength and endurance are exhausted.

11 Be not far from me; for trouble *is* near;
   For *there is* none to help.
12 Many bulls have compassed me:
   Strong *bulls* of Bashan have beset me round.
13 They gaped upon me *with* their mouths,
   As a ravening and a roaring lion.
14 I am poured out like water,
   And all my bones are out of joint:
   My heart is like wax;
   It is melted in the midst of my bowels.
15 My strength is dried up like a potsherd;
   And my tongue cleaveth *to* my jaws;
   And thou hast brought me into the dust of death.
16 For dogs have compassed me:
   The assembly of the wicked have inclosed me:

11. *Be not far from me*] The expostulation of *v.* 1 is turned into a prayer, again repeated in *v.* 19. He urges his plea on the double ground that while Jehovah still stands afar off in seeming indifference, distress is close at hand, and there is no other helper to whom he can look.

12. He compares his insolent enemies to wanton bulls, which "are in the habit of gathering in a circle round any novel or unaccustomed object, and may easily be irritated into charging with their horns" (Tristram, *Nat. Hist. of the Bible*, p. 71). Bashan is here used in a wide sense for the district from the Jabbok to the spurs of Hermon, including part of Gilead. It was famous for its rich pastures (Num. xxxii. 1 ff.; Deut. xxxii. 14; Amos iv. 1).

13. *They gaped* &c.] R.V., **they gape upon me with their mouths** (Lam. ii. 16, iii. 46); like a lion roaring as it prepares to spring upon its prey (vii. 2).

14—17. The effects of anxiety and persecution. Vital strength and courage fail; his frame is racked and tortured; he is reduced to a skeleton.

14. Cp. Josh. vii. 5; Ps. vi. 2 ff. It is the experience of the dying man. Cp. Newman's *Dream of Gerontius*,

"This emptying out of each constituent
And natural force, whereby I come to be."

15. The vital sap and moisture of the body are dried up. Cp. xxxii. 4. Possibly for *my strength* we should read *my palate*. Cp. lxix. 3.

thou hast brought me] **Thou art laying me.** Even in this persecution he can recognise the hand of God. His tormentors are Jehovah's instruments. Cp. Acts ii. 23.

16. A fresh description of his foes. An unclean, cowardly, worrying rabble, like the troops of hungry and half-savage dogs with which

They pierced my hands and my feet.
I may tell all my bones: 17
They look *and* stare upon me.
They part my garments among them, 18
And cast lots upon my vesture.
But be not thou far *from me*, O Lord: 19
O my strength, haste thee to help me.

every oriental city and village still abounds (Tristram, *Nat. Hist.* p. 79), come thronging round him: a gang of miscreants have hemmed him in.

They pierced my hands and my feet] The figure of the savage dogs is still continued. They fly at his feet and hands, and maim them.

The A.V. here rightly deserts the Massoretic text in favour of the reading represented by the LXX, Vulg., and Syr., which have, *they dug*, or, *pierced*. Another group of ancient Versions (Aq. Symm. Jer.) gives *they bound*. (*Fixerunt* in some editions of Jerome is a corruption for the true reading *vinxerunt*.) The Massoretic text has, *like a lion my hands and my feet*. A verb *did they mangle* must be supplied, but the construction is harsh and the sense unsatisfactory. It seems certain that a somewhat rare verb form כָּאֲרוּ (*kā'ărū*), 'they pierced,' has been corrupted into the similar word כָּאֲרִי (*kā'ărī*), 'like a lion.' The Targum perhaps preserves a trace of the transition in its conflate rendering, *biting like a lion*.

The literal fulfilment in the Crucifixion is obvious. But it is nowhere referred to in the N.T.

17. *I may tell*] i.e. **I can count.** He is reduced to a living skeleton. Cp. Job xxxiii. 21.

they look &c.] **While they—they gaze** &c. The original expresses the malicious delight with which these monsters of cruelty feast their eyes upon the sorry spectacle.

18. His brutal enemies are only waiting for his death that they may strip his body, and divide his clothes between them. Already they are settling their respective shares. This is a simpler explanation than to suppose that the Psalmist represents himself as a prisoner stripped and led out to execution, or as waylaid and plundered by robbers (Job xxiv. 7—10; Mic. ii. 8). It need not be supposed that this actually happened to the Psalmist. The language is perhaps proverbial. But it was literally fulfilled in the circumstances of the Crucifixion (John xix. 23, 24; cp. Matt. xxvii. 35, where, however, the reference to the prophecy in the Received Text is an interpolation).

and cast lots &c.] R.V., **and upon my vesture do they cast lots.** The inner garment, the "seamless tunic," which would be spoilt by rending.

19. The prayer for help is repeated after this description of the urgency of his need. **But thou, O LORD** (in emphatic contrast to **they** in *v.* 17), **keep not thou far off.** The sufferer looks away from his numerous tormentors and fixes his gaze upon Jehovah.

O my strength] R.V., **O thou my succour.**

20 Deliver my soul from the sword;
My darling from the power of the dog.
21 Save me from the lion's mouth:
For thou hast heard me from the horns of the unicorns.

22 I will declare thy name unto my brethren:
In the midst of the congregation will I praise thee.

> 20. *from the sword*] From a violent death.
> *my darling*] Lit., *my only one*. The clue to the meaning is given by the use of the word of *an only child* (Gen. xxii. 2; Jud. xi. 34). The word denotes the one precious life which can never be replaced. Cp. xxxv. 17.
> *the dog*] See on v. 16.
> 21. *for thou hast heard me* &c.] Render, **yea from the horns of the wild oxen—thou hast answered me.** A singularly bold and forcible construction. We expect a second imperative, repeating the prayer for deliverance (*rescue thou me*: cp. Jer. *exaudi*). But the conviction that his prayer is heard, nay, answered, flashes upon the Psalmist's soul; prayer is changed into assurance, joyous confidence takes the place of petition. Less forcible is the explanation which assumes a pregnant rather than a broken construction:—*From the horns of the wild oxen thou hast answered* and delivered *me*.
> *unicorns*] The rendering of LXX, Vulg., Jer. But the *re'ēm* was certainly a two-horned animal (Deut. xxxiii. 17, R.V.). The Auerochs or wild ox (*Bos primigenius*), now everywhere extinct, is almost certainly the animal meant. Its strength and untamableness are described in Job xxxix. 9 ff. See Tristram's *Nat. Hist.* p. 146 ff.

> 22—31. Convinced that his prayer is heard, the Psalmist breaks forth with resolutions of public thanksgiving (22—26); and the glorious prospect of Jehovah's universal kingdom opens up before him (27—31). "*Thou answerest not*" (v. 2) is the key-note of vv. 1—21; "*Thou hast answered me* of vv. 22—31". (Cheyne).
> 22. *thy name*] All that Thou hast proved thyself to be. See note on v. 11.
> *my brethren*] By the ties of national and religious sympathy. The author of the Epistle to the Hebrews (ii. 12) puts these words directly into the mouth of Christ, "He is not ashamed to call them brethren."
> *in the midst of the congregation*] Gratitude demands the most public proclamation of Jehovah's lovingkindness. It concerns all the faithful to know what He has wrought, and all the faithful must join in thanksgiving for the deliverance vouchsafed to their fellow and representative. Cp. xl. 9, 10; xxxv. 18.
> *will I praise thee*] Now he can contribute his share to the praises which form Jehovah's throne (v. 3). *Praise* is four times repeated in vv. 22—26.

Ye that fear the LORD, praise him; 23
All ye the seed of Jacob, glorify him;
And fear him, all ye seed of Israel.
For he hath not despised nor abhorred the affliction of the 24
afflicted;
Neither hath he hid his face from him;
But when he cried unto him, he heard.
My praise *shall be* of thee in the great congregation: 25
I will pay my vows before them that fear him.
The meek shall eat and be satisfied: 26

23, 24. Already he can imagine himself standing 'in the great congregation.' These are the words in which he summons them to praise.

23. *ye that fear the* LORD] Possibly coextensive with *the seed of Jacob*, but pointing rather to the inner circle of true believers who are in fullest sympathy with the Psalmist.

seed of Jacob...seed of Israel] Cp. Is. xlv. 19, 25.

fear him] R.V., **stand in awe of Him** (xxxiii. 8).

24. *For he hath not despised* as men do (*v.* 6) *nor abhorred* as something loathsome and abominable (Is. xlix. 7, though the word here is even stronger) *the affliction of the afflicted.* Cp. lxix. 33. The 'servant of Jehovah' (Is. liii. 4, 7) and Zion's future king (Zech. ix. 9) are both described as 'afflicted.' See note on ix. 12.

hid his face] In anger (x. 11, xiii. 1); or abhorrence (Is. liii. 3, R.V.).

25. *My praise* shall be *of thee*] Rather as R.V., **Of thee cometh my praise**. From his fellow-worshippers the Psalmist turns to Jehovah, who is not only the object but the source of his praise. "It is the LORD's doing."

I will pay my vows] Thank-offerings vowed in the time of trouble. Cp. lxvi. 13, cxvi. 14, 18.

26. *The meek shall eat and be satisfied*] The flesh of a sacrifice offered in performance of a vow was to be eaten on the same day on which it was offered, or on the morrow (Lev. vii. 16; Num. xv. 3). The Psalmist will invite the meek to join him in this eucharistic meal. Such an invitation is not indeed prescribed in the Law, but it is in full accordance with the command to invite the poor and needy to share in the tithes (Deut. xiv. 29, xxvi. 12; where the phrase 'eat and be satisfied' occurs), and in the harvest festivals (Deut. xvi. 11, 14). There seems to be no good reason for supposing that the words are to be understood wholly in a figurative and spiritual sense, though on the other hand their meaning is not to be limited to the external performance of a ritual ceremony. At any rate the language of this and the preceding verse is based upon the idea of a sacrifice of thanksgiving of which the worshippers partook (xxiii. 5). 'Eat and be satisfied' is not merely a current formula for the refreshment which

They shall praise the LORD that seek him:
Your heart shall live for ever.
27 All the ends of the *world* shall remember and turn unto the
   LORD:
   And all the kindreds of the nations shall worship before
   thee.
28 For the kingdom *is* the LORD'S:
   And *he is* the governor among the nations.

flows from Divine blessing, the Psalmist anticipating that his own deliverance will lead to the prosperity of all the godly.

that seek him] R.V., **that seek after him.** All Jehovah's devoted followers (see on xxiv. 6) will swell the anthem.

your heart shall live &c.] R.V., **let your heart live for ever.** The entertainer invokes a blessing on his guests. May those who were ready to perish be revived and quickened with an undying energy! With the whole verse cp. lxix. 32.

If the primary and immediate reference is to a sacrificial feast, it is clear that the words reach far beyond the outward rite to the spiritual communion of which it was the symbol; while the Christian reader cannot but see the counterpart and fulfilment of the words in the Holy Eucharist.

27—31. The Psalmist's hopes take a wider range, extending to all mankind and to future ages. He anticipates the time when not he alone, not the seed of Israel only, but all nations to earth's remotest bound, will pay homage to Jehovah. From personal hopes he passes to national hopes, from national hopes to universal hopes, reaching forward into the future from generation to generation. But this establishment of Jehovah's kingdom is not explicitly regarded as the fruit of the Psalmist's sufferings. We are not yet upon the level of Isaiah liii. Perhaps the nations are represented as being attracted by Jehovah's deliverance of His servant, though even this is not clear.

27. *All the ends of the world*] R.V., **of the earth.** The remotest countries. Cp. lxvii. 7; xcviii. 3.

shall remember &c.] There was a knowledge of God, to which the nations might attain through the witness of His works without and the witness of conscience within. But they 'forgot Him' (ix. 17) and turned away from Him to idols of their own imagination (Rom. i. 21, 28). But one day they will 'remember' and 'return.' Cp. Jer. xvi. 19 ff.

all the kindreds of the nations] **All the families of the nations;** realising the patriarchal promise (Gen. xii. 3; xxviii. 14).

28. The reason for this homage. It is but the recognition of the present fact of Jehovah's universal sovereignty. Cp. Obad. 21; Ps. xciii. 1; xcvi. 10; xcvii. 1; Zech. xiv. 16, 17.

and he is *the governor* &c.] R.V., **and he is the ruler over the nations.** Cp. lxvi. 7; ciii. 19.

All *they that be* fat upon earth shall eat and worship: 29
All they that go down to the dust shall bow before him:
And none can keep alive his own soul.
A seed shall serve him; 30
It shall be accounted to the Lord for a generation.

29. A most obscure verse. The first line (according to the present text) may be rendered literally,
All earth's fat ones have eaten and worshipped.
The tense is a 'prophetic perfect'; with the eye of faith the Psalmist sees homage already paid to Jehovah even by the haughty nobles of the earth. They abandon their proud self-sufficiency, and join in the eucharistic meal with the meek (*v.* 26), whom once they despised and persecuted. Then he continues
Before him bow all that were going down to the dust,
Yea he who could not keep his soul alive.
Those who were on the edge of the grave, ready to die from want and misery and trouble, come as guests and gain new life. Rich and poor, strong and weak, alike partake of the feast: for it the rich desert their wealth; in it the poor receive the compensation of their privations; and those who were ready to die find life. Cp. Is. xxv. 6—8.

This seems to be the best explanation of the text as it stands; but it is open to serious objections. The reference to the sacrificial meal is very abrupt; the sense given to 'those that go down to the dust' is questionable; and the last line drags heavily at the end of the verse.

Others suppose that the contrast intended is not between rich and poor, but between the living and the dead. 'Earth's fat ones' are those in the full vigour of life: *eat* means simply 'enjoy life': *all they that have gone down into the dust* are the dead. Quick and dead bow in homage before the universal sovereign. Cp. Phil. ii. 10. Attractive as this explanation is, the idea is foreign to the O. T. See cxv. 17; Is. xxxviii. 18; and Introd. p. lxxv, ff.

But the text is not improbably corrupt. An easy emendation, adopted by several critics, simplifies the first line thus:
Surely him shall all earth's fat ones worship,
and the second line repeats the thought,
Before him shall bow all they that must go down to the dust.

Earth's mightiest are but mortals and must yield their homage to the King of kings. Then the last line should be joined to the next verse thus:
And as for him that could not keep his soul alive,
His seed shall serve Him.

The Psalmist and those who like him were at the point of death will leave a posterity behind them to serve Jehovah. The reading indicated by the LXX, *But my soul liveth unto him, my seed shall serve him,* suits the context less well.

30. *It shall be accounted* &c.] i.e. as R.V. marg., *It shall be counted unto the Lord for* his *generation*. Better, however, as R.V. text, It

31 They shall come, and shall declare his righteousness
Unto a people that *shall be* born, that he hath done *this*.

shall be told of the Lord unto the *next* **generation.** But here again it seems best slightly to alter the text, and following the LXX to connect the first word of v. 31 with v. 30: *It shall be told of the Lord unto the generation that shall come:* for (1) *the generation* needs the qualification which R.V. supplies by inserting *next:* and (2) *they shall come* absolutely in the sense of *they shall come into being* is doubtful.

31. *and shall* &c.] **And they shall declare his righteousness unto a people that shall be born**; i.e. to the next generation. From one generation to another the tradition of Jehovah's righteousness, of His faithfulness to His covenant, will be handed down.

that he hath done this] Or as R.V., **that he hath done it.** The object is not expressed. Cp. xxxvii. 5 (which combines *vv.* 8 and 31); lii. 9; cxix. 126; Is. xliv. 23; Num. xxiii. 19, 23. "Gen. xxviii. 15 unites the first and last lines of the Psalm." *Kay*. He has wrought out His purpose of salvation, interposed on His servant's behalf, proved Himself the living righteous and true God.

The song of praise, begun by the Psalmist (*v.* 22), is taken up by Israel; all the nations of the earth swell the chorus; and the strain echoes on through all the ages. So gloriously ends the Psalm which began in the darkest sorrow. *Per crucem ad lucem.* It is a parable of the history of the individual, of Israel, of the Church, of the world.

PSALM XXIII.

The grateful praise of Jehovah (i) as the Good Shepherd who tends (*vv.* 1, 2), and guides (*vv.* 3, 4) the Psalmist, providing for every want, and protecting him in every danger: (ii) as the bountiful host (*vv.* 5, 6), who entertains the Psalmist as his guest with gracious liberality.

The Psalm is unrivalled for calm serenity and perfect faith. Under Jehovah's loving care the Psalmist knows neither want nor fear. His words admit of the most universal application to all needs, temporal and spiritual, in every age. Their meaning grows in depth as the love of God is more fully revealed through the teaching of the Spirit in the experience of life (Eph. iii. 17—19; Rom. viii. 35 ff.).

The Targum explains the Psalm of God's care for the nation of Israel. This however, though justifiable as a secondary application, can hardly be the original meaning. Its tone is strongly personal. It is an individual realisation and appropriation of the blessings involved in the covenant-relation of Jehovah to His people. Each sheep can claim the care which is promised to the whole flock (Luke xv. 4 ff.).

Was David the author? Many have thought that *vv.* 1—4 are based on the recollections of his early shepherd life; and that *v.* 5 reflects his entertainment by Barzillai (2 Sam. xvii. 27—29). Nor is *v.* 6 decisive against the Davidic authorship. The language is figurative, and the phrase 'house of the LORD' does not necessarily imply the existence of

the temple (Ex. xxiii. 19; Jud. xviii. 31; 1 Sam. i. 7), though it must be admitted that it seems to point to it.
The kindred Ps. xxvii should be carefully compared.

A Psalm of David.

The LORD *is* my shepherd; I shall not want. 23
He maketh me to lie down in green pastures: 2
He leadeth me beside the still waters.
He restoreth my soul: 3
He leadeth me in the paths of righteousness for his name's sake.

1. *The LORD is my shepherd*] How natural a figure in a pastoral country, and for the shepherd-king, if the Psalm is his! Jehovah is often spoken of as the Shepherd of Israel, and Israel as His flock, especially in the Psalms of Asaph. See lxxiv. 1, lxxvii. 20, lxxviii. 52, 70 ff.; lxxix. 13; lxxx. 1, and cp. xcv. 7, c. 3; Mic. vii. 14; and the exquisite description of Jehovah's care for the returning exiles in Is. xl. 11. Jacob speaks of "the God who shepherded me" (Gen. xlviii. 15, cp. xlix. 24). The title of shepherd is also applied to rulers; and in particular to David (2 Sam. v. 2, vii. 7); and to the future king of whom David was a type (Mic. v. 4; Ez. xxxiv. 23); and so Christ appropriates it to Himself (John x. 1; cp. Heb. xiii. 20; 1 Pet. ii. 25).

I shall not want] The language, partly of experience in the present, partly of confidence for the future. So of Israel, looking back on the wandering in the wilderness, "thou hast lacked nothing" (Deut. ii. 7); and looking forward to the Land of Promise, "thou shalt not lack anything in it" (Deut. viii. 9). Cp. Ps. xxxiv. 10, lxxxiv. 11.

2. The figure of the shepherd is expanded. He makes his flock lie down in the noontide heat (Cant. i. 7) *in pastures of tender grass*. For this picture of the shepherd's care cp. Jer. xxxiii. 12.

He leadeth me] The word suggests the idea of *gentle guidance* (Is. xl. 11); sometimes of sustaining and providing (Gen. xlvii. 17 R.V. marg.) So here Vulg. *educavit*. It is specially applied to God's guidance of His people (Ex. xv. 13; Ps. xxxi. 3; Is. xlix. 10).

the still waters] Lit. *waters of rest:* not gently-flowing streams, but streams where they may find rest and refreshment (Is. xxxii. 18). So Jerome: *super aquas refectionis*. The Promised Land was to be Israel's rest (Deut. xii. 9; Ps. xcv. 11). It will be remembered that "the eastern shepherd never *drives*, but always leads his sheep," and that "in the East the sheep requires water daily, owing to the heat and dryness of the climate." Tristram's *Nat. Hist. of the Bible*, pp. 140, 141.

With *vv*. 1, 2 comp. Rev. vii. 17.

3, 4. The shepherd's care as guide and guardian.

3. *He restoreth my soul*] Renews and sustains my life. Cp. xix. 7, note. Not as P.B.V. (after the LXX and Vulg.) *he shall convert my soul*.

he leadeth me] R.V., **he guideth me**: a word often used of God's

4 Yea, though I walk through the valley of the shadow of death,
I will fear no evil: for thou *art* with me;
Thy rod and thy staff they comfort me.
5 Thou preparest a table before me in the presence of mine enemies:

---

guidance of His people collectively (Ex. xv. 13; Deut. xxxii. 12), and individually (Ps. v. 8, xxvii. 11, &c.).

in the paths of righteousness] Usage is decisive in favour of rendering thus, and not, *in straight paths*. The word for *righteousness* nowhere retains its primary physical meaning of *straightness*. For *paths* cp. xvii. 5; and for the whole phrase, Prov. iv. 11, viii. 20, xii. 28.

for his name's sake] In order to prove Himself such as He has declared Himself to be (Ex. xxxiv. 5 ff.).

4. The figure of the shepherd is still continued. "The sheep districts [in Palestine] consist of wide open wolds or downs, reft here and there by deep ravines, in whose sides lurks many a wild beast, the enemy of the flocks" (Tristram, *Nat. Hist.* p. 138). Even in such a dismal glen, where unknown perils are thickest, where deathly gloom and horror are on every side, he knows no fear. Cp. Jeremiah's description of Jehovah's care for Israel in the wilderness (ii. 6). Bunyan's development of the idea in the *Pilgrim's Progress* is familiar to everyone.

the shadow of death] The word *tsalmāveth* is thus rendered in the Ancient Versions, and the present vocalisation assumes that this is its meaning. But compounds are rare in Hebrew except in proper names, and there are good grounds for supposing that the word is derived from a different root and should be read *tsalmūth* and explained simply *deep gloom* (cp. R.V. marg.). It is not improbable that the pronunciation of the word was altered at an early date in accordance with a popular etymology (like our *causeway*, originally *causey*, from Fr. *chaussée*).

for thou art with me] God's presence is His people's strength and comfort. Cp. Gen. xxviii. 15; Josh. i. 5 ff.; &c. &c.

Thy rod and thy staff] The shepherd's crook is poetically described by two names, as the *rod* or club with which he defends his sheep from attack (Mic. vii. 14; 2 Sam. xxiii. 21; Ps. ii. 9); and the *staff* on which he leans. The shepherd walks before his flock, ready to protect them from assault; they follow gladly and fearlessly wherever he leads.

5, 6. The figure is changed. Jehovah is now described as the host who bountifully entertains the Psalmist at his table, and provides him with a lodging in his own house, as Oriental monarchs entertained those to whom they wished to shew special favour. See Gen. xliii. 16; 2 Sam. ix. 7 ff., xix. 33; 1 Kings iv. 27.

5. *in the presence of mine enemies*] Or, **adversaries**, as in vi. 7. The mark of favour is public and unmistakable.

Thou anointest my head with oil; my cup runneth over.
Surely goodness and mercy shall follow me all the days of 6
   my life:
And I will dwell in the house of the LORD for ever.

thou anointest] R.V., **thou hast anointed**. The reference is to the unguents and perfumes which were the regular accompaniment of an Oriental banquet (Amos vi. 6; Ps. xlv. 7, xcii. 10), not to the regal anointing, for which a different word is used.

my cup &c.] See note on xvi. 5: and cp. xxxvi. 8, lxvi. 12, note.
Jehovah is no niggard host, like the Pharisee (Luke vii. 46); He provides for the joys as well as the necessities of life (John ii. 1—11); His guests shall be of a cheerful countenance and a gladsome heart (civ. 15).

6. *Surely*] Or, as R.V. marg., **only**. Nothing but goodness and mercy *shall pursue me*. What a contrast to the lot of the wicked man, pursued by the angel of judgment (xxxv. 6), hunted by calamity (cxl. 11).

And I will dwell] The text as it stands would mean, *and I will return* [to dwell] *in the house of the LORD*. But a comparison of xxvii. 4 leaves no doubt that we should read *shibhtī* or regard *shabhtī* as an exceptional form for it, and explain, *and my dwelling shall be* &c. Clearly the words are to be understood figuratively, and not of actual residence within the precincts of the temple. Cp. xxxvi. 8.

for ever] Lit. *for length of days*. The blessing of long life (xxi. 4) is crowned by the still greater blessing of the most intimate fellowship with God.

PSALM XXIV.

The impregnable stronghold of Zion had fallen. David was master of his future capital. But it was not in his own strength, not for his own glory, that the victory had been won. The city of David was to be "the city of the LORD of Hosts." Its true owner and King must now enter and take possession. The Ark, which was the symbol of His Presence, must be solemnly brought up and installed in the tent which David had prepared for it. For that unique occasion, the greatest day in David's life (see Stanley's *Jewish Church*, Lect. xxiii.), this Psalm appears to have been written. Jehovah comes as a victorious warrior, fresh from the conquest of the impregnable fortress (*vv.* 7—10). The opening assertion of His universal sovereignty as the Creator of the world offers a fitting caution not to suppose that because He has chosen one city for His special dwelling-place, His Presence and activity are limited to it (*vv.* 1, 2); the inquiry what must be the character of His worshippers (*vv.* 3—6), appropriate in any case, gains fresh point in view of the disaster which had for a while deferred the ceremony (2 Sam. vi. 9). The "ancient doors" are the gates of the venerable fortress, now opening to receive their true Lord.

No other occasion, such as the Dedication of the Temple, or the return of the Ark from some victory, explains the whole Psalm equally well.

Some commentators have questioned the original unity of the poem. On the ground of difference in tone and style, and supposed want of coherence, they have maintained that *vv.* 1—6 are taken from a poem of a didactic character, *vv.* 7—10, from a triumphal ode. The variety of style is not however greater than might be expected from the change of subject, and a clear sequence of thought can be traced in the three stanzas of the Psalm.

i. The introductory verses declare the Majesty of Him Who comes to take possession (*vv.* 1, 2).

ii. The conditions of access to His sanctuary are determined (*vv.* 3—6).

iii. The ancient fortress is summoned to admit its true king, and the character of His sovereignty is proclaimed (*vv.* 7—10).

The musical performance of the Psalm probably corresponded to its dramatic character, though the precise arrangement can only be conjectured.

vv. 1—6 were perhaps intended to be sung as the procession mounted the hill; *vv.* 1, 2 by the full choir, the question of *v.* 3 as a solo, the answer of *vv.* 4, 5 as another solo, the response of *v.* 6 in chorus. *vv.* 7—10 may have been sung as the procession halted before the venerable gates of the citadel; the summons of *v.* 7 and *v.* 9 by a single voice (or possibly by the choir), the challenge of *v.* 8*a* and *v.* 10*a* by a voice as from the gates, the triumphant response of *v.* 8*b* and *v.* 10*b* by the full choir.

According to the title in the LXX, which agrees with the liturgical use of the Jewish Church as prescribed in the Talmud, this was the Psalm for the first day of the week. See Introd. p. xxiv.

It is fitly used as a Proper Psalm for Ascension Day.

Psalms xv and lxviii should be compared.

A Psalm of David.

24 The earth *is* the LORD'S, and the fulness thereof; The world, and they that dwell therein.

1, 2. The unique Majesty of Him Who comes to take possession of His chosen dwelling-place. His sovereignty is not limited to a single nation or a single country. He is the Lord of all the world, for He is its Creator.

1. *The earth is the LORD'S*] Better, **Unto Jehovah belongeth the earth.** The natural order of the Heb. fixes the reader's mind first on Him, Whose approach is the theme of the Psalm. For the same thought see Ex. xix. 5; Deut. x. 14 (R.V.); Ps. l. 12, lxxxix. 11. The words are quoted (from the LXX) in 1 Cor. x. 26, to confirm the intrinsic lawfulness of eating whatever is sold in the market.

the world] Properly, the habitable part of the earth (ix. 8); hence naturally supplemented by the mention of its inhabitants. The P.B.V., *the compass of the world*, was probably suggested by the Vulg., *orbis terrarum*.

For he hath founded it upon the seas, 2
And established it upon the floods.
Who shall ascend into the hill of the LORD? 3
And who shall stand in his holy place?
He that hath clean hands, and a pure heart; 4
Who hath not lift up his soul unto vanity,
Nor sworn deceitfully.

2. *For he* &c.] HE is emphatic. It is HE and no other who laid the foundation of the world (civ. 5; Job xxxviii. 4). The land rising out of the water is supposed to rest upon it. Cp. cxxxvi. 6; and the idea of the subterranean abyss of waters in Gen. vii. 11; and "the water under the earth" in Ex. xx. 4. It is a popular or poetic conception derived from phenomena; yet possibly the idea that the earth was firmly fixed upon such a foundation suggested the Creator's power much in the same way as the suspension and motion of the earth in space may do to us.

3—6. The moral conditions required for access to the presence of so great a God. His Holiness corresponds to His Majesty. Ps. xv. 1 ff. and Is. xxxiii. 14 ff. are parallel in substance as well as form.

3. *Who shall ascend*] Often of going up to worship at the sanctuary. See 1 Sam. i. 3, 22; Is. ii. 3, xxxvii. 14, xxxviii. 22.

stand] Not merely appear or remain, but as in i. 5, stand his ground. Cp. 1 Sam. vi. 20.

in his holy place] Synonymous with '*the hill* (or, *mountain*) *of the LORD*' in the preceding line. Cp. ii. 6, iii. 4, xv. 1, xliii. 3; Is. ii. 2, 3, &c.

4. *He that hath clean hands, and a pure heart*] He who is innocent of violence and wrong-doing (xviii. 20, 24); nay, innocent even in thought and purpose as well as in deed. Cp. lxxiii. 1; Matt. v. 8.

Who hath not lift up his soul unto vanity] i.e. who is true and faithful to Jehovah. 'To lift up the soul' means to direct the mind towards (xxv. 1), to set the heart upon (Deut. xxiv. 15), to desire (Hos. iv. 8). 'Vanity' denotes what is transitory (Job xv. 31), false and unreal (Ps. xii. 2), or sinful (Is. v. 18), and may even designate false gods (Ps. xxxi. 6). It includes all that is unlike or opposed to the nature of God. The traditional reading (*Qrī*) however is, *my soul* (so too Cod. Alex. of the LXX.). This reading must be rendered, *Who hath not taken me in vain.* God speaks; and the words are an echo of Ex. xx. 7, with *my soul* (=my being) substituted for *my name*. But this explanation is forced, and cannot be defended even by Am. vi. 8, and Jer. li. 14, where God is said to swear 'by His soul'= by Himself.

nor sworn deceitfully] R.V., **and hath not sworn deceitfully.** The paraphrase of P.B.V., 'nor sworn to deceive his neighbour,' which follows the LXX and Vulg., gives the sense rightly. He has been true to his neighbour, as well as to God. Cp. xv. 4.

5 He shall receive the blessing from the LORD,
And righteousness from the God of his salvation.
6 This *is* the generation of them that seek him,
That seek thy face, O Jacob. Selah.
7 Lift up your heads, O ye gates;
And be ye lift up, ye everlasting doors;
And the King of glory shall come in.
8 Who *is* this King of glory?

    5. *the blessing*] R.V. rightly, **a blessing.**

    righteousness] 'Righteousness' is blessing in another aspect. Jehovah manifests Himself to the godly man, as 'the God of his salvation' (xxv. 5; xxvii. 9); and this 'salvation' is the witness to and reward for his upright conduct. See 1 Sam. xxvi. 23; Ps. xviii. 20, 24; lviii. 11. In the light of N.T. revelation the words receive a deeper meaning. See Matt. v. 6.

    6. *generation*] i.e. class, as in xii. 7; xiv. 5; lxxiii. 15.

    that seek him] R.V., **that seek after him.** Two words for *seek* are used in this verse. Both may be used of the outward act of visiting the sanctuary; but both come to express the inward purpose of the heart as well. So far as the two words can be distinguished the first denotes the attitude of loving devotion, the second that of inquiry or supplication.

    O Jacob] The A.V. marg. and R.V. rightly follow the LXX, Vulg., and Syr. in reading **O God of Jacob.** If the Massoretic text is retained, it must be rendered with R.V. marg., *That seek thy face*, even *Jacob*. These are the ideal Jacob, the true people of God. But the construction is harsh; a vocative is needed after *thy face;* and *Jacob* does not by itself convey this sense.

    7—10. The procession has reached the ancient gates of Zion. They are summoned to open high and wide to admit their true King.

    7. *Lift up your heads*] As though they were too low and mean for the entrance of "the high and lofty one" who comes, and in token that all resistance is at an end.

    ye everlasting doors] Or, *ye ancient doors*, venerable with unknown antiquity.

    and the King &c.] Or, **that the King of glory may come in.** The Ark, "which is called by the Name, even the name of the LORD of hosts that sitteth upon the cherubim" (2 Sam. vi. 2) was the symbol of Jehovah's majesty and the pledge of His Presence among His people (Num. x. 35, 36). When the ark was lost, "the glory departed from Israel" (1 Sam. iv. 21). Cp. xix. 1, note.

    8. Who is the King of glory? may be merely a rhetorical question; but it is far more poetical to suppose that the gates, or the warders, are represented as challenging the comer's right to enter. The choir's response recalls the opening words of the Song of Moses (Ex. xv. 2, 3), "Jah is my strength and song...Jehovah is a man of war:" while the title *King* reflects its closing words (Ex. xv. 18); "Jehovah shall be

The LORD strong and mighty,
The LORD mighty *in* battle.
Lift up your heads, O ye gates;   9
Even lift *them* up, ye everlasting doors;
And the King of glory shall come in.
Who is this King of glory?   10
The LORD of hosts, he *is* the King of glory. Selah.

King for ever and ever." He is now proclaimed as the Victor, who comes as He had purposed, to take His kingdom.

9, 10. Challenge and response are repeated, with some slight variations, and one important change.

9. *even lift* &c.] Yea, **lift them up...that the King of glory may come in.**

10. *The LORD of hosts*] The climax is reached. He claims to enter, not merely as a victorious warrior, but as the Sovereign of the Universe. The great title *Jehovah Tsebāōth* or *LORD of hosts*, which was characteristic of the regal and prophetic period, meets us here for the first time in the Psalter. Originally perhaps it designated Jehovah as "the God of the armies of Israel" (1 Sam. xvii. 45), who went forth with His people's hosts to battle (xliv. 9; lx. 10), and whose Presence was the source of victory (xlvi. 7, 11). But as the phrase "host of heaven" was used for the celestial bodies (Gen. ii. 1), and celestial beings (1 Kings xxii. 19), the meaning of the title was enlarged to designate Jehovah as the ruler of the heavenly powers, the supreme Sovereign of the universe. Hence one of the renderings in the LXX is κύριος παντοκράτωρ, *Lord Almighty*, or rather, *All-sovereign*. See Additional Note on 1 Samuel in this series, p. 235.

PSALM XXV.

An alphabet of prayer and meditation, the utterance of a humble, yet confident faith. It falls into three equal divisions.
 i. Prayer for protection, guidance, and pardon (*vv.* 1—7).
 ii. Reflections on the character of God (*vv.* 8—10) and on His dealings with those who fear Him (12—14), separated by a prayer for pardon, which springs naturally out of *v.* 10.
 iii. Renewed prayer for deliverance in distress (*vv.* 15—21). *v.* 22 is a supernumerary verse, probably a later addition.
Thus the Psalmist begins and ends with prayer, and sustains and kindles faith and devotion by meditating on the truths of revelation.
The speaker is hardly "pious Israel personified." He is an individual, and speaks for and of individuals. Yet it may well be the case that he feels the sins and sufferings of his nation in some measure as though they were his own (e.g. *vv.* 11, 19), and that his prayer for pardon and deliverance reaches beyond his own personal needs.
Thought and language shew the influence of the 'Wisdom,' or religious

philosophy of Israel, embodied in the Book of Proverbs. But the Psalm has no distinct historical background, and might belong to almost any age.

It is one of the nine alphabetic Psalms (see Introd. p. xlviii). Each verse, usually consisting of two lines, begins with a letter of the alphabet. But as the text stands at present, a word (*O my God*) precedes the *Bēth* with which the second line should begin; *Vāv* is omitted, or only represented by the second line of *v.* 5, instead of having a separate verse to itself; *Qōph* is wanting, and instead two verses (18, 19) begin with *Rēsh*; and a supernumerary verse beginning with *Pē* is added at the end. Some of these irregularities may be due to corruption of the text; but it is a curious fact that two of them, the absence of a separate verse for *Vav*, and the supernumerary *Pē* verse, are found again in Ps. xxxiv. The two Psalms are clearly related; the one is a prayer, the other a thanksgiving; and they are probably by the same author.

A Psalm of David.

25 (א) Unto thee, O LORD, do I lift up my soul.
2 O my God, (ב) I trust in thee: let me not be ashamed,
Let not mine enemies triumph over me.
3 (ג) Yea, let none that wait on thee be ashamed:

1—7. Petition for protection, guidance, and pardon.

1. He who may approach Jehovah's sanctuary must be one 'who hath not lifted up his soul unto vanity' (xxiv. 4). Jehovah, and Jehovah alone, is the subject of his desires, his aspirations, his prayers. Cp. lxxxvi. 3; cxliii. 8; Lam. iii. 41.

As the verses are usually distichs, it has been conjectured with much probability that the line "on thee do I wait all the day," which overweights *v.* 5, originally belonged to *v.* 1. *v.* 3 *a* gains point by this transposition.

2. This verse should begin with the letter *Beth* in the word for *in thee*. It has been suggested that the first word *O my God* was disregarded in the alphabetic arrangement; but it is more probable that it originally belonged to the second line of the preceding verse (so codd. אBA of the LXX), which has now been lost or misplaced. Otherwise it must be omitted. Verse 2 then forms a proper distich:

**In thee have I trusted, let me not be ashamed:
Let not mine enemies triumph over me.**

Cp. *v.* 20; xxii. 5; xxxi. 1, 17.

3. Render with R.V.

**Yea, none that wait on thee shall be ashamed:
They shall be ashamed that deal treacherously without cause.**

The words are not a prayer, but the expression of a conviction corresponding to and justifying the prayer of *v.* 2. Cp. Rom. v. 3—5. It certainly gains in point if the last clause of *v.* 5 is joined to *v.* 1, and the

Let them be ashamed which transgress without cause.
(ד) Shew me thy ways, O Lord; 4
Teach me thy paths.
(ה) Lead me in thy truth, and teach me: 5
For thou *art* the God of my salvation;
On thee do I wait all the day.
(ז) Remember, O Lord, thy tender mercies and thy loving- 6
kindnesses;
For they *have been* ever of old.
(ח) Remember not the sins of my youth, nor my trans- 7
gressions:
According to thy mercy remember thou me
For thy goodness' sake, O Lord.
(ט) Good and upright *is* the Lord: 8

Psalmist has already spoken of himself as one of "those who wait on Jehovah."

which transgress] Rather as R.V., **that deal treacherously**: a word used of faithless, treacherous conduct towards men (Jud. ix. 23), or God (Jer. iii. 20): here of the faithless desertion of God which is the opposite of patiently waiting upon Him. Cp. cxix. 158.

without cause] Or, *to no purpose*, without result.

4. *Shew me thy ways*] Lit. *make me to know thy ways:* the prayer of Moses in a moment of perplexity (Ex. xxxiii. 13). Cp. Ps. xxvii. 11. God's 'ways' and 'paths' are the purposes and methods of His Providence; or more specifically, the course of life and conduct which He prescribes for men. Cp. xxvii. 11; cxliii. 8.

5. *Lead me* &c.] R.V., **Guide me in thy truth**: not, as at first sight would seem to be the meaning, into a fuller knowledge of revealed truth. Jehovah's truth, so often coupled with His lovingkindness, means His faithfulness; and the sense is either 'guide me in virtue of thy faithfulness'; or 'let me live in the experience of thy faithfulness' (xxvi. 3).

6. An appeal to Jehovah's unchangeableness (Mal. iii. 6). The love of ancient days cannot be exhausted (Jer. ii. 2; xxxi. 3).

For they have been *ever of old*] Lit., *for they* have been *from everlasting.* Cp. ciii. 17; xciii. 2.

7. The word translated *sins* is derived from a root meaning *to miss the mark* or *lose the way.* It denotes primarily the failures, errors, lapses, of frailty; and so is naturally applied to the thoughtless offences of youth. The word for *transgressions* means literally *rebellions*, and denotes the deliberate offences of riper years.

according to thy mercy] **According to thy lovingkindness**, as in *vv.* 6, 10.

for thy goodness' sake] When Moses desired a revelation of God's glory, he was granted a revelation of His goodness (Ex. xxxiii. 19). Cp. xxvii. 13; Rom. ii. 4; xi. 22.

Therefore will he teach sinners in the way.
9 (ט) The meek will he guide in judgment:
And the meek will he teach his way.
10 (י) All the paths of the LORD *are* mercy and truth
Unto such as keep his covenant and his testimonies.
11 (ל) For thy name's sake, O LORD,
Pardon mine iniquity; for it *is* great.
12 (מ) What man *is* he that feareth the LORD?
Him shall he teach in the way *that* he shall choose.
13 (נ) His soul shall dwell at ease;

> **8—14.** The Psalmist's petitions are grounded upon the revealed character of Jehovah.
>
> **8.** *Therefore*] He who is at once perfectly loving and perfectly upright must needs guide the erring.
> *teach*] R.V. **instruct**: the word from which *torah* ('law,' primarily 'instruction') is derived. See on i. 2.
> **9.** *The meek*] The humble-minded. See note on ix. 12. Humility is indispensable for God's scholars. Cp. 1 Pet. v. 5.
> *in judgment*] The practice of right; often coupled with righteousness and equity; e.g. Prov. i. 3.
> 10. In all His dealings Jehovah proves His loving purpose and His faithfulness to His promises to those who on their part are faithful to Him, keeping the covenant inaugurated by circumcision (Gen. xvii. 2 ff.), and ratified at Sinai (Ex. xix. 5; xxiv. 7, 8); of which the Ark of the Covenant (Num. x. 33) was the outward sign, and the Ten Words written on the Tables of the Covenant were the fundamental charter (Deut. ix. 9). Jehovah's testimonies are His commandments, as witnessing to His will. See note on xix. 7.
> *mercy and truth*] R.V. **lovingkindness and truth**. So He proclaimed Himself to Moses, as a God 'plenteous in lovingkindness and truth' (Ex. xxxiv. 6).
> **11.** The thought of God's requirements (*v.* 10) makes him feel his own shortcomings, and prompts this prayer for pardon. He appeals to Jehovah's revelation of Himself as the God of mercy. The verse combines *vv.* 5 and 9 of Ex. xxxiv. Cp. xxiii. 3, note; Is. xliii. 25; Jer. xiv. 7.
> **12.** *What man* &c.] A rhetorical question, equivalent to *whosoever*. Cp. xxxiv. 12.
> *him shall he teach*] R.V., **him shall he instruct**, as in *v.* 8.
> *in the way* that *he shall choose*] In the course of life which His Providence chooses for him: or, *in the way that he should choose*; what course to take in circumstances of doubt or difficulty; or, *in the way that he chooseth;* he chooses 'the fear of the LORD' which is 'the way of truth,' and Jehovah instructs him in it. This is most in accordance with cxix. 30, 173; Prov. i. 29; iii. 31.
> **13.** Temporal blessings are in store for him. He himself *shall con-*

And his seed shall inherit the earth.
(ס) The secret of the LORD *is* with them that fear him; 14
And he will shew them his covenant.
(ע) Mine eyes *are* ever towards the LORD; 15
For he shall pluck my feet out of the net.
(פ) Turn thee unto me, and have mercy upon me; 16
For I *am* desolate and afflicted.
(צ) The troubles of my heart are enlarged: 17
O bring thou me out of my distresses.
(ר) Look upon mine affliction and my pain; 18
And forgive all my sins.

tinue in prosperity; and his posterity after him **shall inherit the land** (R.V.), in accordance with the promise to Abraham (Gen. xv. 7, 8), and Israel (Ex. xx. 12; Lev. xxvi. 3 ff.; Deut. iv. 1, 40; &c.). Cp. Ps. xxxvii. 11; Prov. ii. 21, 22; and the N. T. counterpart, Matt. v. 5.

14. Mysterious spiritual blessings await him too. To those who fear Him Jehovah reveals His secret counsel. Cp. Prov. iii. 32; Ps. cxi. 10; Prov. i. 7; Matt. xi. 25. For *secret* R.V. marg. gives alternatives *counsel* or *friendship*, ideas included in the word, which denotes the confidential intercourse of intimate fellowship. For examples see Gen. xviii. 17; Am. iii. 7.

and he will shew them] Lit. *make them to know* (as in v. 4), to experience, in ever fuller and deeper measure, the meaning and blessedness of His covenant. We may also render, *and his covenant is to give them knowledge.*

15—21. Renewed prayer, for deliverance and preservation.

15. *Mine eyes* &c.] The attitude of expectant prayer. Cp. cxli. 8; cxxiii. 1 ff.; 1 Thess. v. 17. Prof. Cheyne compares the proper name Elyōēnai or Elyehōēnai, 'Unto Yahvè are mine eyes,' 1 Chr. iii. 23, Ezra viii. 4.

for he shall pluck &c.] Release me from the entanglements and perplexities of life, whether due to my own faults or to the hostility of enemies. Cp. ix. 15; xxxi. 4.

16. *Turn thee*] Or, *look:* the opposite of 'hiding the face' (xxii. 24). Cp. lxxxvi. 16; cxix. 132.

have mercy upon me] **Be gracious unto me.** See iv. 1, note.

desolate] Solitary; without other friend or helper.

17. The verb rendered *are enlarged* cannot mean 'augmented.' It is all but certain that the consonants should be divided and vocalised differently, giving the appropriate sense, **The straitnesses of my heart enlarge thou, and bring me** &c.: i.e. relieve my distress. Cp. xviii. 36; cxix. 32.

18. *Look upon* &c.] **Behold my affliction and my travail.** Cp. ix. 13.
and forgive] Lit. *take away*, sin being regarded as a burden. Cp. xxxii. 1. This verse ought to begin with the letter *Qōph*, and various

19 (ר) Consider mine enemies; for they are many;
And they hate me *with* cruel hatred.
20 (ש) O keep my soul, and deliver me:
Let me not be ashamed; for I put my trust in thee.
21 (ת) Let integrity and uprightness preserve me;
For I wait on thee.
22 (פ) Redeem Israel, O God, out of all his troubles.

emendations have been proposed with the object of restoring it. The simplest change is to add *arise* (iii. 7) at the beginning of the verse.

19. *Consider*] **Behold**, the same word as in *v*. 18.

with *cruel hatred*] Lit. *a hatred of violence*, hatred inspired by and leading to cruelty. Cp. xi. 5; xxvii. 12.

20. *O keep* &c.] **Preserve my soul.** Cp. xvi. 1; lxxxvi. 2.

for I put my trust in thee] **For I have taken refuge in thee.** Cp. vii. 1; ii. 12, note.

21. **Let integrity and uprightness guard me.** May single-hearted devotion to God and honourable behaviour to men be as it were guardian angels at my side (lxi. 7). He prays thus, not on the ground of his own merits, but in virtue of his patient dependence on God. Cp. xl. 11. 'Integrity' is the virtue of the 'perfect' man. See xv. 2; xviii. 23; cp. vii. 8. Job was "perfect and upright" (ii. 3). Cp. xxxvii. 37.

22. A concluding prayer for the nation. The alphabet has been completed, and this is a supplementary distich beginning with *Pē*, which has already been represented in *v*. 16. Ps. xxxiv has the same peculiarity. Lagarde has ingeniously conjectured that these verses contain a reference to the names of the authors, Pedael and Pedaiah. But this is very doubtful; and this verse at any rate is probably a liturgical addition to the original Psalm. The absolute use of *God* instead of *Jehovah* is contrary to the usage of the Psalm, and rare in the First Book of Psalms generally. See Introd. p. xl.

PSALM XXVI.

This Psalm is the appeal of conscious integrity for recognition and vindication. The Psalmist calls upon Jehovah to do him justice, pleading the integrity of his life, and offering himself to the searching scrutiny of the All-knowing, upon whose lovingkindness and faithfulness he grounds his confidence (*vv*. 1—3). He has shunned and will shun the society of the godless, and strives to prepare himself duly for the worship of the sanctuary which is his delight (*vv*. 4—7). And therefore he prays that he may not share the premature fate of the wicked, and declaring his purpose to live hereafter as heretofore in his integrity, concludes with a trustful assurance that his prayer is answered, and a resolution of public thanksgiving (*vv*. 8—12).

This Psalm is linked to Ps. xxv, by several resemblances of thought and expression. Compare the professions of integrity in *vv*. 1, 11 with xxv. 21, and of trust in *v*. 1 with xxv. 2; the prayer for deliverance and grace in *v.* 11 with xxv. 16, 21, 22; the sense of God's loving-kindness and faithfulness in *v.* 3 with xxv. 5, 6, 7, 10. On the other hand, the confessions of sin and prayers for pardon which are a marked feature of Ps. xxv are absent. The Psalmist is contrasting his own sincerity and innocence with the hypocrisy and violence of those whose fate he deprecates, rather than measuring his own defects by the standard of God's holiness.

There are no sufficient grounds for assigning the Psalm to a particular period of David's life, such as Saul's persecution or Absalom's rebellion. More suggestive is Ewald's acute conjecture that it and Ps. xxviii were written in a time of national calamity, probably a pestilence (cp. xxviii. 1), which seemed likely to sweep away righteous and wicked in a common judgment, though his supposition that Josiah was the author is a mere speculation. The Psalmist prays that Jehovah would distinguish between the righteous and the wicked, and save him from sharing the fate of the wicked by a premature death. Yet in the face of the danger his confidence in God is unshaken.

A Psalm of David.

Judge me, O LORD; for I have walked in mine integrity: 26
I have trusted also in the LORD; *therefore* I shall not slide.
Examine me, O LORD, and prove me; 2
Try my reins and my heart.
For thy lovingkindness *is* before mine eyes: 3

1—3. The Psalmist's plea for the recognition of his integrity.

1. *Judge me*] Do me justice; shew me to be in the right; vindicate my integrity by discriminating between me and wicked men. Cp. vii. 8; xxxv. 24; xliii. 1.

for I have walked in mine integrity] Sincerity of purpose and single-heartedness of devotion have been the rule of his life. Cp. vii. 8; xv. 2; xviii. 23; and Introd. p. lxix.

therefore I shall not slide] A possible rendering: but better, as R.V., **without wavering**. The context here requires a description of the character of his trust, rather than of its issue.

2. God knows him already (xvii. 3); and fearlessly he offers himself for a fresh scrutiny. This prayer attests at once the clearness of his conscience, and his desire that if aught of evil remains, it may be purged away. Cp. cxxxix. 23, 24. Three words are used to express the thoroughness of the scrutiny. *Examine me*, as the refiner assays his metal to test its fineness; *prove me*, by bringing me into circumstances in which the reality of my faith may be demonstrated; *try me*, as the refiner smelts gold to get rid of any remaining dross. So God 'proved' Abraham (Gen. xxii. 1); and Israel (Deut. viii. 2, 16). The purpose of such heart-searching is 'to give every man according to his ways' (Jer. xvii. 10).

my reins and my heart] The reins are the seat of the affections, the heart of thought and will. Cp. vii. 9; xi. 4.

3. The ground of the prayers in *vv.* 1, 2. He can pray for a

And I have walked in thy truth.
4 I have not sat with vain persons,
Neither will I go in with dissemblers.
5 I have hated the congregation of evildoers;
And will not sit with the wicked.
6 I will wash mine hands in innocency:
So will I compass thine altar, O LORD:
7 That *I* may publish with the voice of thanksgiving,
And tell of all thy wondrous works.
8 LORD, I have loved the habitation of thy house,

favourable judgment, and submit himself to this scrutiny, because he knows God's lovingkindness and faithfulness. They are the object of his constant meditation, the daily experience of his life. Cp. xvi. 8; xxv. 10, note.

4—7. The proof of his integrity in his conduct in the past, and his purpose for the future.

4. *I have not sat*] Of deliberate and prolonged intercourse, implying community of tastes and interests. Cp. i. 1; Jer. xv. 17.

vain persons] Lit. *men of vanity;* hollowness, falsehood, unreality: the opposite of truth and righteousness. See xii. 2; xxiv. 4.

neither will I go in] To their houses: or an abbreviation for *go in and out*, associate with.

dissemblers] Lit. *those who hide themselves;* hypocrites who disguise their real thoughts and purposes (xxviii. 3).

5. *I have hated*] R.V., I hate.

the congregation of evil doers] Cp. xxii. 16. Is there not a tacit contrast between the congregation which meets for its own evil purposes, and that which assembles for the worship of Jehovah (*v.* 12)?

I will wash mine hands in innocency] "As the priests, before they came near to the altar to minister (Ex. xxx. 17—21). What the priest did in symbolical rite, that the priestly people were to do in spiritual reality." *Kay.* Cp. lxxiii. 13: and for the ceremony as symbolising innocence see Deut. xxi. 6; Matt. xxvii. 24.

compass thine altar] Take my place in the ring of worshippers around it. A reference to solemn processions round the altar is questionable.

7. *That I may publish with the voice of thanksgiving*] Better, as R.V., **that I may make the voice of thanksgiving to be heard.**

thy wondrous works] Or, *marvellous works*. See note on ix. 1.

8—12. His love for God's house is a further reason why he should not be involved in the fate of sinners.

8. Taking up the thought of *vv.* 7, 8, he makes it the ground of his plea in *vv.* 9, 10.

I have loved] R.V., **I love.** It is the correlative of *I hate* in *v.* 5.

And the place where thine honour dwelleth.
Gather not my soul with sinners,   9
Nor my life with bloody men:
In whose hands *is* mischief,   10
And their right hand is full *of* bribes.
But *as for* me, I will walk in mine integrity: 11
Redeem me, and be merciful unto me.
My foot standeth in an even place: 12
In the congregations will I bless the LORD.

the place where thine honour dwelleth] Better, with R.V., **the place where thy glory dwelleth**: lit. *the place of the tabernacle of thy glory;* for the word *mishkan*, rendered *tabernacle*, means properly *dwelling*, the sanctuary where Jehovah *dwelt* among His people (Ex. xxv. 8, 9). Jehovah's *glory* is His manifested Presence, of which the ark was the outward symbol. Cp. Ex. xvi. 7; xxxiii. 18, 22; 1 Sam. iv. 21, 22; Ps. lxxviii. 61.

9. *Gather not*] i.e. *take not away.* Let me not share the fate of those whose society and practices I have ever shunned. How natural a prayer if a pestilence was raging which seemed to strike righteous and wicked indiscriminately! The wicked are described as *men of blood* (v. 6), who do not shrink from violence and murder: *in whose hands is mischief* (vii. 3), they deliberately plan and execute crime; *and their right hand is full of bribes,* which they take to pervert justice (xv. 5). Nobles and men in authority are referred to. Comp. Mic. vii. 2, 3.

11. With such evil-doers the Psalmist contrasts himself. His purpose, if his life is spared, is to shape his conduct as hitherto; and therefore he prays *redeem me* (xxv. 22), deliver me from the fate of the wicked, *and be gracious unto me* (iv. 1, note).

12. Faith realises the answer to its prayer as already granted, and security assured. He has traversed the rough winding path through the gloomy defile, and stands in the open plain, where there is no more fear of stumbling or sudden assault. Life thus prolonged is the reason and the opportunity for public thanksgiving. Cp. xxii. 25.

PSALM XXVII.

Enthusiastic confidence is the keynote of the first six verses of the Psalm. Under Jehovah's guardianship the Psalmist knows no fear in the midst of dangers (*vv.* 1—3). His highest desire is to enjoy Jehovah's fellowship and protection as a guest in His house. He anticipates a speedy triumph over his foes, and promises grateful thanksgiving (*vv.* 4—6). The swing of the rhythm corresponds to the energy of the thought.

Suddenly all is changed: the jubilant rhythm is abandoned; anxious supplication takes the place of joyous faith. Earnestly the Psalmist pleads that Jehovah will not forsake His servant, and appeals to His promises and His past mercies (*vv.* 7—12). Yet in this crisis Jehovah is his only stay, and he concludes by encouraging himself to faith and patience (*vv.* 13, 14).

Thus the Psalm falls into two equal divisions, with a conclusion. If the two parts are by the same poet, he must clearly have written them at different times, and under the influence of different circumstances. When he added the prayer of *vv.* 7—14 to his former song he reaffirmed the faith of happier days, though it had ceased to give joy and comfort in his present distress. But the marked difference in tone, contents, and rhythm, makes it not improbable that two independent Psalms are here combined, or that a later poet appended *vv.* 7—14 to *vv.* 1—6. It is as though he would say: 'I would fain appropriate this bold utterance of faith; but all is dark around me, and I can only pray in faltering tones, and strive to wait in patience.'

The Psalm (or at any rate the first part) has strong claims to be regarded as Davidic, and may best be assigned to the time of Absalom's rebellion, shortly before the final battle. The language of *vv.* 2, 3 is that of a warrior; *v.* 3 breathes the same spirit as iii. 6; and with *vv.* 4 ff. comp. 2 Sam. xv. 25. Jehovah's abode is still a tent (*v.* 6), though it can be called a temple or palace (*v.* 4) as the abode of a king. Comp. 2 Sam. vi. 17. The Sept. addition to the title, *before he was anointed*, would refer it to Saul's persecution, or to the wars of the first seven years of his reign.

Comp. Pss. iii, xxiii, xci.

A Psalm of David.

27 The LORD *is* my light and my salvation; whom shall I fear?
  The LORD *is* the strength of my life; of whom shall I be afraid?
2 When the wicked, *even* mine enemies and my foes, came upon me to eat up my flesh,

1—3. With Jehovah on his side, he knows no fear. This faith, the constant theme of prophet and psalmist, finds its N.T. extension in Rom. viii. 31.

1. *my light*] Illuminating the darkness of trouble, anxiety, and danger; giving life and joy. Cp. iv. 6; xviii. 28; xxxvi. 9; xliii. 3; lxxxiv. 11; Is. x. 17; Mic. vii. 8. Again the N.T. interprets the words for us in a larger spiritual sense. John i. 4, 9; viii. 12; 1 John i. 5.

my salvation] Cp. *v.* 9; Ex. xv. 2.

strength] Or, *stronghold*, a defence against all assaults. Cp. xviii. 2; xxxi. 2, 3.

2. **When evil-doers came near against me to eat my flesh,**
  Even mine adversaries and my foes, they stumbled and fell.

This may refer to past experience, or it may be a confident anticipation of the discomfiture of his foes. According to a common Hebrew idiom the perfect tense may realise their defeat as an accom-

They stumbled and fell.
Though a host should encamp against me, my heart shall 3
   not fear :
Though war should rise against me, in this *will* I *be* con-
   fident.
One *thing* have I desired of the LORD, that will I seek after; 4
That I may dwell in the house of the LORD all the days of
   my life,
To behold the beauty of the LORD, and to inquire in his
   temple.
For in the time of trouble he shall hide me in his pavilion : 5
In the secret of his tabernacle shall he hide me;
He shall set me up upon a rock.

plished fact. See Note IV, p. 223. He compares his assailants to wild beasts, eager to devour him. Cp. iii. 7.
stumbled and fell] Cp. Is. viii. 15; Jer. xlvi. 6.
3. The language may be figurative, but is more natural, if the writer was, like David, actually exposed to war's alarms. Cp. iii. 6.
in this] In the truth of *v.* 1. But it is better to render with R.V., **even then**, in spite of opposing armies.

4—6. To be Jehovah's guest and live secure under His protection is the Psalmist's chief desire; and even now he confidently anticipates deliverance from his foes. *v.* 4 can hardly be understood literally of a lifelong residence in the Temple. Rather, as in xxiii. 4, 5; xv. 1, Jehovah is thought of as the royal host, whose guests are secure under His protection, and enjoy familiar intercourse with Him. But the language is suggested by the possibility of approach to God in His earthly house, and perhaps by the suppliant's right of asylum there.

4. *One* thing *have I desired*] R.V., **One thing have I asked**; above all others as the climax of my petitions.
to behold] The word implies a wondering and delighted *gazing*.
the beauty] Or, *pleasantness;* not merely the outward beauty of the sanctuary and its worship, but the gracious kindliness of Jehovah to His guests. Cp. xvi. 11; xc. 17; Prov. iii. 17.
to inquire in his temple] Investigating His character and dealings with men. For knowledge gained and doubts solved by meditation in the Temple see lxxiii. 17. We may also render, *to consider his temple* (R.V. marg.); to contemplate it, for the sanctuary and its ordinances were to the devout worshipper symbols of heavenly realities. Cp. Is. vi.

**5. For he shall conceal me in his pavilion in the day of trouble,
He shall hide me in the hiding-place of his tent;
Upon a rock shall he lift me up.**
He will be secured from danger as one who is sheltered from heat and storm, or safe from assault in some inaccessible rock fortress.

6 And now shall mine head be lifted up above mine enemies
round about me:
Therefore will I offer in his tabernacle sacrifices of joy;
I will sing, yea, I will sing *praises* unto the LORD.

7 Hear, O LORD, *when* I cry *with* my voice:
Have mercy also upon me, and answer me.
8 *When thou saidst*, Seek ye my face; my heart said unto thee,
Thy face, LORD, will I seek.
9 Hide not thy face *far* from me;
Put not thy servant away in anger:

Cp. xxxi. 20; Is. iv. 6; and the expression *his hidden* or *secret ones* in Ps. lxxxiii. 3.

6. *And now* &c.] In the immediate future he anticipates not protection only but triumphant victory. Cp. iii. 3; cx. 7.

in his tabernacle] Lit. in his tent, as in the preceding verse. There it may simply mean *dwelling*, in a general figurative sense; but here in connexion with the offering of sacrifice, it would seem that the tent which David pitched for the Ark on Mount Zion (2 Sam. vi. 17) must be meant.

sacrifices of joy] A bold expression for *sacrifices of thanksgiving*. *Joy* may mean the jubilant *shouting* with which religious festivities were celebrated (2 Sam. vi. 15; Ps. xxxiii. 3; xlvii. 5); or *trumpet-sound*, such as accompanied certain sacrifices (Num. x. 10); here probably the former.

7—14. The tone of the Psalm changes abruptly to plaintive and anxious supplication. God seems to be on the point of hiding His face.

7. *Have mercy*] Be gracious.
8. The A.V. gives the general sense fairly. But the text as it stands must be rendered:

Unto thee my heart hath said:
'Seek ye my face'; 'Thy face, Jehovah, will I seek.'

In prayer from his innermost heart the Psalmist pleads the invitation which Jehovah addresses to His people, *Seek ye my face;* and responds to it on his own behalf, *Thy face, Jehovah, will I seek.* The construction is bold, but finds a parallel in Job xlii. 3—5, where in *vv.* 3 *a*, 4 Job quotes the Lord's words, and in *vv.* 3 *b*, 5 answers them. We need not assume a reference to any particular passage (e.g. Deut. iv. 29). The invitation is the sum of all revelation. Cp. Matt. vii. 7 ff.

9. Hide not thy face from me (R.V.). A prayer grounded on the divine promise which he has obeyed. Cp. xxii. 24.

put not &c.] Or, *turn not*, like the unjust judge who turns the needy from his right (Job xxiv. 4; Is. x. 2; Luke xviii. 1 ff.).

Thou hast been my help; leave me not,
Neither forsake me, O God of my salvation.
When my father and my mother forsake me, 10
Then the LORD will take me up.
Teach me thy way, O LORD, 11
And lead me in a plain path, because of mine enemies.
Deliver me not over unto the will of mine enemies: 12
For false witnesses are risen up against me, and such as breathe out cruelty.
I had fainted, unless I had believed 13
To see the goodness of the LORD in the land of the living.

in anger] See note on vi. 1.
thou hast been my help] An appeal to past experience. Surely God cannot have changed.
leave me not] R.V., **cast me not off** (xciv. 14; 1 Kings viii. 57).
10. *When my father* &c.] Or, as R.V.,
For my father and my mother have forsaken me, but &c.
A proverbial expression. (Comp. '*bereavement* to my soul,' xxxv. 12). Though he is friendless and forsaken as a deserted child, Jehovah will adopt him and care for him. His love is stronger than that of the closest human relations. Cp. Is. xlix. 15; Ps. ciii. 13.
11. Cp. v. 8; xxv. 12. In the course of life designed for him by God he will be safe. He prays that it may be like a path along a level open plain, free from pitfalls and places where enemies may lurk in ambush. *Plain* is the same word as *even* in xxvi. 12; and *mine enemies* means literally, *those that lie in wait for me*, as in v. 8. Cp. Mk. xii. 13 for illustration.
12. *enemies*] R.V., **adversaries**, as in *v.* 2.
false witnesses] Slanderous calumniators are meant, rather than actual witnesses in court. Cp. xxxv. 11; Prov. vi. 19.
such as breathe out cruelty] Bent on injuring him by their talk. For the phrase cp. Acts ix. 1.
13. The word for *unless* is marked with dots in the Massoretic text as probably spurious, and is not rendered by LXX, Vulg., or Jerome. Omitting it, we must render;
I believe that I shall see &c.
If it is retained, the construction is an aposiopesis:
O! had I not believed &c.;
or an apodosis may be supplied, as in A.V.
to see] The construction of the Heb. verb implies the sense, *to see and enjoy*.
in the land of the living] Here, as in lii. 5; cxvi. 9; cxlii. 5; Is. xxxviii. 11; liii. 8; &c., this life on earth in contrast to Sheol, the land of death: not, as in the natural Christian application of the words and as the Targum already paraphrases, 'the land of everlasting life'.

14 Wait on the LORD:
Be of good courage, and he shall strengthen thine heart:
Wait, I say, on the LORD.

14. The Psalmist addresses himself, and encourages himself to patience. His faith rebukes his faintness.
Be of good courage] R.V., **Be strong, and let thine heart take courage.** Cp. xxxi. 2.; Deut. xxxi. 7; Josh. i. 6, 7, 9, 18.
Wait, I say] R.V., **Yea, wait thou.** Cp. xxv. 3; xxxvii. 9, 34; Prov. xx. 22.

PSALM XXVIII.

An urgent cry for audience (*vv.* 1, 2) is followed by a prayer that the Psalmist may be delivered from sharing the fate of evil-doers and hypocrites, and that they may receive the retribution which is the fitting punishment of their blind disbelief (*vv.* 3—5). Suddenly the Psalmist breaks into joyous thanksgiving. His prayer is answered, or faith guarantees that it will be answered (*vv.* 6, 7); and the Psalm concludes with an intercession for the people (*vv.* 8, 9).

The Psalm is a companion to Ps. xxvi. The circumstances are similar, but here the danger is yet more pressing. Cp. *v.* 3 with xxvi. 9, 10. The Psalmist is in imminent peril of death. He fears that he may share the fate of the godless. Was there a pestilence raging, which threatened to sweep away righteous and wicked without distinction? There he pleads his own integrity, here the iniquity and the godlessness of the wicked, as the reason for discriminating. Jehovah will manifest His justice alike in sparing the righteous and punishing the wicked.

The Psalm is however commonly thought to have been written by David during his flight from Absalom. *v.* 3 then alludes to the character of the treacherous conspirators, and *v.* 5 refers to their obstinate refusal to recognise the hand of Jehovah in David's choice and elevation to the throne; while the concluding prayer is such as the king might well offer for a people torn by intestine quarrels.

A Psalm of David.

28 Unto thee will I cry, O LORD, my rock; be not silent to me:

1, 2. Introductory appeal for a hearing, emphasising the urgency of the need.

1. Render with R.V.,
   Unto thee, O LORD, will I call;
   My rock, be not thou deaf unto me.

He appeals to Jehovah as his *rock*, the ground of his confidence. See xviii. 2 (note), 31.

be not silent unto me] Lit. *from me*; and similarly in the next line. The rendering *be not silent* may stand, as in xxxv. 22; xxxix. 12; or we may render with R.V., **be not thou deaf.** The sense is, 'Turn not

Lest, *if* thou be silent to me, I become like them that go
down into the pit.
Hear the voice of my supplications, when I cry unto thee, 2
When I lift up my hands toward thy holy oracle.
Draw me not away with the wicked, and with the workers 3
of iniquity,
Which speak peace to their neighbours, but mischief *is* in
their hearts.
Give them according to their deeds, 4
And according to the wickedness of their endeavours:

away from me as though thou didst not hear, lest if thou turn away in
unregarding silence, I become ' &c.
like them that go down to the pit] i.e. the dying or the dead. *The
pit* is the grave or Sheol. Cp. xxii. 29; lxxxviii. 4; Prov. i. 12.
How natural a prayer if people were dying of pestilence all round him!
The last line recurs in cxliii. 7.
2. The first line recurs in xxxi. 22.
when I cry] A stronger word than that in *v*. 1, meaning to *cry for
help*.
when I lift up my hands] The attitude of prayer (lxiii. 4; 1 Tim.
ii. 8), the outward symbol of an uplifted heart (xxv. 1).
toward thy holy oracle] Lit., as R.V. marg., *toward the innermost
place of thy sanctuary*, i.e. the most holy place, where the Ark, the
symbol of God's Presence among His people, was. See 1 Kings vi.
16 ff.; viii. 6. The rendering *oracle*, following Jerome's *oraculum*, rests
upon a wrong derivation. The word does not in itself denote the
place where God answers. It is used elsewhere only in the accounts
of the building of the Temple (1 Kings vi—viii; 2 Chr. iii—v). The
worshipper naturally turns as he prays towards Jehovah's dwelling-
place in heaven (1 Kings viii. 22), or its earthly counterpart (1 Kings
viii. 30 ff.). Cp. Ps. v. 7.

3—5. The Psalmist's prayer that he may be distinguished from the
wicked, and that they may be judged as they deserve.

3. *Draw me not away*] Cp. xxvi. 9. But the word here is stronger,
suggesting the idea of criminals being dragged off to execution. He
prays that he may not share the fate of the wicked in the judgment
now being executed.
which speak peace to &c.] Rather, as R.V., **with**. Double-hearted
hypocrites; cp. xii. 2; Jer. ix. 8; and contrast xv. 2.
4. Give them according to their work,
And according to the evil of their doings:
Give them according to the operation of their hands.
This is not a vindictive craving for personal revenge, but a solemn
prayer that Jehovah will openly convict false and wicked men by manifesting His righteous judgments upon them, and punishing them as
they deserve. See Introd. p. lxxii.

Give them after the work of their hands;
Render to them their desert.
5 Because they regard not the works of the LORD,
Nor the operation of his hands,
He shall destroy them, and not build them up.

6 Blessed *be* the Lord, because he hath heard the voice of my supplications.
7 The LORD *is* my strength and my shield;
My heart trusted in him, and I am helped:
Therefore my heart greatly rejoiceth;
And with my song will I praise him.
8 The LORD *is* their strength,
And he *is* the saving strength of his anointed.
9 Save thy people,

Give] Of a judicial sentence. Cp. Hos. ix. 14; Jer. xxxii. 19.
their desert] The word denotes an *action* either good or bad, and its fitting reward.

5. Atheists in practice if not in profession, they deny that Jehovah governs the world, and refuse to discern His working in creation, in providence, and in judgment. Unbelief lies at the root of all their sin. *The works of the LORD* and *the operation of his hands* stand in strong contrast to *their work* and *the operation of their hands* in *v.* 4. Compare the parallels to this and *v.* 4 in Is. i. 16; iii. 8—11; v. 12, 19; xxii. 11.

he shall destroy them] Better with P.B.V. and R.V., **he shall break them down.** Cp. Jer. xxiv. 6.

6, 7. Thanksgiving succeeds to prayer. Are we to suppose that faith realises the answer to its prayer as already granted, and can give thanks accordingly? or that this conclusion was added by the Psalmist subsequently as a grateful memorial of his deliverance? Either alternative is possible; but here and in xxxi. 21—24 we seem to have a record of actual deliverance. vi. 8 ff. is somewhat different.

7. *my strength*] Cp. Ex. xv. 2. *my shield*] See note on iii. 3.
trusted] Better as R.V., **hath trusted.**
greatly rejoiceth] Exulteth. Cp. v. 11; 1 Sam. ii. 1.

8, 9. Concluding intercession for the people. Cf. iii. 8.

8. *their strength*] *Their* must refer to the people. But there is no antecedent for the pronoun, and it is best to follow a few Heb. MSS., the LXX, Vulg., and Syr., in reading, **a strength unto his people.** Cp. xxix. 11.

and he is &c.] R.V., **and he is a strong hold of salvation to his anointed.** Cp. xxvii. 1. *Salvation* is lit. *salvations*, great and manifold deliverance. Cp. xviii. 50; xx. 6.

PSALM XXIX.

And bless thine inheritance:
Feed them also, and lift them up for ever.

9. *thine inheritance*] Israel. Cp. Deut. iv. 20.
feed them] Lit. *shepherd them*. Cp. xxiii. 1; 2 Sam. vii. 7. *Govern them* in the adaptation of this verse in the Te Deum is from the Vulg. *rege*.
lift them up] Exalt them; as the word is used in 2 Sam. v. 12. But we should probably render as in R.V., *bear them up;* either as a shepherd carries his sheep (Is. xl. 11), continuing the idea of the preceding word; or as a father carries his child, a figure often applied to Jehovah's care for Israel. See Deut. i. 31; Is. xlvi. 3, 4; lxiii. 9. Cp. too Ex. xix. 4; Deut. xxxii. 11.

PSALM XXIX.

The devout Israelite's view of Nature was profoundly religious. He did not contemplate its wonder and beauty and variety simply for their own sake. All spoke to him of God's power and glory and beneficence, or supplied him with emblems and figures for the delineation of God's attributes and working. Thus the thunder was to him the Voice of God, and all the terrible phenomena of the storm were an expression of the majesty of the Eternal Sovereign of the Universe. See Ex. xix. 16; xx. 18; Ps. xviii. 7 ff. (and notes there); Is. xxx. 27 ff.; Hab. iii: &c.: and for Nature as the revelation of God see especially Pss. viii, xix, civ.

It must be remembered that storms in Palestine are often far more violent and impressive than storms in this country. See the description of a storm at Sinai quoted in Stanley's *Jewish Church*, Lect. VII. Vol. I. p. 128.

The Psalm falls into three divisions: *vv.* 3—9 form the main part, with a prelude, *vv.* 1, 2, and conclusion, *vv.* 10, 11.

i. The angels are summoned to render their tribute of praise to Jehovah (*vv.* 1, 2).

ii. The special occasion of this summons is the revelation of His majesty on earth, where the thunder of His Voice convulsing all nature proclaims His power and glory (*vv.* 3—9).

iii. But terrible as is this manifestation, His people need not fear. Towards them the might of the Eternal King displays itself in blessing (*vv.* 10, 11).

From the title in the LXX (ἐξοδίου σκηνῆς, Vulg. *in consummatione tabernaculi*) it appears that in the time of the Second Temple this Psalm was sung on the 8th or concluding day of the Feast of Tabernacles (Lev. xxiii. 36; where for 'solemn assembly' the LXX has ἐξόδιον = 'closing festival,' as R.V. marg.). According to the Talmudic treatise *Sopherim* it is the Psalm for Pentecost, and it is now used in the Synagogue on the first day of that festival.

A Psalm of David.

29 Give unto the LORD, O ye mighty,
Give unto the LORD glory and strength.
2 Give unto the LORD the glory due unto his name;
Worship the LORD in the beauty of holiness.

1, 2. Prelude, calling upon the angels to celebrate Jehovah's glory. Cp. xcvi. 7—9, where however the words are differently applied.

1. *O ye mighty*] The phrase *bnē ēlīm* admits of three renderings.

(1) *O ye sons of the mighty* (R.V.), which may mean either powerful nobles, or mighty celestial beings. (2) *O ye sons of the gods* (R.V. marg.), meaning either beings "belonging to the class of superhuman, heavenly powers" (Cheyne); or the nations who "had forgotten their true parentage, and ranged themselves under the protection of deified heroes or invented gods, and are now invited to remember themselves and return to the Lord." (Kay). Cp. xcvi. 7; Jer. ii. 27.

(3) *O ye sons of God* (R.V. marg., taking *bnē elim* as a doubly formed plural of *ben ēl*); i.e. angels, who are called *bnē elōhīm*, 'sons of God,' in Job i. 6; ii. 1; xxxviii. 7. The last rendering is the best; but whichever rendering is adopted, the use of the phrase in Ps. lxxxix. 6 (comp. *vv.* 5 and 7) is decisive for the meaning *angels*. The spiritual beings which surround God's throne in heaven are called upon to render Him their tribute of adoration. Cp. ciii. 20 f.; cxlviii. 1 f.; Job xxxviii. 7. The special occasion of the summons is the manifestation of His glory upon earth which the Psalmist describes in *vv.* 3—9. So the Seraphic chorus in Is. vi. 3 recognise the earth as "full of Jehovah's glory."

Give] i.e. ascribe, attribute. Recognise by your confession and proclamation those attributes of glory and strength which are supremely His. Cp. Deut. xxxii. 3; Ps. lxviii. 34; Lk. xvii. 18; Rom. iv. 20; Apoc. xiv. 7.

The P.B.V., *Bring unto the Lord, O ye mighty, bring young rams unto the Lord*, comes from the LXX through the Vulg. In the present text of the LXX, the first line of the verse is doubly represented. *Ēlīm* may mean *rams*, and an alternative rendering of *bnē ēlīm* as *young rams*, originally placed in the margin, has found its way into the text.

2. *the glory due unto his name*] Lit. *the glory of his name*, particularising the general idea of glory in *v.* 1. *The glory of his name* is His glory as He reveals Himself in the world (v. 11 note); here, as the context shews, especially in Nature.

in the beauty of holiness] Suggestive as this rendering is, it can hardly be right; and the true sense is that given in R.V. marg., **in holy array**. Cp. Ps. xcvi. 9 (= 1 Chr. xvi. 29); 2 Chr. xx. 21 (R.V. marg.); Ps. cx. 3. The ideas of earth are transferred to heaven. As the priests in the earthly temple were clothed in "holy garments for glory and for beauty" (Ex. xxviii. 2), so even the ministrants in the heavenly temple must be arrayed befittingly.

PSALM XXIX. 3—7. 149

The voice of the LORD *is* upon the waters :
The God of glory thundereth :
The LORD *is* upon many waters.
The voice of the LORD *is* powerful ;
The voice of the LORD *is* full of majesty.
The voice of the LORD breaketh the cedars ;
Yea, the LORD breaketh the cedars of Lebanon.
He maketh them also to skip like a calf;
Lebanon and Sirion like a young unicorn.
The voice of the LORD divideth the flames of fire.

3—9. The exhibition of Jehovah's power which is the ground of the opening call to praise. His voice is heard in the pealing of the thunder above the storm-clouds (*vv.* 3, 4); the storm bursts, it shatters the cedars and shakes the mountains in the far north (*vv.* 5, 6); the lightnings flash (*v.* 7); the deserts to the far south with their affrighted denizens tremble (*vv.* 8, 9); and over all resounds the chorus, Glory (*v.* 9 *b*). The seven times repeated *voice of the LORD* is like successive peals of thunder.

3. *The voice of the LORD*] So thunder is called in Ex. ix. 23 ff.; Ps. xviii. 13; &c. Cp. Rev. x. 3 f.

upon the waters] Hardly the sea, as though the storm were represented as coming in from the Mediterranean; but rather the waters collected in the dense masses of storm-cloud upon which Jehovah rides (xviii. 9 ff.; civ. 3; Jer. x. 13).

the God of glory] Cp. "the King of glory" (xxiv. 7 ff.).

the LORD is upon many waters] The idea of the first line is repeated and emphasised. Not Jehovah's voice alone, but Jehovah Himself is there, and the waters are many (or, *great*). The R.V. *Even the LORD upon many waters* is hardly an improvement. The P.B.V. of *vv.* 3, 4 is a free paraphrase of the supposed sense.

4. is *powerful*...is *full of majesty*] Lit. *is with power*...*is with majesty*.

5. *cedars*] The noblest and strongest of the trees of the forest; emblematical of worldly magnificence (Is. ii. 13).

yea, the LORD breaketh] R.V. yea, the **LORD** breaketh in pieces. The idea of the first line is emphasised and particularised in the second. Cp. *v.* 8.

6. *them*] Not the cedars, but the mountains generally, to be understood from *Lebanon* and *Sirion* in the next line. Cp. cxiv. 4, 6; xviii. 7 ff.

Sirion] The old Sidonian name for Hermon (Deut. iii. 9), derived probably from the glistening of the snow on its summit. Lebanon and Sirion are specified as the noblest mountains of Palestine, and also as forming the northern boundary of the land.

unicorn] R.V. **wild ox.** See note on xxii. 21.

7. *divideth the flames of fire*] Better, as in R.V., cleaveth the flames

8 The voice of the LORD shaketh the wilderness;
  The Lord shaketh the wilderness of Kadesh.
9 The voice of the LORD maketh the hinds to calve,
  And discovereth the forests:
  And in his temple doth every one speak of *his* glory.
10 The LORD sitteth upon the flood;
  Yea, the LORD sitteth King for ever.
11 The LORD will give strength unto his people;
  The LORD will bless his people with peace.

of fire; or, as in R.V. marg., *heweth out flames of fire;* a poetical description of the forked lightnings darting from the cloud.

8. *shaketh the wilderness*] Or, **maketh the wilderness tremble.** Cp. xcvi. 9; xcvii. 4; cxiv. 7.

the LORD...the wilderness of Kadesh] Again with poetical effect emphasising and specialising the idea of the previous line. The storm sweeps down to the desert in the far south. Kadesh, famous in the history of Israel's wanderings, was the eastern part of the desert toward the border of Edom (Num. xx. 16), though its exact position is disputed.

9. *maketh the hinds to calve*] Prematurely, in fear; an observed fact. There is no need to emend (though the change required would be very slight), *shaketh* (or, *pierceth*) *the oaks*.

discovereth] i.e. as R.V., **strippeth the forests bare,** of branches, leaves, bark. *Discover* is an archaism for *uncover* (xviii. 15, note).

and in his temple &c.] R.V., **And in his temple everything saith, Glory.** It is tempting to understand *his temple* of heaven and earth, and to regard the line as a summary of the message of the storm; but *temple* (or, *palace*) must mean heaven; and the meaning is better given by rendering
  While in his temple all are saying, Glory.
This is the chant of the angelic worshippers (*vv.* 1, 2) as they watch the manifestation of Jehovah's majesty.

10, 11. Conclusion. The storm passes, but HE whose glory it declares is the Eternal King, the Judge of the world, the Guardian of His people. Awful as is His power, they need not fear. To them it speaks of peace.

10. **The LORD sat** *as king* **at the Flood;**
   Yea, the LORD sitteth as king for ever (R.V.).
According to the A.V. *the flood* appears to mean the deluge of rain which falls in the storm. But the word *mabbûl* is found nowhere else but in Gen. vi—xi, and is best explained by its use there. The storm reminds the poet of the great typical example of judgment and mercy, in which Jehovah's judicial sovereignty was exhibited.

Literally we may render, *sat for the Flood;* took His seat on His throne in order to execute that memorable judgment (Ps. ix. 7).

11. Comp. xxviii. 8, 9; xlvi. 1—3; and the blessing in Num. vi.

24—26. For His own people He is not the God of terror; for them all ends in peace. "This closing word *with peace* is like a rainbow arch over the Psalm. The beginning of the Psalm shews us heaven open, and the throne of God in the midst of the angelic songs of praise; while its close shews us His victorious people upon earth, blessed with peace in the midst of the terrible utterance of His wrath. *Gloria in excelsis* is the beginning, and *pax in terris* the end." *Delitzsch*.

PSALM XXX.

A thanksgiving for recovery from an almost fatal sickness, and a reflection on the lessons which it was sent to teach. Cp. cxix. 67. The Psalmist praises Jehovah for preserving his life in answer to his prayer (1—3), and calls upon the godly to join him in thanksgiving (4, 5). He goes on to relate his own experience of God's mercy. In prosperity he had grown presumptuous, till God withdrew His favour, and trouble came (6, 7). Then he pleaded that his life might be spared (8—10): his prayer was answered; his life was prolonged that he might praise Jehovah, and in thanksgiving will he employ the remainder of his days (11, 12).

The Psalm is entitled, **A Psalm; a Song at the Dedication of the House**; *a Psalm of David* (R.V.): and this title has generally been supposed to refer to the occasion for which the Psalm was written. But commentators are not agreed whether *the House* means the Temple or David's Palace. The term *dedication* is used of a house (Deut. xx. 5), or city walls (Neh. xii. 27), as well as of sacred things and places (Num. vii. 10 ff.; 1 Kings viii. 63; Ezra vi. 16, 17). Some refer it to David's palace in Zion (2 Sam. v. 11), and suppose that he had recently recovered from a severe illness: others to the dedication of the site of the Temple (1 Chr. xxi. 26; xxii. 1) after the great Plague, regarding the allusions to sickness in the Psalm as not literal but figurative of the anguish which the king felt for the sufferings of his people.

But it is most probable that the title does not refer to the occasion of the Psalm at all, but to its liturgical use at the Dedication of the Second Temple (Ezra vi. 16), or in later times at the Feast of the Dedication, to which it is assigned in the Talmudic treatise *Sopherim*. Comp. the title of Ps. xcii, and of xxix in the LXX. The title appears to be a composite one. The words *A Song at the Dedication of the House* are inserted awkwardly between *A Psalm* and *of David*. The Feast of the Dedication (John x. 22) was instituted by Judas Maccabaeus in B.C. 165, to commemorate the purification of the Temple after its desecration by Antiochus Epiphanes, and the erection of the new altar of burnt-offering (1 Macc. iv. 52 ff.; 2 Macc. x. 1 ff.).

But it does not follow that the Psalm was written for either of these occasions. More probably it was already familiar, and was selected as appropriate to the circumstances. The very existence of the nation had been at stake; it had been suddenly and unexpectedly freed from a crushing tyranny and as it were restored to life; and this Psalm supplied it with fitting language in which to give thanks for its deliverance. The experience of the individual had been repeated in that of the nation.

This thanksgiving corresponds to the prayer of Ps. vi. Comp. *v.* 2 *b* with vi. 2 *b*; *v.* 5 *a* with vi. 1 *a*; *v.* 7 *b* with vi. 2, 3, 10; *v.* 9 with vi. 5. Hezekiah's prayer (Is. xxxviii. 10—20) seems to contain reminiscences of it; comp. especially *vv.* 18—20 with *vv.* 9 ff.

A Psalm *and* Song *at* the dedication of the house of David.

30 I will extol thee, O LORD; for thou hast lifted me up,
And hast not made my foes to rejoice over me.
2 O LORD my God, I cried unto thee, and thou hast healed me.
3 O LORD, thou hast brought up my soul from the grave:
Thou hast kept me alive, that I should not go down *to* the pit.
4 Sing unto the LORD, O ye saints of his,

1—3. Thanksgiving for deliverance from death in answer to prayer.

1. *I will extol thee*] Or, *exalt*, as the word is rendered in Ex. xv. 2; Ps. xxxiv. 3; Is. xxv. 1; &c. The same word is used of God's exalting men to high estate (1 Sam. ii. 7), or lifting them up out of danger into safety (ix. 13; xxvii. 5); and man's return is to exalt God by proclaiming His supreme exaltedness.

thou hast lifted me up] R.V., **thou hast raised me up**, a peculiar word, meaning literally, *thou hast drawn me up*, from the depths of trouble, or the pit of Sheol.

and hast not made my foes to rejoice over me] His death would have been the occasion for the triumph of his enemies. For the malignant delight of enemies enhancing the bitterness of misfortune see xxxv. 19, 24 ff.; xxxviii. 16; Lam. ii. 17.

2. *healed me*] Best taken literally of restoration from sickness.

3. So desperate was his sickness that his recovery was as life from the dead, a veritable resurrection from the grave.

from the grave] R.V. **from Sheol**. See note on vi. 5. Cp. 1 Sam. ii. 6.

thou hast kept me alive that I should not go down to *the pit*] Better, **thou hast restored me to life from among them that go down to the pit**. He was already as good as dead, when Jehovah raised him up again. Cp. ix. 13; lxxxviii. 4 ff. This is the reading of the *K'thîbh*, which is supported by the LXX and Syr., and by xxviii. 1. The A.V. *that I should not go down* follows the *Qrî*, which is supported by the Targ. and Jer., but involves an anomalous grammatical form, and gives a less vigorous sense.

4, 5. An invitation to the godly to join in thanksgiving, in view of those attributes of Jehovah of which the Psalmist has just had experience. Cp. ix. 11; xxii. 23.

4. *Sing*] **Sing praise** (R. V.); or, *sing psalms*.
saints] See note on iv. 3.

And give thanks at the remembrance of his holiness.
For his anger *endureth but* a moment; in his favour *is* life: 5
Weeping may endure for a night, but joy *cometh* in the morning.
And in my prosperity I said, 6

at the remembrance of his holiness] Lit. *to the memorial of his holiness*, and so virtually, as R.V., **to his holy name**. For His name is that which brings to remembrance all that He is and does. See Ex. iii. 15; and cp. Ps. xcvii. 12; cxxii. 4. It is here called the memorial of his *holiness*, because the mercy and faithfulness which the Psalmist is celebrating are rays out of the light of holiness. Cp. xxxiii. 21.
 5. Literally, *For a moment in his anger;*
 life in his favour:
which is generally explained to mean, as in R.V. marg.,
 For his anger is but for a moment;
 His favour is for a life-time:
on the ground that the parallelism requires the contrast between *a lifetime* and *a moment*. But this is a maimed and inadequate explanation. The parallelism is (as is often the case) incomplete; *life* is not the antithesis to *a moment* but to the adversity which comes in Jehovah's anger. If the thought of the lines were expanded it would be:
 For in his anger is adversity for a moment;
 In his favour is life for length of days.
The A.V. may therefore be retained as a tolerable paraphrase. *Life* carries with it the ideas of light and joy and prosperity. Cp. xvi. 11; xxi. 4; xxxvi. 9.
 weeping &c.] Literally;
 Weeping may come in to lodge at even,
 But in the morning there is singing.
Sorrow is but the passing wayfarer, who only tarries for the night; with dawn it is transfigured into joy, or joy comes to takes its place. Note the natural and suggestive contrast between the dark night of trouble and the bright morn of rejoicing. Cp. xlix. 14; xc. 14; cxliii. 8; and for the truth expressed by the whole verse, which is a commentary on Ex. xxxiv. 6, 7, see ciii. 8 ff.; Is. liv. 7, 8; Mic. vii. 18; John xvi. 20; and indeed the whole of the O. T. and N. T.

 6, 7. The Psalmist relates his own experience of the truth stated in the preceding verse. His presumption had required the correction of chastisement.
 6. Render with R.V.
 As for me, I said in my prosperity.
 The word translated *prosperity* includes the idea of careless security, resulting from uninterrupted good fortune. Comp. Prov. i. 32; and for the carnal pride that is apt to spring from prosperity, see Deut. viii. 10 ff.; xxxii. 15; Dan. iv. 27 ff.

I shall never be moved.

7 LORD, by thy favour thou hast made my mountain to stand strong:
Thou didst hide thy face, *and* I was troubled.
8 I cried to thee, O LORD;
And unto the LORD I made supplication.
9 What profit *is there* in my blood, when I go down to the pit?
Shall the dust praise thee? shall it declare thy truth?
10 Hear, O LORD, and have mercy upon me:
LORD, be thou my helper.

I shall never be moved] Forgetting his dependence upon God, and approaching perilously near the godless man's self-confident boast (x. 6).

7. R.V., **Thou, LORD, of thy favour hadst made my mountain to stand strong**; lit. *hadst established strength for my mountain*. Zion, strong by position and art, may be thought of, partly in itself, partly as an emblem of the Davidic kingdom. Fortress and kingdom alike derived their real strength from Jehovah. Cp. 1 Kings xv. 4; 2 Chron. ix. 8. But the reading is doubtful. The LXX, Vulg., and Syr. represent, *hadst established strength for my majesty*. The Targum, which rarely departs from the Massoretic Text, gives *hadst made me stand upon strong mountains;* a figure for security. Cp. xviii. 33; xxvii. 5.

thou didst hide thy face] Withdrawing the light of thy favour. Then *I was troubled* (omit *and* which A.V. inserts): a strong word, expressing the confusion and helplessness of terror, as in vi. 2, 3, 10 (A.V. *vexed*); civ. 29.

8—10. By trouble he learnt whence his strength came, and betook himself to prayer. *vv.* 9, 10 are the words of his prayer.

8. The tense in the original is inadequately represented by a simple perfect, though its precise force is not easy to define. It may express the frequent repetition of the prayer, or, like a historic present, it may set the action vividly before us as in actual progress (Note IV, p. 223); or possibly throwing himself back into the past, the Psalmist gives the words of his resolution: [I said,] *Unto thee, O Jehovah, will I call* (=xxviii. 1); *yea, unto the Lord* (the best attested reading is *Adonai*) *will I make supplication* (cxlii. 1).

9. What advantage would it be to Thee to slay me? Nay, Thou wouldest lose Thy servant's praises. For the form of the question cp. Job xxii. 3. The same motive is appealed to in Hezekiah's prayer, Is. xxxviii. 18, 19. Cp. Ps. vi. 5; lxxxviii. 10 ff.; cxv. 17. On this gloomy view of death as the interruption of communion with God, see Introd. p. lxxv ff.

the dust] Not the dust into which the body is dissolved, but the grave, as in xxii. 15, 29.

thy truth] God's faithfulness (xxv. 5), which is the object of the praises of the faithful.

Thou hast turned for me my mourning into dancing: 11
Thou hast put off my sackcloth, and girded me *with* gladness;
To the end that *my* glory may sing *praise* to thee, and not 12
  be silent.
O LORD my God, I will give thanks unto thee for ever.

11, 12. Prayer answered: life prolonged, and its purpose.

11. Better, **Thou didst turn...didst loose...and gird.** He looks back to the moment when his prayer was answered.

mourning...dancing] The gestures of sorrow and joy are contrasted, for mourning means literally the beating of the breast (*planctus*). Cp. Lam. v. 15. In place of the sackcloth which was the mourner's garb, gladness clothes him like a festal garment. Cp. Is. lxi. 3.

12. my *glory*] My soul, as in vii. 5 (note); lvii. 8.

for ever] All the days of my life. See 1 Sam. i. 22 compared with *v.* 28. But the Psalmist's words had a larger meaning than he could as yet know (Rev. xxii. 3 ff.).

PSALM XXXI.

Worn out in mind and body, despised, defamed, and persecuted, the Psalmist casts himself upon God. Faith upholds him as he recalls past mercies; despondency overwhelms him as he thinks of his present distress; till the clouds clear, and the sunlight of God's goodness floods his soul.

The Psalm falls into three divisions.

i. Professions of trust and prayers for deliverance grounded upon the experience of past mercies (1—8).

ii. Urgent pleading, with a pathetic description of the extremity of his need (9—18).

iii. Grateful celebration of God's goodness, once more demonstrated in the deliverance of the Psalmist, who looks back in surprise upon his own faint-heartedness, and concludes by exhorting all the godly to take courage (19—24).

Most of the earlier commentators suppose that the Psalm was written by David in the wilderness of Maon, and point to the coincidence between *in my haste* (*v.* 22), and "David *made haste* to flee" (1 Sam. xxiii. 26). The Sept. translators appear to have seen in that verse a reference to the occasion of the Psalm, for they add ἐκστάσεως (*for desperation*) to the title, and ἐν τῇ ἐκστάσει μου (*in my desperation*) is their rendering in *v.* 22.

But the situation of the Psalmist and the tone of the Psalm would rather suggest that Jeremiah, or some prophet in similar circumstances of persecution, was its author. Comp. *v.* 10 with Jer. xx. 18; 'the broken vessel' (*v.* 12) with Jer. xxii. 28; xlviii. 38; *v.* 13 with Jer. xx. 10; *v.* 17 with Jer. xvii. 18; *v.* 22 with Lam. iii. 54. Still it is quite possible that Jeremiah may be using the words of the Psalm which was familiar to him.

The striking difference in the tone of *vv*. 9—18 from that of 1—8 and 19—24 suggests the possibility that these verses may be a later addition: and it is noteworthy that the parallels with the Book of Jeremiah occur almost exclusively in *vv*. 9—18, while the first and third divisions resemble Psalms which have good claims to be regarded as Davidic. But the change of tone may only correspond to a change of situation.

The latter part of the Psalm has several parallels with Ps. xxviii. With *v*. 21 *a* comp. xxviii. 6 *a*; with *v*. 22 *b* cp. xxviii. 2, 6; with *v*. 23 cp. xxviii. 4. Comp. too *v*. 22 (*as for me*) with xxx. 6; and the invitation in *v*. 23 with xxx. 4.

To the chief Musician, A Psalm of David.

31 In thee, O LORD, do I put my trust;
    Let me never be ashamed:
    Deliver me in thy righteousness.
2 Bow down thine ear to me; deliver me speedily:
    Be thou my strong rock,
    For a house of defence to save me.
3 For thou *art* my rock and my fortress;
    Therefore for thy name's sake lead me, and guide me.
4 Pull me out of the net that they have laid privily for me:
    For thou *art* my strength.

1—8. The prayer of faith. *vv*. 1—3 are repeated in that beautiful mosaic, Ps. lxxi; and *v*. 1 *a* forms the close of the *Te Deum*.

1. *do I put my trust*] **Have I taken refuge.** Cp. vii. 1 (note); xi. 1; xvi. 1; xxv. 20.

let me never be ashamed] Disappointed and confounded by finding that my trust was vain. Cp. v. 17; xxv. 2, 20; xxii. 5.

in thy righteousness] To desert His servant (*v*. 16) would be inconsistent with Jehovah's righteousness.

2. *Bow down*] Or, *incline*, as in xvii. 6; &c.

2, 3. *Be thou* &c.] Lit. *Become* (LXX γενοῦ) *to me a stronghold-rock, a fortress-house to save me: for* (he goes on to give the ground of his prayer) *thou art my cliff and my fortress:* i.e. prove Thyself to be what I know Thou art. "It is the logic of every believing prayer." *Delitzsch*. For the figures see note on xviii. 2.

therefore &c.] **And for thy name's sake thou wilt lead me and guide me.** A further expression of trust rather than a petition. By gentle and unerring guidance God will shew Himself all that He has declared Himself to be. Cp. the same words in xxiii. 2, 3, and see notes there.

4. **Thou wilt bring me out of the net...for thou art my strong hold.** He compares his insidious enemies to hunters or fowlers, as in ix. 15; xxv. 15.

Into thine hand I commit my spirit: 5
Thou hast redeemed me, O LORD God of truth.
I have hated them that regard lying vanities: 6
But I trust in the LORD.
I will be glad and rejoice in thy mercy: 7
For thou hast considered my trouble;
Thou hast known my soul in adversities;
And hast not shut me up into the hand of the enemy: 8

5. *I commit* &c.] Or, as P.B.V. and R.V., **I commend my spirit**. To God's care he entrusts as a precious deposit the life inbreathed by God Himself (Job x. 12; xvii. 1). The context makes it plain that it is for the preservation of his life that he thus entrusts himself to God; but the further application of the words to the departing spirit is obvious and natural, and it is sanctioned and consecrated by our Lord's use of them on the Cross (Luke xxiii. 46). Cp. the noble words of Wisdom iii. 1; "The souls of the righteous are in the hand of God:" and John x. 28 f.; 2 Tim. i. 12; 1 Peter iv. 19 (noting how *a faithful Creator* corresponds to *thou God of truth* here). "The many instances on record, including St Polycarp, St Basil, Epiphanius of Pavia, St Bernard, St Louis, Huss, Columbus, Luther, and Melancthon—of Christians using these words at the approach of death, represent how many millions of unrecorded cases!" *Kay*.

The words, **Thou hast redeemed me, O LORD, thou God of truth**, give the double ground of this confidence, in his own past experience, and the known character of Jehovah as the God of faithfulness. *Redeemed* primarily means *delivered* from temporal distress (2 Sam. iv. 9); but for the Christian the word must bear a deeper significance.

6. *I have hated*] Better, as R.V., **I hate**. He disclaims all sympathy and fellowship with the worshippers of false gods. But the LXX, Vulg., Syr., Jer. read, **thou hatest** (cp. v. 5). This reading gives the contrast required by the next line, which must be rendered, **but as for me, I trust in Jehovah**.

that regard lying vanities] Cp. Jonah ii. 8. False gods are *vanities of nothingness*, having no real existence, and deluding their worshippers; the exact opposite of the *God of truth*, Who IS, and constantly proves His faithfulness (Deut. xxxii. 4, 21). *Vanity* is a common expression for false gods in Jeremiah (viii. 19; &c.). For *regard* = pay respect to, worship, see lix. 9 (A.V. *wait upon*); Hos. iv. 10 (A.V. *take heed to*).

7. **Let me be glad and rejoice in thy lovingkindness:**
For thou hast seen my affliction;
Thou hast taken knowledge of the distresses of my soul.
An entreaty, based upon past experience. Here, and in *v.* 8, as well as in 5 *b*, it is more natural to understand the perfect tenses to refer to past mercies, rather than as a confident anticipation of future deliverance. With the second line cp. ix. 13.

8. *hast not shut me up into the hand of the enemy*] Hast not

Thou hast set my feet in a large room.
9 Have mercy upon me, O LORD, for I am in trouble:
Mine eye is consumed with grief, *yea*, my soul and my belly.
10 For my life is spent with grief, and my years with sighing:
My strength faileth because of mine iniquity, and my bones are consumed.
11 I was a reproach among all mine enemies,
But especially among my neighbours, and a fear to mine acquaintance:
They that did see me without fled from me.
12 I am forgotten as a dead man out of mind:
I am like a broken vessel.

surrendered me into his power. Cp. Deut. xxxii. 30; 1 Sam. xxiii. 11, 12 (A.V. *deliver up*).

thou hast set &c.] Lit. *thou hast made my feet to stand in a large* (or, *wide*) *place;* enabled me to move and act with freedom. Cp. iv. 1; xviii. 19; xxvi. 12. *Room* in A.V.=space, place.

9—18. The tone of the Psalm changes. The recollection of past mercies brings present suffering into sharper relief. "A sorrow's crown of sorrow is remembering happier things." This part of the Psalm reminds us of Ps. vi, and of Jeremiah's complaints.

9. Be gracious unto me, O Jehovah, for I am in distress:
Mine eye is wasted away because of provocation, yea, my soul and my body.

Cp. vi. 7 *a*; amplified here by the addition of *my soul and my body* (xliv. 25).

10. *grief*] R.V. **sorrow**, as in xiii. 2; Jer. viii. 18.
sighing] Or, *groaning*, as in vi. 6.
my strength &c.] **My strength totters because of mine iniquity, and my bones are wasted away.** There was then some sin which called for chastisement, or required the discipline of suffering. But the LXX, Syr., and Symmachus read *affliction* instead of *iniquity*. With the last clause cp. vi. 2 (*note*); xxxii. 3.

11. Because of all mine adversaries I am become a reproach,
Yea, unto my neighbours exceedingly. (R.V.)

The original is as awkward as the translation, and we should probably connect *because of all mine adversaries* with the previous verse, and read, *I am become a reproach unto my neighbours exceedingly:* or else, with Lagarde, Cheyne, and others, read *a shaking of head* (xliv. 14, cp. 13), in place of *exceedingly*. Cp. xxii. 6, 7; Jer. xx. 7, 8.

they that did see me &c.] Those who met him in public avoided him, afraid of incurring persecution themselves by any sign of sympathy.

12. As a dead man passes out of men's minds, so he is forgotten.

For I have heard the slander of many: 13
Fear *was* on every side:
While they took counsel together against me,
They devised to take away my life.
But I trusted in thee, O LORD: 14
I said, Thou *art* my God.
My times *are* in thy hand: 15
Deliver me from the hand of mine enemies, and from them
 that persecute me.
Make thy face to shine upon thy servant: 16
Save me for thy mercy's sake.
Let me not be ashamed, O LORD; for I have called upon 17
 thee:
Let the wicked be ashamed, *and* let them be silent in the
 grave.
Let the lying lips be put to silence; 18
Which speak grievous things proudly and contemptuously
 against the righteous.

Cp. Job xix. 14. He is like a broken (lit. *perishing*) vessel, flung aside contemptuously and no more remembered. Cp. (though the phrase there is different) Jer. xxii. 28 (R.V.).
 13. **For I have heard the defaming of many,**
   Terror on every side (R.V.).
 Jeremiah uses these very words to describe his plight (xx. 10). *Terror on every side* is a favourite phrase with him (vi. 25; xx. 3, 4; xlvi. 5; xlix. 29; Lam. ii. 22).
 they devised &c.] Jer. xi. 19 ff.; xviii. 20 ff., supply an illustration.
 14. Render:
   But as for me, on thee do I trust O LORD:
   I have said, &c.
 Men turn from him, but he turns to God. Cp. *v.* 6; xvi. 2; cxl. 6.
 15. *My times* &c.] Cp. 1 Chr. xxix. 30. The vicissitudes of my life are all under Thy control.
 16. Comp. the paraphrase in P.B.V., *Shew thy servant the light of thy countenance:* and see note on iv. 6.
 for thy mercy's sake] R.V. **in thy lovingkindness,** as in *vv.* 7, 21.
 17. The prayer of *v.* 1 is repeated. While my prayers are answered, let my enemies be silenced and consigned to Sheol. A similar prayer in xxv. 2, 3; Jer. xvii. 18.
 18. **Let the lying lips be dumb;**
   Which speak against the righteous arrogantly,
   In pride and contempt.
Cp. xii. 3; xciv. 4.

19 O how great *is* thy goodness, which thou hast laid up for them that fear thee;
   Which thou hast wrought for them that trust in thee
   Before the sons of men!
20 Thou shalt hide them in the secret of thy presence from the pride of man:
   Thou shalt keep them secretly in a pavilion from the strife of tongues.
21 Blessed *be* the Lord: for he hath shewed me his marvellous kindness in a strong city.
22 For I said in my haste, I am cut off from before thine eyes:
   Nevertheless thou heardest the voice of my supplications when I cried unto thee.

19—24. Can the author of this serenely joyous thanksgiving be the despised and downcast sufferer of *vv.* 9—18? If so, it was surely not at the same moment. An interval has elapsed; his prayer has been answered; the danger is past.

19, 20. God's goodness to those who fear Him is like an inexhaustible treasure stored up, and at the proper time brought out and used for *them that take refuge* (as *v.* 1) in Him; and this publicly in the sight of man. Cf. xxiii. 5. With R.V. place a comma after *trust in thee*, and connect *before the sons of men* with *wrought*.

20. Thou shalt hide them in the hiding-place of thy presence from the plottings of man:
   Thou shalt conceal them in a pavilion from the strife of tongues.

With the whole verse cp. xxvii. 5; but *the hiding place of thy tent* is here spiritualised into *the hiding place of thy presence* (lit. *face* as in *v.* 16). No darkness of evil can penetrate into the light of God's countenance.

21, 22. Thanksgiving: but is it for deliverance anticipated by faith or for deliverance already experienced? Surely the latter.

21. *Blessed be the Lord*] Cp. xxviii. 6.
   he hath shewed me his marvellous kindness] Lit. *he hath made marvellous his lovingkindness to me*, as in xvii. 7.
   in a strong city] Either, *as in a strong city*, putting me out of the reach of my enemies as it were in a fortified city; or, *as a strong city*, proving Himself my fortress (*vv.* 2, 3). The words may also mean *in a besieged city*, which might be taken as a metaphor for trouble generally. Some commentators understand the words literally of David's escape from Keilah, or of his establishment in Ziklag; or of Jeremiah in Jerusalem during the siege.

22. *For I said* &c.] **But as for me, I said in my haste** (or, *alarm*). Humbly he confesses his want of faith in the hour of trial, when he thought himself out of God's sight, and contrasts it with God's goodness. Cp. xxx. 6; cxvi. 11. With 22*a* cp. Jon. ii. 4: with 22*b* cp. xxviii. 2.

O love the LORD, all ye his saints: 23
For the LORD preserveth the faithful,
And plentifully rewardeth the proud doer.
Be of good courage, and he shall strengthen your heart, 24
All ye that hope in the LORD.

23, 24. Concluding exhortation to the faithful. Cp. xxx. 4; xxvii. 14; xxxii. 11.
preserveth the faithful] Or, *keepeth faithfulness*. Cf. Ex. xxxiv. 7, note.
plentifully rewardeth the proud doer] The judgment of the wicked is, in the view of the O. T., the necessary complement of the triumph of the saints. See Introd. p. lxxiii.
24. **Be strong, and let your heart take courage** (R.V.), as in xxvii. 14.
all ye that hope in the LORD] Or, *wait for*. The phrase links this Psalm to Ps. xxxiii. See *vv.* 18, 22. Comp. too xxxiii. 18 with *v.* 22.

PSALM XXXII.

With a fervour which is unmistakably the fruit of experience the Psalmist describes the blessedness of forgiveness, and teaches that penitence is the indispensable condition for receiving it (1, 2). He had sinned grievously, and so long as he refused to acknowledge his sin he suffered inward torture (3, 4). But confession brought instant pardon (5). Arguing then from his own experience he exhorts the godly to timely prayer (6). Professing his trust in Jehovah, he receives from Him a gracious promise of guidance (7, 8). Then addressing himself to men in general, he warns them against the folly of resisting God's will (9), and contrasts the lot of the godly and the wicked (10). The Psalm concludes with an exhortation to the righteous to rejoice (11).

This Psalm is generally thought to have been composed by David after his adultery with Bathsheba and the murder of Uriah. For almost a year he stubbornly refused to acknowledge his sin, in spite of the accusing voice of conscience, and, it may be, the admonitions of sickness (*vv.* 3, 4); until the prophet's message struck home to his heart, and opened the fountain of penitential tears. Ps. li may be the first heartfelt prayer for pardon; while this Psalm, written somewhat later, when he had had time calmly to survey the past, records his experience for the warning and instruction of others, in fulfilment of the promise in li. 13.

The lessons of the Psalm are summed up in Prov. xxviii. 13; or 1 John i. 8, 9.

It is the second of the seven 'Penitential Psalms' (see Introd. to Ps. vi), and is appointed for use on Ash-Wednesday. It was a favourite with St Augustine, who "often read this Psalm with weeping heart and eyes, and before his death had it written upon the wall which was over against his sick-bed, that he might be exercised and comforted by it in his sickness." His words "intelligentia prima est ut te noris peccatorem"—the beginning of knowledge is to know thyself to be a sinner—might be prefixed to it as a motto.

A Psalm of David, Maschil.

32 Blessed *is* he whose transgression *is* forgiven,
    whose sin *is* covered.
2   Blessed *is* the man unto whom the LORD imputeth
    not iniquity,
    And in whose spirit *there is* no guile.
3   When I kept silence, my bones waxed old
    Through my roaring all the day long.
4   For day and night thy hand was heavy upon me:
    My moisture is turned into the drought of summer. Selah.

On the title *Maschil* see Introd. p. xviii.

1, 2. The blessedness of forgiveness. See Rom. iv. 6 ff. for St Paul's use of these verses.

Blessed] Or, *Happy*. Cp. i. 1. The first beatitude of the Psalter is pronounced on an upright life; but since "there is no man that sinneth not" (1 Kings viii. 46), there is another beatitude reserved for true penitence.

transgression—sin—iniquity] The words thus rendered describe sin in different aspects (1) as rebellion, or breaking away from God: (2) as wandering from the way, or missing the mark: (3) as depravity, or moral distortion. Cp. *v.* 5; li. 1—3; Ex. xxxiv. 7. Forgiveness is also triply described (1) as the taking away of a burden; cp. John i. 29, and the expression 'to bear iniquity': (2) as covering, so that the foulness of sin no longer meets the eye of the judge and calls for punishment; (3) as the cancelling of a debt, which is no longer reckoned against the offender: cp. 2 Sam. xix. 19.

and in whose spirit there is *no guile*] No deceitfulness. The condition of forgiveness on man's part is absolute sincerity. There must be no attempt to deceive self or God. Cp. 1 John i. 8.

3, 4. The illustration of this truth from the Psalmist's own experience. He kept silence, refusing to acknowledge his sin to himself and to God; but meanwhile God did not leave him to himself (Job xxxiii. 16 ff.); His chastening hand was heavy upon him (xxxviii. 2; xxxix. 10), making itself felt partly by the remorse of conscience, partly perhaps by actual sickness. He suffered and complained (xxii. 1; xxxviii. 8); but such complaint was no prayer (Hos. vii. 14), and brought no relief, while he would not confess his sin.

my bones] See note on vi. 2.

my moisture &c.] R.V. **my moisture was changed as with** (marg., **into**) **the drought of summer**: the vital sap and juices of his body were dried up by the burning fever within him. Cp. xxii. 15; Prov. xvii. 22.

Selah] The musical interlude here may have expressed the Psalmist's distress of mind, and prepared the way for the change in the next verse.

I acknowledged my sin unto thee, 5
And mine iniquity have I not hid.
I said, I will confess my transgressions unto the LORD;
And thou forgavest the iniquity of my sin. Selah.
For this shall every one *that is* godly pray unto thee in a 6
time when thou mayest be found:
Surely in the floods of great waters they shall not come
nigh unto him.
Thou *art* my hiding place; thou shalt preserve me from 7
trouble;
Thou shalt compass me about *with* songs of deliverance.
Selah.

5. The way of restoration. Lit. *I began to make known to thee my sin, and mine iniquity did I not cover.* The tense of the first verb graphically represents the confession being made (xxv. 8, note): the second verb is the same as that in *v.* 1. Not until man ceases to hide his sin will it be hidden from God. "Quantum tibi non peperceris," says Tertullian, quoted by Abp. Leighton, "tantum tibi parcet Deus." "The less you spare yourself, the more will God spare you."

and thou forgavest] THOU is emphatic, and the form of the sentence expresses the immediateness of the pardon. "Vox nondum est in ore et vulnus sanatur." *St Augustine.*

The musical interlude may have expressed the joy of forgiveness, and served to separate this record of experience from the application which follows.

6. An exhortation based upon experience.

For this &c.] Rather, **Therefore let every one** &c.

in a time when thou mayest be found] This is the most probable explanation of the Heb., which means literally *in a time of finding*, and is obscure from its brevity. So "in a time of acceptance" (lxix. 13). Comp. Deut. iv. 29 with Jer. xxix. 13; and see Is. lv. 6. Let no one delay, for there is also a time of *not* finding (Prov. i. 28). The words may also be explained as in R.V. marg., *in the time of finding out* sin, when God makes inquisition; cp. xvii. 3; or, *in the time when* sin *finds* them *out;* cp. Num. xxxii. 23: but these explanations are less obvious.

surely &c.] R.V., **surely when the great waters overflow they shall not reach unto him.** In a time of calamity and judgment he will not be overwhelmed, but will be safe like one who stands secure upon a rock out of reach of the raging flood. For the figure cp. xviii. 16; Is. xxviii. 2, 17; xxx. 28; Nah. i. 8.

7. The Psalmist addresses Jehovah, appropriating to himself the promise of the preceding verse.

my hiding place] The same word as in xxvii. 5; xxxi. 20; xci. 1.

thou shalt preserve me &c.] **Thou wilt guard me** (xii. 7; xxv. 21; xxxi. 23) **from distress** (xxxi. 9); **thou wilt compass me about with**

8 I will instruct thee and teach thee in the way which thou shalt go:
I will guide thee with mine eye.
9 Be ye not as the horse,
Or as the mule, *which have* no understanding:
Whose mouth must be held in with bit and bridle,
Lest *they* come near unto thee.
10 Many sorrows *shall be* to the wicked:

shouts (*v.* 11) of deliverance. Occasions for rejoicing arise wherever he turns: or possibly the glad shouts of the godly rejoicing at his deliverance are meant.

8. Who is the speaker? The Psalmist or God? Most commentators suppose that it is the Psalmist, who now assumes the part of teacher, as in xxxiv. 11, and fulfils the promise of li. 13. But surely it must be God who speaks in answer to the Psalmist's profession of trust.

Would any human teacher venture to say, **I will counsel thee with mine eye upon thee,** as the last line must be rendered with R.V.? For the ever-wakeful 'eye' of God's loving Providence see xxxiii. 18; xxxiv. 15; Jer. xxiv. 6. The view that God is the speaker is confirmed by the parallels in xxv. 8, 12; xvi. 7; lxxiii. 24; and it avoids the abruptness of the transition from *v.* 7 to *v.* 8, and the awkwardness of the change to the plural in *v.* 9, which the other explanation involves.

9, 10. A warning addressed to all not to resist God's will, and neglect instruction.

> **Be not like horse like mule with no understanding,**
> **With trappings of bit and bridle must they be curbed:**
> **Else will they not come near unto thee.**

The Heb. is obscure and possibly corrupt in some points; but the general sense is clear. Brute animals without reason must be controlled and compelled by force to learn to submit to man's will. If man will not draw near to God and obey Him of his own free will, he lowers himself to the level of a brute, and must expect to be treated accordingly and disciplined by judgment (Is. xxvi. 9—11).

For the thought that man who will not listen to God's teaching 'becomes brutish' see Jer. x. 14, 21; Ps. xlix. 10, 12, 20; lxxiii. 22. The word rendered *mouth* in A.V., *trappings* in R.V., is of doubtful meaning. Some explain, *whose* **wild spirit** *must be curbed* &c.; but this is less probable. The A.V. of the last line, *lest they come near unto thee,* to hurt thee, gives no suitable point of comparison, and must certainly be rejected.

10. The warning given in the preceding verse is confirmed by the contrast between the lot of the ungodly and the faithful.

many sorrows] Calamities and chastisements. The LXX has μάστιγες, *scourges.* Cp. Job xxxiii. 19.

But he that trusteth in the LORD, mercy shall compass him
about.
Be glad in the LORD, and rejoice, ye righteous: 11
And shout for joy, all *ye that are* upright in heart.

mercy] **Lovingkindness** (xxxi. 7, 16, 21; xxxiii. 5, 18, 22). The
clause may also be rendered, *with lovingkindness will he compass him
about*. Cp. *v.* 7.
11. Cp. *v.* 11; xxxiii. 1; Neh. viii. 10; Phil. iii. 1, iv. 4; 1 Thess.
v. 16. All kindred spirits must share the joy of a pardoned soul, and
rejoice in the contemplation of God's gracious dealings with His
people.

PSALM XXXIII.

The Psalm begins by repeating the call to praise with which the
preceding Psalm closed, and recites the grounds on which Jehovah is
worthy to be praised. It stands here as an answer to the invitation of
xxxii. 11, an example of the "songs of deliverance" spoken of in xxxii.
7. Yet it differs widely in character from Ps. xxxii. That Psalm is
an instruction based upon a particular personal experience; this is a
congregational hymn of praise, arising (if indeed any special event
inspired it) out of some national deliverance.

Contrary to the general rule in Book I (Introd. p. xxxix), it has no
title in the Hebrew, though the LXX ascribes it to David.

It may commemorate some national deliverance from heathen enemies (*vv.* 10, 11, 16 ff.), but it is impossible to fix its date or occasion.
It does not, like cxlvii, which has many points of resemblance to it,
contain clear references to the Restoration. There are echoes of it
in Ps. cxliv, partly in later language.

The structure is symmetrical. To the introductory call to praise
(1—3) corresponds the concluding profession of trust in Jehovah
(20—22). Between these comes the main body of the Psalm, reciting
the grounds upon which Jehovah is worthy of praise and trust. This
falls into two equal parts. i. Generally, He is to be praised for His
moral attributes (4, 5), for His creative Omnipotence (6—9), for His
sovereign rule (10, 11). ii. Specially, He is to be praised for His
choice and care of His people in the midst of the nations (12—15);
material force is a delusion (16, 17), but He is the sure Protector of
His people (18, 19). Verses 4—19 are arranged in couplets or in
quatrains.

Rejoice in the LORD, O ye righteous: 33

1—3. Introductory call to praise.

1. *Rejoice*] **Shout for joy**: the same verb as in xxxii. 11 *b*, though
in a different form. As in that verse, *the righteous* and *the upright*, the
true Israelites, are addressed. Praise is their duty and their honour: in
their mouths alone is it seemly.

For praise is comely for the upright.
2 Praise the LORD with harp:
Sing unto him with the psaltery *and* an instrument of ten strings.
3 Sing unto him a new song;
Play skilfully with a loud noise.
4 For the word of the LORD *is* right;
And all his works *are done* in truth.
5 He loveth righteousness and judgment:
The earth is full *of* the goodness of the LORD.
6 By the word of the LORD were the heavens made;
And all the host of them by the breath of his mouth.

for *praise &c.*] Omit *for.* Cp. cxlvii. 1 *b*.
**2. Give thanks unto the LORD with harp:
Sing praises unto him with the psaltery of ten strings** (R.V.).
The harp and psaltery were both stringed instruments, differing somewhat in form.
3. *a new song*] Fresh mercies demand a fresh expression of gratitude. See xl. 3; and cp. xcvi. 1; xcviii. 1; cxlix. 1; Is. xlii. 10; Judith xvi. 13; Rev. v. 9. Ps. cxliv. 9 reproduces 2 *b*, and 3 *a*.
with a loud noise] Referring either to the music itself, or to the accompanying shouts of joy. See note on xxvii. 6, where the same word is rendered *joy* in A.V.

4—11. The grounds of praise.

4, 5. The moral attributes of Jehovah. Jehovah's word is **upright**: the same word as in *v.* 1; cp. xix. 8; xxv. 8; xcii. 15; Hos. xiv. 9: **and all his work is in faithfulness**: cp. Deut. xxxii. 4; Ps. xxxvi. 5; xcii. 2. *Word* and *work* need not be limited; they include all the expressions of the Will of Him Who is always consistent with Himself (James i. 17).

5. *Righteousness* is the principle of justice; *judgment* the application of it in act. Cp. xxxvi. 6; ciii. 6; and for *loveth* cp. xi. 7.
goodness] Better, as R.V., **lovingkindness.** This line recurs in cxix. 64.

6—9. Jehovah's creative omnipotence. Word is the expression of thought; command of will: He had but to think and will, and the Universe came into being.

6. *The breath of his mouth* is synonymous with *the word of the LORD:* together they represent *and God said* in Gen. i. 3 ff. The parallelism and the addition *of his mouth* seem to exclude a reference to *the spirit of God* in Gen. i. 2, though the word in the original is the same. The germ of the doctrine of the Word in John i. 1, 3 may be found here, though of course the Psalmist had no idea of a personal Word. Cp. cvii. 20; and Ecclus. xliii. 26, " By his word all things consist." *The*

He gathereth the waters of the sea together as a heap: 7
He layeth up the depth in storehouses.
Let all the earth fear the LORD: 8
Let all the inhabitants of the world stand in awe of him.
For he spake, and it was *done;* 9
He commanded, and it stood fast.
The LORD bringeth the counsel of the heathen to nought: 10
He maketh the devices of the people of none effect.
The counsel of the LORD standeth for ever, . 11
The thoughts of his heart to all generations.

host of heaven (Gen. ii. 1) are the sun moon and stars, marching forth like an army in ordered array at God's command (Is. xl. 26).

7. The separation of land and water (Gen. i. 9, 10). The present tense (*gathereth...layeth up*) expresses the continued action of maintenance as well as the original creation. The comparison *as an heap* probably refers to the appearance of the sea from the shore, and may have been derived from Ex. xv. 8; cp. Josh. iii. 13, 16; Ps. lxxviii. 13.

But all the Ancient Versions render *as in a bottle*, reading *nôd* for *nēd*. To the infinite power of the Creator the bed of the sea is but as the water-skin which a man carries with him for a journey. See Is. xl. 12, 15. Cp. "the pitchers of heaven" (Job xxxviii. 37).

the depth] Better as R.V., **the deeps**: the vast masses of water stored away in subterranean abysses (Gen. vii. 11; Ps. lxxviii. 15). So we read of the storehouses of the wind (cxxxv. 7=Jer. x. 13), of the snow and hail (Job xxxviii. 22).

8, 9. With what awe should man regard such an Almighty Creator! Cp. the argument of Amos, iv. 13; v. 8; ix. 6. Emphasis is laid on the wonder of the method of creation, by the simple divine *fiat*.

9. **For HE** (emphatic) **spake, and it was** (cp. Gen. i. 3, 7, &c.); **HE commanded and it stood**; came into existence and stood there before Him ready to obey His commands; or simply, stood firm. Cp. cxlviii. 5; cxix. 90, 91; Is. xlviii. 13.

10, 11. Jehovah's sovereignty in the world.

10. *bringeth...maketh*] Or, *hath brought...hath made*, with particular reference to some recent event. But it agrees better with the argument of *vv.* 4—11 to regard the words as expressing a general truth, though quite possibly it had been verified by recent experience.

11. The A.V. obscures the parallelism between *vv.* 10 and 11. **The counsel of the nations** and **the thoughts of the peoples** are contrasted with **the counsel of Jehovah** and **the thoughts of his heart**. His counsel stands fast like His work in creation (*v.* 9). Cp. Jer. xxxiii. 20, 21. With *v.* 10, cp. Is. viii. 10; Neh. iv. 15; with *v.* 11, cp. Is. v. 19; xix. 17; xlvi. 10, 11; Mic. iv. 12; Is. lv. 8, 9; Jer. xxix. 11; and generally, Prov. xix. 21; xxi. 30. To us the words may suggest that "through the ages one increasing purpose runs," and point forward to

12 Blessed *is* the nation whose God *is* the LORD;
And the people *whom* he hath chosen for his own inheritance.
13 The LORD looketh from heaven;
He beholdeth all the sons of men.
14 From the place of his habitation he looketh
Upon all the inhabitants of the earth.
15 He fashioneth their hearts alike;
He considereth all their works.
16 There is no king saved by the multitude of a host:
A mighty *man* is not delivered by much strength.

"The one far-off divine event
To which the whole creation moves."

The addition in P.B.V., *and casteth out the counsels of princes*, is derived through the Vulg. from the LXX.

12—19. From the nations the Psalmist turns to the chosen people. Jehovah's care for Israel constitutes His special claim on their praise. Happy the nation which is the particular object of the choice and care of the omniscient observer of men.

12. *Blessed*] Or, **happy**; see note on i. 1. This 'beatitude' is based on Deut. xxxiii. 29; cp. Deut. iv. 6—8. The first line of the verse recurs (with some variations) in cxliv. 15; with the second cp. xxviii. 9.

13, 14. The Psalmist dwells upon Jehovah's all-seeing omniscience in order to emphasise the peculiar privilege of His people. Throned in heaven (1 Kings viii. 39 ff.) He surveys all mankind. Cp. xi. 4; xiv. 2; cii. 19, 20.

14. *looketh*] R.V. **looketh forth**; a rare word, different from that in *v.* 13.

15. **Even he who formeth the hearts of them all,**
Who considereth all their works.

He Who created man must know man's heart (xciv. 9). As God 'formed' man originally (Gen. ii. 7, 8), so He continues to 'form the hearts' of individuals and of races (Zech. xii. 1). All are in some sense subservient to His plan and purpose.

16—19. The delusiveness of material resources is contrasted with Jehovah's care for His people. The discomfiture of Pharaoh with his host and horses and chariots (Ex. xiv. 17; xv. 4) may have been in the poet's mind; and 'saved' again recalls Deut. xxxiii. 29.

16. **A king is not saved by a numerous host**; or, **by greatness of power**, including other forces beside forces of soldiers. See xx. 7; xliv. 3 ff.; lx. 11 f.; and comp. the noble expression of this truth in 1 Macc. iii. 19; "The victory of battle standeth not in the multitude of an host; but strength cometh from heaven."

A horse *is* a vain thing for safety: 17
Neither shall he deliver *any* by his great strength.
Behold, the eye of the LORD *is* upon them that fear him, 18
Upon them that hope in his mercy;
To deliver their soul from death, 19
And to keep them alive in famine.
Our soul waiteth for the LORD: 20
He *is* our help and our shield.
For our heart shall rejoice in him, 21
Because we have trusted in his holy name.
Let thy mercy, O LORD, be upon us, 22
According as we hope in thee.

17. *A horse*—to the Israelites cavalry seemed the most formidable part of an army—*is but a vain thing*—lit. *a lie*, a delusion—*for safety*—for victory (xxi. 1): *neither can it give escape by the greatness of its power:* it cannot even secure its rider's escape in case of defeat. Cp. Prov. xxi. 31.

18. *the eye of the LORD*] Cp. xxxii. 8, note; xxxiv. 15; Ezra v. 5; Job xxxvi. 7; 1 Pet. iii. 12.
that hope in his mercy] Or, *that wait for his lovingkindness* (xxxi. 24).

19. *death*] Violent death by war or pestilence is meant, as the parallel line shews. Famine was a common scourge in Palestine (xxxvii. 19).

20—22. The people's concluding profession of patient trust and hope, corresponding to the introductory invitation of *vv.* 1—3, and springing naturally out of the consideration of Jehovah's character in *vv.* 12—19.

20. *waiteth*] R.V. **hath waited**; a different word from that in *vv.* 18, 22; found in the Psalter again only in cvi. 13; but used in Is. viii. 17; xxx. 18; lxiv. 4; &c.
our help and our shield] Cp. again Deut. xxxiii. 29, "the shield of thy help"; Ps. iii. 3; xxviii. 7; and cxv. 9, 10, 11.

21. *his holy name*] See note on xxx. 4.

22. **Let thy lovingkindness** (*vv.* 5, 18), **O LORD, be upon us, According as we have hoped in thee** (or, *waited for thee*).
Comp. xxxi. 1, 24; Rom. v. 4, 5.

PSALM XXXIV.

Another song of praise (cp. *v.* 1 with xxxiii. 1). The Psalmist gratefully celebrates, and invites others to join him in celebrating, Jehovah's care for those who fear Him, manifested towards himself and many another afflicted saint (1—10). Then, assuming the tone of a teacher, he sets forth the essential characteristics of the fear of Jehovah, and commends it by a consideration of the blessings which He bestows on those who fear Him (11—22).

The verses for the most part run in pairs.

The Psalm is closely related to Ps. xxv. Both are alphabetic Psalms, with the peculiarity that the verse beginning with *Vav* is omitted[1], and a supplementary verse beginning with *Pē* added at the end to make up the number of letters in the alphabet (22). For the ingenious though improbable conjecture that these verses record the names of the authors, see note on xxv. 22. Both Psalms moreover shew a striking affinity in thought and language to the Book of Proverbs; and this Psalm corresponds to Ps. xxv as thanksgiving to prayer.

The title assigns the Psalm to David, *when he feigned madness* (lit. *changed his reason*) *before Abimelech; and he drove him away, and he departed*. The incident referred to is related in 1 Sam. xxi. 11 ff., where however the Philistine king is called *Achish*. After Saul's massacre of the priests at Nob, David fled to Gath. It was a desperate expedient: he was discovered, and only escaped with his life by feigning madness. Ps. lvi is connected by its title with the same occasion.

Most modern commentators peremptorily reject the title as of no value. The Psalm, they think, does not suit the supposed occasion; it manifestly bears the stamp of a later age; and the scribe or compiler who prefixed the title took it from 1 Samuel, substituting Abimelech for Achish by a slip of memory.

It is however hard to suppose such ignorance or carelessness on the part of a compiler; and the facts that the title does not agree with 1 Sam., and that there is nothing in the Psalm to suggest that particular occasion, are really in favour of regarding the title as resting upon some independent authority, and not upon mere conjecture. Can it have been derived, as Delitzsch thinks, from the *Annals of David*, one of the older works from which the Book of Samuel was compiled? The difference in the names might easily be accounted for if Abimelech was a dynastic name or royal title, like Agag among the Amalekites, or Pharaoh in Egypt. Cp. Gen. xx; xxi; xxvi.

But it must be acknowledged that thought and style are those of the Book of Proverbs, and apparently of a later age. Was the Psalm written by some poet-sage, who thought of that perilous episode in David's life as one of the most striking illustrations of the truth which he wished to enforce?

It was one of the Eucharistic Psalms of the early Church; a use no doubt suggested by *v.* 8. See Bingham's *Antiq.* v. 460.

Vv. 1 and 15 connect the Psalm with xxxiii. 1 and 18; *v.* 7 links it to xxxv. 5, 6.

---

[1] In Dr. Scrivener's edition, from which the text of the present edition is taken, the letter *Vav* is prefixed to the second line of *v.* 5. But throughout the Psalm each letter has a complete distich, and it is preferable to suppose that *Vav* is omitted as in Ps. xxv. rather than that *Hē* and *Vav* have only a single line each.

PSALM XXXIV. 1—5.

A Psalm of David, when he changed his behaviour before Abimelech; who drove him away, and he departed.

(א) I will bless the LORD at all times: 34
His praise *shall* continually *be* in my mouth.
(ב) My soul shall make her boast in the LORD: 2
The humble shall hear *thereof*, and be glad.
(ג) O magnify the LORD with me, 3
And let us exalt his name together.
(ד) I sought the LORD, and he heard me, 4
And delivered me from all my fears.
(ה) They looked unto him, and were lightened: 5
(ו) And their faces were not ashamed.

1, 2. Resolution of praise.

1. *His praise*] Cp. xxxiii. 1.

2. *In the* LORD stands emphatically at the beginning of the sentence in the original; in Him, and not in any of the worldling's objects of self-congratulation (xlix. 6; Jer. ix. 23, 24), shall be my boast.

the humble &c.] Probably, *let the humble* (or, *meek*) *hear and be glad*. Cp. v. 11. He claims the sympathy of those who have learned humility in the school of suffering. See note on ix. 12.

3, 4. Addressing the humble, he invites them to join in thanksgiving for his deliverance.

3. *magnify*] Man *makes* God *great* by acknowledging and celebrating His greatness (Deut. xxxii. 3), and *exalts* His Name by confessing that He is supreme above all. See note on xxx. 1.

4. *When I sought Jehovah* (with earnest devotion, see note on xxiv. 6), *he answered me, and rescued me from all my terrors* (xxxi. 13).

5, 6. Such experience of Jehovah's help is not limited to the Psalmist.

5. *They looked* &c.] The subject is to be supplied from the verb. *They that looked unto him looked, and were brightened.* The earnest gaze of faith and confidence was not in vain. For the phrase cp. Is. xxxi. 1; and for illustration see Num. xxi. 9; Zech. xii. 10. The Heb. word for *brightened* is a rare word, found in Is. lx. 5 (R.V.); but this, not *flowed* unto him (A.V. marg.) is the right sense. In most editions *They flowed* is wrongly marked as the alternative to *They looked.* For the thought cp. xxxvi. 9.

were not ashamed] R.V. **shall never be confounded**, lit. *put to the blush* with disappointment: a word which has not met us before in the Psalter, but recurs twice in Ps. xxxv. (*vv.* 4, 26), and elsewhere.

The reading of the Massoretic text gives a fair sense, but the ancient Versions (except the Targum) read an imperative in the first clause, and *your faces* in the second. We should then render, *Look unto him*

6 (ז) This poor *man* cried, and the LORD heard *him*,
And saved him out of all his troubles.
7 (ח) The angel of the LORD encampeth
Round about them that fear him, and delivereth them.
8 (ט) O taste and see that the LORD *is* good:
Blessed *is* the man *that* trusteth in him.
9 (י) O fear the LORD, ye his saints:
For *there is* no want to them that fear him.
10 (כ) The young lions do lack, and suffer hunger:

and be brightened, that your faces may not be confounded. This reading is in itself probable, and is supported by grammatical considerations. The connexion of thought in *vv.* 5, 6 will then be exactly the same as in *vv.* 3, 4; an invitation, followed by the statement of a fact which supports it.

6. This afflicted man (see note on ix. 12) **called, and Jehovah heard, and saved him out of all his distresses.** Cp. *v.* 17; xxxi. 7. Does the poet point to himself, or to one here and another there who had been instances of God's protecting care?

7. *The angel of the LORD*] That mysterious Being who appears as Jehovah's representative in His intercourse with man, called also *the angel of His presence* (Is. lxiii. 9). See especially Ex. xxiii. 20 ff. Only here and in xxxv. 5, 6 is he mentioned in the Psalter. He protects those who fear Jehovah like an army encamping round a city to defend it (Zech. ix. 8); or perhaps, since he is 'the captain of Jehovah's host' (Josh. v. 14), he is to be thought of as surrounding them with the angelic legions at his command. See for illustration Gen. xxxii. 2 (God's *camp*); 2 Kings vi. 16 f. For an examination of the doctrine of the angel of the Lord see Oehler's *O. T. Theology*, §§ 59, 60.

8. *O taste* &c.] Make but trial, and you will perceive what His goodness is toward them who fear Him. Cp. xxvii. 13. The adaptation of the words in 1 Pet. ii. 3 follows the rendering of the LXX, ὅτι χρηστὸς ὁ Κύριος. It is significant that the words are there applied to *Christ*. See Bp. Westcott's *Hebrews*, pp. 89 ff.

blessed &c.] Or, *happy is the man that taketh refuge in him*. Cp. ii. 12; and i. 1; xxxii. 2; but the word for *man* here is a different one. It means properly *a strong man*, and suggests the thought that be he never so strong in himself, man's only true happiness is in dependence on Jehovah.

9, 10. His saints want for nothing.

9. *saints*] Not the word commonly so rendered, e.g. in xxx. 4; xxxi. 23; but as in xvi. 3, *holy ones:* those whose character corresponds to their calling as members of the holy nation (Ex. xix. 6; Lev. xi. 44, 45).

want] A word found here only in the Psalter, but eight times in Proverbs.

10. *The young lions*] Best understood literally, not as a metaphor

But they that seek the LORD shall not want any good *thing*.

(ל) Come, ye children, hearken unto me: 11
I will teach you the fear of the LORD.
(מ) What man *is he that* desireth life, 12
And loveth *many* days, that *he* may see good?
(נ) Keep thy tongue from evil, 13
And thy lips from speaking guile.
(ס) Depart from evil, and do good; 14

for the rich (LXX πλούσιοι, though possibly from a different reading), or powerful oppressors (xxxv. 17). The sense is that the strongest beasts of prey, most capable of providing for themselves, may suffer want (Job iv. 11); not so God's people. Cp. xxiii. 1.

For the touching connexion of these words with St Columba's last hours see Ker's *Psalms in History and Biography*, p. 62. He was transcribing the Psalter, and at this verse he laid down his pen. "Here at the end of the page I must stop; what follows let Baithen write." "The last verse he had written," says his biographer Adamnan, "was very applicable to the saint who was about to depart, and to whom eternal good shall never be wanting; while the one that followeth is equally applicable to the father who succeeded him, the instructor of his spiritual children."

11 ff. If such are the blessings promised to those who fear the LORD, how essential to know what the fear of the LORD is! Accordingly the poet adopts the language of a teacher and addresses his *sons*. So the teacher in Prov. i—viii constantly addresses his disciples as *sons* (iv. 1), or *my son*.

11. *the fear of the LORD*] Including both the devout reverence which is essential to a right relation of man to God, and the conduct which it demands. The phrase is characteristic of Proverbs, occurring in that book almost as often as in all the rest of the O. T. See especially viii. 13; ix. 10; and cp. Is. xi. 2, 3; 1 Pet. i. 17.

12. The challenge with its answer in *vv.* 13, 14 is a vivid and forcible equivalent for *Whosoever desires...let him &c.* Cp. xxv. 12.

life] Not mere existence, but life worthy of the name (xvi. 11; xxx. 5); again a word characteristic of Proverbs, and connected there too with the fear of the LORD (xiv. 27; xix. 23; xxii. 4).

and *loveth*] Lit., *loving days for seeing good*, explaining and emphasising the preceding line. Cp. *v.* 10; iv. 6. *Days*=length of days (Prov. iii. 2; x. 27).

13. *Keep*] **Guard.** Cp. Prov. xiii. 3 (R. V.); xxi. 23; Ps. xxxix. 1; James iii. 2 ff.

guile] Deceit. Cp. xxxv. 20; xxxvi. 3.

14. The first line recurs in xxxvii. 27. Comp. the character of Job, the ideal righteous man (i. 1, 8; ii. 3); and Job xxviii. 28; Prov. xvi. 17.

Seek peace, and pursue it.
15 (ע) The eyes of the LORD *are* upon the righteous,
And his ears *are open* unto their cry.
16 (פ) The face of the LORD *is* against them that do evil,
To cut off the remembrance of them from the earth.
17 (צ) *The righteous* cry, and the LORD heareth,
And delivereth them out of all their troubles.
18 (ק) The LORD *is* nigh unto them that are of a broken heart;
And saveth such as be of a contrite spirit.

pursue it] Do not be discouraged if it should need prolonged effort to overtake it. Cp. the *pursuit* of righteousness (Prov. xxi. 21; Is. li. 1); and see Rom. xiv. 19; Heb. xii. 14. In P.B.V. *eschew* and *ensue* are archaisms for *avoid* and *follow after*.

15 ff. The fear of the LORD is commended by the consideration of His favour toward the righteous, which is contrasted with His displeasure against the wicked.

15. With the first line cp. xxxiii. 18. More literally, **toward the righteous**, as R. V. renders here but not there, though the prepositions are the same.

his ears &c.] Lit., *his ears are toward their cry for help:* cp. *my cry for help was in his ears* (xviii. 6).

16. *The face of the LORD* means the manifestation of His Presence, either as here in wrath (cp. ix. 3), or as in Num. vi. 25, in blessing. See Oehler's *O. T. Theology*, § 57. Comp. "The LORD *looked forth* upon the host of the Egyptians...and discomfited them" (Ex. xiv. 24).

the remembrance of them] Or, *their memorial;* even the name by which they might be remembered. Cp. ix. 5, 6; Job xviii. 17. Contrast cxii. 6.

17. **They cried, and Jehovah heard;**
And rescued them out of all their distresses.

We may understand a subject from the verb, *they who cried cried,* as in v. 5, i.e., when any cried: or with LXX and Vulg. supply *the righteous*. (Had the LXX this reading, or did they merely insert the word from v. 15?) It has been conjectured that vv. 15 and 16 should be transposed, so that *the righteous* in v. 15 would be the natural subject to v. 17. This transposition deserts the present order of the letters of the alphabet, but is justified by Lam. ii, iii, iv, and Prov. xxxi according to the LXX, where *Pē* precedes *Ayin*. But it may be doubted if the rearrangement is a gain.

18. *nigh* &c.] Cp. cxix. 151; Is. l. 8; and the contrast, Ps. x. 1. *The broken in heart* and *crushed in spirit* are those who have been broken down and crushed by sorrow and suffering (cxlvii. 3; Is. lxi. 1; Jer. xxiii. 9); in whom, it is implied, affliction has borne fruit, and all

(ר) Many *are* the afflictions of the righteous:　19
But the LORD delivereth him out of them all.
(ש) He keepeth all his bones:　20
Not one of them is broken.
(ת) Evil shall slay the wicked:　21
And they that hate the righteous shall be desolate.
(פ) The LORD redeemeth the soul of his servants:　22
And none of them that trust in him shall be desolate.

self-asserting pride has been subdued and replaced by true contrition and humility.

19. No exemption from *evils* is promised to the righteous man, but out of them all the LORD *rescues* him (*vv.* 4, 17).

20. As *breaking the bones* is a forcible metaphor for the torture of pain that racks the bodily framework (li. 8; Is. xxxviii. 13), or for cruel oppression (Mic. iii. 3), so *keeping* them denotes the safe preservation of the man's whole being. See note on vi. 2. This passage as well as Ex. xii. 46 may have been present to the Evangelist's mind as fulfilled in Christ (John xix. 36). The promise to the righteous man found an unexpectedly literal realisation in the passion of the perfectly Righteous One.

21. While the righteous is rescued out of all evils (*v.* 19), evil brings the wicked to his death. His evil ways work out their own punishment, and divine retribution overtakes him. (Rom. vi. 21, 23.)

21, 22. *shall be desolate*] R.V. **shall be condemned**; or, marg., *held guilty.* Cp. v. 10.

22. A second verse beginning with *Pē*, like xxv. 22, where see note.

PSALM XXXV.

Relentless enemies are seeking the Psalmist's life. Their hostility is groundless, and its maliciousness is aggravated by their ingratitude. He appeals to Jehovah to do him justice and deliver him.

Each of these points is strikingly illustrated by the narrative of David's persecution by Saul.

(1) Saul was seeking David's life. With *vv.* 4, 7, cp. 1 Sam. xx. 1; xxiii. 15; xxiv. 11; xxv. 29.

(2) Saul's enmity had been fomented by the malicious slanders of courtiers who were jealous of David; men with whom no doubt he had been on friendly terms at the court. Again and again he protests his innocence of the charges of disloyalty brought against him. With *vv.* 7, 11 ff., 19, cp. 1 Sam. xix. 5; xx. 1; xxiv. 9, 11; xxvi. 18, 19; and Saul's confession of ingratitude, xxiv. 17 ff.

(3) With the appeal to God as the judge, *vv.* 1, 23, 24, cp. 1 Sam. xxiv. 12, 15.

But it is not against Saul himself that the Psalm (if it is David's) is directed, but against the men who fomented Saul's insane jealousy.

Envious of David's sudden rise, they left no means untried to bring about his fall. Comp. Introd. to Ps. vii.

Attention has however been called to the points of contact with Jeremiah, and the Psalm has been attributed to him by some commentators. Thus *v.* 6 finds a parallel in Jer. xxiii. 12; *v.* 12 in Jer. xviii. 20, 22; *vv.* 21 *b*, 25 in Lam. ii. 16; &c. But it may well be questioned whether Jeremiah is not merely borrowing the language of the Psalm; and it should be noted that the military figures of *vv.* 1—3, which would not be natural for him, find no parallel in his book.

The Psalm falls into three divisions, each ending with a vow of thanksgiving.

i. *vv.* 1—10. Appeal to Jehovah to arm himself as the Psalmist's champion (1—3): prayer for the repulse and rout of his enemies (4—6), and for the recoil of their groundless hostility upon themselves (7, 8); with a concluding vow of thanksgiving (9, 10).

ii. *vv.* 11—18. The base ingratitude of his persecutors. They accuse him falsely, and return evil for good (11, 12); for while in their trouble he shewed the most friendly sympathy (13, 14), they requite him with slander and hatred (15, 16). Prayer for deliverance and vow of thanksgiving (17, 18).

iii. *vv.* 19—28. Renewed prayer that Jehovah will not allow such malignant and spiteful foes to triumph but will do him justice; that he and all who hold with him may rejoice in the manifestation of Jehovah's favour.

The points of contact with Pss. vii; xxii; xxxviii—xl; lxix; should be noticed.

On prayer for the destruction of enemies, see Introd. p. lxx ff.

A Psalm of David.

35 Plead *my cause*, O LORD, with them that strive with me:
Fight against them that fight against me.
2 Take hold of shield and buckler,

1—3. Appeal to Jehovah to arm himself as the Psalmist's champion.

1. *Plead* my cause] There is as it were a suit between him and his enemies. He appeals to Jehovah the Judge to do him justice (cp. *vv.* 23, 24). But the court in which the cause is to be tried is the field of battle; and therefore (dropping the figure of a suit) he calls on Jehovah to arm on his behalf. So in ix. 4 victory is regarded as a judicial decision. Cp. 1 Sam. xxiv. 15; xxv. 39. The renderings **strive with them that strive with me** (R. V.); or, (as Is. xlix. 25), *contend with them that contend with me*, obscure this point, and miss the connexion with *v.* 23. *Plead my cause with them that implead me* (Cheyne) represents the original better.

2, 3. 'Anthropomorphic' language of remarkable boldness, expanding the idea of Jehovah as "a man of war" (Exod. xv. 3: cp. Deut. xxxii. 41 f.).

shield and buckler] See note on v. 12. The mention of both together is part of the poetical picture.

And stand up for mine help.
Draw out also the spear, and stop *the way* against them that 3
persecute me:
Say unto my soul, I *am* thy salvation.
Let them be confounded and put to shame that seek after 4
my soul:
Let them be turned back and brought to confusion that
devise my hurt.
Let them be as chaff before the wind: 5
And let the angel of the LORD chase *them.*
Let their way be dark and slippery: 6
And let the angel of the LORD persecute them.

stand up for mine help] Rather, **Arise as my help.** Arise (see notes on iii. 7; vii. 6) in the character and capacity of my helper (xxvii. 9).
Draw out] From the armoury, or more probably from the spear-holder in which it was kept when not in use (Gr. δουροδόκη, Hom. *Od.* i. 128). The word is used of drawing a sword from its sheath (Ex. xv. 9).
stop the way] All the ancient versions render the word *s'gor* as an imperative; and this gives a good sense. First the enemy are checked in their pursuit; then (*vv.* 4 ff.) put to flight. But an ellipse of *the way* is harsh; the verb *shut* is not so used elsewhere; and the preposition *against* seems to imply attack. Hence many modern commentators regard the word as the name of a weapon not mentioned elsewhere in the O. T., *battle-axe* (R. V. marg.) or, *dirk* (Cheyne); the equivalent of the *sagaris* mentioned by Greek historians as the characteristic weapon of Persians, Scythians, and other Asiatics.
that persecute me] Rather, **that pursue me** (R. V.). Cp. 1 Sam. xxiv. 14; &c.
say unto my soul &c.] Give me the comforting assurance of thy interposition for my deliverance. Cp. iii. 2, 8 and notes there. The primary meaning of the words is of course temporal not spiritual.

4—6. Prayer for the repulse and rout of his enemies. No doubt the language might be entirely figurative, but it is more naturally explained if a literal fulfilment was at least a possibility.

4. Ashamed and dishonoured be they that seek my life;
  Turned back and confounded be they that devise my hurt.
For *that seek my life* (or, *soul*) cp. 1 Sam. xx. 1; &c. Let them be disappointed in their aim, repulsed with ignominy in their attack. Cp. *v.* 26; xl. 14; vi. 10.

5, 6. **Let them be as chaff before the wind,**
  The angel of Jehovah thrusting them down.
  Let their way be all dark and slippery,
  The angel of Jehovah pursuing them.
A terrible picture of a pell-mell rout. Does it not read like a recollection of some incident in a warrior's life, perhaps some defeat of the

7 For without cause have they hid for me their net *in* a pit,
  Which without cause they have digged for my soul.
8 Let destruction come upon him at unawares;
  And let his net that he hath hid catch himself:
  Into that *very* destruction let him fall.
9 And my soul shall be joyful in the LORD:
  It shall rejoice in his salvation.
10 All my bones shall say,
  LORD, who *is* like unto thee,

Philistines? Helpless as chaff before the wind (i. 4: lxxxiii. 13) they are driven headlong down a dark and slippery track, where they can neither see nor keep their footing, with the dread Angel smiting them down as they vainly strive to escape. "The tracks down the limestone hills of Palestine are often worn as smooth as marble" (*Kay*).

Most probably the participles should be transposed. *Pursuing* suits the image of the storm-driven chaff (Is. xvii. 13); *thrusting down* (xxxvi. 12; cxviii. 13; cxl. 4) agrees better with the picture of the stumbling fugitives. For *the angel of Jehovah* see note on xxxiv. 7. Cp. the reminiscence of this passage in Jeremiah xxiii. 12.

7, 8. The causelessness of their insidious enmity is the ground for such a prayer. May their schemes recoil on their own heads.

7. The word for *pit* must be transposed from the first line, where it is superfluous and awkward, to the second line, where it is required. Render
  For without cause have they hid a net for me:
  Without cause have they dug a pit for my soul (*life*).
The metaphors from the hunter's nets and pitfalls express the insidious character of their secret plots. Cp. again Jer. xviii. 20, 22.

8. Let his mischief recoil upon his own head. Cp. vii. 15; ix. 15; lvii. 6; and with the first line cp. Is. xlvii. 11. Does the singular individualise each one of the enemies, or particularise one above all the rest, or speak of them collectively in the mass? It is less easy to decide here than in vii. 2.

into that very destruction let him fall] R.V. renders, **With destruction let him fall therein**, retaining A.V. in the marg. But neither rendering is satisfactory; and it is possible (especially in view of the almost certain textual errors in *vv.* 5, 6, 7) that the original reading was, *and his pit that he hath dug, let him fall therein*.

9, 10. Rejoicing for deliverance.

10. *All my bones*] The bodily frame feels the thrill of joy as it feels the pain of sorrow. Cp. li. 8; and see note on vi. 2.

who is *like unto thee*] Incomparable for power and goodness. Cp. Ex. xv. 11; Mic. vii. 18.

Which deliverest the poor from him that is too strong for
him,
Yea, the poor and the needy from him that spoileth him?
False witnesses did rise up; 11
They laid to my charge *things* that I knew not.
They rewarded me evil for good 12
To the spoiling of my soul.
But *as for* me, when they were sick, my clothing *was* sack- 13
cloth:
I humbled my soul with fasting;
And my prayer returned into mine own bosom.

the poor] **The afflicted,** often coupled with *the needy* (xxxvii. 14;
xl. 17; lxxxvi. 1; &c.)

11—18. The causelessness of the Psalmist's persecution and the
ingratitude of his persecutors are urged as reasons for God's inter-
ference on his behalf.

11. *False witnesses*] Rather, **unrighteous,** or, **malicious, witnesses
rise up**; lit., *witnesses of violence,* as in Ex. xxiii. 1; Deut. xix. 16.
Cp. Ps. xxvii. 12 (A.V. *cruelty*).

they laid to my charge &c.] R.V. **they ask of me things that I
know not**: calling me to account for crimes, of which I have not
even any knowledge. Cp. lxix. 4. The phraseology is that of a court;
not that the Psalmist is to be thought of as actually put upon his
trial. David was falsely and maliciously accused of treason and conspiracy against the king's life (1 Sam. xxiv. 9). Cp. Mt. xxvi. 59 ff.

12. *They rewarded* &c.] Better, as R.V., **they reward.** As in
the preceding verse he speaks of what is still going on. His enemies
are guilty of the basest ingratitude. Cp. xxxviii. 20; cix. 5; Prov.
xvii. 13. Saul confessed that he had treated David thus (1 Sam.
xxiv. 17 ff.).

to the spoiling of my soul] Render as R.V., **to the bereaving of
my soul**: or perhaps, *it is bereavement to my soul.* Such conduct makes
him feel as desolate as the childless mother.

13. The 'good' he had done to them. His sympathy when they
were in trouble was no mere formality. He prayed for their recovery,
humbling himself before God with mourning and fasting (lxix. 10,
11; 2 Sam. xii. 16; Joel ii. 12), that their sin might be forgiven and
their sickness removed.

humbled] R.V., **afflicted.** It is the technical term for fasting in
the Law. See Lev. xvi. 29, 31; xxiii. 27, 32; Num. xxix. 7; Is. lviii.
3, 5.

and my prayer returned into mine own bosom] An obscure phrase;
not to be explained of the attitude of earnest prayer with head bent
down on the bosom so that the prayer which came from his heart
seemed to return thither again (1 Kings xviii. 42 does not justify this

14 I behaved myself as though *he had been* my friend *or* brother:
I bowed down heavily, as one that mourneth for his mother.
15 But in mine adversity they rejoiced, and gathered themselves together:
Yea, the abjects gathered themselves together against me, and I knew *it* not;
They did tear *me*, and ceased not:
16 With hypocritical mockers in feasts,
They gnashed upon me *with* their teeth.

explanation): nor again, that his prayer returned to him without effecting its object (Matt. x. 13), for there would be no point in his prayer being unanswered: but rather, **my prayer shall return into mine own bosom.** They have recompensed him evil for good; but his prayer will not be unrewarded. As the causeless curse returns with interest into the bosom whence it issues (lxxix. 12), so the prayer at least brings back a blessing to its offerer (Jer. xviii. 20).

14. Better with R.V.,
**I behaved myself as though it had been my friend or my brother:
I bowed down mourning, as one that bewaileth his mother.**
Had they been his nearest and dearest, he could not have displayed deeper grief.

The verse would be improved by a slight transposition (which is supported by xxxviii. 6), thus; *I bowed down* (descriptive of the mourner's gait with the head bowed down by the load of sorrow)...*I went mourning* (like Lat. *squalidus*, of all the outward signs of grief, dark clothes, tear-stained unwashed face, untrimmed hair and beard—see 2 Sam. xix. 24).

15. But at my halting they rejoice, and gather themselves together. Limping, like stumbling, is a figure for misfortune. Cp. xxxviii. 17; Jer. xx. 10.

Yea, *the abjects*] The word rendered *abjects* is of doubtful meaning and possibly corrupt. (1) According to the rendering of A.V., retained by R.V., the sense is, that with his other enemies were associated the lowest outcasts, a rabble of men whom he knew not (Job xxx. 8 ff.); for the last words of the line must be rendered with R.V. marg., *and* those whom *I knew not*. (2) But the form of the sentence rather points to a description of the conduct of the men who have been mentioned already: so (retaining or slightly altering the present text), *they gather themselves together smiting me unawares*, or, *for things that I know not*. The wounds of slander are meant (Jer. xviii. 18). So the Targum: *wicked men who smite me with their words*. (3) Various emendations have been proposed. One that has found some favour, *strangers*, is foreign to the rest of the Psalm.

they did tear me &c.] **They rend** me, **and cease not.** Like beasts of prey (Hos. xiii. 8); or as we talk of tearing a man's reputation to shreds.

16. Like (less probably, *among*) **the profanest of mocking para-**

Lord, how long wilt thou look on? 17
Rescue my soul from their destructions,
My darling from the lions.
I will give thee thanks in the great congregation: 18
I will praise thee among much people.
Let not them that are mine enemies wrongfully rejoice 19
over me:
Neither let them wink *with* the eye that hate me without
a cause.
For they speak not peace: 20
But they devise deceitful matters against *them that are* quiet
in the land.
Yea, they opened their mouth wide against me, 21
And said, Aha, aha, our eye hath seen *it*.

sites, they gnash &c.; a gesture of rage, as though they would devour their victim (*v.* 25). The obscure phrase in the first line is generally explained to mean *mockers for a cake*, buffoons who purchase entertainment for themselves by scurrilous jests (Gr. κνισσοκόλακες, ψωμοκόλακες, Lat. *buccellarii*). Another explanation is, *like* (or, *among*) *the profanest of perverse mockers*.

17, 18. A cry for help, and a vow of thanksgiving.

17. *wilt thou look on*] Lit. *wilt thou see*, as in *v.* 22, and not interfere. A.V. gives the sense rightly.

rescue my soul] Restore, lit., *bring back*, my life, for it is all but lost.
my darling] Lit. *my only one*, i.e. my precious life. See on xxii. 20.
The lions are his savage persecutors (lvii. 4).

18. Another parallel to Ps. xxii, *vv.* 22, 25. Cp. xl. 9, 10.
much people] Or, *a mighty people* (R. V. marg.). The publicity of the thanksgiving is the point.

19—28. Renewed prayer in a somewhat calmer tone.

19. *wrongfully*] Lit., *falsely* (xxxviii. 19; lxix. 4); the grounds they allege for their enmity being untrue.

neither *let them wink*] The insertion of the negative is grammatically justifiable, and probably right; though the clause may also be rendered, *they wink* &c., describing the confederates' malicious signals of satisfaction at his misfortune (Prov. vi. 13; x. 10).

that hate me without a cause] Cp. lxix. 4. Our Lord refers to these words as 'fulfilled' in Himself (John xv. 25).

20. Their conduct is just the opposite of 'the fear of the LORD' (xxxiv. 13, 14). *For it is not peace that they speak, but against them that are quiet in the land they imagine words of guile*, accusing them of being 'troublers of Israel' and disturbers of the peace.

21. And they open…a gesture of contempt (Is. lvii. 4), rather than

22 *This* thou hast seen, O LORD: keep not silence:
O Lord, be not far from me.
23 Stir up thyself, and awake to my judgment,
Even unto my cause, my God and my Lord.
24 Judge me, O LORD my God, according to thy righteousness;
And let them not rejoice over me.
25 Let them not say in their hearts, Ah, so would we have it:
Let them not say, We have swallowed him up.
26 Let them be ashamed and brought to confusion together that rejoice at mine hurt:
Let them be clothed with shame and dishonour that magnify *themselves* against me.
27 Let them shout for joy, and be glad, that favour my righteous cause:
Yea, let them say continually, Let the LORD be magnified,
Which hath pleasure in the prosperity of his servant.
28 And my tongue shall speak of thy righteousness

of murderous intent (*v.* 25): **they say, Aha, aha, our eye hath seen:** seen its desire, seen the fall of the man whose rise excited our envy.

22. He turns their taunt into a plea: **Thou hast seen, O Jehovah.** Cp. *v.* 17, note.

keep not silence] The same word as in xxviii. 1, where R. V. renders, *be not thou deaf unto me.* With *be not far from me*, cp. xxii. 11; &c.

23. **Arouse and awake for my judgment,**
O my God and my Lord, for my cause.

Interpose to do me justice, and defend my cause. Cp. *v.* 1, and see note on vii. 6.

24. *Judge me*] Do me justice. Cp. vii. 8; and for the plea, *according to thy righteousness*, see vii. 17; xxxi. 1.

25. *Ah, so would we have it*] Lit. *Aha, our desire!*

We have swallowed him up] Destroying every trace of his existence. Cp. cxxiv. 3; Prov. i. 12; Lam. ii. 16.

26. A repetition of *v.* 4, with some variations, occurring again in xl. 14.

27. Cp. xl. 16.

that favour my righteous cause] Lit. *that delight in my righteousness;* that welcome the vindication of my innocence.

which hath pleasure in the prosperity of his servant] More exactly, **which delighteth** (2 Sam. xv. 26; Ps. xviii. 19, xxii. 8) **in the welfare** (lit. *peace*) **of his servant.**

28. *shall speak*] 'Shall speak *musingly*, in the low murmur of one entranced by a sweet thought.' *Cheyne.*

of thy righteousness] For Jehovah's righteousness (*v.* 24) will have been manifested in delivering His servant.

And of thy praise all the day long.

all the day long] 'Tota die Deum laudare quis durat? Suggero remedium, unde tota die laudes Deum, si vis. Quidquid egeris bene age, et laudasti Deum....In innocentia operum tuorum praepara te ad laudandum Deum tota die.' *St Augustine.*

PSALM XXXVI.

This Psalm presents two contrasted pictures: one of the godless principles and conduct of the man who has made deliberate choice of evil; the other of the universal and inexhaustible lovingkindness of God. From the prevailing wickedness around him (to which he is in danger of falling a victim, *v.* 11), the Psalmist turns for relief and comfort to contemplate the goodness of God. The wicked man may deny God's Providence and defy His judgments, but to the eye of faith His goodness is supreme, and His judicial righteousness will ultimately be triumphant. The contemplation of that goodness brings the folly of deserting God into strong relief, and suggests the greatness of the loss which man incurs by his apostasy.

The abruptness of the transition from *vv.* 1—4 to *vv.* 5 ff. has suggested the hypothesis that we have here parts of two Psalms, which have been combined by an editor. But the hypothesis is unnecessary. The two parts are related like the two members of an antithetic proverb (e.g. Prov. xiv. 22); and the reader is left to interpret the connexion for himself. Moreover the connexion of thought and language in *vv.* 11, 12 with *vv.* 1—4 is decidedly in favour of the unity of the Psalm.

The structure of the Psalm is clear and simple.
 i. The principle of godlessness (1, 2), and the practical results to which it leads (3, 4).
 ii. The gloriousness of God's attributes (5, 6), and His beneficence to man (7—9).
 iii. Prayer for blessing (10), and protection (11); and confident anticipation of the overthrow of the wicked (12).

For the title *servant of the* LORD in the inscription comp. the inscription of Ps. xviii; and xxxv. 27.

To the chief Musician, *A Psalm* of David the servant of the LORD.

The transgression of the wicked saith within my heart,   **36**
That there is no fear of God before his eyes.

1, 2. The ground of the godless man's security in his sin.

1. As the Psalmist reflects on the conduct of the wicked man, it becomes clear to him that practical atheism is the guiding principle of his life. So the reading of the Massoretic Text, followed in the A. V., may be explained. But it is unnatural to regard transgression as uttering its oracle in the Psalmist's heart; and the reading of the LXX, Vulg., Syr., and Jerome, **within his heart,** is certainly preferable. The verse

2 For he flattereth himself in his own eyes,
    Until his iniquity be found to be hateful.
3 The words of his mouth *are* iniquity and deceit:
    He hath left off to be wise, *and* to do good.

may then be rendered either (1), **Saith Transgression to the wicked within his heart**, (that) **there is** &c.; the second line giving the words of Transgression's oracle: or (2) **Transgression uttereth its oracle to the wicked within his heart**; **There is** &c.; the second line being the statement of the Psalmist, and hinting at the substance of the oracle.

The word rendered *saith*, or, *uttereth its oracle*, is regularly used of solemn divine utterances in the phrase *saith the* LORD (Gen. xxii. 16; and frequently in the prophets). Occasionally though rarely, it has a human speaker for its subject (Num. xxiv. 3 ff.; 2 Sam. xxiii. 1; Prov. xxx. 1). Transgression—more precisely, *rebellion* or *apostasy*,—is here personified (cp. Gen. iv. 7, R.V.; Zech. v. 8; Rom. vi. 12, 13, R.V.). The wicked man has made it his God, and it has become a lying spirit within him (1 Kings xxii. 21 ff.; 2 Thess. ii. 11, 12).

no fear of God] Rather, **no terror of God**. The word *pachad* denotes terror inspired by God, not reverence for God (Is. ii. 10, 19, 21, R.V.). Transgression persuades the wicked man that there is no need for him to dread God's judgments. Cp. x. 4, 5, 6, 11, 13: xiv. 1; and contrast Ps. xviii. 22; cxix. 120: Job xiii. 11; xxxi. 23. With these words St Paul sums up his description of the character and condition of fallen man in Rom. iii. 18.

2. A much disputed verse. Three renderings of the first line deserve consideration. (1) Taking the wicked man as the subject, we may render as the A. V. (2) Taking Transgression as the subject, we may render, **For It flattereth him in his eyes**. (3) Taking God as the subject, we may render, **For He flattereth him in his eyes**.

The third rendering, whether it is explained to mean, 'God treats him gently, so he imagines,' (Cheyne) or, 'God's threatenings seem to him mere idle words,' can hardly be supported by the usage of the word. The first agrees best with the reading *my heart* in *v.* 1, giving the ground of the Psalmist's conviction expressed there. But if the better reading, *his heart*, is adopted, the second rendering gives the best connexion. It explains how Transgression goes to work. It 'speaks smooth things and prophesies deceits' to him, *concerning the finding out of his iniquity and hating it*, i.e. as R. V.,

That his iniquity shall not be found out and be hated:
dragged to light in order to be punished, and exposed in its true hatefulness. The word *find out* is frequently used of detection with a view to punishment. See xvii. 3: 1 Kings i. 52.

3, 4. The fruits of this reckless atheism described.

3. *iniquity and deceit*] Cp. v. 5, 6; x. 7.

he hath left off &c.] Or, *he hath ceased to be wise to do good*. Cf. Jer. iv. 22. He inverts the prophetic exhortation, Is. i. 16, 17. The word here rendered *to be wise* is specially used of the intelligence which

He deviseth mischief upon his bed ;
He setteth himself in a way *that is* not good ;
He abhorreth not evil.
Thy mercy, O LORD, *is* in the heavens ;
And thy faithfulness *reacheth* unto the clouds.
Thy righteousness *is* like the great mountains ;
Thy judgments *are* a great deep :
O LORD, thou preservest man and beast.
How excellent *is* thy lovingkindness, O God!

leads to right and successful conduct. Cp. xiv. 2 (*understand*); ci. 2 (*behave myself wisely*).
4. *mischief*] **Iniquity,** as in *vv.* 3, 12.
upon his bed] In the stillness of the night, the time for repentance (iv. 4), and recollection of God (lxiii. 6), he is restlessly planning his crimes. For illustration see Mic. ii. 1 ff.
he setteth himself &c.] Evil courses are his deliberate choice; conscience is blunted, and wrong excites no abhorrence. Cp. i. 1; Prov. xvi. 29; Is. lxv. 2.

5—9. From the grievous spectacle of human perversity the Psalmist takes refuge in adoring contemplation of the character of God, the only source of life and light, who deals blessing liberally to all His creatures.

5. O LORD, thy lovingkindness *reacheth* **to the heavens;**
Thy faithfulness even unto the skies.
God's lovingkindness (*vv.* 7, 10) and faithfulness cannot be measured. For the comparison see Job xi. 8; xxii. 12; xxxv. 5: and cp. lvii. 10; ciii. 11: Eph. iii. 18.

6. Jehovah's righteousness—His faithfulness to His character and covenant (v. 8), manifested alike in mercy and in judgment—is **like the mountains of God** (*El*), immovably firm (cxi. 3), eternally unchanged, majestically conspicuous. God's works proclaim their Author, and reflect His attributes. Cp. civ. 16; lxv. 9; lxxx. 10. *The great mountains* is a paraphrase which obscures the meaning.
a great deep] Mysterious, unfathomable, inexhaustible, as the vast subterranean abyss of waters (xxxiii. 7; Gen. vii. 11; Job xxviii. 14; xxxviii. 16). Cp. Rom. xi. 33.
preservest] Or, *savest*. The lower animals are the objects of God's care as well as man. See civ. 14, 27, 28; cxlvii. 9; Jon. iv. 11; Matt. vi. 26 ff.; x. 29 ff.

7. *How excellent*] **How precious** (R.V.). It is the Psalmist's treasure. Cp. cxxxix. 17.
O God] The substitution of *God* for *Jehovah* is significant. The Psalmist is speaking of a love which extends beyond the limits of the chosen people, and embraces all mankind. *The children of men*—lit. *sons of man* (xiv. 2) are men regarded as earthborn and mortal in contrast to God.

Therefore the children of men put their trust under the shadow of thy wings.
8 They shall be abundantly satisfied with the fatness of thy house;
And thou shalt make them drink *of* the river of thy pleasures.
9 For with thee *is* the fountain of life:
In thy light shall we see light.
10 O continue thy lovingkindness unto them that know thee;
And thy righteousness to the upright in heart.
11 Let not the foot of pride come against me,
And let not the hand of the wicked remove me.

therefore &c.] **And the children of men take refuge** &c. (R. V.). Cp. xvii. 7, 8, note; Ruth ii. 12.

8. God is more than a protector. He is a bountiful host, who provides royal entertainment for His guests. Cp. xxiii. 5, 6; xxvii. 4; lxv. 4. The metaphor is derived from the sacrificial meal, in which God receives the worshipper at His table[1] (Lev. vii. 15; Jer. xxxi. 14). That welcome is the sacramental expression of His relation to man.

the river of thy pleasures] Or, *the stream* (Am. v. 24) *of thy delights:* a different word from that in xvi. 11, and derived from the same root as *Eden*.

9. The expectation of *v.* 8 is no idle dream, for God is the source of life and light. From Him springs all that constitutes life (xxxiv. 12), physical and spiritual (cp. Jer. ii. 13; xvii. 13): from Him proceeds all that makes up true happiness (cp. iv. 6). Golden sayings like this anticipate the revelation of the Gospel. It is only in the light of the Incarnation that their depth of meaning begins to be understood. Cp. John i. 4, 9.

10—12. Concluding prayer for the continuance of God's lovingkindness and for protection from the wicked, with a confident anticipation of the final downfall of evil-doers. *v.* 10 springs naturally out of *vv.* 5—9, and *vv.* 11, 12 clearly revert to *vv.* 1—4.

10. A prayer for the continued exercise of the attributes which have been celebrated in *vv.* 5—9. All God's bounty to man flows from His lovingkindness, yet His righteousness also is concerned in the fulfilment of His covenant and promise.

them that know thee] With an effectual knowledge which must issue in loving obedience (ix. 10; xci. 14); and entitles its possessors to be called *upright in heart* (vii. 10; xi. 2; xxxii. 11).

11. Let me not be trampled under foot by proud oppressors, or driven from my home by wicked violence. This verse clearly refers to *vv.* 1—4. The Psalmist is himself in danger of falling a victim to the ruthless oppressors there described.

remove me] R. V. **drive me away,** from hearth and home to become

---

[1] See Bp. Westcott's *Hebrews*, p. 292.

There are the workers of iniquity fallen : 12
They are cast down, and shall not be able to rise.

a wanderer and a vagabond. The word may be used of exile (2 Kings xxi. 8; Jer. iv. 1); but there is not the slightest hint here of an impending invasion. What the Psalmist fears is treatment like that described in Mic. ii. 9, leaving him a homeless beggar (Job xv. 23; Ps. cix. 10).

12. With the eye of faith he beholds the certain and irreparable ruin of the "workers of iniquity" (*vv.* 3, 4: cp. v. 5; vi. 8; xiv. 4). *There* points to the scene of their discomfiture. Cp. xiv. 5; lxiv. 8.

they are cast down] R. V. **they are thrust down** (v. 10; xxxv. 5), and overthrown for ever. Cp. Is. xxvi. 14. Such judgments are an earnest of the final triumph (Rom. xvi. 20).

PSALM XXXVII.

In the preceding Psalm the Psalmist found relief and hope in the presence of high-handed iniquity by the contemplation of the inexhaustible lovingkindness of God. Here he assumes the character of a teacher, and bids the godly man not be disquieted by the sight of the prosperity of the wicked, for they are doomed to speedy destruction, while enduring happiness is in store for the righteous. "Hence Tertullian calls the Psalm, *providentiae speculum* (A mirror of providence), Isidore, *potio contra murmur* (An antidote to murmuring), Luther, *vestis piorum, cui adscriptum: Hic sanctorum patientia est* (A garment for the godly, with the inscription, 'Here is the patience of the saints')." *Delitzsch.*

The prosperity of the wicked was one of the enigmas of life which most sorely tried the faith of the godly Israelite[1]. No light had as yet been cast upon the problem by the revelation of a future state of rewards and punishments. Sometimes, as we see in Ps. lxxiii, he was in danger of losing all belief in the providential government of the world: at all times he was liable to be tempted to murmuring and envy.

It is with the more obvious and common danger that the Psalmist here deals. The consolation which he has to offer is of a simple and elementary kind. He affirms the popular doctrine of recompence and retribution which Job found so unsatisfactory. Trust in the LORD: wait His time: all will be well in the end: the wicked will be destroyed and the righteous rewarded. There is an element of truth in this doctrine, for God's judgments are constantly distinguishing between the righteous and the wicked (Mark x. 30; 1 Tim. iv. 8). The verdict of history and experience is, in the long run, in favour of righteousness. But the doctrine is inadequate, as Job felt, for retribution does not invariably and immediately overtake the wrong-doer in this world, nor is the righteous man always visibly rewarded.

In order, however, fairly to estimate the Psalmist's teaching and its value for those whom he addressed, we must bear in mind that personal individuality was comparatively unrecognised in early ages, while the solidarity of the family was realised to an extent which we find it hard

[1] See Oehler's *Old Testament Theology,* § 246.

to understand. A man lived on in his posterity: his posterity represented him: and the instincts of justice were satisfied if the law of retribution and recompence could be traced in the destinies of the family if not of the individual.

The consolation here offered was no doubt real to the mass of the Psalmist's contemporaries, in virtue of the element of truth which it contains. But it was only a partial and provisional solution of the problem. Through trials of faith and imperfect answers to their questionings God was on the one hand leading men to a truer ideal of happiness, on the other hand preparing them to receive the revelation of a future state of rewards and punishments. The author of Ps. lxxiii makes a distinct step forward. Though he still looks for the visible punishment of evil-doers, he is taught to find his own highest joy and comfort in fellowship with God, independently of the prospect of temporal felicity. The author of the Book of Job is carried still further, and forced to the conclusion that this world must be but one act in the drama of life.

The Psalm should be studied in connexion with Ps. lxxiii (cp. also Ps. xlix) and the Book of Job. The unquestioning confidence of the teacher who speaks here presents a striking contrast to the touching record in Ps. lxxiii of faith sorely tried but finally victorious.

The close relation of the Psalm to the Book of Proverbs must also be noticed. It forms a connecting link between lyric poetry and the proverbial philosophy of the 'Wise Men' whose teaching was such an important influence in Israel. See especially Prov. x. 27—32; xxiv. 15 ff. The promises of the Psalm should also be compared with the prophetic expectation of the Messianic age of peace and righteousness.

The Psalm is alphabetic in structure. The stanzas commence with the letters of the alphabet in regular succession, and usually consist of two distichs connected in sense. In three instances the stanza consists of a tristich instead of two distichs (*vv.* 7, 20, 34); and in three instances it consists of five lines (*vv.* 14, 15; 25, 26; 39, 40).

The same fundamental ideas recur throughout; but four symmetrical divisions of 11, 9, 11, 9 verses respectively, in each of which a particular thought is prominent, may be observed.

i. Counsel to avoid murmuring, and trust in Jehovah (1—11):
ii. For the triumph of the wicked is shortlived (12—20):
iii. And the reward of the righteous sure and abiding (21—31).
iv. The final contrast of retribution and recompence (32—40).

A Psalm of David.

37 (א) Fret not thyself because of evildoers,
Neither be thou envious against the workers of iniquity.

1—11. Warnings and counsels for times of temptation.

1, 2. Stanza of *Aleph*, stating the theme of the Psalm;—an exhortation against discontent and envy at the prosperity of the wicked, on the ground that it is only transitory.

1. *Fret not thyself*] Lit., *incense not thyself:* be not angry or indignant or discontented.

neither be thou envious &c.] **Neither be envious of them that do**

> For they shall soon be cut down like the grass, 2
> And wither as the green herb.
>
> (ב) Trust in the LORD, and do good; 3
> So shalt thou dwell in the land, and verily thou shalt be fed.
> Delight thyself also in the LORD; 4
> And he shall give thee the desires of thine heart.

unrighteousness, and for the time prosper (*v.* 7). The severity of the temptation is attested by lxxiii. 3. The warning, repeated in *vv.* 7, 8, is found again in Prov. xxiv. 19. Cp. Prov. iii. 31; xxiii. 17; xxiv. 1. The phrase rendered in A. V. *workers of iniquity* is a different one from that in xxxvi. 12. It is the opposite of *doing good* (*vv.* 3, 27). The LXX rendering is τοὺς ποιοῦντας τὴν ἀνομίαν, words which occur in Matt. xiii. 41 in a context which should be compared with this Psalm. Cp. 1 John iii. 4.

2. *The grass* and *the green herb* are a common image for what is transient and perishable. See note on *v.* 20; and cp. xc. 5 f.; ciii. 15 f.; Is. xl. 6 ff.

be cut down] Or, *fade*. Cp. Job xiv. 2; xviii. 16 (R. V. marg.).

3, 4. Stanza of *Beth*. The antidote to envious discontent is patient trust in Jehovah, and perseverance in the path of duty. Render

> **Trust in Jehovah, and do good;**
> **Dwell in the land, and follow after faithfulness:**
> **So shalt thou delight thyself in Jehovah,**
> **And he shall grant thee thy heart's petitions.**

Remain in the land of promise where God has placed thee: "the land of Jehovah's presence, which has not only a glorious past, but a future rich in promise, and will finally become the inheritance of the true Israel in a more complete manner than under Joshua" (*Delitzsch*): there, and there alone, shalt thou find thy true satisfaction in Him. It would seem that the poorer Israelites, oppressed or driven from their homes by powerful neighbours (xxxvi. 11), were tempted to seek their fortunes in foreign lands, and forfeit their national and religious privileges. Cp. 1 Sam. xxvi. 19.

Here, as in *vv.* 9, 11, 22, 29, 34, *the land* is Canaan, the land of promise. The rendering of A. V. in *vv.* 9, 11, 22, *the earth*, is misleading so far as the primary meaning of the Psalm is concerned.

It is best to take *v.* 3 as virtually a series of conditions in the form of exhortations, and *v.* 4 as the promise depending on the fulfilment of the conditions. The A. V. *so shalt thou dwell*, &c., is inadmissible on grammatical grounds: and though it is possible to render *Delight thyself also* &c., in *v.* 4, the balance of the clauses, and the parallels in Job xxii. 26, Is. lviii. 14 are decisive in favour of the rendering, *so shalt thou delight thyself* &c. The renderings of the last clause of *v.* 3, *verily thou shalt be fed*, or, *feed securely* (R. V. marg.) are in themselves questionable, and fall to the ground when the true construction of the verses is adopted. With *follow after faithfulness* (R. V.) cp. cxix. 30 (R. V.).

5 (ג) Commit thy way unto the LORD;
Trust also in him; and he shall bring *it* to pass.
6 And he shall bring forth thy righteousness as the light,
And thy judgment as the noonday.

7 (ד) Rest in the LORD, and wait patiently for him:
Fret not thyself because of him who prospereth *in* his way,
Because of the man who bringeth wicked devices to pass.

8 (ה) Cease from anger, and forsake wrath:
Fret not thyself in any wise to do evil.
9 For evildoers shall be cut off:
But those that wait upon the LORD, they shall inherit the earth.

5, 6. Stanza of *Gimel.* The reward of faith.

5. *Commit* &c.] Lit. *Roll thy way upon Jehovah:* shake off and devolve upon Him all the burden of anxiety for life's course. Cp. Prov. xvi. 3; 1 Pet. v. 7.

and he shall bring it *to pass*] With forcible brevity in the Heb. simply, **and HE** (emphatic) **will do** (*ipse faciet*, Vulg.) all that is needful. Cp. lii. 9; cxix. 126; 1 Thess. v. 24. This verse combines *vv.* 3 and 31 of Ps. xxii.

**6. And he shall make thy righteousness go forth as the light,
And thy judgment as the brightness of the noonday.**

The result of that divine working. The justice of thy cause has been hidden, but it shall shine forth like the sun rising out of the darkness of night; thy right has been obscured, but it shall be clear as the full light of the noonday. Cp. Job xi. 17; Prov. iv. 18; Is. lviii. 10; Matt. xiii. 43.

7. Stanza of *Daleth.* The remedy for impatience.

Rest in the LORD] Or, *Be still before* (Heb. *be silent to*) *the* LORD (R.V. marg.), in the calmness of faith. Cp. lxii. 1, 5; and for illustration see Is. vii. 4; xxx. 15.

who bringeth wicked devices to pass] Lit. *who doeth* (cp. *v.* 1 *b*, and contrast *vv.* 3, 5 *b*) *crafty devices.*

8, 9. Stanza of *Hê.* The warning of *vv.* 1, 2 repeated and emphasised.

8. Render with R.V., **Fret not thyself,** *it tendeth* **only to evildoing.** Discontent is not only foolish and useless, but dangerous. It may lead the man who yields to it to deny God's providence, and cast in his lot with the evil-doers. See Ps. lxxiii. 2 ff., 13 ff.

9. *the earth*] Rather, as in *v.* 3, **the land;** and so in *vv.* 11, 22, 29, 34. As the nations were "cut off" before Israel (Deut. xii. 29; xix. 1), that Israel might possess the Promised Land, so will the wicked be destroyed, that the true Israel may have undisturbed enjoyment of their inheritance. Cp. xxv. 13.

(ו) For yet a little while, and the wicked *shall* not *be*: 10
Yea, thou shalt diligently consider his place, and it *shall* not *be*.
But the meek shall inherit the earth; 11
And shall delight themselves in the abundance of peace.

(ז) The wicked plotteth against the just, 12
And gnasheth upon him *with* his teeth.
The Lord shall laugh at him: 13
For he seeth that his day is coming.

(ח) The wicked have drawn out the sword, and have bent 14
their bow,
To cast down the poor and needy,
And to slay such as be of upright conversation.

10, 11. Stanza of *Vāv;* expanding the preceding verse.
10. Cp. *v.* 36: Is. xxix. 20.
his place] His abode. Cp. Job vii. 10; viii. 18; xx. 9.
and it shall *not* be] Better, as R.V., **and he shall not be**.
11. The promise is reaffirmed in a larger sense in the beatitude of Matt. v. 5, the language of which reproduces the rendering of the LXX here: οἱ δὲ πραεῖς κληρονομήσουσιν γῆν.
in the abundance of peace] Cp. lxxii. 7; cxix. 165; Is. xxxii. 17.

12—20. Disappointment and destruction are the destiny of the wicked.

12, 13. Stanza of *Zayin.* The impotent rage of the wicked.
12. **The wicked deviseth mischief against the righteous.** Cp. *vv.* 7, 32.
gnasheth &c.] Like a furious wild beast, eager to seize its prey. Cf. xxxv. 16.
13. **Doth laugh** (ii. 4 note)...**for he hath seen.** The punishment of the wicked has been foreseen and foreordained from the first.
his day] The appointed day of retribution and ruin. Cp. cxxxvii. 7; Obad. 12; 1 Sam. xxvi. 10; Job xviii. 20.
14, 15. Stanza of *Cheth.* The machinations of the wicked recoil upon themselves. Cp. vii. 15 ff.; ix. 15 ff.
14. *Sword* and *bow* are not merely figurative expressions for any means of inflicting injury. The Psalm deals with a state of society in which the poor and defenceless were in constant danger of actual violence (*v.* 32). Cp. Prov. i. 10 ff.
the poor and needy] Or, *the afflicted and needy.* See notes on ix. 12, 18: and cp. Am. viii. 4; Is. xxxii. 7; Jer. xxii. 16.
such as be of upright conversation] Lit. *the upright of way:* those whose life and conduct are upright. Cp. cxix. 1. The LXX however reads *upright in heart* (xxxvi. 10, and often).

15 Their sword shall enter into their own heart,
And their bows shall be broken.

16 (ט) A little that a righteous *man* hath
Is better than the riches of many wicked.

17 For the arms of the wicked shall be broken:
But the LORD upholdeth the righteous.

18 (י) The LORD knoweth the days of the upright:
And their inheritance shall be for ever.

19 They shall not be ashamed in the evil time:
And in the days of famine they shall be satisfied.

20 (כ) But the wicked shall perish,
And the enemies of the LORD *shall be* as the fat of lambs:

conversation, as in l. 23, has the obsolete sense of *manner of life, behaviour*.

16, 17. Stanza of *Teth*. The nature of true wealth.

16. **Better is a little that the righteous hath
Than the abundance of many wicked.** (R.V.)

Abundance, lit. *tumult* (a different word from that in v. 11), suggests the idea of noisy, ostentatious opulence. Cp. Prov. xv. 16; xvi. 8; and Tobit xii. 8; "a little with righteousness is better than much with unrighteousness." The P.B.V. *great riches of the ungodly* follows the LXX, Vulg. and Jer.: but the present Heb. text cannot be so rendered.

17. *For the arms* &c.] All the power which they have misused for evil will be rendered impotent. Cp. x. 15; Job xxxviii. 15.

upholdeth] When the wicked strives to make him fall (*vv.* 14), and at all times. See *vv.* 24, 31. Cp. iii. 5; liv. 4; lxxi. 6.

18, 19. Stanza of *Yôd*. Jehovah's care for the godly.

18. Jehovah knoweth, and the Omniscient is also the All-Sovereign (see on i. 6), **the days of the perfect**: each fraction of the lives of those who are devoted to Him (see on xv. 2), with all that it brings. Cp. *my times* (xxxi. 15); Matt. vi. 8.

and their inheritance shall be for ever] The righteous man lives in his posterity, who continue in possession of the ancestral inheritance, while the posterity of the wicked perish (*vv.* 28, 38; xxxiv. 16). The Psalmist's view is still limited to earth (cp. *v.* 19). The eternal inheritance reserved in heaven is beyond his horizon.

19. Cp. Job v. 19, 20.
in the evil time] R.V. **in the time of evil**, i.e. calamity.

20. Stanza of *Kaph*. The end of the wicked.
the enemies of the LORD] For His people's enemies are His enemies. Cp. xcii. 9.

as the fat of lambs] A rendering derived from the Targum. But the consumption of the fat of the sacrifice upon the altar would be a

They shall consume; into smoke shall they consume *away*.

(ל) The wicked borroweth, and payeth not again: 21
But the righteous sheweth mercy, and giveth.
For such as be blessed of him shall inherit the earth; 22
And they that be cursed of him shall be cut off.

(מ) The steps of a *good* man are ordered by the LORD: 23
And he delighteth in his way.

strange simile for the evanescence of the wicked: and we must render **as the excellency of the pastures**, or, (R.V.) **as the splendour of the meadows**. The gay show of flowers, so quickly vanishing, is an apt emblem for the short-lived pomp of the wicked.

The force of the comparison is hardly realised in our moist northern climate, where verdure is perpetual. "But let a traveller ride over the downs of Bethlehem in February, one spangled carpet of brilliant flowers, and again in May, when all traces of verdure are gone; or let him push his horse through the deep solid growth of clovers and grasses in the valley of the Jordan in the early spring, and then return and gallop across a brown, hard-baked, gaping plain in June,...and the Scriptural imagery will come home to him with tenfold power." Tristram's *Natural History of the Bible*, p. 455. Cp. *v.* 2; Matt. vi. 29, 30; James i. 10, 11.

they shall consume &c. Lit. **they are consumed; in smoke** (or, *like smoke*) **are they consumed away**. *Smoke* is in itself a natural figure of speedy and complete disappearance (Hos. xiii. 3): possibly, however, the idea of the preceding line is continued, and we are to think of "the grass of the field, which to-day is, and to-morrow is cast into the oven" (Matt. vi. 30). The perfect tense, as in xxxvi. 12, forcibly expresses the realising certainty of faith.

21—31. God's care for the righteous.

21, 22. Stanza of *Lamed*. The wicked are impoverished, while the righteous are enriched. Cp. Prov. iii. 33.

21. At first sight it may seem that the Psalmist intends to contrast the dishonesty of the wicked with the liberality of the righteous. But *v.* 22 makes it clear that this is not the meaning. Looking forward, he foresees the future which awaits them. He sees the wicked man falling into debt and forced to contract loans which he cannot repay, while the righteous man has enough and to spare, and makes a bountiful use of his wealth. The promise to Israel as a nation finds its analogy within the nation (Deut. xv. 6; xxviii. 12, 44).

sheweth mercy] Better as R.V., **dealeth graciously**. Cp. *v.* 26.

22. *For* &c.] The wicked man's ruin and the righteous man's ability to do good proceed respectively from the curse and the blessing of God.

23, 24. Stanza of *Mem*. God's directing and upholding care.

23. It seems best to take *v.* 23 in close connexion with *v.* 24, as (virtually) the condition of the promise:

24 Though he fall, he shall not be utterly cast down:
 . For the LORD upholdeth *him with* his hand.

25 (נ) I have been young, and *now* am old;
Yet have I not seen the righteous forsaken,
Nor his seed begging bread.
26 *He is* ever merciful, and lendeth;
And his seed *is* blessed.

27 (ס) Depart from evil, and do good;
And dwell for evermore.
28 For the LORD loveth judgment,
And forsaketh not his saints;

> When a man's goings are established of Jehovah,
> And he delighteth in his way;
> Though he fall &c.

The second line may be understood of Jehovah's satisfaction in the good man's life (*He delighteth in his way:* cp. xviii. 19; xxii. 8); or of the good man's willing acceptance of Jehovah's guidance (*he delighteth in His way*). The latter explanation is supported by Prov. x. 29, which occurs in a context parallel to this Psalm. Cp. *v.* 34; cxix. 35.

24. *shall not be utterly cast down*] Or, **shall not lie prostrate.** Cp. Prov. xxiv. 16.

upholdeth him with his hand] Better, as R. V. marg., **upholdeth his hand.** Cp. *v.* 17; Is. xli. 13; li. 18.

25, 26. Stanza of *Nun*. An appeal to the experience of a long life in confirmation of the preceding stanzas. He has never seen the righteous permanently deserted by God, or his children reduced to homeless beggary (cix. 10). Cp. *vv.* 28, 33; ix. 10; Gen. xxviii. 15. Temporary impoverishment and apparent abandonment for a time need not be supposed to be excluded.

26. **All the day long he dealeth graciously and lendeth** (R. V.). Cp. *v.* 21; cxii. 5. The righteous not only have abundance, but know how to use it (Is. xxxii. 5—8).

27, 28 *a, b*. Stanza of *Samech*.

27. Once more the teacher addresses his disciple, as in *v.* 3 ff. The first line is identical with xxxiv. 14 *a* (see note): the second line is virtually a promise, and might be rendered *so shalt thou dwell* &c. But as Delitzsch observes, the imperative retains its force in constructions of this type, as an exhortation to participate in the blessing by the fulfilment of the duty. Peaceable occupation of the land by successive generations is meant (cp. *v.* 29). The individual lives on in his descendants.

28 *a*. Cp. xxxiii. 5. For *saints* see note on iv. 3.

28 *c, d*, 29. Stanza of *Ayin*. The verses are wrongly divided. It is evident from the regular structure of the Psalm that the last two lines of *v.* 28 together with *v.* 29 should form a stanza commencing with the

(לְע) They are preserved for ever:
But the seed of the wicked shall be cut off.
The righteous shall inherit the land,   29
And dwell therein for ever.

(פ) The mouth of the righteous speaketh wisdom,   30
And his tongue talketh of judgment.

letter *Ayin*. If the Massoretic text is sound, the *Ayin* is represented by the second letter of the word *l'ōlām*, 'for ever',—the prefixed preposition *l* being disregarded, as is the prefixed *and* in v. 39. But a comparison of the LXX makes it all but certain that the first word of the verse has been lost, and a further corruption taken place in consequence[1]; and that the original reading was:
    The unrighteous are destroyed for ever,
    And the seed of the wicked is cut off.
With this reading a full stop must of course be placed after *saints*, and the couplet forms the antithesis to v. 29. The perfect tenses, as in v. 20 c, express the Psalmist's conviction of the certainty of the event. Cp. v. 38.

30, 31. Stanza of *Pē*. The secret of security.
30. **The mouth of the righteous meditateth wisdom,**
    And his tongue speaketh judgment.
Cp. Prov. x. 31, 32. The word rendered *meditateth* combines the ideas of meditation and meditative discourse. Vulg. *meditabitur sapientiam*. Cp. i. 2; xxxv. 28; Josh. i. 8.

---

[1] The LXX reads thus: εἰς τὸν αἰῶνα φυλαχθήσονται· ἄνομοι δὲ ἐκδιωχθήσονται (אB ἄμωμοι ἐκδικηθήσονται), καὶ σπέρμα ἀσεβῶν ἐξολοθρευθήσεται, 'They shall be preserved for ever; but the lawless shall be driven out (אB, the perfect shall be avenged), and the seed of the ungodly shall be destroyed.' The reading of the Sinaitic and Vatican MSS. appears to be a correction or corruption, and must be abandoned in favour of that found in (apparently) all other MSS., and supported by the Vulg., *iniusti punientur*. We have then the words ἄνομοι δὲ ἐκδιωχθήσονται, *but the lawless shall be driven out*, in addition to a rendering of the Massoretic text. These words might represent an original עֲוָלִים נִשְׁמָדוּ. If the original reading (written defectively) was עולם לעלם נשמדו, *the unrighteous are destroyed for ever*, the process of corruption is easily intelligible. עוֹלָם was omitted, either accidentally from its resemblance to לְעֹלָם, or because the transcriber did not recognise a somewhat rare word, and supposed it to be an erroneous repetition. When once it had disappeared, the change of נִשְׁמָדוּ (*destroyed*) into נִשְׁמָרוּ (*preserved*) followed as a matter of course, 'his saints' in the preceding line being the only possible subject. The word עֲוָלִים does not occur elsewhere in the Psalter, but is found four times in the Book of Job, with which this Psalm is so closely connected. Cp. too the substantive עַוְלָה in v. 1. A case like this, in which the acrostic structure of the Psalm demands a correction for which the LXX supplies clear evidence, is a convincing argument for the temperate employment of the LXX for the correction of the Massoretic Text. This or some similar correction is adopted by most editors.

31 The law of his God *is* in his heart;
None of his steps shall slide.

32 (צ) The wicked watcheth the righteous,
And seeketh to slay him.

33 The LORD will not leave him in his hand,
Nor condemn him when he is judged.

34 (ק) Wait on the LORD, and keep his way,
And he shall exalt thee to inherit the land:
When the wicked are cut off, thou shalt see *it*.

35 (ר) I have seen the wicked in great power,
And spreading himself like a green bay tree.

36 Yet he passed away, and lo, he *was* not:
Yea, I sought him, but he could not be found.

31. Cp. cxix. 11. God's law, treasured in his heart, regulates all his conduct. Without wavering or variation he pursues the path of right. Cp. xxvi. 1; lxxiii. 2.

32—40. The final contrast.

32, 33. Stanza of *Tsadi*. Malice defeated.

32. Cp. x. 8 ff.: Prov. i. 11 ff. The next verse shews that wrong by judicial corruption (Is. v. 23) as well as actual violence is meant.

33. *will not leave him*] Lit. *will not forsake him*, as in *v.* 28, and leave him *in the hand*, i.e. power, of the wicked.

nor condemn him &c.] Will not suffer him to be unjustly condemned. The explanation, that though men may condemn him unjustly, God the supreme judge will acquit him, does not satisfy the context. The Psalmist looks for a temporal deliverance.

34. Stanza of *Qoph*. The Psalmist again addresses his disciple. For a while he may be crushed and down-trodden, but ultimately he will be exalted and the wicked cut off.

keep his way] Cp. v. 23, note; xviii. 21.

thou shalt see it] With satisfaction at the vindication of God's righteous government. Cp. lii. 6; lviii. 10, 11. See Introd. p. lxxiii.

35, 36. Stanza of *Resh*. The transitoriness of the wicked. Cp. *v.* 10; lii. 5 ff.; Job viii. 16 ff.

35. *I have seen*] Comp. the similar appeal to experience in *v.* 25; and the close parallel in Job v. 3.

in great power] Or, **in his terribleness**, inspiring terror by tyrannical oppression. Cp. the cognate verb in x. 18 (R.V.).

like a green bay tree] R.V. **like a green tree in its native soil**, some deeply-rooted giant of the primeval forest, apparently secure from all danger of sudden disturbance.

36. *Yet he passed away*] R. V. **But one passed by.** Better, with LXX, Vulg., Syr., Jer.; **And I passed by.**

(שׁ) Mark the perfect *man*, and behold the upright: 37
For the end of *that* man *is* peace.
But the transgressors shall be destroyed together: 38
The end of the wicked shall be cut off.

(ת) But the salvation of the righteous *is* of the LORD: 39
He is their strength in the time of trouble.
And the LORD shall help them, and deliver them: 40
He shall deliver them from the wicked,
And save them, because they trust in him.

37, 38. Stanza of *Shin*. The future of the wicked and the righteous.
Mark] I.e. observe. The P.B.V., *Keep innocency, and take heed unto the thing that is right*, follows the LXX, Vulg., Symm., Jer., Syr., Targ., in a doubtful rendering.
for the end &c.] R.V. **for the latter end** &c. But the marginal alternatives certainly give the right construction of the sentence: *there is a reward* (or, *future*, or, *posterity*) *for the man of peace*. *Achărīth* means 'an after', 'a sequel' (Prov. xxiii. 18; xxiv. 20): hence 'reward' or 'posterity'; and *v.* 38 points to the latter sense here. 'The man of peace' lives on in his posterity: the wicked man's family become extinct. P.B.V., *for that shall bring a man peace at the last*, appears to be a paraphrase of Jerome's *quia erit in extremum viro pax*.
38. **But transgressors are destroyed together:**
   The posterity of the wicked is cut off.
Cp. *v.* 28; cix. 13; Job xviii. 13—21. To the Israelite, with his strong sense of the continuity of life in the family, childlessness or the loss of posterity was a virtual annihilation. In the light of N. T. revelation the contrast between the 'after' of the righteous and the wicked is still more solemn and significant.
39, 40. Stanza of *Tav*. Jehovah's faithfulness to His own.
39. *their strength*] R. V. **their strong-hold** (xxvii. 1); or perhaps *their asylum*.
40. **And the LORD helpeth them, and rescueth them:**
   He rescueth them from the wicked, and saveth them,
   Because they have taken refuge in him (R.V.).

PSALM XXXVIII.

Tortured by pain of body and anguish of mind, deserted by his friends, mocked and menaced by his enemies, the Psalmist lays his cause before God. In his sufferings he recognises the merited punishment of his sins: he submits to the insults of his enemies with a meek resignation which is a distinguishing feature of the Psalm. For the most part he simply pleads the extremity of his plight as an argument to move God's compassion: only at the opening and close does he directly ask for relief (*vv.* 1, 21, 22), and at the beginning of each division (*vv.* 9, 15), addresses God with words of faith and hope.

PSALM XXXVIII.

The Psalm is closely related to Ps. vi and Ps. xxxix. Delitzsch regards Pss. vi, xxxviii, li, xxxii, as a chronological series, the occasion of which was David's adultery with Bathsheba. Others suppose that it was written by Jeremiah, at the time when he was scourged and put in the stocks by Pashur (Jer. xx). Others find in it the utterance, not of an individual, but of the nation. It is suffering Israel which confesses its sin, acknowledges the justice of its punishment, and appeals to the mercy of Jehovah.

The remarks already made on Ps. vi apply here. The allusions are not sufficiently definite to enable us to refer the Psalm to any particular author or occasion. The *application* of it, in liturgical use, to the nation, was easy and natural, but there is no hint that the speaker is other than an individual, who relates his own experience. The best illustration of the Psalm is to be found in Job's description of his sufferings[1], though the Psalmist's temper of mind differs absolutely from his: and the portraiture of Job, even if ideal, must have been intended to be, in the main, true to life. The striking parallels, and not less striking points of difference, between the Psalm and the portrait of the suffering servant of the Lord in Is. liii should also be studied.

This is the third of the 'Penitential Psalms,' in use on Ash-Wednesday.

The Psalm falls into three divisions, each beginning with an address to God; and the verses are generally arranged in pairs. The use of the divine names should be noted: first *Jehovah* (v. 1); then *Adonai* (v. 9); then both combined with the addition of *my God* (v. 15), and the three repeated (vv. 21, 22).

   i. The Psalmist's bodily and mental sufferings described (1—8).
   ii. The desertion of friends, and the threats of enemies (9—14).
   iii. Pleadings for deliverance (15—22).

The title *to bring to remembrance*, prefixed also to Ps. lxx, has commonly been explained to refer to the contents of the Psalm, as a record of suffering, or as a prayer intended to bring the suppliant to God's remembrance. But more probably it should be rendered, *to make memorial* (R. V. marg.), or, *for making the memorial*, and explained as a note of the liturgical use of the Psalm either in connexion with the offering of incense, or at the offering of the *Azkara*. Comp. the phrase *to make a memorial of incense* (Is. lxvi. 3, marg.), and for the connexion of prayer and offering of incense see Num. xvi. 46 ff.: Luke i. 9, 10. The *Azkara* or *Memorial* was a technical term in the Levitical ritual (1) for the portion of the 'meal-offering' mixed with oil and burnt with incense on the altar (Lev. ii. 2); (2) for the incense placed on the shewbread and afterwards burnt (Lev. xxiv. 7). Though probably the term originally meant only 'a fragrant offering' (see Dillmann on Lev. ii. 2) it was interpreted to mean 'a memorial' (LXX. μνημόσυνον, Vulg. *memoriale*)

---

[1] See e.g. Job's description of his sickness, ch. vii. 5, ix. 17; God has attacked him, xvi. 12 ff.; and esp. cp. vi. 4, vii. 20, xvi. 12, 13, with v. 2 of the Ps.; he is deserted by friends, xvi. 20, xix. 13 ff.; insulted and even assaulted by enemies, xvi. 10 f., xvii. 2, 6, xxx. 9 ff., 12 ff.; he connects his sufferings with sin, though he knows of no special sin which can account for the severity of the punishment, vii. 21, x. 6, 14, xiii. 23, 26, xiv. 16, 17.

as bringing the offerer to God's remembrance. There may be an allusion to the use of Psalms in connexion with the *Azkara* in 1 Chr. xvi. 4, where *to celebrate* (R. V.) is the same word as that used here.

The LXX has "For a memorial for the Sabbath," an addition which confirms the liturgical explanation. The liturgical use must have arisen in days of national distress and persecution, such as the time of Antiochus Epiphanes (1 Macc. i): and implies the application of the Psalm to the nation.

A Psalm of David, to bring to remembrance.

O LORD, rebuke me not in thy wrath: **38**
Neither chasten me in thy hot displeasure.
For thine arrows stick fast in me, 2
And thy hand presseth me sore.
There is no soundness in my flesh because of thine anger; 3
Neither *is there any* rest in my bones because of my sin.
For mine iniquities are gone *over* mine head: 4
As a heavy burden they are too heavy for me.
My wounds stink *and* are corrupt 5
Because of my foolishness.

1—8. The chastisement of sin.

1. In words almost identical with vi. 1 the Psalmist deprecates the severity of a chastisement which seems to proceed from an angry Judge rather than from a loving Father. The emphasis is on *in thy wrath... in thy hot displeasure.* Cp. Jer. x. 24. For similar expressions of a sense of guilt under suffering, see xxv. 18; xxxi. 10; xxxix. 10 ff.; xl. 12.

2. God's 'arrows' are His judgments in general (vii. 12: Deut. xxxii. 23); here in particular pain and sickness (Job vi. 4; xvi. 12, 13; Lam. iii. 12, 13). Blow after blow from God's 'hand' (xxxii. 4; xxxix. 10) has lighted upon him. *Stick fast* and *presseth sore* are renderings of different voices of the same verb, meaning literally *to come down, to light upon.*

3. His own sin is the cause of the divine indignation which inflicts the chastisement; and while God's wrath assaults him from without, the fever of sin consumes him from within. With this verse and *v.* 5, comp. Isaiah's description of the deep-seated disease of Israel's body corporate (Is. i. 5, 6).

anger] Better as R. V. **indignation**, as in vii. 11; cii. 10.

rest] R. V. **health**; lit., wholeness or peace. For *in my bones* see vi. 2, note.

4. His sins are like a flood which overwhelms (cxxiv. 4, 5); like a burden which crushes (Gen. iv. 13; Is. liii. 4; Job vii. 20).

5. *My wounds*] Or *stripes* (=*bruises*, Is. i. 6, A. V.): for he has been as it were scourged by God.

my foolishness] Sin is essentially foolishness. Cp. cvii. 17. The

6 I am troubled ; I am bowed down greatly;
I go mourning all the day long.
7 For my loins are filled *with* a loathsome *disease:*
And *there is* no soundness in my flesh.
8 I am feeble and sore broken :
I have roared by reason of the disquietness of my heart.
9 Lord, all my desire *is* before thee ;
And my groaning is not hid from thee.
10 My heart panteth, my strength faileth me :
As for the light of mine eyes, it also is gone from me.
11 My lovers and my friends stand aloof from my sore ;
And my kinsmen stand afar off.

word occurs only once again in the Psalter (lxix. 5), and elsewhere only in Proverbs, where it is common (e.g. v. 23; xix. 3).

6. I am bent, I am bowed down exceedingly, as one whose frame is contracted and drawn together by pain, or whose gestures indicate mental anguish. Cp. xxxv. 14; Is. xxi. 3. Notice the vigorous archaism *wried* in A. V. margin, i.e. *twisted*.

mourning] In the guise of a mourner. See note on xxxv. 14.

In later times at any rate it was customary for the accused to appear before the court in mourning. "Whosoever comes before this court of the Sanhedrin to take his trial, presents himself in the guise of humility and fear, appealing to your compassion, with hair neglected, and clad in black garments." (Josephus, *Antiq.* XIV. 9. 3). If the custom prevailed in earlier times, *in mourning garb* may suggest that he feels himself, like Job, under the divine accusation. Cp. Zech. iii. 1 ff.

7. with *a loathsome* disease] R. V. **with burning**; fever and inflammation. Cp. Job xxx. 27, 30.

8. I am faint and sore bruised (R. V.). Cp. li. 8; Is. liii. 5, 10.

I have roared &c.] Lit. *I have roared* (xxii. 1; xxxii. 3; Job iii. 24) *from the moaning of my heart.* The inward moaning of his heart must needs find utterance in loud cries of distress.

9—14. The neglect of friends and the scorn of enemies augment his sufferings.

9. God knows what he needs (x. 17; Matt. vi. 8).

10. *panteth*] R. V. excellently, **throbbeth.**

as for the light of mine eyes &c.] His eyes are dim and dull with weakness and weeping. Cp. vi. 7; xiii. 3, note; xxxi. 9; Job xvii. 7; Lam. ii. 11.

11. *from my sore*] R. V. **from my plague.** The word is specially used of the plague of leprosy (Lev. xiii. 3, &c.). His friends treat him as a leper, standing *over against him,* within sight but at a distance. Even his *near kinsmen* falsify their name by standing *afar off.* (LXX. οἱ ἔγγιστά μου μακρόθεν ἔστησαν.)

Comp. xxxi. 11—13; lxix. 8; lxxxviii. 18; Job xix. 13 ff.; Is. liii. 4.

12. Pitiless enemies beset him. Comp. xxxv. 4, 26.

They also that seek after my life lay snares *for me:* 12
And they that seek my hurt speak mischievous things,
And imagine deceits all the day long.
But I, as a deaf *man*, heard not; 13
And *I was* as a dumb *man that* openeth not his mouth.
Thus I was as a man that heareth not, 14
And in whose mouth *are* no reproofs.
For in thee, O Lord, do I hope: 15
Thou wilt hear, O Lord my God.
For I said, *Hear me*, lest *otherwise* they should rejoice 16
  over me:
When my foot slippeth, they magnify *themselves* against me.
For I *am* ready to halt, 17
And my sorrow *is* continually before me.

mischievous things] Lit. *destructions*. See note on v. 9.
imagine] Lit. *meditate*. Contrast xxxvii. 26, 30.
13, 14. Conscious of guilt he must keep silence and commit his cause to God, resigned and patient as though he did not hear the insults, or had no power to answer them. Cp. xxxix. 9; Is. liii. 7; 1 Pet. ii. 23.
But I &c.] R. V. **But I, as a deaf man, hear not; and I am as a dumb man,** &c. He is describing his present situation.
14. **Yea, I am become like a man that hath no hearing;**
And in whose mouth are no arguments.
No arguments for his own defence. Cp. Job xxiii. 4, where Job desires to argue with God.

15—22. Fresh pleadings with God.
15. The motive of silence and resignation.
in thee...do I hope] Or, *for thee do I wait*. Patience and hope are inseparable. Cp. xxxix. 7; Mic. vii. 7.
thou wilt hear] **Thou, thou wilt answer.** The pronoun is emphatically expressed. It is possible to complete the sense by supplying *me*, with reference to the prayer of which v. 16 speaks: or *for me* (P.B.V.) with reference to v. 14. But the one involves the other. An answer to his prayer must be a refutation of the taunts of his enemies.
16. **For I said, Lest they rejoice over me** (R. V.). This was the plea which he urged in his prayer (xxv. 2; xxxv. 19). The enemies of the godly man rejoice at his calamities, for they see in them a proof of God's disfavour (xli. 11).
when my foot slippeth] Lit. *is moved*, a metaphor for misfortune of any kind (xiii. 4).
magnify themselves] Cp. xxxv. 26.
17. *For* &c.] A further argument for a speedy hearing. For the metaphor cp. xxxv. 15.
my sorrow &c.] I.e. my suffering is unceasingly present with me. Cp. li. 3.

18 For I will declare mine iniquity;
   I will be sorry for my sin.
19 But mine enemies *are* lively, *and* they are strong:
   And they that hate me wrongfully are multiplied.
20 They also that render evil for good are mine adversaries;
   Because I follow *the thing that* good *is*.
21 Forsake me not, O LORD:
   O my God, be not far from me.
22 Make haste to help me,
   O Lord my salvation.

18. *For* &c.] Sin, he confesses, is the cause of that suffering.

I will be sorry] Or, *I will be troubled.* Jer. *sollicitus ero:* v. l. *contristabor.*

19. *mine enemies* are *lively*] He contrasts their vigour with his own weakness. But the expression is somewhat strange; and a comparison of xxxv. 19 suggests that we should read **without cause**, corresponding to *wrongfully* in the next line, in place of *are lively.* The Hebrew words are very similar (חנם—חיים).

wrongfully] Lit. *falsely.* Their hatred is based on misconception and misrepresentation.

20. Yea, and rewarding evil for good
They are adversaries unto me, for my following of good.

Not, in return for my pursuit of good in general, but, in return for the good I have striven to do for them. The point is their base ingratitude. Cp. xxxv. 12, 13, note.

21, 22. Concluding prayer.

21. Cp. xxii. 1; x. 1.

"The light has not yet dawned upon the darkness of God's wrath. *Fides supplex* is not yet transformed into *fides triumphans.* But the difference between Cain's repentance and David's repentance is shewn in the concluding words. True repentance includes faith: it despairs of itself, but not of God." *Delitzsch.*

22. *Make haste* &c.] Cp. xxii. 19; xl. 13.

O Lord my salvation] Cp. lxii. 2; li. 14.

PSALM XXXIX.

This Psalm, which is pronounced by Ewald to be "indisputably the most beautiful of all the elegies in the Psalter," is a sequel to the preceding one. The situation of the Psalmist is in the main the same. Prolonged sickness has brought him to the very edge of the grave. But the crisis of suffering is over, and the taunts of his enemies have ceased for the time.

The Psalm consists of four stanzas, the first three containing three verses each, and the fourth four verses, which fall into two pairs.

The outline of the contents is as follows:

i. As he compares his lot of suffering with the prosperity of the wicked, the Psalmist is tempted to murmur, and resolves to meet the temptation by silence. But the fire of emotion refuses to be suppressed (1—3).

ii. He is forced to seek relief in prayer that he may be taught to understand the transitoriness of human life and the vanity of worldly aims (4—6).

iii. Thus he is brought to feel that his only hope is in Jehovah, to Whom he turns in silent resignation (7—9).

iv. Then, pleading the frailty and the shortness of human life, he prays for relief and respite (10—13).

In order rightly to understand this Psalm, as well as Ps. xxxviii, it must be remembered (1) that sickness was popularly regarded as a proof of God's displeasure: (2) that to ancient Israel it seemed that death must be an interruption of fellowship with God (Introd. p. lxxxv ff.).

This Psalm, like Pss. xxxviii and xl, has been regarded by some critics as the utterance of the nation rather than of an individual. But however well it may admit of such an application, this can hardly have been the original meaning.

The Psalm is closely connected in thought and language with Ps. xxxviii. Cp. *vv*. 2, 9 with xxxviii. 13, 14; *v*. 7 with xxxviii. 15; *v*. 8 with xxxviii. 16; *vv*. 10, 11 with xxxviii. 1—3, 11. It is also related to Ps. lxii. Both Psalms are marked by the same hope in God, and the same view of the vanity of life: and in both the word *ak*, 'only' or 'surely,' is characteristic. The parallels with the Book of Job should also be noticed. See note on *v*. 13.

The title should be rendered, *For the Chief Musician Jeduthun*. Jeduthun, whose name appears again in the titles of Pss. lxii and lxxvii, is mentioned in 1 Chr. xvi. 41 f.; xxv. 1 ff.; 2 Chr. v. 12; xxxv. 15, along with Heman and Asaph, as one of the directors of the Temple music. He appears to have been also called Ethan (1 Chr. xv. 17 ff.).

To the chief Musician, *even* to Jeduthun, A Psalm of David.

39 I said, I will take heed to my ways,
That *I* sin not with my tongue:

1—3. The resolution of silence in the presence of temptation.

1. *I said*] To myself: I resolved, as the result of self-communing. Cp. xxx. 6; xxxi. 14.

I will take heed to my ways] Lit. *I will keep my ways:* keep watch and ward over thought word and action. Cp. Prov. xvi. 17; and the often repeated exhortation in Deuteronomy to 'take heed' (iv. 9; &c.). He fears that he may sin with his tongue (Job xxxi. 30) by murmuring against God as he contrasts the prosperity of the wicked with his own lot of trial. Cp. Job i. 22; ii. 10; and generally Pss. xxxvii and lxxiii.

I will keep my mouth with a bridle,
While the wicked *is* before me.
2 I was dumb *with* silence, I held my peace, *even* from good;
And my sorrow was stirred.
3 My heart was hot within me,
While I was musing the fire burned:
Then spake I with my tongue,

4 LORD, make me to know mine end,
And the measure of my days, what it *is;*
That I may know how frail I *am.*
5 Behold, thou hast made my days *as* a handbreadth;

I will keep &c.] Lit. *I will keep a muzzle for my mouth.* Cp. cxli. 3. Perhaps with the LXX, we should read *I will put...on.*

while the wicked is before me] For the sight of their prosperity is a temptation. Cp. Hab. i. 3. This seems to be the sense, rather than that he was afraid of giving way to complaints in the hearing of the wicked, which might give occasion for ridicule or blasphemy.

2. *silence*] The word carries with it the idea of mute submission. Cp. lxii. 1; xxxvii. 7; Lam. iii. 26.

even from good] I kept absolute silence, speaking neither good nor bad (Gen. xxxi. 24). Less probably as R. V. marg., *and had no comfort.*

my sorrow was stirred] The effort to suppress his feelings only aggravated the pain. Cp. xxxii. 3. So Ovid, *Trist.* v. 1. 63, 'Strangulat inclusus dolor atque exaestuat intus.'

3. *burned*] Better, as R.V. from Coverdale and P.B.V., *kindled.* The smouldering fire of passion within could no longer be restrained from bursting into a flame of words. Comp. (though the cause was different) Jer. xx. 9.

4—6. Silence has proved impossible. He must give vent to his emotions, and he breaks out into a prayer that he may be taught so to understand the frailty of his life and the vanity of human aims, that he may be led back from selfish, envious, murmuring thoughts, to rest in submission to God's will. Cp. xc. 12.

4. His prayer is not that he may know how much of life is left him; as the P.B.V. *that I may be certified how long I have to live,* paraphrasing the LXX. ἵνα γνῶ τί ὑστερῶ ἐγώ: *ut sciam quid desit mihi,* Vulg.: but that he may realise how surely life must end, and how brief it must be at best. *What it is*=how short it is.

that I may know] Better, as R.V., **let me know**. *Frail,* lit. *ceasing,* transitory.

5. *as a handbreadth*] Better, *a few handbreadths long.* The shortest measure is enough to reckon life by. The 'handbreadth'=four 'fingers' (Jer. lii. 21 compared with 1 Kings vii. 26) or less than half a 'span.'

And mine age *is* as nothing before thee :
Verily every man at his best state *is* altogether vanity. Selah.

Surely every man walketh in a vain shew : 6
Surely they are disquieted in vain :
He heapeth up *riches*, and knoweth not who shall gather them.
And now, Lord, what wait I for ? 7
My hope *is* in thee.
Deliver me from all my transgressions : 8

mine age &c.] The same word as that rendered 'world' in xvii. 14, denoting life in its fleeting, transient aspect. In the sight of the Eternal man's existence shrinks into nothing. Cp. Is. xl. 17.

verily &c.] The particle *ak*, which is characteristic of this Ps. and of Ps. lxii, may be used affirmatively to introduce the whole clause (*verily*, or *surely*, as in *vv.* 6, 11), or restrictively, to emphasise the words which immediately follow it (*only*). The order of the words points to the latter sense here. 'Only altogether a breath', i.e. *nought but mere vanity are all men at their best estate:* lit. *when standing firm :* however securely they may seem to be established. Cp. cxliv. 4; James iv. 14.

**6. Only as a phantom doth each walk to and fro:
Only for vanity do they turmoil :
One heapeth up, and he will not know who doth gather the hoard.**

Man is an unsubstantial phantom (or *shadow*, lit. *image*), lxxiii. 20: σκιᾶς ὄναρ, 'a dream of shadow' as Pindar calls him (Pyth. VIII. 95). With unreal aim and unenduring result do men disturb themselves. The word expresses the idea of restless noisy bustle and uproar. Cp. 'a *tumultuous* city' Is. xxii. 2, and see note on 'abundance', xxxvii. 16. *Shew* (A. V.) must be taken to mean 'appearance,' not 'display' or 'pomp.'

One heapeth up riches, treasures, possessions of all kinds (Job xxvii. 16), *and he will not know* after his death *who gathers* these hoards as his harvest, or rather, *who carries them off* as his spoil (Is. xxxiii. 4). Cp. Luke xii. 20.

7—9. Man's life being thus transient, and earthly treasures thus deceitful, the Psalmist turns to God, as the one sure stay in life.

7. *And now*] Or, *Now therefore* (ii. 10), introduces a conclusion from a preceding statement.

what wait I for] What have I waited and still am waiting for? or, What (else) could I have waited for? the form of the question implying that nothing else was possible.

wait...hope] The words form a link between the preceding (*v.* 15) and the following (*v.* 1) Psalms.

8. The Psalmist prays to be delivered not merely from his present afflictions but from the power of the sins which he recognises as the

Make me not the reproach of the foolish.
9 I was dumb, I opened not my mouth;
Because thou didst *it*.
10 Remove thy stroke away from me:
I am consumed by the blow of thine hand.
11 When thou with rebukes dost correct man for iniquity,
Thou makest his beauty to consume away like a moth:
Surely every man *is* vanity. Selah.

12 Hear my prayer, O LORD,
And give ear unto my cry;
Hold not thy peace at my tears:

cause of them. Sin gets hold of its victim and brings him into punishment. Cp. xl. 12; Job viii. 4.

the reproach of the foolish] **The fool** (xiv. 1 note) regards the sufferings of the godly as a mark of God's wrath, and taunts him accordingly (xxxviii. 16; xxii. 8; xxxi. 11). Cp. the plea of the nation, xliv. 13 ff.; lxxiv. 18, 22.

9. This verse may refer to the silence with which he bore the taunts of his enemies (*v.* 2; xxxviii. 13, 14): or it may be the expression of perfect resignation to the will of God: **I am dumb, I will not open my mouth, for THOU hast done it.** Cp. Lam. i. 21. "He has risen out of the moody silence of impatience to the contrite silence of evangelical faith, recognising at once his sin and God's holy love." *Kay.*

10—13. Petition for relief (10, 11) and respite (12, 13).

10. *stroke*] The same word as that rendered *plague* in xxxviii. 11. Cp. Job ix. 34.

I am consumed &c.] **By the conflict of thy hand am I consumed.** 'I' stands in emphatic contrast with 'thy hand'. When the power of the Almighty contends with me, I, frail mortal that I am, must needs perish. Cp. Job x. 2 ff.

11. When thou with rebukes dost chasten a man for iniquity,
Thou wastest like a moth his desirableness:
Nought but vanity are all men.

The A. V. obscures the correspondence of the first line with xxxviii. 1; vi. 1. As easily as the moth-grub, working unseen, destroys 'goodly raiment' (Gen. xxvii. 15), so easily does God's chastisement destroy a man's 'goodliness,' the bodily strength and beauty which make him attractive (Is. liii. 2). It is God's consuming 'hand' which is compared to the 'moth' (Hos. v. 12); not, as the A. V. might seem to imply, the ephemeral duration of man's goodliness. Cp. Job xiii. 28; Is. l. 9; li. 8.

12. *hold not thy peace*] Restoration to health will be an answer. But the word may be rendered, as in R. V. of xxviii. 1, *be not deaf.* So Jerome, *ne obsurdescas.*

It is a Rabbinic saying that there are three kinds of supplication,

For I *am* a stranger with thee,
And a sojourner, as all my fathers *were.*
O spare me, that I may recover strength, 13
Before I go hence, and be no more.

each superior to the other; prayer, crying, and tears. Prayer is made in silence, crying with a loud voice, but tears surpass all. "There is no door, through which tears do not pass," and, "The gates of tears are never locked." Cp. Heb. v. 7.

a stranger with thee, and *a sojourner*] Omit *and.* 'Stranger' and 'sojourner' were the technical terms for aliens residing in a country to which they did not belong, and where they had no natural rights of citizenship (Gen. xxiii. 4). The words suggest the idea of a temporary residence, dependent on the good-will of the actual owners. The Israelites were taught to regard themselves as 'strangers and sojourners' in the land of Canaan, which belonged to Jehovah (Lev. xxv. 23): and here the idea is extended to man in general. The earth is God's, and man is His tenant upon it (cxix. 19). This being so, the Psalmist appeals for a hearing on the ground that he is but a temporary resident on the earth (Gen. xlvii. 9), God's guest for a while only in the upper world, where alone His Presence can be enjoyed. And further, as the strangers and sojourners among them were specially commended to the care of Israel (Ex. xxii. 21; &c.), he would plead to be treated by God with a corresponding clemency.

The words are placed in David's mouth by the Chronicler (1 Chr. xxix. 15), and applied by St Peter (1 Pet. ii. 11) to the Christian's position in the world, παρακαλῶ ὡς παροίκους καὶ παρεπιδήμους, the words used in the LXX here. Cp. Heb. xi. 13.

as all my fathers] Cp. Elijah's words, 1 Kings xix. 4.

13. *O spare me*] So Jerome, *parce mihi.* But more exactly, **Look away from me.** Cheyne renders, 'avert thy frown.'

that I may recover strength] Lit. *brighten up,* as the sky when the clouds clear.

Parallels for every phrase in the verse are to be found in Job. See Job vii. 19; xiv. 6; x. 20, 21; vii. 8 (R. V.).

It is, as Delitzsch remarks, the heroic character of Old Testament faith, that in the midst of the enigmas of life, and in full view of the deep gloom ensbrouding the future, it throws itself unconditionally into the arms of God.

PSALM XL.

This Psalm consists of two parts, differing widely in tone and character. In the first part (*vv.* 1—11) thanksgiving for deliverance and its true expression in the devotion of obedience to God's will are the prominent ideas: in the second part (*vv.* 12—17) the Psalmist is still the victim of a cruel persecution, from which he prays for deliverance.

The first part is marked by singular vigour and spirituality; the second part consists mainly of phrases found elsewhere, and *vv.* 13—17 recur separately in Book ii as Ps. lxx.

It seems most probable that two Psalms or parts of Psalms have been combined by a compiler, with reference to his own needs or for liturgical purposes, at a time when he himself or the nation looked back upon past deliverance from the midst of present trials. Still it is possible that the author of *vv.* 1—11 himself added *vv.* 12—17 at a later time under changed circumstances, making use of language which he had employed before in time of distress. There are links of connexion between the two parts. *Be pleased* (*v.* 13) takes up *thy good pleasure* (*v.* 8); *taketh thought for me* (*v.* 17) glances back to *thy thoughts to us-ward* (*v.* 5); *they are more* (*v.* 12) is found in *v.* 5: and such repetition of a word already used in a different connexion is characteristic of the author of the first part: e.g. *restrain not thou* (*v.* 11) corresponds to *I will not restrain* (*v.* 9); *thy lovingkindness and thy truth* (*v.* 11) to the same words in *v.* 10.

If the Psalm is David's, it would seem to belong to the later years of his outlaw life, shortly before he became king, rather than to the time of Absalom's rebellion. It has been well pointed out that the words of *vv.* 6 ff. gain fresh force if they are taken in connexion with 1 Sam. xv. 22. The self-devotion of the king after God's own heart is the exact opposite of the self-will which was the ground of Saul's rejection.

The ascription of the Psalm to Jeremiah rests mainly on the supposed reference of *v.* 2 to Jeremiah's imprisonment (Jer. xxxviii. 6), but the language is certainly figurative and not literal.

Some regard the speaker in this, as in the two preceding Psalms, as "either pious Israel personified, or (virtually the same thing) a representative pious Israelite" (Cheyne), who speaks in the name of the nation. But though Israel in later times may well have appropriated to itself the words of the Psalm, the personal origin of it appears to be unmistakable. There is not the slightest hint that the enemies referred to are heathen, or that those who are won by the sight of God's mercy (*v.* 3) are distant nations.

The first part falls into four approximately equal stanzas. The following is an outline of the contents.

A. i. After long and patient waiting prayer has been answered occasion given for fresh thanksgiving (1—3).

ii. Once more it has been proved that trust in God is th source of true happiness. The goodness of God to His people is and incomparable (4, 5).

iii. What shall be man's response to that love? Not sacrifice, but the service of glad obedience (6—8).

iv. The Psalmist has not failed publicly to confess what proved Himself to be, and confidently anticipates the contin His favour (9—11).

B. Suddenly the scene changes. The Psalmist represents h overwhelmed by afflictions, and pleads for speedy help, and the fiture of his malicious enemies. Yet even in the midst of distress his trust remains unshaken (12—17).

This Psalm is one of the Proper Psalms for Good Friday. Its appropriateness is obvious, as describing in *vv.* 6 ff. the fundamental nature of the sacrifice which was consummated upon the Cross.

PSALM XL. 1—4.

To the chief Musician, A Psalm of David.

I waited patiently for the LORD; **40**
And he inclined unto me, and heard my cry.
He brought me up also out of a horrible pit, out of the miry **2**
  clay,
And set my feet upon a rock, *and* established my goings.
And he hath put a new song in my mouth, *even* praise unto **3**
  our God:
Many shall see *it*, and fear, and shall trust in the LORD.
Blessed *is that* man that maketh the LORD his trust, **4**
And respecteth not the proud, nor such as turn aside to lies.

1—3. The reward of patient waiting upon God.

1. *I waited patiently*] Such renderings as *I waited, yea I waited,* or, *I waited waitingly* (Vulg. *expectans expectavi*) are closer to the original. Cp. xxxviii. 15; xxxix. 7: and the confession of the Church in the day of Redemption, Is. xxv. 9.

he inclined unto me] As it were, 'bent down towards me.' To 'incline' or 'bow down *the ear*' is the usual phrase (xxxi. 2; cxvi. 2).

my cry] Cp. xxxix. 12; xviii. 6.

2. And brought me up out of a pit of destruction, out of the miry slough:
And set my feet upon a rock, made firm my steps.

A literal reference to Jeremiah's imprisonment in the dungeon can hardly be intended. The second line, *set...rock*, makes it plain that the whole verse is to be understood figuratively. He compares his pl⁞ ⁞o that of a prisoner in a dungeon (Lam. iii. 53, 55), or even a dead man in the grave (xxviii. 1; lxxxviii. 4, 6); to that of a traveller ⁞ering in a morass, or quicksand. Quagmires, 'treacherous to the c⁞ ⁞egree,' are common in Palestine. Thomson's *Land and the Book*, Job ⁞ Now he has been given firm footing (xxvii. 5), and the possi- ⁞of secure advance (xvii. 5; xxxvii. 31).

I⁞ ⁞uch deliverance is a fresh theme of praise. Cp. xxxiii. 3. The faith⁞ pronoun, '*our God*,' implies that others were interested in the deep ⁞ ⁞t and his fortunes.

the a⁞ *shall see* it] Omit *it*, which only weakens the expression. The ⁞lation of God's mercy in the deliverance of His servant, and ⁞ ⁞wer in the discomfiture of his enemies which that deliverance Th⁞ will inspire a reverent awe, and lead to trust. Cp. lii. 6; and ⁞y, xxii. 22 ff.

4, 5. The blessedness of such a trust.

4. Happy is the man that hath made Jehovah his trust,
And hath not turned unto the arrogant, and false apostates.

The word for *man* is that used in xxxiv. 8, where see note. For the opposite to 'making Jehovah the object of trust' see Ps. lii. 7.

respecteth not] Rather, as above, **hath not turned unto:** *non est*

5 Many, O LORD my God, *are* thy wonderful works *which* thou hast done,
And thy thoughts *which are* to us-ward:
They cannot be reckoned up in order unto thee:
If I would declare and speak *of them*,
They are moe than can be numbered.

aversus ad...Jerome. The word is specially used of turning away from God to idols or false objects of confidence (Deut. xxix. 18; Hos. iii. 1; Ezek. xxix. 16).

the proud &c.] The word for 'proud' suggests the idea of overbearing arrogance and ostentatious self-assertion: 'such as turn aside to lies', or as R. V. marg., *fall away treacherously*, are those who desert God and the right cause for false objects of reliance and false aims. Idolatry does not appear to be meant, at any rate exclusively. Happy the man who is not misled by appearances to despise God's help, and seek the patronage of worldly men who boast of their own power.

5. **Abundantly hast Thou wrought, even Thou, O Jehovah my God, Thy marvellous works and Thy thoughts to us-ward: There is none to be compared unto Thee.**

Multa fecisti tu Domine Deus meus mirabilia tua et cogitationes tuas pro nobis. Jerome. *Thou* is emphatic. Jehovah is contrasted with all such objects of reliance as those mentioned in the preceding verse. His 'marvellous works' (ix. 1 note) are the embodiment of His 'thoughts' or purposes of love toward His people. Cp. xcii. 5; Is. lv. 8, 9; Jer. xxix. 11. The rendering of R. V. marg., *there is none to be compared unto thee*, an exclamation of reverent wonder (cp. lxxxix. 6; lxxi. 19), is decidedly preferable to that of the A. V., and that of R. V. text, *they cannot be set in order unto thee*. The P.B.V. *and yet there is no man that ordereth them unto thee* (cp. Is. xl. 14) is improbable.

they are moe than can be numbered] Or, *than I can tell of* (xxvi. 7). *Moe* as the comparative of *many* is an archaism which has disappeared from modern editions of the Bible. The word for *they are more* may mean *they are mightier*. Their number and their greatness alike baffle human powers to celebrate. Cp. John xxi. 25.

6—8. True service consists not in material sacrifices but in obedience to the will of God. The stanza is an answer to the implied question, How should man express his gratitude? It affirms the common prophetic doctrine that sacrifice was in itself of no value apart from the dispositions of heart which it was intended to represent. The new commandment of the Exodus was not sacrifice but obedience (Ex. xv. 26). See Ps. l. 7 ff.; li. 16 ff.; 1 Sam. xv. 22; Hos. vi. 6; Micah vi. 8; Jer. vii. 21 ff.

6. The various kinds of offerings are described according to their material, as *sacrifice* of slain animals, and *offering* ('meal-offering') of the fruits of the earth (Lev. ii. 1 ff.); and according to their purpose, as *burnt-offering*, symbolising the dedication of the worshipper to God,

PSALM XL. 6—8.

Sacrifice and offering thou didst not desire;   6
Mine ears hast thou opened:
Burnt offering and sin offering hast thou not required.
Then said I, Lo, I come: 7
In the volume of the book *it is* written of me,
I delight to do thy will, O my God: 8

and *sin-offering*, for the reconciliation of the offender and the restoration of interrupted communion.

thou didst not desire] R. V. **thou hast no delight in.** It is the same word as in *v*. 8, and in the parallel passages Hos. vi. 6; Is. i. 11; cp. 1 Sam. xv. 22.

mine ears hast thou opened] Lit. *ears hast thou dug* (or, *pierced*) *for me*. This unique phrase can hardly be an equivalent for the common expression to 'uncover' or 'open the ear,' to be explained as a parenthetical exclamation that this truth has been impressed upon the Psalmist by a special revelation. It is best to regard it as a statement preparing the way for *v*. 7, and placed between the two parallel clauses of *v*. 6 for poetic effect. God has endowed man with the faculty of hearing, and the endowment implies a corresponding duty of obedience. 'Ears' need not be limited to the physical organ, but may include 'the ears of the heart.' The same Hebr. word means *to hear* and *to obey*. Cp. the repeated appeals to Israel to hear; Deut. iv. 1; vi. 4; &c.

The language does not suggest any reference to the custom of boring the slave's ear (Ex. xxi. 6; Deut. xv. 17) in the sense, 'Thou hast bound me to Thyself for perpetual service.'

hast thou not required] Lit. *asked*. Cp. Deut. x. 12; Mic. vi. 8.

7. *Then said I*] This was his answer when he became aware of God's requirements.

Lo, I come] Rather as R. V., **Lo, I am come**: (LXX. ἰδοὺ ἥκω) the servant's response to his master's summons (Num. xxii. 38; 2 Sam. xix. 20): like 'Behold me,' or, 'Here I am' (Is. vi. 9). The object of the coming is not expressed, but is clear from the context.

in the volume of the book it is *written of me*] Better, **in a roll of a book is it prescribed to me**: though the rendering of A. V., which is that of the LXX, is possible. The exact phrase 'roll of a book' occurs only in Jer. xxxvi. 2, 4; Ezek. ii. 9; 'roll' only in Jer. xxxvi; Ezek. iii. 1—3; Zech. v. 1, 2; Ezra vi. 2[1]. Cp. however Is. xxxiv. 4. The context points to Deuteronomy, or at any rate the nucleus of the teaching contained in it, as the book referred to. The absence of the article seems to emphasise the fact that a *written* document is referred to (*in a book*, cp. Hos. viii. 12), rather than to single out a particular document as '*the* book' *par excellence*, as the A. V. seems to imply.

8. *I delight*] Cp. *v*. 6. What is God's delight is his delight. Contrast the delight of the wicked in evil, *v*. 14.

---
[1] 'Roll' in Is. viii. 1 (A.V.) should be *tablet*.

Yea, thy law *is* within my heart.
9 I have preached righteousness in the great congregation:

thy will] Thy good pleasure: what Thou approvest (Prov. xv. 8; Ps. xix. 14).

thy law is *within my heart*] Lit. *in the midst of my body*, as though God's law were itself the heart which gives life to his whole being (xxii. 14). Such was God's demand of Israel (Deut. vi. 6); such is the characteristic of the righteous (Ps. xxxvii. 31; Is. li. 7): such is to be the universal condition in the Messianic age (Jer. xxxi. 33). The law will be graven not on tablets of stone (Ex. xxxii. 15f.), but on the tablet of the heart (Prov. iii. 3; vii. 3).

Vv. 6—8 *a* are quoted in Heb. x. 5—7 according to the LXX[1], with some slight variations. The writer is contrasting Christ's perfect obedience with the inefficacy of the sacrifices of the Law, and he puts these words into His mouth as the most fitting expression of the purpose of His life. The willing obedience which the Psalmist of old was taught to recognise as the divine requirement for himself and Israel was carried to its completion, was 'fulfilled,' in Christ. The variation of the LXX from the Hebrew may seem to present a serious difficulty. But the appropriateness of the quotation does not depend on this particular clause, and the rendering of the LXX, whatever its origin, has in effect a sense analogous to the sense of the original. As the ear is the instrument for receiving the divine command, so the body is the instrument for fulfilling it. The possession of a body implies the duty of service, in the same way that the possession of hearing implies the duty of obedience. See Bp. Westcott's note.

9—11. Beside the sacrifice of himself, he has not failed to render the sacrifice of praise and thanksgiving, by the fullest public proclamation of Jehovah's goodness, which he trusts he will still continue to experience.

9. *I have preached righteousness*] R. V. **I have published**: better, as R. V. marg., **I have proclaimed glad tidings of**, εὐηγγελισάμην δικαιοσύνην (LXX). His theme was 'righteousness;' all the facts which are the concrete manifestation and evidence of God's righteousness (*v.* 10). The good news which he can proclaim is the certainty of the just moral government of the world, and Jehovah's faithfulness to His people. And this he has done *in the great congregation*, with the utmost publicity (xxii. 25; xxxv. 18), perhaps, as the prophets often delivered their messages, on some festival (Jer. xxvi. 2).

---

[1] The reading of the LXX is σῶμα δὲ κατηρτίσω μοι, *a body didst thou prepare for me*. This reading is attested by the Vulgate. *Aures* in the Gallican Psalter is a correction. καταρτίζεσθαι occurs in the LXX as the rendering of several Hebrew words, and might easily have been chosen to represent the obscure *thou hast dug*. 'Body' for 'ears' may then have been a free paraphrase. But the reading may have originated in an ancient corruption of the Greek text. Through a repetition of the final C of the preceding word and the change of ΩΤΙΑ into ΩΜΑ, ΗΘΕΛΗCΑCΩΤΙΑ might easily have become ΗΘΕΛΗCΑCCΩΜΑ.

Lo, I have not refrained my lips,
O LORD, thou knowest.
I have not hid thy righteousness within my heart;   10
I have declared thy faithfulness and thy salvation:
I have not concealed thy lovingkindness and thy truth from
  the great congregation.
Withhold not thou thy tender mercies from me, O LORD: 11
Let thy lovingkindness and thy truth continually preserve me.
For innumerable evils have compassed me about: 12
Mine iniquities have taken hold upon me, so that I am
  not able to look *up;*

I have not refrained] R. V. restores Coverdale's **I will not refrain**: but the words refer rather to what he did in the past than to what he resolves to do in the future. By rendering **I did not restrain**, the connexion with *v.* 11 may be brought out.

thou knowest] For the appeal to God's omniscience, cp. lxix. 5; Jer. xv. 15.

10. Neither indolence nor ingratitude nor fear of man has deterred him from openly celebrating those fundamental attributes of the divine character which have been once more manifested in his deliverance. For *thy righteousness*, see v. 8, note; for *lovingkindness, faithfulness, righteousness*, cp. xxxvi. 5, 6, 7, 10; for *truth* and *salvation*, xxv. 5; *lovingkindness* and *truth*, xxv. 10.

11. THOU, O Jehovah, wilt not restrain Thy tender mercies from me,
  Thy lovingkindness and thy truth shall continually guard me.
The words are not a prayer but an expression of confidence in the certainty of God's response (Matt. x. 32). **Thou** is emphatic. God on His part will not fail. The double correspondence with *vv.* 9, 10 should be noted. As he has not *restrained* his lips, so, he trusts, God will not *restrain* His tender mercies: as he has not ceased to acknowledge God's lovingkindness and truth, so that lovingkindness and truth will not cease to protect him. Cp. xxv. 21; lxi. 7; Is. lxiii. 15.

12—17. The scene is changed. The sky is overclouded. Supplication for speedy help in time of danger takes the place of joyous thanksgiving.

12. This verse is somewhat loosely attached to *v.* 11 by *for*. The rendering of *v.* 11 as a prayer makes the connexion appear closer and more natural than it is.

evils] Afflictions (xxxiv. 19), which are trials of faith or chastisements for sin.

have compassed me about] The use of the word in 2 Sam. xxii. 5 suggests that the true meaning is 'have overwhelmed me like a flood.' Cp. Jonah ii. 5.

have taken hold upon me] R. V. **have overtaken me.** Sin pursues

They are moe than the hairs of mine head, therefore my
heart faileth me.
13 Be pleased, O LORD, to deliver me:
O LORD, make haste to help me.
14 Let them be ashamed and confounded together that seek
after my soul to destroy it;
Let them be driven backward and put to shame that wish
me evil.
15 Let them be desolate for a reward of their shame
That say unto me, Aha, aha!
16 Let all those that seek thee rejoice and be glad in thee:

the sinner like an avenging Nemesis, till it gets him into its power and punishes him. Cp. xxxviii. 4; Deut. xxviii. 15; Job viii. 4 (R. V.); Prov. v. 22.

so that I am not able to look up] The only rendering justified by usage is, **and I cannot see.** In the extremity of terror and faintness sight fails him. Cp. xxxviii. 10; lxix. 3, and note that the next line contains parallels to both passages.

than the hairs of my head] As in lxix. 4. (A different word is used there for *they are more:* here it is the same as in *v.* 5.)

therefore &c.] Lit. **and my heart hath forsaken me.** Courage utterly fails. Cp. xxxviii. 10.

13. *Vv.* 13—17 recur as Ps. lxx, with some verbal variations.

Be pleased] An echo of 'thy good pleasure' ('thy will') in *v.* 8. The word is omitted in Ps. lxx, and in the first line, though not in the second, *God* is substituted for *LORD*, according to the usual rule in Book II. See Introd., p. xl f.

make haste to help me] Cp. xxxviii. 22; xxii. 19.

14. The whole verse is a repetition, with variations, of xxxv. 4, 26 (cp. xxxviii. 12); and *vv.* 15—17 recall *vv.* 21, 25, 27, 10 of the same Psalm. *Together* and *to destroy it* are omitted in lxx. 2.

let them be driven backward &c.] Render, as in Ps. xxxviii;
    Let them be turned back and brought to dishonour
    That delight in my hurt.
Contrast xxxv. 27 with the last line.

15. R. V., **Let them be desolate** (Lam. i. 16) **by reason of their shame**, the defeat of their malicious plans: or, less probably, *let them be astonished* (Lev. xxvi. 32) *for a reward of their shame*, at the shame which is their recompence. Ps. lxx. 4 reads *let them turn back*, as in vi. 10. The difference of reading probably arose out of the confusion of sound or form between M and B (ישבי־ ישמו).

Aha, aha] The exclamation of malicious pleasure at another's misfortune. Cp. xxxv. 21, 25.

16. Cp. xxxv. 27. The discomfiture of the wicked gives occasion for the righteous to rejoice in God, not merely because they are set free

Let such as love thy salvation say continually, The LORD
be magnified.
But I am poor and needy; yet the Lord thinketh upon me: 17
Thou art my help and my deliverer;
Make no tarrying, O my God.

from persecution, but because they see in it the proof of God's righteous sovereignty and the unfolding of His purposes of salvation.

such as love thy salvation] Cp. *v.* 10: and the corresponding N. T. thought in 2 Tim. iv. 8.

17. The Psalmist reverts to his own need, but in calm assurance that he is not forgotten.

But I, who am afflicted and needy:—
The Lord will take thought for me.

For *afflicted and needy*, see ix. 18; xxxv. 10; xxxvii. 14; lxxxvi. 1; cix. 22. With *will take thought for me*, cp. *v.* 5 (*thoughts*): Jonah i. 6. Ps. lxx. 5 reads *O God, make haste unto me*, probably an alteration suggested by the parallelism, *make no tarrying*. *My help*, as in xxvii. 9: *my deliverer*, as in xviii. 2, 48 (a different word from *deliver* in *v.* 13).

make no tarrying] Cp. Daniel's prayer, ix. 19 (A.V. *defer not*); and the promise, Is. xlvi. 13.

PSALM XLI.

The Psalmist is suffering from an illness which threatens to be fatal. Treacherous enemies, and among them one who had been a trusted friend, eagerly anticipate his death. But his confidence in Jehovah remains unshaken.

It is much disputed whether the Psalmist is to be thought of as still lying on his sick-bed, or as restored to health and recording his past experience. In the latter case 'I said' in *v.* 4 must be supposed to govern *vv.* 4—12, or at least *vv.* 4—10. But the former alternative appears preferable, for it is unnatural to regard the prayer of *v.* 10 as part of a narrative, and the verb in *v.* 4 can be rendered 'I have said', or 'I say'.

The Psalm consists of four stanzas, of which the second and third cohere closely.

i. The first stanza is an expansion of the beatitude, 'Blessed are the merciful, for they shall obtain mercy.' The language is general, but the Psalmist is thinking of himself. Conscious, like Job (xxx. 25), of having shewn compassion towards others, he trusts that he may receive the blessings promised to the compassionate. And further, the picture of the spirit which wins divine approval emphasises the wickedness of the treatment which he is himself experiencing (1—3).

ii. iii. A prayer for restoration introduces the description of his present situation. The malice and hypocrisy of his enemies are vividly delineated. The climax of all is the perfidy of a trusted friend (4—9).

iv. From his enemies he turns to God with renewed prayer for restoration, and expression of confidence in the continuance of His favour (10—12).

If David was the author of the Psalm, the false friend can hardly be other than Ahithophel, and the Psalm must have been written shortly before the outbreak of Absalom's rebellion. Ahithophel's sneer at Hushai (2 Sam. xvi. 17) well illustrates the confidential relation of a trusted counsellor to the king, and the depth of his own perfidy.

It is true that the narrative in 2 Sam. makes no reference to an illness such as is here described; but that narrative necessarily passes over many details. Such an illness would account for the remissness in attending to his official duties, which Absalom's words to the suitors for justice seem to imply (2 Sam. xv. 3). It would account also for the strange failure of David's natural courage which his flight from Jerusalem at the first outbreak of the rebellion appears to indicate.

Unnerved by sickness, in which he recognised a just punishment for his sins, David watched the growing disloyalty of his courtiers, and in particular of Ahithophel, without feeling able to strike and crush the conspiracy before it came to a head. Comp. generally, Ps. lv.

To the chief Musician, A Psalm of David.

41 Blessed *is* he that considereth the poor:
  The LORD will deliver him in time of trouble.
2 The LORD will preserve him, and keep him alive;
  And he shall be blessed upon the earth:
  And thou wilt not deliver him unto the will of his enemies.

1—3. The blessings in store for the compassionate man.

1. *Blessed*] Or, *happy*, as in *v.* 2, and in i. 1. The word is to be distinguished from *blessed* in the doxology of *v.* 13, the tribute of human reverence to divine majesty. The last Psalm in Book I begins like the first with a beatitude.

that considereth the poor] Behaves considerately and intelligently towards those in affliction, shewing kindness and sympathy, and not judging them harshly. Cp. for illustration xxxv. 13, 14; James i. 27. The word rendered *poor* is different from that in xl. 17. It means *weak*, and includes the sick as well as the poor. The sequel shews that it is the sick that the Psalmist has chiefly in mind. The P.B.V. *the poor and needy* follows the LXX, which may have been influenced by xl. 17.

in time of trouble] R.V. **in the day of evil**, though *in the day of trouble* is given in xxvii. 5 for the same phrase.

2, 3. It is possible to render as in P.B.V. and R. V. marg., *The LORD preserve him...the LORD support him:* but it is more natural to regard these clauses as descriptive of the blessings which await the compassionate man, rather than as a prayer on his behalf.

he shall be blessed upon the earth] He shall be made prosperous, or more probably, counted happy (Job xxix. 11; Ps. lxxii. 17), **in the land**. Cp. xxxvii. 3 ff.

and thou wilt not deliver him] Rather, as R. V., **and deliver not**

The LORD will strengthen him upon the bed of languishing: 3
Thou wilt make all his bed in his sickness.
I said, LORD, be merciful unto me : 4
Heal my soul; for I have sinned against thee.
Mine enemies speak evil of me, 5
When shall he die, and his name perish?
And if he come to see *me*, he speaketh vanity: 6

thou him. Cp. xxvii. 12. The language of promise passes into that of prayer, doubtless with a tacit reference to the Psalmist's own need.

3. The LORD will support him upon the couch of languishing (R. V.), uphold him (xviii. 35) and preserve him from sinking into the grave.

thou wilt make all his bed] Lit. **thou hast turned** (or, **changed**) **his lying down**: changed his sickness into health. Cp. xxx. 11. Instead of a general truth a particular example is appealed to: or perhaps faith pictures the result as already attained. 'The LORD will support...nay, thou hast already raised him up.'

The verse is commonly explained as a metaphor from the nurse supporting the patient's head and shifting the bed and pillows to give ease and relief, but usage does not seem to warrant this interpretation.

4—6. The foregoing sketch of the blessedness of the compassionate man serves to introduce the Psalmist's description of his own case, partly as a foil and contrast to the heartless treatment he is experiencing, partly because he feels that he can himself plead for a share in the mercy promised to the merciful.

4. *I said*] Or, **I, even I, have said.** This has been and is my prayer. *v.* 10 seems to imply that the sickness is not yet a thing of the past.

be merciful] **Be gracious** (iv. 1; &c.).

heal my soul] The soul is the man's whole 'self;' the living personality which results from the union of spirit and flesh. See Oehler's *Old Test. Theology*, § 70. The bodily sickness is the sign and symptom of spiritual disease: he would fain be healed of both. Cp. vi. 2, 3; Jer. xvii. 14.

for I have sinned against thee] Cp. li. 4; xxxi. 10. He has offended against God; the chastisement comes from Him; and He alone can heal. Cp. Hos. vi. 1.

5. *speak evil of me*] R. V. **against me.** *v.* 5 takes up *v.* 2, as *v.* 4 answers to *v.* 3.

When &c.] The words of the enemies, expressing their impatient eagerness for his death, and even for the extinction of his posterity. Cp. cix. 13; 2 Sam. xviii. 18; Ps. ix. 6.

6. And if one *of them* **comes to see** *me*, **he speaketh falsehood.** If one of these enemies comes to visit him, as was usual in sickness (2 Kings viii. 29), he speaks vanity or falsehood (xii. 2), makes hypocritical professions of sympathy; though all the time *his heart is gathering*

His heart gathereth iniquity to itself;
When he goeth abroad, he telleth *it*.
7 All that hate me whisper together against me:
Against me do they devise my hurt.
8 An evil disease, *say they*, cleaveth fast unto him:
And *now* that he lieth he shall rise up no more.
9 Yea, mine own familiar friend, in whom I trusted,
Which did eat *of* my bread,
Hath lift up *his* heel against me.

iniquity or *mischief;* he is collecting materials for fresh slander, or feeding his malice on the sight of the sick man; and then *he goeth abroad, he telleth* what he has seen.

7. The scene outside the house is graphically depicted. We see the associates waiting, eager for news. With a transparent pretence of secrecy they whisper together, and divert themselves with anticipating the worst.

do they devise my hurt] Or, *imagine evil for me*, indulging in uncharitable speculations as to the cause of his illness (cp. Job xxii. 5 ff.), and hoping for a fatal issue of it. The next verse is a summary of their malevolent conversation.

8. Render: **A deadly mischief is poured out upon him.** The phrase *a thing of belial* is variously explained to mean *an incurable disease* or *a matter of wickedness* (cp. note on xviii. 4). The use of it in ci. 3 (*base thing*), and Deut. xv. 9 (*base thought*) points to the latter as the primary sense. But probably the speakers do not distinguish between the moral cause—some monstrous crime—and the physical effect—a fatal illness—; but include the latter in the former. Cp. Shimei's taunt, 2 Sam. xvi. 7.

cleaveth fast unto him] R. V. marg., *is poured out upon him;* perhaps, *is molten*, or, *welded fast upon him*. He will never be free from his guilt and its punishment.

The rendering in P.B.V., *Let the sentence of guiltiness proceed against him*, is quite impossible.

now *that he lieth* &c.] Now that he has taken to his bed he will never leave it again.

9. *mine own familiar friend*] Lit. *the man of my peace*. Cp. vii. 4; Jer. xx. 10; xxxviii. 22; Obad. 7; and the similar complaints of ingratitude in xxxv. 12 ff., lv. 12 ff. (where the Heb. for *familiar friend* is quite different).

which did eat of my bread] Bound to me by the tie of hospitality; and, if the speaker is David, by the honour of entertainment at the royal table. Cp. 2 Sam. ix. 10 ff.; 1 Kings xviii. 19; 2 Kings xxv. 29.

hath lift up his heel against me] Lit. *made great the heel:* spurned me with brutal violence, exerted himself to trip me up and throw me down. Cp. lv. 12; Jer. ix. 4.

The words 'he that eateth my bread lifted up his heel against me' are quoted by Christ in John xiii. 18 as fulfilled by the treachery of Judas.

But thou, O LORD, be merciful unto me, 10
And raise me up, that I may requite them.
By this I know that thou favourest me, 11
Because mine enemy doth not triumph over me.
And *as for* me, thou upholdest me in mine integrity, 12
And settest me before thy face for ever.

The words of the Psalm are not a direct prediction, but the treachery and the fate of Ahithophel foreshadowed the treachery and the fate of Judas. What saints of old time had suffered by the desertion of friends must be suffered with an aggravated bitterness by the Son of Man. Their experience must be fulfilled in His. Cp. John xvii. 12; Acts i. 16.

10—12. After describing his urgent need, the Psalmist resumes his prayer from *v.* 4, and affirms his confident assurance of God's favour.

10. *But thou, O Jehovah*, in contrast to their malignity, *be thou gracious unto me:* though they say 'he shall rise up no more,' *raise me up.*
that I may requite them] The words have a vindictive ring, which is startling, and seems inconsistent with vii. 4; Prov. xx. 22. Yet if the speaker was David, conscious of his divine appointment to be king, he might well pray that he might be restored to punish traitors as they deserved. For the most part he would leave vengeance to Jehovah (1 Sam. xxv. 33; 2 Sam. iii. 39), yet in this instance he might feel that he would be acting as Jehovah's instrument, in punishing those who were conspiring to resist His purposes. See Introd. p. lxxii f.

11. **By this I know that thou delightest in me.**
In the confidence of faith he can use the present: *I know*. Cp. xx. 6. For *delightest in me*, cp. xviii. 19; xxii. 8; xxxv. 27; 2 Sam. xv. 26.
doth not triumph] Lit. *raise a shout of victory.* Cp. xxv. 2 (a different Heb. word); xxx. 1; xxxv. 19; xxxviii. 16.

12. Cp. xxvi. 11; lxiii. 8. *Thou upholdest* (lit. *hast upheld*) is either a reference to past mercies, or more probably a retrospect from the standpoint of deliverance granted. *In mine integrity* is no contradiction to *v.* 4. Integrity (vii. 8; xv. 2) is not synonymous with sinlessness.
and settest me before thy face for ever] His enemies hope that his name will perish. He knows that he will be admitted to stand in the presence of the King of Kings. Cp. xi. 7 (note); xvi. 11; xvii. 15; lxi. 7; and the fundamental promise in 2 Sam. vii. 16 (read *before me* with LXX).

Thus the first book of the Psalter ends with a hope, destined to be illuminated with a new light by the revelation of the Gospel. See Rev. xxii. 4.

13 Blessed *be* the LORD God of Israel from everlasting, and to everlasting. Amen, and Amen.

13. This doxology is of course no part of the Psalm, but stands here to mark the close of Book i. Cp. lxxii. 18, 19; lxxxix. 52; cvi. 48.

Blessed be *the LORD God of Israel*] Better as R. V., **Blessed be the LORD, the God of Israel.** *LORD* answers to the Name Jehovah, and is not an attribute to *God of Israel.* Cp. David's doxology, 1 Kings i. 48; 1 Chr. xxix. 10; and Solomon's, 1 Kings viii. 15; also Ezra vii. 27; Neh. ix. 5; Luke i. 68.

from everlasting, and to everlasting] From all eternity in the past to all eternity in the future: in the eternal present of the divine existence. Cp. xc. 2; xciii. 2; ciii. 17.

Amen, and Amen] So it is: the response of the congregation, affirming the ascription of praise on their own behalf (cvi. 48).

APPENDIX.

Note I.

On the word Chāsīd.

The word *chāsīd* is characteristic of the Psalter, in which it is found 25 times. Elsewhere it occurs only in Deut. xxxiii. 8; 1 Sam. ii. 9; Prov. ii. 8; Jer. iii. 12; Mic. vii. 2. (2 Sam. xxii. 26, and 2 Chr. vi. 41 are of course not independent passages.) It is variously rendered in A.V., 'godly,' 'merciful,' or, after the Sept. ὅσιος, Vulg. *sanctus*, 'holy,' 'saints.' Its exact meaning, however, is disputed. Is it (1) active, denoting the character of the man who practises dutiful love (*chesed*) to God and to his fellow-men (A.V. and R.V. 'godly' or 'merciful'): or (2) passive, denoting the state of one who is the object of God's lovingkindness (R.V. marg., 'one that He favoureth:' cp. A.V. marg. to lxxxvi. 2)? The form of the word is not decisive between the two senses, and appeal must be made to the usage of the word. In favour of (1) it is urged that the word certainly has an active sense in cxlv. 17 and Jer. iii. 12, where it is applied to God: and also in Ps. xii. 1; xviii. 25; xliii. 1; Mic. vii. 2; where it is used of the quality of lovingkindness between man and man.

On the other hand in favour of (2) it may be urged that the substantive *chesed* from which the adjective *chāsīd* is derived denotes in the Psalter almost without exception God's lovingkindness to man. It occurs there 127 times, and in three cases only is it used of man's love to man (cix. 12, 16; cxli. 5), though this sense is common elsewhere. It is never used in the Psalter of man's love to God, and indeed it is doubtful whether it is really so used at all. The passages generally quoted (Hos. vi. 4, 6; Jer. ii. 2) are not decisive.

If the primary meaning of *chāsīd* is to be governed (as seems reasonable) by that of *chesed* in the Psalms, it must certainly mean 'one who is the object of Jehovah's lovingkindness.' And this sense suits the predominant usage of the word best. It is used 15 times with a pronoun to express the relation of the covenant people, or individuals in it, to Jehovah (My, Thy, His *chasīdīm*), in connexions where the position into which they have been brought by Jehovah's grace is a more appropriate thought than that of their response to that grace either by love to God or love to their fellow-men. It is not man's love to God or to his fellow-man which is pleaded as the ground of acceptance or urged as the motive for duty, but the fact that Jehovah by His free lovingkindness has brought the nation and its members into covenant with Himself. In its primary sense then the word implies no moral praise or merit; but it came, not unnaturally, to be connected with the idea of *chesed* as 'loving-kindness' between man and man, and to be used of the character which reflected that love of which it was itself the object; and finally was applied even to God Himself.

NOTE II.

ON THE TITLE 'MOST HIGH.'

The usage of the title 'Most High' (*Elyōn*) should be carefully examined.

(1) As used by non-Israelites, it appears as the designation of the Supreme God in the mouth of the Canaanite priest-king Melchisedek (Gen. xiv. 18—22); it is employed by Balaam (Num. xxiv. 16); it is put into the mouth of the presumptuous king of Babylon (Is. xiv. 14).

(2) Its application to Jehovah from the Israelite standpoint is limited to poetry. It occurs in Deut. xxxii. 8 (note the connexion with the partition of the earth among the *nations*); Lam. iii. 35, 38; and 21 times in the Psalter [and in 2 Sam. xxii. 14 = Ps. xviii. 13], always, with one exception (cvii. 11), in the first four books. It is nowhere found in the Prophets.

(3) In the Aramaic of the Book of Daniel it occurs, in one peculiar passage (vii. 18—27) in the plural of majesty; and a synonymous word is used frequently, but, with one exception. (vii. 25), in the mouth of Nebuchadnezzar or Belshazzar, or in words addressed to them. It comes to be a favourite word with the author of Ecclesiasticus (ὕψιστος, without the article), and occurs also in 2 Macc. iii. 31.

NOTE III.

ON XI. 1.

There are two readings here: the Qrī, *flee thou* (fem.): the Kthībh, *flee ye*. If *flee thou* is addressed, as it is natural to suppose, to David's soul, it must be explained as a bold combination of direct and indirect speech, equivalent to 'that she should flee as a bird to your mountain,' i.e. join you in your mountain retreat. Or David and his adherents may be addressed. 'Flee, O birds (fem. collective), to your mountain!' The second reading, 'flee ye, like birds (or, ye birds), to your mountain,' is simpler. David and his companions are exhorted to seek the mountain which is their natural or accustomed place of refuge. But it must be admitted that the plural 'flee ye' is harsh, and that we should expect the poet's soul to be addressed; while at the same time if the singular 'flee thou' is read, the plural 'your mountain' can only be explained by the assumption of a bold construction, or an abrupt transition from sing. to plur. And when we find that all the ancient versions give the verb in the singular, and none of them express *your*, it becomes almost certain that by a very slight change of text we should read 'Flee (thou) as a bird to the mountain.' (נודי הר כמו צפור).

Note IV.

On the Hebrew Tenses.

The English reader may be at a loss to understand how it can so often be doubtful whether a verb should be rendered by the past or the future tense. The uncertainty arises from the peculiar character of the Hebrew Tenses, which denote *mode* of action rather than *time* of action. The fundamental idea of the 'perfect' (sometimes called the 'past') is *completed* action: the fundamental idea of the 'imperfect' (sometimes called the 'future') is *incomplete* action.

In simple narrative prose the 'perfect' usually refers to the past, and the 'imperfect' to the future. But in the higher styles of poetry and prophecy both tenses are used with much greater freedom.

(1) A future event may be regarded as having already taken place, either in order that it may be more forcibly presented to the mind, or because it is contemplated as being absolutely certain to happen; and in such cases the perfect tense, sometimes called the 'perfect of certainty,' or 'prophetic perfect,' is used. See Ps. xxii. 29; xxxvii. 20.

(2) A past event may be regarded, for the sake of vivid description, as being still in progress, and the 'imperfect' tense may be employed with reference to it. Thus in Ps. vii. 15, 'the ditch *he was making*' (imperf.) represents the wicked man as still engaged upon his plot when it proves his own ruin. This usage corresponds to the 'historic present,' and is very common in poetry.

The 'imperfect' is also used as a frequentative, of repeated action, and to express general truths.

Hence it is often doubtful, as in numerous instances in Ps. xviii, whether a Hebrew imperfect refers to the past or the future, and should be rendered by past, present, or future. The decision must be regulated by the context and the general view taken of the sense of the passage. Not seldom the peculiar force of the Hebrew tenses cannot be expressed in an English translation without awkward circumlocutions.

NEW TESTAMENT QUOTATIONS FROM THE FIRST BOOK OF THE PSALMS.

Psalm		
ii. 1, 2	quoted	Acts iv. 25, 26.
ii. 7	,,	Acts xiii. 33; Heb. i. 5, v. 5.
ii. 8, 9	,,	Rev. ii. 26, 27; xii. 5; xix. 15.
iv. 4	,,	Eph. iv. 26.
v. 9	,,	Rom. iii. 13.
viii. 2	,,	Matt. xxi. 16.
viii. 4—6	,,	Heb. ii. 6—8.
viii. 6	,,	1 Cor. xv. 27.
x. 7	,,	Rom. iii. 14.
xiv. 1 c, 2 b, 3	,,	Rom. iii. 10—12.
xvi. 8—11	,,	Acts ii. 25—28.
xvi. 10 b	,,	Acts xiii. 35.
xviii. 2 b	,,	Heb. ii. 13.
xviii. 49	,,	Rom. xv. 9.
xix. 4	,,	Rom. x. 18.
xxii. 1	,,	Matt. xxvii. 46; Mk. xv. 34.
xxii. 8	,,	Matt. xxvii. 43.
xxii. 18	,,	John xix. 24 [Matt. xxvii. 35].
xxii. 22	,,	Heb. ii. 12.
xxiv. 1	,,	1 Cor. x. 26 [28].
xxxi. 5 a	,,	Lk. xxiii. 46.
xxxii. 1, 2	,,	Rom. iv. 7, 8.
xxxiv. 12—16	,,	1 Pet. iii. 10—12.
xxxv. 19 b	,,	John xv. 25.
xxxvi. 1 b	,,	Rom. iii. 18.
xxxvii. 11 a	,,	Matt. v. 5.
xl. 6—8	,,	Heb. x. 5—7.
xli. 9	,,	John xiii. 18.

This list includes a few passages which are not formally introduced as quotations, though they are taken directly from the Psalms: but it does not attempt to collect the numerous indirect allusions and references to the thought and language of the Psalms which are to be found in the New Testament.

INDEX.

Absalom's rebellion, 13 ff., 140, 144, 216
acrostic Psalms, xlviii
afflicted, 47
Ahithophel, 216
Alāmōth, xxii
alloweth, 59
alphabetic Psalms, xlviii
angel of the LORD, 172, 177
angels, 148
anthropomorphism, 90
Aquila, liv
Arabic poetry, xxxi
Aramaic language, liii
Ark, symbol of Jehovah's presence, 47, 130; translation of to Zion, 69, 127
Augustine, St, 161
Authorised Version, lvi
Azkara, 198

bones, meaning of, 26, 175, 178
bribes, 72
bring back the captivity, meaning of, 69

Calvin, 27
chāsīd, 18, 61, 221
Cherubim, 90
Chief Musician, xix
Columba, St, 173
covenant of the LORD, 134
Coverdale's Bible, lvi
Cush, 29

daughter of Zion, 49
David, Psalms of, meaning of the title, xxix
David the founder of the Psalter, xxxii ff.; Psalms illustrating his life, 20, 25, 36, 42, 113, 124, 151, 155, 170, 208; at Saul's court, 57, 60; during Saul's persecution, 29, 60, 63, 72, 78, 170, 175; referring to events of his reign, 42, 69, 84, 106, 127; to his fall, 161, 198; to Absalom's rebellion, 13, 20, 25, 36, 140, 144, 216
death, view of, 27, 48, 154, 207
Dedication, Feast of the, 151
Degrees, Songs of, xxv

Ecclesiasticus, prologue to, xii
El, 22
Eloah, 96
Elohistic Psalms, xl

face of the LORD, 44, 60, 83, 174
faith of Psalmists, 55, 207
family, solidarity of the, 187
fear of the LORD, 105
figurative language; derived from experiences of David's outlaw life, 87; from warfare, 176; from hunting, 35
fool, meaning of term, 66
freebooters, 53
future life, view of, lxxv ff., 27, 78, 154

generation, 63
Gittith, xxiii
glory=soul, 31
glory of God, 102
God, Hebrew words for; *El*, 22, 101; *Eloah*, 96; *Elohim*, xl: the Name of, 25, 37, 46, 75, 107, 148: Jehovah (=LORD), 101; LORD of Hosts, 131; Most High, 35, 91, 222; the living God, 99; Rock, 87; Creator, 101 ff., 129, 166; Lawgiver, 101 ff.; King, 59; Judge, 32, 44, 46, 49, 59, 79, 176; Goel, 47; His moral attributes, 166, 185, 212; righteousness, 23; truth, 133; holiness, 116, 153: His knowledge, 5; Providence, 5; anger, 31, 112, 199; vengeance, 99; glory, 102, 139, 148; sovereignty in the world, 128, 167; care for Israel, 168; care for mankind, 185; the good Shepherd, 125; the bountiful host, 126, 141, 186; description of His Advent, 89; revealed in Nature, 35 ff., 101, 147; law of His dealings with men, 94; His covenant, 134; may be known by the nations, 50; and is to be celebrated among them, 100
godly, meaning of word, 18, 61, 221
Great Bible, lvi

heart, 33, 137
heathen, 8

PSALMS   15

Hebrew language, mode of writing, li
Hebrew tenses, 223
Hebrew poetry, various kinds of, ix; form of, xliv ff.; strophical arrangement, xlvii; alphabetic or acrostic Psalms, xlviii
Hebrew Text of O. T., xlix ff.; date of MSS., xlix; history of, l; imperfections of, l; two recensions of Ps. xviii, 86. See 12, 32, 37, 48, 73, 88, 91, 98, 100, 109, 119, 123, 130, 171, 183, 195, 202, 222, &c.
Hexapla, Origen's, liv
Hezekiah, xxxiv
historical allusions; Sodom and Gomorrah, 60; Exodus, 68; Sennacherib, 69; the Flood, 150; Exile, 69
house of the LORD, 20
humble, 47

interpretation of Messianic Psalms, lxiv

Jeduthun, xxiii
Jehoshaphat, xxxiv
Jeremiah, Psalms of, xxxiv, 113, 155, 176, 198, 208
Jerome, lv
Job, Book of, Psalms related to, x, 188, 198, 203

Kadesh, 150
king, position and typical significance of the Israelite, 6; lofty language applied to, 110
Korah, Psalms of the sons of, xxix
Krī. See *Qrī*
K'thībh, li, 47, 55, 77, 96, 100, 129, 152, 222

lamp, metaphor of, 95
land of Canaan, 135, 189 ff.
Latin Versions, lv
Law, meaning of word, 3; references to the, 3, 101 f., 104, 212
leasing, 18
life, 77; desire for long, 111, 143
LORD of hosts, 131

Maccabaean Psalms, xxxv ff.
man: Hebrew words for, 39; the wonder of creation, 35; his true destiny, 36; corruption of, 65 f.
marvellous works, 44
Maschīl, xviii
Massora, xlix
Massoretic Text, xlix
Matthew's Bible, lvi
meek, 47
memorial, 198
Messianic hope, lviii ff.; the royal Messiah, lviii, 6, 110; the suffering Messiah, lxi, 112 ff., 219; the Son of God, 6; the Son of Man, lxii, 36, 212; the Advent of God, lxiii; the destiny of the nations, lxv, 7, 100, 122

Messianic references in the Targum, liv
Michtam, xviii
mizmor, xiii, xvii
moe, 210
moth, 206
Musician, the chief, xix

nations, destiny of, lxv ff.; relation of Israel to, lxvi; capable of knowing God, 50, 67, 122; Jehovah's praise to be celebrated among, 47, 100
Nature the revelation of God, 35, 101; O. T. view of, 147
Negīnōth, xxii
Nehīlōth, xxii
nobles, oppression of, 53, 80

Old Testament, position of Psalter in, xii; triple division, xii; order of Books, xiii; text of, xlix ff.; Versions of, li ff.; limitations of view in, lxxii; some ruling ideas in, lxxiii f.; relation to N. T., lxix ff., lxxv
oracle, 145
oral tradition, xxxi
Origen, liv

parallelism, xlv ff.
penitential Psalms, 26
perfect, meaning of word, 70
Peschito, liv
poor, 47
posterity, desire for, 83, 197
Praises, as a name for the Psalms, xiv
Prayer-Book Version, lvi
Prayers, as a name for the Psalms, xiv
prevent, 92
prophecy, connexion of the Psalms with, x; 'double sense' of, lxiv f. See *Messianic Hope*.
prosperity of the wicked a cause of discontent, 187, 204
Proverbs, Book of, Psalms related to, x, 1, 132, 170, 188
psalm, xiii
Psalms, Book of, general characteristics, ix; relation to other books of O. T. x; historical importance, xi; critical study, xi; devotional use, xi; position in O. T., xii; names, xiii; numbering, xiv; division into books, xvi; collection and growth, xxxix; steps in formation, xliii; date of collection, xliii; previous collections, xliv; Messianic Hope in, lviii ff; theology of, lxvii ff.
Psalms, titles of, xvii ff.; oral transmission of, xxxi; adapted and altered, xxxi; authorship and age of, xxxi ff.; arrangement, xliv; alphabetic or acrostic, xlviii; Maccabaean, xxxv; Elohistic, xl; poetical form of, xliv; strophical arrangement, xlvii; imprecatory, lxx ff.; related to Proverbs, x, 1, 132, 170, 188; related to the Book of Job,

x, 188, 198, 203; supposed to be written in the name of the nation, 26, 114, 124, 131, 198, 203, 208
Psalms of Solomon, xxxvii
psalter, xiv. See Psalms, Book of

Qrî, li, 47, 55, 77, 96, 100, 129, 152, 222
Quotations from the Psalms in the N.T., 7, 19, 36, 38, 67, 77, 103, 114, 115, 117, 120, 128, 157, 162, 172, 173, 181, 191, 207, 212, 218

reins, 33, 76, 137
Resurrection, hope of in O.T., lxxvi f., 73, 78, 83 f.
retribution, desire for in the O.T., lxxiii ff.
Revised Version, lvii
righteousness, 126; of God, 23, 60, 124, 130; of man, 17, 19, 83

sacrifice, lxviii; various kinds of, 210; true sacrifice, 210; before a war, 108
sacrificial feast, 121
salvation, meaning of word, 16
scorner, 2
Selah, xx
Septuagint, li ff.; its history, li; MSS. lii; value, liii; influence on P. B. V., lvi. See 67, 106, 119, 129, 130, 148, 183, 195, 196, &c.
servant of the LORD, 86
Shemīnīth, xxiii
Sheol, 27, 49, 88
shield, 25
Shiggaion, xix
Shîr, xviii
sickness, regarded as a sign of God's displeasure, 25
simple, 104
sin, 105; different words for, 133, 162; confessed and repented of, 161 ff.
sin and suffering, popular view of the relation of, lxx, 25, 158, 201, 206, 218

Sirion, 149
Solomon, references to, 5 f.
Solomon, Psalms of, xxxvii
song, xviii
Songs of Degrees, xxv
soul, 14, 59, 129, 217
symbolism, character of Hebrew, 90
Symmachus, liv
Syriac Version, liv

Targum, liii; Messianic references in, liv
Temple, reference to, lxviii, 141; meaning of word, 21
Theodotion, liv
Theology of the Psalms, lxvii ff.; relation to ordinances of worship, lxvii; alleged self-righteousness of the Psalmists, lxix f., 33, 93; imprecatory Psalms, lxx ff.; future life, lxxv ff., 27, 78, 154; view of death, 48, 154, 207; destruction of the wicked why desired, lxxiii, 25, 42, 161, 187
Titles of Psalms, xvii ff.; referring to character of poem, xvii; musical setting or performance, xix; instruments, xxii; pitch of music, xxii; melody, xxiii; liturgical use, xxiv; authorship, xxvi; occasion, xxvi; value of the titles, xxvi ff.
tōrāh=law, 3

unicorn, 120
usury, 72

Versions, Ancient, li ff.
,, English, lv ff.
Vulgate, lv

week, Psalms for days of, xxiv
'Wisdom' of Israel, x
worship, meaning of word, 15

Zion, 10, 15, 47